The Lutheran Church
and the East German State

The Lutheran Church
and the East German State

POLITICAL CONFLICT AND CHANGE
UNDER ULBRICHT AND HONECKER

ROBERT F. GOECKEL

Cornell University Press

ITHACA AND LONDON

Copyright © 1990 by Cornell University

All rights reserved. Except for brief quotations in a review, this book, or parts thereof, must not be reproduced in any form without permission in writing from the publisher. For information, address Cornell University Press, 124 Roberts Place, Ithaca, New York 14850.

First published 1990 by Cornell University Press.

International Standard Book Number 0-8014-2259-0
Library of Congress Catalog Card Number 90-31313

Printed in the United States of America

Librarians: Library of Congress cataloging information appears on the last page of the book.

⊗The paper used in this publication meets the minimum requirements of the American National Standard for Permanence of Paper for Printed Library Materials Z39.48—1984.

To my parents
for the inspiration and
support they have provided

Contents

Preface

This book examines the role of the Protestant Lutheran church in East Germany under the governments of Walter Ulbricht and Erich Honecker. The case of East Germany, formally the German Democratic Republic (GDR), is unique: only in the GDR has a Communist regime faced a largely Protestant population, or at least a Protestant political culture. Most other regimes in the Communist world confront traditionally Catholic societies, such as Poland and Hungary, or traditionally Orthodox ones, such as Soviet Russia, Romania, and Bulgaria. Yugoslavia and Czechoslovakia must deal with confessionally mixed societies; Protestant minorities are found in almost all Communist systems. Yet no other regime has inherited a national culture in which a Protestant church is predominant, as it is in the GDR. I aim here to illuminate the distinctive features of this particular nexus of Lutheran Protestantism and Soviet-style Leninism.

I also intend to shed light on broader issues, yielding generalizations regarding church-state relations in Communist political systems, the nature and changes of the inter-German relationship, the impact of international organizations on Communist systems, and the issue of political change in Communist systems generally. The East German government has often been considered a Stalinist regime, but it has experienced considerable political change in its policy toward religion and the church. The regime has granted institutional legitimacy to the church; the church has granted legitimacy to the GDR as a political community and accepted socialism as its environment. I describe this change, particularly the crucial years of transition in the 1970s, and analyze the causal factors operating to produce it.

This book focuses primarily on the Honecker era, particularly on the period before Mikhail Gorbachev came to power in the USSR in 1985. The reform process he set in motion there has engendered profound changes in East Europe. Until 1989, however, the East German regime had rejected the notions of *glasnost* and *perestroika,* and this truculence had caused a chill in the state's relationship with the church. The end of the Honecker era and collapse of the authority of the Communist party in late 1989 leaves a fluid situation in which the future direction of the entire political system, let alone that of church-state relations, is unclear. Certainly the spillover effects of the Gorbachev reforms reinforce one of my major conclusions, namely that Soviet policy remains an important contextual factor for church-state relations in the GDR.

The genesis of this project can be traced to my studies, at the University of Michigan and Harvard University, of Eastern Europe and the role of religion in Communist systems. The interest in these subjects inspired by Zvi Gitelman and Erich Goldhagen provided a context for my further research. Discussions with German scholars, including the late Peter Christian Ludz, convinced me of the need for and political relevance of such a study, and the supportiveness of Karl Deutsch enabled me to complete an early version of this manuscript. I am deeply grateful to them all for nurturing the undertaking.

This book would have been impossible without research facilities in Germany, West and East. In West Berlin I benefited greatly from use of the press archive of the Evangelical Press Center, Consistory of the Evangelical Church of Berlin (West), and the personal archives of its director, Reinhard Henkys. Numerous conversations with him and his associates, in particular Hans-Juergen Roeder, were invaluable in putting together the pieces of this fascinating puzzle. The assistance and congenial work atmosphere provided by the archivists, Gerd Buessing and the late Hans-Ulrich Hampel, made my research a pleasure.

The facilities of the Central Institute for Social Science Research of the Free University of Berlin also proved useful in my background research. My thanks go to its director, Hartmut Zimmermann, and his associates for their stimulating insights and comments on my work.

In the German Democratic Republic under the auspices of an IREX exchange, I benefited greatly from the advice and assistance of my advisers, Helmut Dressler and Herbert Trebs, both of Humboldt University. Access to the archive of the Executive Committee of the Christian Democratic Union of Germany (East) proved invaluable. I thank the archivist, Jochen Franke, and the director of the Department of Church Questions, Wulf Trende, for their assistance.

I thank those who have read and commented on the manuscript or my related work. In particular the advice of Norman Naimark, Thomas Baylis, Melvin Croan, Henry Krisch, Marilyn Rueschemeyer, and Adam Ulam was invaluable. The stimulating atmosphere of the Russian Research Center at Harvard University served to promote this project at key stages.

The editors at Cornell University Press deserve great credit for their invaluable assistance in revision of the original manuscript. In particular I thank John Ackerman, Roger Haydon, and David Nelson Blair.

Finally, I express my gratitude to my colleagues at the State University of New York at Geneseo, in particular Kenneth L. Deutsch and Alan Shank, for creating a supportive environment for such research. I also thank my secretary, Elizabeth Ancker, for her assistance.

I gratefully acknowledge the financial support of the German Academic Exchange Service, the Center for European Studies at Harvard University, the Free University of Berlin (West), and the International Research and Exchanges Board. Additional research regarding the Luther celebration in 1983 and the peace and environmental movements was made possible by a University Awards Fellowship from the State University of New York.

All translations from German are my own. Likewise I alone assume responsibility for the accuracy of the account and validity of the interpretation.

ROBERT F. GOECKEL

Geneseo, New York

Abbreviations and German Terms

Abbreviations

BS	*Berliner Sonntagsblatt*
CDU	Christian Democratic Union of Germany (East)
CPC	Christian Peace Conference (Prague)
CSCE	Conference on Security and Cooperation in Europe
DA	*Deutschland Archiv*
DAS	*Deutsche Allgemeine Sonntagsblatt*
Diakonie	Home Mission and Church Relief Agency (East)
DW	*Die Welt*
EKD	Evangelical Church in Germany (now only FRG)
EKU	Evangelical Church of the Union
FAZ	*Frankfurter Allgemeine Zeitung*
FDJ	Free German Youth, official youth organization
FR	*Frankfurter Rundschau*
FRG	Federal Republic of Germany (West)
GDR	German Democratic Republic (East)
Kirchenbund	Federation of Evangelical Churches in the GDR
KiS	*Kirche im Sozialismus*
KJ	*Kirchliches Jahrbuch fuer die Evangelische Kirche in Deutschland* (Church yearbook of EKD)
LWF	Lutheran World Federation (Geneva)
ND	*Neues Deutschland* (organ of the SED)
NVA	National People's Army (East)

NZ	*Neue Zeit* (organ of the CDU, East)
PCR	Program to Combat Racism of World Council of Churches
Pfarrerbund	Federation of Evangelical Pastors in the GDR
RFE	Radio Free Europe
RWF	Reformed World Federation
SED	Socialist Unity Party (Communist party, GDR)
SDZ	*Sueddeutsche Zeitung*
SPD	Social Democratic Party of Germany (West)
VELKD	United Evangelical Lutheran Church in Germany (West)
VELKDDR	United Evangelical Lutheran Church in the GDR
WCC	World Council of Churches (Geneva)
WTO	Warsaw Treaty Organization

German Terms

Abgrenzung	delimitation
Bausoldaten	unarmed construction units
Gleichschaltung	elimination of opposition
Jugendweihe	youth consecration ceremony
Kirchenpolitik	state policy toward the churches
Kirchwerdung	church unification process
Landeskirche	church province
Volkskirche	national church

The Lutheran Church
and the East German State

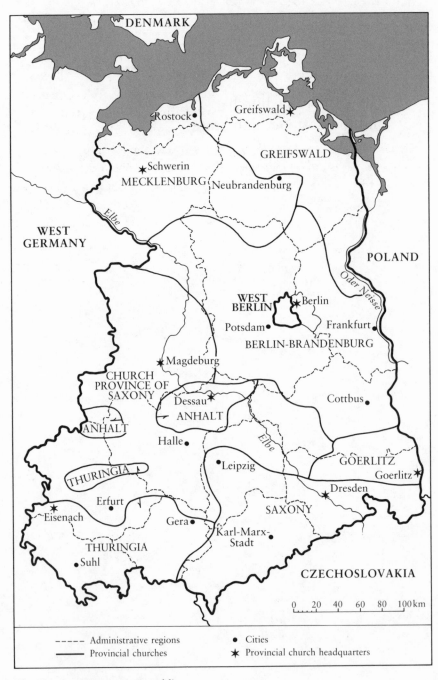

The German Democratic Republic

1 Introduction

Jesus answered and said unto them, Destroy this temple and in three days I will raise it up.

—John 2:19

Suddenly the Church Fits the GDR's Conception. In Order to Lend the Proper Effect to a New Prestige Building, the East Berlin Cathedral Is to Be Restored.

—headline, *Sueddeutsche Zeitung*
December 20, 1974

Much water has flowed under the bridges of the Spree River in Berlin since the partial destruction of the Berlin Cathedral in the final days of World War II. But though the reconstruction of East Berlin's temple may have required somewhat more time than Christ's resurrection, it nonetheless retains an element of the miraculous. The pharisees of the newly formed German Democratic Republic in 1949 doubtless would have similarly mocked any modern-day prophet who spoke of rebuilding the East Berlin cathedral. It is, of course, ironic that this latter-day Sanhedrin, commonly known as the Politburo of the Socialist Unity Party (SED), should be frustrated in its original intention of destroying the cathedral completely because of damage that would have resulted to the surrounding government buildings.[1] That the state should find itself in the position of actually supporting the cathedral's

---

[1] Based on discussion with the former bishop of Berlin-Brandenburg, Kurt Scharf. Scientific studies apparently revealed that razing the cathedral would destabilize government buildings, possibly causing them to sink into the Spree River.

reconstruction further compounds the irony. But Christ surprised his own disciples with his resurrection, so perhaps the often-resigned Christians in the GDR were among those most incredulous of the cathedral's reconstruction. Indeed, it is not surprising that the reconstruction, though dramatic, required so long; with spontaneity a taboo in GDR-style socialism, miracles must necessarily be planned, too. The reconstruction decision followed long negotiations and represented only one step in the long-term rapprochement between the state and the Evangelical churches during the era of SED chief Erich Honecker.

Rapprochement during the Honecker era reached a high point at the March 6, 1978, meeting between Honecker and the leadership of the Federation of Evangelical Churches in the GDR (Kirchenbund). The state under Honecker sought to come to terms with the continued existence and attraction of the churches and thereby to realize practical economic and political benefits. It sought to do so without allowing the leading role of the party to be challenged (as in Poland) and without compromising the ideological tenet of materialistic atheism (as in the Italian Communist party). In pursuing their spiritual and social tasks, the churches sought in the Honecker period to focus on the secularized conditions of their socialist environment and to consolidate common ground with the state wherever possible. They tried to avoid sacrificing the interests of the institution or its individual Christians and compromising the credibility of their organizational and theological independence from the state.

At the same time, the agreement to reconstruct reveals the general dilemmas that confronted both the churches and the state in this process. Both sides obtained practical benefits from the cathedral's reconstruction: the state was pleased to eliminate the eyesore and obtain the windfall of needed hard currency from the West German churches; the churches benefited from the West German–funded program for the building of new churches, which they had successfully linked to the cathedral negotiations. Yet both sides no doubt harbored some ambivalence toward the package deal. Some in the church were uneasy about restoring a church structure so identified with Wilhelmine Germany, so inappropriate to the contemporary needs of the GDR churches, and so awkwardly located near the state's own temple, the Palace of the Republic. Likewise, some in the state and SED doubtless had second thoughts about restoring old structures and building new ones for a "dying remnant of bourgeois society." Thus the rapprochement posed credibility problems for both state and church.

This book describes and explains this change in the church-state relationship, focusing particular attention on the period 1968–74.[2] The point of departure was the creation of the Kirchenbund in 1969. Previously the eight GDR Landeskirchen (provincial churches) were members of the all-German umbrella organization, the Evangelical Church in Germany (EKD). Throughout the 1940s and much of the 1950s, the state accepted the legitimacy of this all-German organization, although internally the Stalinization process entailed periodic campaigns against religious adherence and institutional church prerogatives. After 1958, however, the state withdrew its recognition of the EKD and increasingly tried to abrogate this border-transcending institution. The East German churches eventually accommodated this demand, although their separation from the West German churches was far from total and significant formal and informal ties continued. The creation of the Kirchenbund resulted in a more unified position by the churches vis-à-vis the state.

The state's response to the churches' actions was initially cool. It did not recognize the new Kirchenbund for two years; indeed the accession to power of Honecker in 1971 actually heralded heightened ideological conflicts with the churches. However, after 1973 the state began to grant the church concessions of an institutional nature and reconciled itself to the remaining inter-German church ties. For its part, the church increasingly focused on its role as a "church within socialism."

Yet the rapprochement brought little benefit initially to the individual believer. Only after the problems of grassroots Christians were graphically demonstrated by the public suicide of a clergyman in 1976 did the state move to defuse the situation on this level as well. The new relationship was symbolized by an unprecedented summit between Honecker and the Kirchenbund leadership in March 1978. After that meeting cooperation flourished in a variety of areas, including the massive state celebration of the five hundredth anniversary of Luther's birth in 1983.

In the 1980s the new relationship was challenged by the rise of nonreligious dissent, focusing largely on the issues of security and peace, the environment, and alternative lifestyles. As an autonomous institu-

[2]Robert F. Goeckel, "Detente and Conservatizing Liberalization: The State and the Evangelical Churches in the German Democratic Republic, 1968–74" (Ph.D. diss., Harvard University, 1982).

tion, the church facilitated such dissent by acting as an umbrella for these secular movements; at the same time it channeled and domesticated them to a certain extent. Thus the church's ambiguous role in the face of these movements confirms the symbiotic relationship that developed between church and state.

Examination of the changing church-state relationship in the GDR yields significant findings relevant to broader issues in the study of Communist systems.

First, it sheds light on the relationship between changes in the international system and the domestic system in a Communist state. The GDR was a state born of the Cold War and the tight bipolarity characterizing the international system after World War II.[3] Internally it avoided the worst excesses of Stalinism, as well as the instability accompanying de-Stalinization in several other East European states. Yet by the late 1960s it was one of the most regimented societies and strictest political systems in the Soviet bloc. It was also one of the strongest opponents of any relaxation of tensions between East and West, fearing the domestic consequences of detente, particularly those involving greater contact with and exposure to West Germany.

Yet, as a result of the loosening bipolarity in Europe in the 1960s and foreign policy changes by the Federal Republic of Germany (FRG) stemming from changes in the governing coalition, the GDR was faced with just this prospect.[4] For some time, East German leader Walter Ulbricht was able to use deviations, such as the independent foreign

---

[3] Numerous historical treatments of the founding of the GDR and the Stalinist transformation process exist. See the thorough review by David Childs, *The German Democratic Republic: Moscow's German Ally* (1983), particularly the relatively mild Stalinization process (pp. 20–33) and the limited de-Stalinization under Ulbricht (pp. 37–66). Other sources include Arthur Hanhardt, *The German Democratic Republic* (1968), pp. 43–66; Martin McCauley, *The German Democratic Republic since 1945* (1983), pp. 6–102; and Hermann Weber, *Kleine Geschichte der DDR* (1980), pp. 47–136. The immediate takeover process in the Soviet Zone is well analyzed in Henry Krisch, *German Politics under Soviet Occupation* (1974), and Gregory Sandford, *From Hitler to Ulbricht: The Communist Reconstruction of East Germany, 1945–46* (1983). See also Henry Krisch, *The German Democratic Republic: The Search for Identity* (1985).

[4] For analysis of Ulbricht's reluctance to engage in detente with West Germany and Honecker's greater forthcomingness on the Ostpolitik, see Melvin Croan, "The Development of GDR Political Relations with the USSR," and Siegfried Kupper, "Political Relations with the FRG," both in *GDR Foreign Policy*, ed. Eberhard Schulz et al. (1982), pp. 198–214, 290–304. Also see William Griffith's account of GDR intransigence in his *The Ostpolitik of the Federal Republic of Germany* (1978), particularly pp. 178–79.

policy pursued by Romania, and crises, such as that in Czechoslovakia in 1968, to brake a favorable Soviet response to the incipient West German Ostpolitik. By 1969 Ulbricht's luck and political adroitness began to wane, and Soviet–West German detente blossomed at Ulbricht's expense. The East Germans did not embrace detente until 1971, after Ulbricht's ouster by the Soviets. The church-state relationship reveals the effects on GDR domestic policy of this international change from Cold War to detente, focusing on one actor, the church. More narrowly, it indicates the effect on the churches as the GDR's foreign policy lagged behind the Soviets'.

This dimension is particularly important to West German foreign policy. A fundamental assumption of the West German Ostpolitik, particularly as conceived by Willy Brandt and Egon Bahr, was that domestic change in the GDR would flow from international rapprochement.[5] Even under the CDU today, the Ostpolitik continues to assume that concessions to the GDR may be legitimately linked to the domestic situation there. One highly visible benchmark of this situation is the treatment of the churches and Christians by the state. An improvement in their status as a result of the Ostpolitik would seem to vindicate the West German initiative; conversely, no change or a worsening of their position would cast doubt on the assumptions behind Ostpolitik.

Of course, East Germany diametrically opposed any linkage between international detente and domestic liberalization as an interference in its domestic sovereignty.[6] The regime sought to prevent such a linkage or, if this proved impossible, to limit the negative effects of the domestic changes made necessary by Ostpolitik. Thus a study of the church-state relationship reveals the ability of the GDR to limit the domestic damage from detente.

This discussion of a hypothesized relationship between international

---

[5]This was encapsuled in Bahr's slogan "Change through rapprochement." For a discussion of what Griffith calls the "flexible left" position, see Griffith, pp. 116–20. For the views of its leading theoreticians, see Richard Loewenthal, ed., *Die Zweite Republik: 25 Jahre Bundesrepublik—Eine Bilanz* (Stuttgart: Seewald, 1974), and Walter Hahn, "West Germany's Ostpolitik: The Grand Design of Egon Bahr," *Orbis* 16 (Winter 1973): 859–80.

[6]An East German and Soviet goal in the period of detente was to limit the domestic fallout from increased contacts with the West. This has taken the form of heightened emphasis on *Abgrenzung* and socialist integration. See James F. Brown, "Detente and Soviet Policy in Eastern Europe," *Survey* 20 (Spring–Summer 1974): 46–58; Croan in Schulz, pp. 214–26; and David Childs, "The Ostpolitik and Domestic Politics in East Germany," in *The Ostpolitik and Political Change in Germany*, ed. Roger Tilford (1975), pp. 59–76.

change and domestic change leads to a second significant aspect of this book, namely its relationship to the German question. The issue of linkage discussed above is much more salient to West German policy than to American policy.[7] For the FRG, unlike the United States, domestic liberalization in the GDR is not only intrinsically desirable but also instrumental to its constitutionally mandated and politically expedient goal of German reunification. Liberalization in the GDR and continuing ties between the two Germanies are a means of maintaining the unity of the nation pending a potential reunification. From Wehner to Weizsaecker, West German statesmen have viewed the inter-German ties of the churches as evidence of this continuing unity, even if primarily in terms of a cultural nation (*Kulturnation*).

Again, the East German view of the national question differed from the West German.[8] Following its creation, the GDR experienced a legitimacy deficit, recognized by few states internationally and viewed as provisional by many of its own citizens. For many years it too acknowledged a single German nationality and supported German unity, blaming the failure to realize such unity on the FRG. Despite this rhetorical

---

[7]U.S. foreign policy has alternated on this issue. During the Nixon-Ford Kissinger era, linkage to domestic policy in the Soviet bloc was quite limited. Under Carter, linkage to human rights in the Soviet bloc became a high priority. Under Reagan, linkage to the domestic situation in the bloc again declined as a policy goal.

In the FRG, on the other hand, the West German Basic Law, affirmed by the Letters on German Unity attached to the Moscow and Warsaw treaties by the FRG, precludes diplomatic recognition of the GDR and stipulates the goal of eventual reunification. See Ulrich Scheuner, "The Problem of the Nation and the GDR's Relationship with the FRG," in Schulz, pp. 47–50. With the decreasing likelihood of reunification as a *state*, this commitment to reunification shifted to focus on the continued existence of the German *nation*. Hence, Brandt's formula of "two states, one nation."

[8]The official GDR interpretation of the "nation" shifted particularly in response to the heightened West German focus on the continued existence of the nation. Currently the regime admits the GDR is German in its nationality, but the 1974 Constitution refers only to the "socialist state of workers and peasants." This view allows the GDR to demarcate itself from the FRG, yet claim links with German history. For the official SED view of the nation, see Alfred Kosing, *Nation in Geschichte und Gegenwart* (Berlin/GDR: Dietz Verlag, 1976). West German analyses of the GDR view of the nation can be found in Federal Ministry for Inner-German Relations, *DDR-Handbuch* (1985), pp. 924–27, and Ulrich Scheuner in Schulz, pp. 39–66.

Empirical evidence seems to contradict this official view of the creation of a separate socialist nation, at least in terms of substituting for German nationality. Peter Ludz found that in 1975 two-thirds of the GDR still did not view the FRG as a foreign country. See Peter Christian Ludz, *Die DDR zwischen Ost und West: Politische Analysen 1961–1976* (1977), p. 224. On the other hand, Gebhard Schweigler stresses the creation of a separate political consciousness in the GDR, supportive of the regime; see his *National Consciousness in Divided Germany* (1975).

stand, however, the GDR increasingly sought to create a separate East German identity, eventually even an East German nationality, based on the alleged differences in class character between East and West Germany. Thus the earlier incorporation of the German nation in the 1949 Constitution gave way to the concept of a "socialist state of the German nation" in the 1968 Constitution. Since 1971 this too has been replaced by reference to the "socialist nation," shaped by the working class, tied to other "fraternal socialist nations," and in opposition to the "bourgeois nation." This goal led to a policy of *Abgrenzung,* or delimitation, from the FRG in the 1960s and early 1970s. At different times the churches, through their international work and domestic pronouncements, either accelerated or retarded the state's efforts. But at other times the state tried to influence the public debate in the FRG, in which case special all-German ties became useful. Thus development and changes in the church's inter-German ties will tell a great deal about the GDR's policy on the national question, as well as about the success of the West German policy of "two states, one nation."

Third, an understanding of church-state relations facilitates analysis of the relationship between international organizations—in particular international non-governmental organizations (INGOs)—and a Communist state. As with the debate surrounding transnational actors, the fundamental question is to what extent activities of INGOs erode the sovereignty of states over foreign and domestic policy.[9] Some argue that sovereignty is at bay; others claim that states still control the access of INGOs to the state and that INGO activities may enhance sovereignty by helping states achieve their goals. In this case, it is perhaps more useful to couch the question in terms of the relative costs for the GDR of a policy of openness, versus one of closure, vis-à-vis INGOs. The GDR Evangelical-Lutheran churches are members of various INGOs, most notably the World Council of Churches, the Lutheran World Federation, and the Council of European Churches. In contrast to the Catholic church, a transnational actor with a unified hierarchy, the Evangelical-Lutheran churches are only loosely organized above the state level; member churches in these INGOs retain financial and organizational

[9]Raymond Vernon, *Sovereignty at Bay: The Multinational Spread of U.S. Enterprise* (New York: Basic, 1971); Samuel P. Huntington, "Transnational Organizations in World Politics," *World Politics* 25 (April 1973): 333–68; Robert O. Keohane and Joseph S. Nye, eds., *Transnational Relations and World Politics* (Cambridge, Mass.: Harvard University Press, 1971).

autonomy.[10] However, like transnational actors they may affect the foreign and domestic policies of states by pursuing a private foreign policy, setting the policy agenda, or acting as instruments of state policy.[11] Potential costs to the state of a policy of openness include a strengthening of the churches' position in society and increased criticism of human rights policy. Potential benefits to the state include increased international recognition and legitimacy for the GDR and support on certain foreign policy issues. A study of the GDR church-state relationship indicates how the regime has managed this tradeoff over time and sheds light on the INGO-state relationship.

Fourth, analyzing the change in state policy toward the GDR churches and comparing it with church-state relations in other Communist systems yields conclusions regarding the causal effect of certain domestic variables. First, the effect of internal church factors on the relationship can be studied. For example, the fact that the GDR is the only state in the Soviet bloc with a dominant Protestant tradition allows one to test the role of theological tradition. Chapter 2 describes the East German Lutheran tradition of political passivity tempered by the experience of the Third Reich and Barthian social activism.[12] In addition, comparison of the GDR, a confessionally homogeneous society, with confessionally heterogeneous socialist states may indicate the impact of confessional distribution on the likelihood for rapprochement between church and state, as shown by tables 1.1 and 1.2.[13] Finally, a comparison of the

[10]Ivan Vallier, "The Roman Catholic Church: A Transnational Actor," *International Organization* 25 (Summer 1971): 479–502; Kjell Skjelsbaek, "The Growth of International Non-Governmental Organization in the Twentieth Century," *International Organization* 25 (Summer 1971): 420–42. Dennis Dunn addresses the tension between the Vatican and its "national units" in his *Detente and Papal-Communist Relations, 1962–1978* (Boulder, Colo.: Westview, 1979). The view that INGO participation strengthens the organizational independence in Soviet bloc churches is made by Darrel Hudson, *The World Council of Churches in International Affairs* (1977), pp. 265–70, 279; J. A. Hebly, *The Russians in the World Council of Churches* (1978), p. 8; and William Fletcher, *Religion and Soviet Foreign Policy, 1945–1970* (1970), pp. 150–53.

[11]Joseph S. Nye, Jr., "Multinational Corporations in World Politics," *Foreign Affairs* 3 (October 1974): 153–75.

[12]The minority status of Lutheran churches in Hungary, Poland, Romania, and the USSR has left them overshadowed by larger denominations in the state's policy, except during periods of state campaigns against the majority churches.

[13]Religion as a political cleavage in Western democracies is dealt with in Seymour M. Lipset and Stein Rokkan, "Cleavage Structures, Party Systems, and Voter Alignments: An Introduction," in *Party Systems and Voter Alignments*, ed. Seymour M. Lipset and Stein Rokkan, pp. 50–53, and Richard Rose and Derek Urwin, "Social Cohesion, Political Parties, and Strains in Regimes," *Comparative Political Studies* 2 (April 1969): 7–67.

Table 1.1. Population of the GDR by confession (census data), 1939–1964

	1939	1946	1950	1964
Total Population (ooos)	16,452 100%	18,488 100%	18,338 100%	17,004 100%
No Response	8 0%	28 0.2%	27 0.2%	56 0.3%
No Confession	1,198 7.3%	1,077 5.8%	1,400 7.6%	5,361 31.6%
Members of a Religious Organization	15,246 92.7% (100%)	17,383 94.0% (100%)	16,961 92.2% (100%)	11,587 68.1% (100%)
Evangelical	14,012 85.2% (91.9%)	14,963 80.9% (86.1%)	14,802 80.5 (87.3%)	10,092 59.3% (87.1%)
Catholic	1,083 6.6% (7.1%)	2,233 12.1% (12.8%)	2,021 11.0% (11.9%)	1,375 8.1% (11.9%)
Other	151 0.9% (1.0%)	187 1.0% (1.1%)	138 0.7% (0.8%)	120 0.7% (1.0%)

Note: Percentages without parentheses refer to the percentages of the total population in the respective category; percentages within parentheses refer to the portion of the religious identifiers in the respective category.

Source: Alfred Reinhold, "Jeder dritte Mitteldeutsche ohne Konfession," *Deutschland Archiv* 2, no. 10 (October 1969), p. 1119.

relatively democratic, decentralized GDR church to other more hierarchical churches in the bloc permits analysis of the impact of internal church structure on the relationship with the state. The comparison may suggest the relative advantages of a united front, as opposed to rank-and-file criticism and accountability, for the church in dealing with a centralized state.

Examination of the church-state relationship will also demonstrate the impact of secularization and decline in church adherence. As indicated in table 1.1 and discussed further in chapter 2, the GDR is not only confessionally homogeneous but highly secularized. Church adherence is perhaps the lowest in Eastern Europe. Thus the church has found itself in an increasingly weak position in terms of organizational maintenance. In such a situation, an organization faces two alternatives. It can pursue internal changes to adapt to its environment—for example, making structural reforms that reduce dependence on external

Table 1.2. Affiliated religious adherents in Eastern Europe as a percentage of population, 1970

	Bulgaria	Czechoslovakia	GDR	Hungary	Poland	Romania	USSR	Yugoslavia
Catholic	0.7	67.0	7.90	59.20	88.60	6.3	1.80	34.20
Orthodox	65.2	1.4	0.10	0.60	1.60	79.9	31.00	39.80
Lutheran	—	3.9	59.20	4.40	0.37	1.1	0.29	0.44
Reformed	—	3.2	0.05	18.90	0.02	3.4	0.05	0.15
Other Protestant	0.6	4.4	0.03	0.01	0	3.2	2.40	0.36
Jewish	0.1	0.1	0	0.90	0	0.5	1.20	0
Muslim	11.0	—	—	0	0	1.2	11.50	11.00

Note: The remainder are nonreligious, atheist, or members of sects.
Source: David B. Barrett, ed., World Christian Encyclopedia (Nairobi: Oxford University Press, 1982), pp. 198–201, 257–62, 310–14, 363–67, 569–74, 584–88, 689–97, 753–57.

support or change the incentives for membership—or it can seek to alter its environment to ameliorate the conditions threatening the maintenance of the organization. Comparison of the GDR case of dramatic decline in church adherence with other cases of decline (e.g., Hungary) or stability (e.g., Poland) reveals the effect of this factor on the churches' relationship with its respective regime.

The study of the church-state relationship also sheds light on the extent to which state policy is guided by its constitutional and legal framework. The East German constitution guarantees certain rights to all citizens, including equal rights, freedom of belief and conscience, right to religious practice. The churches are guaranteed the right to "spiritual ministry and activities useful to the community," although separation of church and state is not mentioned.

During the period under study, the state was officially guided by its leading force, the Communist party (in this case, the Socialist Unity party), and its ideology of Marxism-Leninism, of which scientific atheism is an integral component. It is reasonable to hypothesize that state policy would reflect fundamental ideological antagonism toward religion and the churches. Moreover, the Marxist-Leninist ideology brooks no opposition to the leading role of the party, which exercises the dictatorship of the proletariat. Even if there were no differences in worldview between the churches and the state, the state might still seek to weaken the churches' challenge to political monopoly. The case provides the opportunity to test the consistency with which the ideology is pursued and the role that it plays in changes in state policy.

Finally, the church-state relationship allows one to analyze the role of Soviet and bloc policy regarding religion in determining GDR policy. As the hegemonic power in the region, the Soviets might be expected to replicate their rather harsh policy toward the churches throughout the region or to pursue a uniform policy throughout the bloc, even if at variance with the Soviet policy.[14] Thus comparison of the GDR with other Soviet bloc states on dimensions of institutional church strength,

---

[14]During the early postwar period of Soviet hegemony, Stalinist foreign policy dictated replication of Soviet domestic policy in Eastern Europe. See Zbigniew Brzezinski, *The Soviet Bloc: Unity and Conflict* (Cambridge, Mass.: Harvard University Press, 1967), especially 485–512, and Hugh Seton-Watson, *The East European Revolution* (New York: Praeger, 1956), pp. 230–318.

treatment of religious adherents, and relative political strength reveals Soviet influence and goals regarding domestic policy in the bloc.

The change in the church-state relationship in the GDR yields insight into the conditions for and nature of political change in Communist systems. Can the church, a relatively autonomous actor outside the official system, nonetheless act as a source of change in the system? If so, does this represent a fundamental change in the character of the system? Or is this marginal change, designed to foreclose more fundamental political change and liberalization in the Communist system? Can this change be replicated by other institutions or in other Soviet-style systems? Or is this change unique, and hence limited to the conditions obtaining in the GDR? Although I cannot claim to build grand theory in this book, I do seek to contribute to a middle-range theory understanding the process of effective change in Communist systems.

2 Church and State

To analyze the extent of change in the church-state relationship and the factors responsible for the change, it is necessary to understand the structures and beliefs of both church and state that affect their respective self-definitions and their policies toward each other. The organizational structure, theology, and social presence of the churches are significant dimensions of their role in the GDR. For the state, the Marxist-Leninist ideology, particularly as it deals with religion, the legal-constitutional framework, and the instruments and means of the state's policy are relevant to a study of the changing relationship.

THE "REAL EXISTING CHURCH"

The Organization of the Churches

Three aspects of the organization of the churches are relevant to the state's Kirchenpolitik: the confessional distribution of religious adherence, the interchurch structure of the Evangelical-Lutheran confession, and the internal structure of the church.

Religious adherents in the GDR are overwhelmingly Evangelical-Lutheran. Catholics are a small, yet distinct minority; other independent Protestant denominations are minuscule.

As table 2.1 indicates, this confessional distribution contrasts sharply with both that of prewar Germany, in which the Evangelical/Catholic

Table 2.1. Confessional distribution in prewar Germany, West Germany, and East Germany

Confessional distribution in prewar Germany (1939)		
Protestant	41,396,437	(60.7%)
Catholic	22,583,998	(33.1%)
Other	4,250,583	(6.2%)
Confessional distribution in West Germany (1946)		
Protestant	22,283,166	(49.7%)
Catholic	20,734,022	(46.3%)
Other	1,792,387	(4.0%)
Confessional distribution in East Germany, excluding Berlin (1946)		
Protestant	14,963,000	(80.0%)
Catholic	2,233,000	(12.0%)
Other	187,000	(1.0%)

Source: *Kirchliches Jahrbuch der Evangelische Kirche in Deutschland,* 1959, pp. 561–64.

proportion was roughly two to one, and that of the FRG, in which the Evangelical and Catholic confessions are roughly equal in strength.[1] Thus the division of Germany had major consequences for the GDR; for the first time, a modern German state faced an overwhelmingly Evangelical population. Though the transnational Roman Catholic Church and the less visible independent Protestant denominations pose in some ways more interesting problems, the Evangelical churches without doubt bulk most heavily in the state's Kirchenpolitik.

In terms of interchurch structure, however, the Evangelical denomination is by no means a unified entity, due to the strong tradition of parochial states in German history. The basic unit of the Evangelical Church is the territorial church, or Landeskirche. The territorial principle—church boundaries equated with state boundaries—derived from the increasing control of the rulers over the churches in their states after the Peace of Augsburg (1555) and the rise of the modern state.[2] As part

[1]The 1970 FRG census records 49.1% Protestants and 44.7% Catholics. See Statistisches Bundesamt, *Statistisches Jahrbuch 1981 für die Bundesrepublik Deutschland* (Stuttgart und Mainz: W. Kohlhammer, 1981), pp. 50, 62. Although by 1981 Catholics outnumbered Evangelical/Protestants, the balance in confession remains. For the prewar German confessional distribution, see Statistisches Reichsamt, *Statistik des Deutschen Reichs, Band 522, 3, Volks-, Berufs- und Betriebszaehlung vom 17. Mai 1939* (1941), cited in Frederic Spotts, *The Churches and Politics in Germany* (1973), pp. 48–49.
[2]*Evangelisches Staatslexikon* (1975), p. 1143.

of the Napoleonic reforms in the early nineteenth century, the three hundred Landeskirchen were subsumed into approximately thirty. However, despite the political centralization brought about by unification of Germany in 1871 and the Nazi regime, the basic organizational unit of the German church has remained the Landeskirche.

There are eight Landeskirchen in the GDR:

Anhalt Berlin-Brandenburg (East) Church Province of Saxony (Magdeburg) Gorlitz Greifswald	members of the EKU
Mecklenburg Saxony (Dresden) Thuringia	members of the VELKDDR

Five Landeskirchen form the Evangelical Church of the Union (EKU), known until after 1945 as the Old Prussian Union. It reflects the Prussian drive for German unification in the nineteenth century and the merger of Lutheran and Reformed churches in Prussian areas. The remaining three Landeskirchen, outside the Prussian sphere until later in the nineteenth century, have remained purely Lutheran. Although linked loosely in the United Evangelical Churches in the GDR (VELKDDR), they have retained their particularistic traditions. Initiatives aimed at greater unity, such as the Deutscher Evangelischer Kirchenbund (1922), the Deutsche Evangelische Kirche (1933), and most recently the Evangelical Churches in Germany or EKD (1948) have made only minimal progress in overcoming the geographic and confessional particularism associated with the Landeskirche.

Internally the Evangelical Landeskirchen reflect both hierarchical and democratic principles. The democratic principle takes the form of the synod, which was adapted from the Reformed churches acquired by Prussia in the nineteenth century. The synod is largely elected in a democratic process that begins in the local parish councils. The synod in turn chooses the bishop, or church president, along with the church leadership. Thus the leaders of the Landeskirchen are subject to a certain amount of democratic input and control from below. However, simply by the nature of their offices, the bishop and church leadership play an executive role, especially in conjunction with the full-time bureaucracy in the chancellory of each Landeskirche. This hierarchical tendency is heightened by the attention that the centralized state has paid to the church leaderships. Moreover, despite the Lutheran tenet of the priesthood of all believers, a hierarchical element is inherent in the distinction between clergy and laity. Clergy are better informed and more active in church affairs than laity and often tend to dominate synods and church leaderships. The democratic, decentralized character of the church has made it easier for the state to exert pressure on oppositional church leaders, but has also strengthened the negotiating hand of moderate church leaders.

Theological Traditions of the Churches

Nor is the church monolithic in terms of theology. Although the overwhelming majority of congregations are Lutheran, there are some Reformed congregations, residuals of the waves of immigration into Prussia from France and other German states in the seventeenth and eighteenth centuries. This theological division manifests itself structurally in the form of the five Union Landeskirchen and the three purely Lutheran Landeskirchen. Such confessionalism has hindered efforts to overcome these largely anachronistic theological differences.

More to the point, however, are the two strains of theological thought regarding the church's relationship to worldly authority: the Two Kingdoms Doctrine and the Lordship of Christ Principle, associated with Lutheran and Reformed traditions respectively. In addressing the Two Kingdoms Doctrine, one must look first at the thought of Luther, who molded the doctrine. Luther saw the world divided into two kingdoms, that of the devil and that of God.[3] This dualism is reflected in two governments, in Luther's words: the spiritual, "by which the Holy Spirit produces Christians," and the temporal, "which restrains the un-Christian and wicked so that . . . they are obliged to keep still and to maintain an outward peace." Thus, just as Christians are to submit to

[3] According to Luther, "now all of us dwell in the devil's kingdom until the coming of the Kingdom of God. . . . There is of course no one who will not find some trace of the devil's kingdom in himself." The English texts for Luther are taken from the American edition of Luther's works, reprinted in Karl H. Hertz, ed., *Two Kingdoms and One World: A Sourcebook in Christian Social Ethics* (1976), pp. 31–32, 54.

God, they are also to submit to world authority, since it is ordained by God and necessary to control sin on earth. Although Luther considered the state corrupt and inferior to spiritual power, the state was needed to maintain domestic order required for propagation of the Gospel.[4] According to Luther, the Bible brings no new laws into the world; the measure of a state is the law of nature. Luther posits thus that the obligation to obey authority applies to any authority, whether Christian, Turk, or heathen. Indeed, on the basis of the natural law standard, it can occur that Turkish rule is more just than Christian rule.[5] Such submission to the worldly authority, therefore, could result in deference to such un-Christian regimes as the Nazis or Communists.

Reformed theology, rooted in Calvin's thought, is less submissive to secular authority than Luther's doctrine. In modern times it has come to be identified by the term "Lordship of Christ Principle." Calvin did not share Luther's dualism, believing that God's kingdom was to be revealed in this worldly life as well. He speaks of the churches' role in sanctifying this world, of developing the Holy Community.[6] His view of the state is correspondingly quite different from Luther's, in the view of church historian Ernst Troeltsch: "The State, in particular, in the chief passages in which Calvin refers to it, is never recorded as a mere antidote to the fallen State and a penalty for evil, but is always chiefly regarded as a good and holy institution appointed by God himself." Although the church and the state are allowed to retain their own character, they enjoy a theocratic union, both working together in common obedience to the word of God. The individual in Calvin's thought is to participate in politics and government, not out of obligation to authority, as in Luther's thought, but "to glorify God, to produce the Holy Community." Moreover, Calvin gives a limited right of resistance: if the "supreme authority fails in its duty, [a Divine Commission] can intervene for the good of society and the truth of religion." Though Calvin does not grant this right to individuals, it nonetheless represents a marked difference from Luther's submission to authority.

[4]Ernst Troeltsch, *The Social Teachings of the Christian Churches* (1931), pp. 517–19.
[5]Philipp Melanchthon, *Apologia Confessionis Augustanea*, trans. Horst Georg Pohlman (Gutersloh: Gerd Mohn, 1967), pp. 178–80; Martin Luther, "Secular Authority: To What Extent It Should Be Obeyed," and "An Appeal to the Ruling Class of German Nationality as to the Amelioration of the State of Christendom," in *Martin Luther: Selections from His Writings* (1961), ed. John Dillenberger, pp. 363–402, 472.
[6]Troeltsch, pp. 590–92, 607, 613, 616, 617.

Despite the waves of immigration that brought Calvin's Reformed thought to Germany, the history of German Protestantism has been one of submission to the state, molded primarily by Luther's Two Kingdoms Doctrine. Although Luther had foreseen relative autonomy for church and state, in practice the church became dependent on the ruler for its defense. With the rise of the modern state in the seventeenth century, this dependence grew. The dualistic understanding of church and state came to an end, and the churches became adjuncts of the state in Constantinian fashion. The state exercised prerogatives over the designation of church personnel and administration of church possessions.[7] Especially following the process of the unification of Germany in the nineteenth century, the Two Kingdoms Doctrine was used to legitimate the monarchy. The deference to authority, which the Lutheran theological tradition promoted, served to facilitate the state-led industrialization process in Germany.[8] The churches paid scant attention to the plight of the growing working class and limited their social responsibility to caritative work.[9] This strong emphasis on dualism and submission to worldly authority continued into twentieth-century Germany and contributed to the churches' considerable acquiescence to the Third Reich.[10]

The experience of the Third Reich greatly discredited the Two Kingdoms Doctrine. Under the attack of the Nazi heresy and struggle against the churches, or *Kirchenkampf*, the German churches became influenced by the Calvinistic thought of Karl Barth. Barth, a leading German theologian forced into exile in Switzerland during the Nazi period, was a major force behind the Barmen Theological Declaration (1934). This declaration rejected as false teaching that "there were areas of our life, in which we do not own Jesus Christ, but other Masters."[11] Barth called for resistance against any government that acted against the will of

---

[7]This state control is referred to as the *Landesherrliches Kirchenregiment. Evangelisches Staatslexikon* (1975), p. 1143.

[8]Erich Fromm, *Escape from Freedom* (New York: Rinehart and Co., 1941), pp. 62–102.

[9]Hertz, p. 157.

[10]Spotts, p. 120; George Brand, "Accommodation and Resistance: A Study of Church-State Relations in the German Democratic Republic" (Ph.D. diss., Colgate University, 1974), pp. 8–9.

[11]"Barmer Theologische Erklaerung," *Theologisches Lexikon*, ed. Hans-Hinrich Jenssen and Herbert Trebs (1978), p. 51.

Christ and for Christian political engagement in democracy to put into practice the ideas of Christ.[12] Barth's extension of God's kingdom to include social and political life contrasts greatly with the Two Kingdoms Doctrine and even goes beyond Calvin in his allowance for individual action. Based largely on the thought of Barth and Dietrich Bonhoeffer, the Confessing Church resisted the coopted official church hierarchy, Hitler's German Christian movement, and fascism in general. Its numbers remained limited, but its effect on postwar theology has been great, particularly in the GDR.[13] In part this is due to the fact that adherents of the Confessing Church, such as Bishop Schoenherr, Bishop Scharf, and Bishop Jaenicke, have held important positions in the postwar church; but it is also a response to the widespread revulsion against the devastating results of the churches' political passivity. Given this historical legacy of nationalistic wars and authoritarian state, the churches have undergone a theological reconsideration of their historical political passivity and ties to political authority.

The Barthian emphasis on the churches' political responsibility has not erased the traditional Lutheran passivity of the GDR churches, but it has modified it considerably. It has led some to espouse total opposition to a state that they see as a continuation of Nazi-style totalitarian rule. Paradoxically it has led others to give the state the total "yes to socialism" which it seeks. Many have sought to walk the *via media* of "critical solidarity," criticizing state policies within the context of a general acceptance of socialism.

The Social Presence of the Churches

To evaluate the change in the church-state relationship, we need a benchmark for the church's presence in society. Although the Evangeli-

[12]"Karl Barth," in Jenssen and Trebs, pp. 51–54; Spotts, p. 9; Reinhard Stawinski, "Theologie in der DDR–DDR Theologie?" in *Die Evangelischen Kirchen in der DDR*, ed. Reinhard Henkys (1982), p. 91.

[13]Six thousand of 18,000 pastors were active in the Confessing Church according to Carl Friedrich and Zbigniew K. Brzezinski, *Totalitarian Dictatorship and Autocracy* (Cambridge: Harvard University Press, 1965), p. 308. Twenty percent of the pastors signed the Barmen principles and 3,000 were arrested, according to Spotts, p. 9. Barth exercised direct influence in the church debates in the 1950s. See his exchange with prominent East German theologian Johannes Hamel in Karl Barth and Johannes Hamel, *How to Serve God in a Marxist Land*

cal churches have lost membership, they have long maintained a considerable social presence.

Secularization has eroded church adherence as measured in traditional terms. In the 1950s and 1960s this decline occurred precipitously, primarily as a result of members leaving the church (see table 2.2). In recent times the decline has been more moderate but has resulted from the failure to gain new members via baptism of children. As table 2.3 indicates, the decline extends to practically all measures of church adherence, with the exception of burials. Olof Klohr has estimated that only 10 percent to 20 percent of the youth are religious.[14] This decline in church adherence has naturally led to other problems for the churches, such as a shortage of pastors and a reduction in church income.[15]

This decline has twin causes: the secularization common to most industrial societies and the state's discrimination against Christians. With the highest per capita national income in the Soviet bloc, higher indeed than many states in the industrialized West, the GDR has experienced the processes of modernization and the concomitant weakening of ties to religion. In fact this secularization, or de-Christianization, was already well advanced prior to the advent of communism in Germany; the decline in church adherence among the German working class in the late nineteenth century has been well documented.[16] After a brief re-

---

(1959) and the discussion of it in Richard Solberg, *God and Caesar in East Germany* (1961), pp. 278–82.

[14]Olof Klohr, "Tendenzen . . . ," cited in *Kirchliches Jahrbuch*, 1974, p. 573.

[15]For example, in Berlin-Brandenburg (East) in 1972 almost 35% of the pastoral positions were vacant; in the church as a whole, roughly 29% were unfilled in 1973.

[16]For evidence of secularization among the working class in the nineteenth century, see Andrew L. Drummond, *German Protestantism since Luther* (1951), pp. 220–22. For an empirical study documenting working-class alienation from the church, see Paul Piechowski, *Proletarischer Glaube* (1927).

Recent studies indicate lower church adherence in urban regions—such as Berlin, Leipzig, Dresden—than rural ones, such as Suhl, Schwerin, and Neubrandenburg. Also, church adherence appears negatively correlated with level of education. These differences are contained in *epd* (Evangelische Pressedienst) *Landesdienst Berlin*, 22 October 1968, which contains the results of the 1964 census by region.

The term "secularization" requires clarification in this context. Developmentalists, such as Donald Smith, use the term primarily in terms of the increasing independence and dominance of the state and nation over the church and religion. See his "Religion and Political Modernization: Comparative Perspectives," in *Religion and Political Modernization*, ed. Donald E. Smith (New Haven: Yale University Press, 1974), pp. 1–28. The term is used in this work to refer to the decline in subjective religious adherence. For others using the term in this context, see Peter L. Berger, *The Social Reality of Religion* (London: Faber and Faber, 1967), pp. 105–25, and David Martin, *A General Theory of Secularization* (New York: St. Martin's, 1977), pp. 231–32.

Table 2.2. Numbers officially terminating church membership in the GDR, 1952–1960

Provincial church	1952	1953	1956	1957	1958	1959	1960
Pomerania	—	1,321	2,913	2,805	8,584	4,978	—
Silesia	1,973	1,960	1,555	1,159	3,576	2,601	2,159
Anhalt	3,143	3,162	3,373	1,888	5,966	4,306	—
Saxony	35,748	36,578	42,806	46,235	101,515	66,698	54,838
Thuringia	10,347	10,200	10,603	8,548	25,042	—	—
Mecklenburg	3,612	3,159	5,704	3,352	14,053	8,889	7,157
TOTALS	54,823	56,380	66,954	63,987	158,736	87,472	64,154

Source: *Kirchliches Jahrbuch der Evangelischen Kirche Deutschlands* 1955, pp. 438–39; 1958, p. 405; 1959, p. 377; 1960, p. 344; 1961, pp. 430–31.

Table 2.3. Church adherence in two landeskirchen, selected years

Berlin-Brandenburg			Mecklenburg		
	1961	1971		1955	1969
Baptisms	21,112	8,231	Baptisms	11,377	2,790
Marriages	7,791	3,143	Marriages	4,247	798
Religious instruction	80,415	66,957	Confirmations	11,139	3,642
Burials	28,345	25,614	Burials	app. 6,000	app. 6,000

Sources: For Berlin-Brandenburg, "Ostberlin," Broschure der Landeszentrale fur Politische Bildungsarbeit zur Thema "Kirche in der DDR"; for Mecklenburg, "Zahl der Kirchlichen Trauungen in der DDR zuruckgegangen," *Der Tagesspiegel* 10 February 1971.

vival of interest in the church following World War II, this trend resumed, stimulated by a second factor, official discrimination against Christians. The dramatic decline in church membership in the late 1950s demonstrated in table 2.2 reflected state pressure on individuals in leading positions to sever their church ties, as well as the creation of a generalized atmosphere of anxiety in which church ties were seen to hinder educational and career opportunities.

Despite this decline, the churches have historically been committed to providing social services under the rubric of diakonia. They retain 51 hospitals, 89 homes for the disabled and the retarded, 226 nursing homes for the aged, 11 homes for infants, 21 orphanages, 117 retreat centers, 12 hotels, 326 kindergartens, and 19 special day care centers for the mentally retarded.[17] These institutions employ approximately fifteen thousand persons and represent a sizable portion of the health care delivery system in the GDR, especially in the area of care for the disabled and mentally retarded.

The church also figures prominently in the cultural life of the GDR. Musically it represents the tradition of Bach. Organ and choral concerts in the churches are invariably well-attended. The Evangelical academies in Berlin and Meissen offer various programs stimulating intellectual life, as do the meetings of the student parishes at the various universities. The youth parishes offer social activities and compete with the state's youth organization, the Free German Youth. The church has historically played a significant role in the educational system also. The state educates future pastors at theology sections at the six state universities, providing both the budget for the sections and the stipends for the students. But the churches have been permitted to retain several educational institutions, primarily for the education and training of pastors and catechism instructors. The social service agencies also train nurses and support personnel.

The churches are allowed access to the media. They publish their own news service and five weekly newspapers, obtainable by subscription only. Also the churches publish a monthly magazine for church workers. On average, the Evangelical Publishing House publishes 220 titles yearly.[18] The state permits the broadcast of a worship service each Sunday over state radio and, since 1978, once-monthly reporting of church news. Also, since 1978, the state has granted television time to the churches six times per year. In each of these media, the distribution is limited and subject to state censorship. Nonetheless, the media exposure is considerably greater than in other Communist systems.

The churches also enjoy a social presence from various other activities. For example, based on historical possessions, the churches retain considerable land and are active in the forestry economy. Church conventions and youth conventions, often entailing the participation of

[17]The 6,700 beds provided by church hospitals represent approximately 4% of all beds in the GDR. The 10,000 places in church nursing homes represent 8.5% of the GDR total. Half of all rehabilitation of the handicapped in the GDR is undertaken by the church. See Martin Reuer, "Diakonie als Faktor in Kirche und Gesellschaft," in Henkys, *Evangelischen Kirchen*, pp. 219–38, and Federal Ministry for Inner-German Relations, *DDR Handbuch*, p. 562.

[18]Hans-Juergen Roeder, "Churches and Religious Groups in the GDR: An Overview in Figures," *KiS* 5 (June 1979): 33, citing Lutheran World Federation statistics.

thousands, attract public attention. The twice-yearly public street collections, for international aid and diaconical work, yield sizable contributions.

Thus, the churches enjoy considerable social presence in the GDR, which the state must reckon with. This social presence yields bases for cooperation, as well as conflict, between the churches and the state.

THE "REAL EXISTING STATE"

The Ideology of the State

Through its leading force, the SED, the state was officially guided by the ideology of Marxism-Leninism during the period under study. Atheism is an integral component of the dialectical materialist philosophy that is the basis of this ideology. The thought of the founding fathers—Marx, Engels, and Lenin—serves as the bible for the ideological interpretation of religion and policy toward religion and the churches. As with the Christian Bible, it is sometimes vague and often goes unpracticed.

Marxian dialectical materialism draws from two intellectual currents, the materialism of Feuerbach and the historical method of Hegel. Its two tenets are: (1) Every form of social consciousness is a superstructural reflection of the material base which is defined by the social relations characterizing the processes of production, and (2) History is the record of class struggle, with each class having a different type of social consciousness.

To Marx, the origins of religion lie in the alienation inherent in the social relations characterizing the base in the capitalist mode of production. Religion, he said, is thus "true," since it reflects the base: "This state, this society, produce religion, a reversed consciousness, because they are a reverse world."[19]

Engels differs in his adherence more to the rationalist explanation of religion. According to Engels, "all religion . . . is nothing but the fantastic reflection in men's minds of those external forces which control their

---

[19]Unless otherwise noted, references to the writings of Marx and Engels refer to Karl Marx and Friedrich Engels, *On Religion*, introduction by Reinhold Niebuhr (1964). For this reference, see "Contribution to the Critique of Hegel's Philosophy of Right: Introduction," p. 41.

daily life, a reflection in which the terrestrial forces assume the form of supernatural forces."[20] Religion thus originates in man's sense of powerlessness in the face of "blind forces."

Religion plays a twofold function, according to Marx. For those who are exploited, it is a solace in lives of economic misery and alienation. In effect, it dampens their will to rebel, becoming the "opiate of the masses." Religion is at once "the expression of real distress and the protest against this real distress."[21] For the exploiters, religion is not only instrumental in preventing revolution. It also satisfies their subjective desire to enter heaven despite the evilness of their exploitation.[22]

Certain long-term prognoses flow from the analysis of the origins and functions of religion of Marx and Engels. According to Marx, with the elimination of exploitation and alienation as a result of the change from the capitalist to the socialist mode of production, the anesthetizing function of religion will cease and hence religion itself will disappear. Engels likewise envisioned an endpoint in which religion would be extinct, but he seems to have emphasized the independent role of the scientific revolution in this process: "Only real knowledge of the forces of nature ejects the gods or God from one position after another. This process has now advanced so far that, theoretically, it may be considered concluded."[23] Yet in another passage, Engels takes a position closer to that of Marx: "And when this act has been accomplished, when society, by taking possession of all means of production and using them on a planned basis, . . . only then will the last alien force which is still reflected in religion vanish; and with it will also vanish the religious reflection itself." The policy implications in both cases are relatively passive: any direct struggle against religion is both ineffective and misdirected, since, according to Marx, "the religious reflection of the real world can only disappear when the relations of practical work-day life of people represent visably reasonable relations to one another and to nature."[24] In fact, a struggle against religion may force it from the public to the private sphere and, in Engels's words, "help it to martyrdom and a prolonged lease on life."[25]

---

[20]Engels, "Anti-Duehring," p. 147.
[21]Marx, "Contribution to the Critique . . . ," p. 42.
[22]J. M. Bochenski, "Marxism-Leninism and Religion," *Religion and Atheism in the USSR and Eastern Europe*, eds. Bohdan R. Bociurkiw and John W. Strong (1975), p. 9.
[23]Engels, "Anti-Duehring," pp. 151, 149.
[24]Marx, "Das Kapital," p. 136.
[25]Engels, "Anti-Duehring," p. 149; Marx and Engels, *Werke*, vol. 2 (1958), p. 118.

Two directives followed from this general analysis. First, Marx rejected the militant atheism of some—for example, Feuerbach—who made the attack on religion an end in itself. They were not "radical" enough.[26] Second, on a more pragmatic level, he urged cooperation with Christian workers in the revolutionary struggle. Militant atheism may antagonize these elements, without converting them, thus hindering the short-term goal of revolution. Because of his deterministic ideology, Marx could afford to be pragmatic in the short term.

Despite this apparent mildness in Marx's position on religion, some see militant atheism as latent in Marx.[27] According to Lobkowicz, Marx's vision required man's struggle to achieve it, a struggle which would necessarily attack anything that impeded others from joining in that struggle. However, others maintain that Marx used atheism in a utilitarian manner, as a weapon in the struggle for revolution.[28] According to this view, atheistic dogma as a component of Marxist ideology should decline over time, especially in societies that have successfully undergone socialist transformation.

Lenin, like Marx, saw the existence of religion as a response by the masses to the relations of exploitation inherent in capitalist society.[29] However, this standard Marxian determinism appears contradicted in other passages, in which Lenin's tactical voluntarism and concern with organization imply greater emphasis on the decline of religion in the entire revolutionary process.

Lenin's view of the social function of religion with respect to the working class is consistent with the Marxian opiate-of-the-masses interpretation. Like Marx, Lenin held that religion teaches the bourgeoisie to be "charitable," thus providing a justification for exploitation and a cheap ticket to heaven.[30] But in contrast to Marx, for whom religion was a secondary issue, Lenin considered religion a key weapon of the bourgeoisie. The intensity of his atheism was accordingly greater than that of Marx.

[26]Marx, "Theses on Feuerbach," pp. 69–72. For Marx, the goal was broader, namely the elimination of man's alienation, a return of man from religion, family, etc., to his social mode of existence. "The abolition of religion as the illusory happiness of the people is required for their happiness." Marx, "Contribution to the Critique . . . ," p. 42.

[27]Nicholas Lobkowicz, "Marx's Attitude towards Religion," in *Marx and the Western World*, ed. Nicholas Lobkowicz (1967), pp. 334–35.

[28]James Luther Adams, "Is Marx's Thought Relevant to the Christian? A Protestant View," in Lobkowicz, pp. 375–76.

[29]All citations of Lenin refer to V. I. Lenin, *Religion* (1933). Lenin, "The Attitude of the Workers' Party towards Religion," p. 19.

[30]Lenin, "Socialism and Religion," pp. 11, 16.

From his relatively limited writings on religion, Lenin seems to have propounded vague and contradictory policies. For example, he advocated a separation of church and state but at the same time maintained that the party could not abandon its atheistic tenets.[31] Since Russia had not experienced a bourgeois democratic revolution, he agreed that the party was forced to lead this revolution, including its concomitant anticlericalism. This anticlericalism was, however, subordinate to the class goals of the party.[32] Lenin thus endorsed freedom of religion without discrimination and an end to financial ties linking the church to the state.[33] In Russia, Lenin's support for separation of church and state, and his corollary support of sects, was aimed to break the dominant position of the Russian Orthodox Church. On the other hand, Lenin attacked the bourgeois separation of church and state in liberal democracies as strengthening the hold of religion on the masses.

Second, juxtaposed with this antagonism toward the state church, is what J. M. Bochenski calls Lenin's "principle of the outstretched hand."[34] Lenin maintained that those sympathetic to the goals of the party should be enlisted, even though they may not share the materialist philosophy of the party. In a position somewhat inconsistent with previously cited passages, he argued that religious questions are of "third-rate importance, which are rapidly losing all political significance, and which are being steadily relegated to the rubbish heap by the normal course of economic development."[35] Lenin thus appears to have shared Marx's aversion to militant atheism and to have supported his pragmatic policy of alliance with Christians: "A union in that genuinely revolutionary struggle of the oppressed class to set up a heaven on earth is more important to us than a unity in proletarian opinion about the imaginary paradise in the sky."[36]

[31]In "Socialism and Religion," p. 12, Lenin asserted that "we demand that religion be regarded as a private matter as far as the State is concerned, but under no circumstances can we regard it as a private matter in our party."

[32]Bohdan Bociurkiw, "Lenin on Religion," in *Lenin—the Man, the Theorist, the Leader, a Reappraisal,* eds. Leonard Schapiro and Peter Reddaway (1967).

[33]Lenin, "Socialism and Religion," p. 12; Lenin, "On the Significance of Militant Materialism," and "The Attitude of the Classes and Parties toward Religion," pp. 27–28, 31, 39; Bociurkiw in Schapiro and Reddaway, pp. 120–21.

[34]Bochenski, in Bociurkiw and Strong, pp. 12–13.

[35]Lenin, "Socialism and Religion," p. 15.

[36]For example, Lenin justified the lack of atheism in the party program as necessary to avoid the controversy over the question of religion. He endorsed admitting priests and workers of

Lenin also seemed to take a moderate line on religion in his references to policy toward religion in the postrevolutionary state.[37] In one writing he condemned Duehring's pseudo-revolutionary notion that religion would be prohibited in socialist society. Though the party cannot be indifferent to religion, according to Lenin, it "fights against the religious fog with purely ideological and only with ideological weapons—our press, our word."

However, Lenin was not willing to let religion decline derivatively, as foreseen by Marx. He advocated militant atheism as a tactic. He was thus not only anticlerical, but like Machiavelli he was antireligious, viewing a pure and disinterested clergy as more influential, as more dangerous in perpetrating this control than an egotistical, powerful, calculating clergy.[38] Elsewhere Lenin urged a broad antireligious campaign using the eighteenth-century atheistic literature, which, he argued, was more persuasive to illiterates and peasants than the dry Marxist attacks on religion. But to withstand the manipulation of the bourgeoisie, all materialism must have a scientific philosophical basis.[39]

In this Lenin seems to have transformed the struggle against religion from a side effect of proletarian revolution into a means to achieve that revolution. He states: "The more religious prejudices give place to the socialist consciousness, the nearer will be the day of the victory of the proletariat—the victory that will emancipate all the oppressed classes from the slavery they endure in modern society."[40] As Bohdan Bociurkiw puts it, "Lenin upgrades the importance of 'consciousness,' of the active struggle against religious ideology as a means, if not a condition, of a successful struggle against political and economic oppression."[41] This seems to turn on its head the analysis of Marx that religion would die away as a result of the revolution.

Thus one finds in Lenin several seeming contradictions: advocacy of separation of church and state, yet distance from bourgeois anticlericalism; pragmatic cooperation with the Christian proletariat, yet militant

Christian belief into the party. He underscored Engels's attacks on the anarchists' war on religion. See Lenin, "Socialism and Religion," and "The Attitude of Classes and Parties towards Religion," pp. 14, 22–23.

[37]Lenin, "The Attitude of Classes and Parties towards Religion," pp. 13, 17.
[38]Lenin, "Two Letters to A. M. Gorky," p. 50.
[39]Lenin, "On the Significance of Militant Materialism," pp. 37, 40.
[40]Lenin, "What is Religion Good For?" p. 43.
[41]Bociurkiw in Schapiro and Reddaway, p. 110.

atheism. The ambiguity of his position and his attempt to walk the middle road are revealed in his simultaneous attacks on anarchists, those favoring a war on religion, as well as opportunists, those indifferent to religion.[42] He tried to retain Marx's theoretical determinism while introducing his own characteristic voluntarism.

The official GDR ideology during this period reproduced the ambivalent stance found in the Marxist-Leninist ideology, especially in the Leninist.[43] The official ideology described religion as "a fantastic, illusory, misguided representation of objective reality," which results "from the antagonistic class societies with their relations of exploitation and repression of the majority by the minority. In socialism religion loses its social basis, but because of the sustaining power of tradition and external influences, it continues to exist." Yet the SED proclaimed that socialist society guarantees "full freedom of belief and conscience" and the "complete separation of church and state." It also called for the "cooperation of Marxists and Christians for the elimination of capitalism and building of socialism." Yet it propagated Marxism-Leninism "in all its component parts" including materialistic atheism and maintained that the disappearance of religion, although "the result of an objective social process, does not occur spontaneously" and requires education in the atheistic worldview. However, this education was to take the form of "intellectual debate, without hurting the feelings of religious people."

The Stance of the Working Class Movement prior to 1945

The SED's position regarding religion derived not only from its Marxist-Leninist ideology, but also from the historical inheritance of the German working class movement. The movement's position was hardly consistent and uniform, but rather was subject to internal divisions and tactical adaptation to the changing political context.

Of course, Germany possessed a long tradition of anticlerical "free

[42]Lenin, "The Attitude of the Workers' Party towards Religion," p. 21.
[43]Manfred Buhr and Alfred Kosing, eds., *Kleines Woerterbuch der Marxistisch-Leninistischen Philosophie* (Berlin, GDR: Dietz Verlag, 1975), pp. 245–48; Olof Klohr, "Ursachen und Tendenzen des Absterbens von Religion und Kirche im Sozialismus," *Voprosy Filosofi*, no. 3 (1974): pp. 147–54; Olof Klohr, *Marxismus-Leninismus, Atheismus, Religion* (1978), p. 107.

thinkers" associated with the Enlightenment and liberal thought. This intellectual current spread to parts of the working class with the advent of industrialization in the late nineteenth century.[44] The Lassallian and Eisenacher wings of the workers' movement debated the correct position toward religion but assumed a moderate stance, particularly after the merger of the two wings to form the Social Democratic Workers' Party of Germany (later to become the Social Democratic Party of Germany, or SPD) in 1875. In its founding program, the Gotha Program, the SPD declared religion to be a "private matter."[45] Although the period of the SPD's illegality from 1878 to 1890 left it more radical in some respects, its Erfurt Program of 1891 reaffirmed the private nature of religion. In addition the program called for churches to be treated as private associations, independent of the state, and it advocated the secularization of schools—both liberal positions.

Despite this avoidance of programmatic commitment to atheism, the leading Social Democrats inveighed against religion and the church in their public pronouncements. Particularly in the 1870s, the SPD carried on a militantly atheistic campaign against Christianity, thereby undercutting in practice the tolerance expressed at Gotha. August Bebel, an early leader of the SPD, and other polemicists attacked religion as "the main bastion of antisocialism, the breeding ground of all social evil."[46] Unlike attacks by liberal freethinkers, this critique of religion was based on the social role of the church and religion rather than its theological/doctrinal weakness. With the Anti-Socialist Law of 1878, the SPD moderated its atheistic attacks to avoid alienating religious workers, particularly Catholics. This tactical shift in the face of repression was aided by the exile of hard-line atheists in the party and the increasing attention to the views of Engels, who had demoted religion to a secondary issue in his *Anti-Duehring*.

As the SPD increasingly pursued a parliamentary strategy in Wilhelmine Germany, the issue of religion receded in importance.[47] Although

---

[44]Paul Kosok, *Modern Germany* (Chicago: University of Chicago Press, 1933), p. 204.

[45]Gotha Program and Erfurt Program, as reprinted in Vernon L. Lidtke, *The Outlawed Party: Social Democracy in Germany, 1878–1890* (Princeton: Princeton University Press, 1966), pp. 334, 337.

[46]Vernon L. Lidtke, "August Bebel and German Social Democracy's Relationship to the Christian Churches," *Journal of the History of Ideas* 27 (April–June 1966): p. 251.

[47]Heiner Grote, *Sozialdemokratie und Religion* (Tuebingen, FRG: J. C. B. Mohr, Paul Siebeck, 1968), pp. 110–13.

pervaded by a materialistic Weltanschauung, the party sought to avoid controversy over the issue. For example, proposals to make legal renunciation of church membership a requirement of membership failed to obtain majority support in party congresses. The SPD's reformist line seemed to be rewarded with electoral success, particularly among Protestant voters.

Despite its electoral and organizational success, the SPD had been riven with factions, including a Revisionist wing under Eduard Bernstein and a Left-Radical wing under Rosa Luxemburg and Karl Liebknecht. But it took the issue of World War I to bring these to the point of schism.[48] The November revolution in 1918 and the differing responses of the centrist SPD and the revolutionary Spartacist League led to the creation of two opposing working class parties in the Weimar period. It was to be expected that the successor to the Spartacists, the Communist Party of Germany, or KPD, would pursue a harsher policy toward religion than the SPD. To be sure, its founding program made no mention of the issue, concentrating on revolutionary changes in the economy, military and the political system. With its heightened criticism of the SPD and the progressive bolshevization of the KPD in the 1920s, however, it articulated an anticlerical and antireligious position, leading the drive for resignation from church membership among workers. The 1925 Action Program, for example, sharply criticized the church's role in education.[49] The Program of the Communist International (1928), binding on all sections including the KPD, affirmed dialectical materialism as the basis of the ideology and called for the creation of a new culture that "will bury for all time mysticism and religion, prejudices and superstitions and thereby give a powerful impetus to the development of victorious scientific findings."[50] Leading theorists in the KPD and the party's daily newspaper continued unabated the attacks on religion as a "pre-scientific worldview."[51] Even while the SPD was

[48]On this schism, see Carl E. Schorske, *German Social Democracy, 1905–1917* (Cambridge: Harvard University Press, 1955), and Ben Fowkes, *Communism in Germany under the Weimar Republic* (London: Macmillan, 1984).

[49]Zentralkommittee des Kommunistischen Bundes Westdeutschlands, *Kampf um das Programm der Revolution in Deutschland: Der Weg der KPD* (Kuehl, FRG: Verlagsgesellschaft Kommunismus und Klassenkampf, 1977), pp. 249, 250.

[50]Hermann Weber, ed., *Der deutsche Kommunismus: Dokumente* (Cologne: Kiepenheuer and Witsch, 1963), pp. 48–50.

[51]Hartmut Nowacki, *Zwischen Lebensphilosophie und Stalinismus: Philosophische Ansaetze in der Kommunistischen Partei Deutschlands (1918–1933)* (Munich: Profil Verlag,

electing practicing Christians to leading positions in the party, the KPD precluded membership to them.[52] Rather than opening to the SPD, middle class, and the churches, the Weimar KPD responded in Stalinist fashion to the growth of Nazism by appealing to German hypernationalism and revisionism.

The Nazi takeover in 1933 and the realization that it was a long-term phenomenon led to a tactical shift in the party line dictated by Moscow: the promotion of a popular front of antifascist forces and concomitant de-emphasis on ideological orthodoxy.[53] In the context of illegality and repression, the KPD made overtures to the religious sector of the population. At the Brussels Party conference (1935) the KPD recognized freedom of belief and conscience as a fundamental right and pledged to fight for its restoration. The resolution of the Bern Party conference (1939) reaffirmed this commitment and pledged a secure role in a socialist Germany for the church "which has been freed from inherited structures." In 1937 the Central Committee hailed the Confessing Church and the opposition Catholics as part of the "great freedom fight of the German people" and called for support of church resistors and greater cooperation with Christian workers. In the context of the Hitler tyranny, the KPD thus downplayed its traditional critique of religion. This cooperative position—as manifested in the National Committee for a Free Germany operating out of Moscow during the war and the commiseration of Communists and Christians imprisoned in Germany— provided the point of departure for the Communists upon their return to legality in occupied Germany following the war.

Thus the working class movement had early assumed a materialist-atheist position hostile to religion and the churches. However, this early hostility moderated over time; earlier in the case of the SPD as a result of its parliamentary, reformist strategy in Wilhelmine Germany; later in the case of the KPD as a result of the confrontation with fascism. In both cases this shift was a matter of tactics rather than principles. Both parties appealed primarily to de-Christianized workers in secularized

---

1983), pp. 163, 168. One study found that most Communist street fighters in Weimar Berlin had left the church. See Eve Rosenhaft, *The German Communists and Political Violence, 1929–33* (Cambridge: Cambridge University Press, 1983), pp. 198–99.

[52]Kosok, p. 206; Richard N. Hunt, *German Social Democracy, 1918–1933* (New Haven: Yale University Press, 1964), p. 54.

[53]Horst Daehn, *Konfrontation oder Kooperation? Das Verhaeltnis von Staat und Kirche in der SBZ/DDR, 1945–1980* (1982), p. 19. Weber, *Kleine Geschichte*, pp. 328, 379–81.

industrial society. However, by 1945 the SPD had considerably more practice in the toleration of Christians than the KPD.

The Legal Framework of Church-State Relations

The constitution of the GDR provides the general legal framework for church-state relations. The original 1949 constitution was replaced by a new version in 1968, which in turn was amended in 1974. Because the 1974 amendments dealt primarily with the issue of the German nation, the 1949 and 1968 constitutions will serve as the basis for this discussion.

Two preliminary points should be made. First, constitutions in socialist states have traditionally been designed to reflect the current stage of socioeconomic development of the society as well as to lay the groundwork for the next stage toward the final goal of a Communist society. Thus, unlike liberal democratic constitutions, they have been changed more readily and indeed have served a change-producing function themselves.[54]

Second, the Marxist-Leninist ideology has provided the context of the constitution. In particular the separation of church and state and the guarantees of freedom of belief and conscience, as endorsed by Marx and Lenin at various times, could be expected to find their place in a socialist constitution.

Both the 1949 and the 1968 constitutions guarantee equal rights to all citizens. However, the 1949 formulation (Article 6), similar to the Weimar and FRG constitutions, singled out religion for special mention as a protected category. In contrast, the 1968 constitution (Article 20) merely cites religion as one among several social categories—for example, nationality and race—that were to be accorded equal rights and duties.[55]

Both constitutions guarantee freedom of belief and conscience, as per the Marxist-Leninist ideology, although again the 1968 version proved less liberal than the 1949 version. The 1949 right of the churches to take positions on critical issues was excluded in 1968. Moreover, the clause guaranteeing freedom of belief and conscience was included in the final 1968 version only after public pressure. Finally, the constitution defines

---

[54]Dietrich Mueller-Roemer, *Die neue Verfassung der DDR* (1974), p. 28.
[55]Klaus Sorgenicht et al., eds., *Verfassung der Deutschen Demokratischen Republik: Dokumente, Kommentar.* (1969), 2:29f.

freedom of conscience in terms of one's social responsibility, not one's individual rights.[56]

Both constitutions contain a guarantee of the right to religious practice, although the 1949 wording is somewhat broader. This freedom presumes that socialist society "closes out every misuse of religion and the church for political purposes by the state or economic power groups."[57]

In contrast to these relatively cosmetic changes, the rights of the churches were altered drastically in the new constitution. The Weimar constitution had ended the state church and allowed self-determination in the churches. Yet they had retained the legal status of public organizations, which guaranteed them certain privileges (e.g., state support via the church tax). In this vein, the 1949 constitution also guaranteed various church activities. For example, it protected the churches' rights regarding the church tax, religious instruction, public subsidies, and church property/institutions. It gave churches access to hospitals and prisons, among other institutions. This specific regulation of the church-state relationship was replaced in the 1968 constitution by a general clause (Article 39.2) stating that "the churches are to order their business and activity in agreement with the constitution and legal dictates of the GDR" and that "further agreement between the churches and the state could be the subject of separate negotiations." Many of the 1949 guarantees had become anachronistic since the state had unilaterally abrogated certain provisions of the constitution during the 1950s. For example, the state had long since ceased to collect the church tax or guarantee religious instruction. In 1968 the state rejected a detailed specification of church rights. In his speech presenting the proposed new constitution, Ulbricht identified only two areas of legally protected church activity: spiritual ministry and activities useful to the community.[58] Thus, the elimination of these formal rights of the church was designed to legalize the de facto shrinkage of the churches' presence in the public sphere without explicitly incorporating the principle of separation of church and state. The GDR has remained one of the few East European states without such a nominal constitutional provision.

[56]Ibid.
[57]Article 41 of the 1949 Constitution protects "undisturbed religious practice," whereas Article 39.1 of the 1968 Constitution only guarantees "the right to exercise religious practice." See Sorgenicht et al., 2:171f.
[58]Sorgenicht et al., 2:171f; Sorgenicht et al., 1:75.

The contradictions that one finds in the Marxist-Leninist ideology regarding religion and the churches have been mirrored in the legal reality as well. Administrative measures and laws have been used to reduce the official privileges for the churches; yet the state has not affirmed constitutionally the separation of church and state and, in many policy areas, has shown little interest in doing so. The constitution guarantees equal rights and freedom of conscience; but such rights are defined in terms of duties as well. The churches are charged generally with ordering their own affairs; but they are to do so in conformity with the legal dictates of the GDR.

The Instruments of the State's Kirchenpolitik

As in other policy areas in the period under study, the final voice in the Kirchenpolitik was that of the Socialist Unity Party (SED). Under the SED's guiding principle of democratic centralism, this meant that the Politburo and the Secretariat of the Central Committee effectively determined the Kirchenpolitik. Policy did not necessarily originate there, but any policy differences within the party or state were resolved there, if indeed they were resolved at all. The party did not necessarily have an interest in eliminating all policy differences. Although the Politburo had one member whose responsibility included the Kirchenpolitik, the key monitoring and decision point on a standing basis was the Department of Church Questions of the Secretariat of the Central Committee.

The churches seldom came into contact with this level of the party, however; the state dealt with the churches primarily through the State Secretariat for Church Questions, a government bureau.[59] This state secretariat communicated state policy and negotiated directly with the churches. The state secretariat was created in 1958. Prior to this, responsibility for the Kirchenpolitik was divided between the office of Deputy Minister Otto Nuschke (CDU) under Minister President Otto Grotewohl (SED) and a department for church affairs in the Ministry of the Interior. After numerous disputes over bureaucratic competence, the state moved in 1957–58 to consolidate the oversight of the Kirchenpoli-

[59]Federal Ministry for Inner-German Relations, *DDR-Handbuch*, pp. 1299–1300. Hans Seigewasser was head of the State Secretariat until his death in 1979; his successor, Klaus Gysi, held the office until 1988.

tik into one agency directly responsible to the chairman of the Council of Ministers. In 1960 this office received its current title, State Secretary's Office for Church Questions.

Although the state secretary's office was the primary government agency that executed the Kirchenpolitik, it was not the sole one. Because the churches have an extensive social presence and are composed of individual Christians, other bureaucracies necessarily had a direct or indirect impact on the Kirchenpolitik. The Ministry of Health dealt with church hospitals and other service agency institutions; the Ministry of Higher and Technical Education was responsible for the theology sections at the state universities; the Ministry of Construction affected construction of churches; and the Ministry of Culture oversaw church publications. The Ministry of the Interior also played a large role in the Kirchenpolitik, since relations with the churches on the local and district levels were handled by the respective deputy chairman of the interior.[60] Other bureaucracies had an indirect impact on the church-state relationship by affecting individual Christians. For example, treatment of Christians in the education system and the military was affected by the ministries of Education and Defense, respectively. Of course, the Ministry for State Security maintained a special oversight role vis-à-vis the church establishment and individual Christians. With this variety of actors involved, the potential for intentional or unintentional inconsistencies in the Kirchenpolitik—both horizontally across state agencies and vertically between Berlin and the provinces—is obvious.

In addition to the party and the government apparatus, the state possessed several other instruments in its Kirchenpolitik. Most important of these was the Christian Democratic Union Party of Germany (East), or CDU. The Soviets permitted the formation of this political party almost immediately following the end of the war.[61] Building largely on the base of the Catholic Center Party from the Weimar Republic, it enjoyed rapid growth in membership and considerable electoral success in the 1946 regional elections.[62] Between 1946 and 1948, however, the SED purged various CDU leaders in the Soviet Zone, namely those who opposed such SED initiatives as land reform. Realizing the CDU's threat to its own political control, the SED formed

[60]Ibid., pp. 1299–1300.
[61]Ibid., pp. 256–58.
[62]Spotts, pp. 296–97.

other bloc parties to compete with the CDU for the "bourgeois" element, a standard ploy in the Communists' subversion of democratic processes in Eastern Europe. The fixed allocations to the parties in the Democratic Bloc list in the 1950 elections guaranteed the political impotence of the CDU (East) and its separation from the CDU (West). The CDU's rejection of Christian socialism at its Meissen congress in 1951 and its agreement to the SED's drive for the construction of socialism in 1952 undermined its ideological independence as well.[63] Thereafter, the CDU ceased to function as an autonomous political party in the Western sense.

Despite the advance into socialism and the alleged concomitant decline of the social differences that these parties normally represent, the SED found it expedient to retain them. For the ideological and historical underpinning of its alliance policy, the SED cited Lenin's advocacy of cooperation and the United Front policies of the mid-1930s.[64] But more important, these parties served certain functions: they communicated the SED policy to various sectors; they received feedback from below; and they generated support for the political system by assuming responsibility for state policy, without exercising corresponding input into the formulation of such policy. What distinguished the CDU from the other bloc parties, however, was its target group, Christians. The other bloc parties in large part lost their target groups due to social-economic change; collectivization and socialization eliminated the independent economic base of the peasantry and small bourgeoisie, thus eroding the base of the Peasant Party and the Liberal Democratic Party, respectively. The National Democratic Party was predestined to gradually lose its target group, former National Socialists. The CDU too saw its bourgeois base eroded. But the CDU also focused on a group not defined exclusively in socioeconomic terms, namely Christians and the churches. Although they declined in strength, these target groups did not die out. Because of this, the CDU retained its raison d'existence.

The CDU's function in the state's Kirchenpolitik was twofold: vis-à-vis the church leadership, it communicated state policy, often polemically, and mobilized support for the GDR and state policy; vis-à-vis the church grass roots, it mobilized support for the GDR and state policy in

---

[63]Roderich Kulbach and Helmut Weber, *Parteien im Blocksystem der DDR* (1969), pp. 27–30.
[64]Ibid., pp. 9–12.

order to undercut the base of support that the church leadership enjoyed in its criticism of state policy.

Although largely a transmission belt of the SED, the CDU did have greater leeway in some areas than others. It maintained a certain economic presence itself—for example, in publishing. Membership in the CDU afforded some political protection to small businessmen and creative "space" for those in the fine arts.[65] In fact, CDU membership, long kept low under SED pressure, increased from roughly seventy thousand in the 1960s to 120,000 in the early 1980s.[66] The CDU traditionally carried considerable weight in the state's policy regarding university sections of theology. In other policy areas, individual leaders exercised influence on particular issues at certain times (e.g., Nuschke as deputy minister in the 1950s), and local-level CDU officials on occasion affected policy. But in most policy-making the CDU's limits were clearly and narrowly drawn, as demonstrated in the 1980s on questions of peace and the militarization of GDR society.[67]

The "Christian Circles," working groups of the National Front of the GDR, represented another satellite organization. These groups—attached to the committees of the National Front at the local, district, and national levels—met regularly using a lecture-and-discussion format. Although CDU members played a prominent role in them, they were designed to attract and mobilize clergy and Christians on a broader, nonpartisan basis. Indeed the CDU and the National Front sometimes showed a tendency to compete.

Other mobilization organizations included the Federation of Evangelical Pastors in the GDR (or Pfarrerbund) and the Christian Peace Conference—GDR Regional Conference (CPC). Formed in 1958 under direct SED tutelage, the Pfarrerbund sought to mobilize pro-regime, "progressive" pastors and pressure the church leadership. As will be discussed in chapter 5, it was officially dissolved in 1974, although a rump organization remained active. The CPC, founded in Prague in 1958 with Jozef Hromadka as its head, is the Soviet-sponsored organi-

[65]Gerhard Schmolze, "Das Elend der Ost-CDU," in *Das Elend der Christdemokraten,* ed. Gerd-Klaus Kaltenbrunner (1977), pp. 85–87; Heinz Hofman, *Mehrparteiensystem ohne Opposition* (Bern: Herbert Lang, 1977), pp. 72–78.

[66]Federal Ministry for Inner-German Relations, *DDR-Handbuch,* p. 256.

[67]Schmolze in Kaltenbrunner, pp. 77–78; Klemens Richter, "Erziehung zum Frieden? DDR-CDU und sozialistische Wehrerziehung," *Deutschland Archiv* 14 (September 1981): 899–902.

zation designed to mobilize churches and Christians for peace. The Soviet and East European churches have predominated, as has the Soviet conception of peace. Though wracked and discredited by purges following the invasion of Czechoslovakia in 1968, it has continued to function. Neither the Pfarrerbund nor the CPC attracted much interest among the clergy in the GDR.[68] Partly as a result, the "progressives" active in these various satellite organizations often found themselves spread too thinly and the political effectiveness of these organizations accordingly suffered.

The Tactics of the State's Kirchenpolitik

The state had four basic tactics at its disposal in pursuit of its goals in the Kirchenpolitik: atheistic propaganda, political mobilization, administrative measures, and cadre policy.

Atheistic propaganda involved the propagation in the education system and mass media of scientific atheism as part of the party's basic philosophy of dialectical materialism. This led to conflict with the churches over whether the schools should require simply a knowledge of Marxism-Leninism or should insist on an affirmation of Marxism-Leninism by the students. In contrast with the 1950s, public atheistic propaganda became much less aggressive, and its role as a means in the GDR's Kirchenpolitik diminished. Within the SED, of course, such propaganda continued unabated.[69]

The major activity of the state representatives and satellite organizations was to promote the political mobilization of Christians and the churches—namely, social/political engagement and support for the GDR and its policies with the goal of building "socialist consciousness." This agitation work, conducted through private discussions, public events, and the mass media, was designed to dampen any criticism by the churches.

Administrative measures took two forms, constraints and rewards. Constraints ranged from the actual closing of churches, prohibition of certain church activities, or arrest of individuals (particularly pastors) to

---

[68]Federal Ministry for Inner-German Relations, *DDR-Handbuch*, p. 258.
[69]Reinhard Henkys, "Der Atheismus fehlt im SED-Programm," *KiS* 2 (February 1976): 9–13; Hans-Juergen Roeder, "Kirche und Gesellschaft in der DDR—Versuch einer Bestandsaufnahme," Mimeographed, Evangelical Press Center, West Berlin.

measures hindering church activities such as religious instruction and church congresses to denial of visas for ecumenical travel and reduction in funding or construction capacity for the churches. The rewards consisted of foregoing these prohibitions and arrests, as well as accommodating church needs. These included institutional needs, such as repair or construction of churches, or the financial needs of church educational and service organizations. It also took the form of favorable responses on policy issues, such as treatment of conscientious objectors or environmental activists. Because there are so many areas of church life that require an interface with the state, the churches could not escape the use of state administrative measures. Whereas in the 1950s the state tended to rely on constraints, more recently the state shifted to greater reliance on rewards, reflecting a change in strategy from curtailing the church to coopting the church.

Cadre policy refers to the personnel files on individuals, which were used in decisions regarding educational and career advancement. These often contained information on the individual's participation in mass organizations and state activities, such as the youth dedication ceremony (or *Jugendweihe*), and even on participation in confirmation and church membership. By using this cadre policy to limit the advancement of individual Christians, the state exerted pressure on the church adherence and political stance of individual Christians.[70]

The relationship between church and state in the period under study was thus set in a certain historical, ideological, and organizational context. The state faced a church that has historically been characterized by a decentralized yet democratic structure and by a theology that has stressed deference to the authority of the state. However, the church's theology has become more pluralistic as a result of the experience of the Third Reich and the Barthian influence. The church in turn faced a Communist party guided by an ideology that both affirmed scientific atheism yet allowed a certain tactical flexibility. The church also confronted a strong state which, despite its rather liberal constitution, was armed with various levers of influence over the church and believers.

[70]For a study of the cadre policy of the GDR, see Gerd-Joachim Glaessner, *Herrschaft durch Kader: Leitung der Gesellschaft und Kaderpolitik in der DDR am Beispiel des Staatsapparates* (Wiesbaden: Westdeutscher Verlag, 1977).

3 Socialist Transformation and the German Question, 1945–1958

The change in church-state relations that occurred in the 1970s can be understood only against the backdrop of the immediate postwar years and the periods of Stalinist transformation and de-Stalinization. The initial postwar years, known officially as the antifascist-democratic transformation, saw a relatively mild policy toward religion and the churches, not unlike that in other so-called people's democracies. The Stalinist period, from roughly 1949 to 1953, was characterized by harsher treatment of the churches, although milder than in most other Soviet bloc states. Finally, the de-Stalinization process of 1953 to 1958 was incomplete in the GDR, and consequently pressure on the churches remained unabated. Moderating the state's policy toward the churches during this entire period were the continuing ties to West Germany and the GDR's interest in influencing the FRG's international commitments.

THE ANTIFASCIST-DEMOCRATIC PERIOD, 1945–1949

The period of antifascist-democratic transformation brought considerable economic and political change to the Soviet Occupation Zone.[1] The defeat of the Nazi regime brought a collapse of civil author-

---

[1] For discussion of this period, see Weber, *Kleine Geschichte,* pp. 9–46; Dietrich Staritz, *Sozialismus in einem halben Land* (Berlin: Verlag Klaus Wagenbach, 1976), pp. 12–126; Childs, pp. 1–37; Hanhardt, pp. 3–43; McCauley, pp. 6–41.

ity, which the Soviet command sought to reconstruct along new lines. Denazification of the state and society began early under Soviet aegis. Political parties that could demonstrate opposition to fascism, such as the KPD, SPD, and CDU, were granted official status in June 1945. Likewise, provincial administrations were soon reconstituted with the approval of the Soviet Military Administration in Germany. Economic change ensued, although it was hardly dramatic compared with what was to come. Large agricultural states were confiscated and redistributed to small farmers and refugees from the Eastern territories in the land reform of 1946. Nazi-owned industrial property was also confiscated and placed under Russian, eventually zonal authority control. The forced fusion of the SPD and KPD in 1946 and the *Gleichschaltung* of the bloc parties created the political conditions for the later Stalinization of the economy and society.

Despite these political and economic changes promoted by the Soviet authorities, their policy toward the churches was a relatively mild one.[2] As in the Western zones, the Soviets found that in the early postwar period the churches were often the only intact organizations that were relatively untainted by collaboration with the Nazis. Moreover, just as Stalin reversed his antireligious campaign during the war in order to strike a pragmatic alliance with the Russian Orthodox Church, so too the German Communists, particularly in Soviet exile, made religious elements part of their antifascist resistance in the National Committee for a Free Germany, or NKFD.[3] The Soviets' recognition of the churches' not inconsiderable opposition to Hitler's rule and the personal experience of German Communists jailed with members of the Confessing Church—along with the force of circumstance—led them to grant the church a honeymoon. The impact of this common anti-Nazi collaboration on later regime policy is often labeled the "concentration camp effect."[4] The honeymoon took several forms. For example, the Soviets allowed the churches to conduct their own internal denazification process. The churches were permitted to publish church newspapers. The Christian Democratic Union Party was licensed soon after the war.

The SED's policy toward the churches likewise was characterized by

[2]Daehn, pp. 11–33.

[3]The prominent role of future Bishop Friedrich Wilhelm Krummacher of Pomerania in the NKFD brought him and the church somewhat greater credibility with the postwar regime. See his *Ruf zur Entscheidung: Predigten, Aussprachen, Aufsaetze, 1944–1945* (1965).

[4]Solberg, pp. 30–33.

conciliation.[5] To a certain extent, in the current of antifascist cooperation, the SED underscored its earlier exile resolutions at the Brussels and
Bern conferences supporting freedom of religion and conscience as
basic rights and a role for churches in the future order. The fusion
congress of the SED affirmed this view, but also proclaimed the separation of church and state as its goal. On August 27, 1946, the Central
Secretariat of the SED declared on the issue "SED and Christianity":
"The Socialist Unity Party categorically rejects subordinating itself to
the church, just as the church with justification rejects taking itself in a
partisan sense."

It was this policy of separation of church and state that led to early
conflicts with the churches, specifically in the area of education. With
the purpose of limiting the churches' influence in certain areas, the state
in 1946 proclaimed the goal of secularized "uniform schools." Despite
the support by the CDU and the churches for the right of parents to
determine the education of their children, the state emerged victorious.[6]

Despite this issue of conflict, the SED in general pursued a mild policy
toward the churches. Some pastors who had been members of the SPD
prior to Nazi rule were allowed to remain in the newly formed SED,
despite the ideological inconsistency. The SED, too, recognized the
churches' role in opposition to Hitler. Its economic and social policies in
this phase were hardly radical. Indeed, the 1949 constitution guaranteed freedom of religion and conscience and the churches' status as
bodies in public law.[7]

The churches also pursued a conciliatory policy during this period.[8]
Denazification within the churches, focusing particularly on the "German Christian" leaders, occurred swiftly as the Confessing Church
leaders assumed control over the provincial church structures and were
legitimized by reconstituted provincial synods. The churches, both the
Confessing Council of the Brethren and the nascent Evangelical Church
in Germany, admitted their collective guilt in the rise of Hitler and
World War II.[9] The church's stance toward the Soviet occupiers and the

[5]Daehn, p. 20; Hans-Gerhard Koch, *Staat und Kirche in der DDR* (1975), pp. 30–33.
[6]Ibid., p. 22.
[7]To be sure, during the debate surrounding the constitution, the SED attempted to strike this
clause regarding the churches' legal status, but reconsidered this move. Daehn, p. 24; Koch,
Staat und Kirche, pp. 35–45.
[8]Daehn, pp. 26–29; Solberg, pp. 25–41.
[9]Spotts, pp. 93–95, 121.

SED was one of modest cooperation and support for policies of the zonal authorities. By and large, for example, the churches supported the land reform, limiting their criticism to the periodic harshness of its implementation, in particular confiscation of land of non-Nazis without compensation.[10] The Saxon church supported the referendum on the confiscation of Nazi property. The churches supported political participation in the reconstruction process by clergy and parishioners. Although they forbade clergy from running for elective office, they supported party membership by clergy. In terms of providing support service to and raising the morale of the population, the churches' role in the early postwar period can hardly be underestimated.

Storm clouds did appear in the form of the issue of education and schools, harbingers of intense future conflict between the church and state. The churches questioned, "who gave the state, in particular those who currently govern the state, the right to determine in what spirit our children should be raised?" Bishop Otto Dibelius, to become a leading actor in the church-state conflict, opposed a "purely secular, in other words purely political 'unified school,'" and the churches insisted upon Christian schools in those areas where the majority of parents wished them. The state rejected this position and in the school legislation determined that "the formal education of children is exclusively the competence of the state. Religious instruction is the competence of the religious communities."[11] However, the provision of religious instruction by the churches themselves became more difficult as the school authorities made it impossible for the churches to use schoolrooms for religious instruction.

With this exception, the effect of this initial period in the church-state relationship was to restore the traditional role and rights of the church.[12] The church tax, the primary means of financing the church, was retained, and the state assumed the legal responsibility for collecting the tax. The state agreed to pay subsidies to the churches that were based on long-standing legal agreements dating from the Prussian era. Moreover, the land reform, which caused such upheaval, exempted the

[10]Bishop Beste of Mecklenburg, a province particularly subject to land reform, voiced his support for the program.
[11]Quotes from Daehn, pp. 29–33.
[12]Ibid., pp. 98–99; Reinhard Henkys, "Kirche—Staat—Gesellschaft," in Henkys, *Evangelischen Kirchen*, pp. 37–39.

not inconsiderable land holdings of the churches. Church publications were licensed. Church meetings, both within the Soviet Zone and interzonal, were allowed, even fostered. Internal church autonomy regarding personnel and policy was not challenged; indeed the state recognized the churches' right to its own work laws providing "official bureaucratic status" (*Beamten*) for church personnel, even while the state began to dismantle such status in the secular sector. Finally, the authorities made little attempt to indoctrinate scientific atheism in society or to restrict Christians' roles in society. The early period of antifascist-democratic transformation (1945–1949) thus saw, for the most part, a mild conciliatory policy toward the churches, rooted in wartime cooperation against fascism and the relatively cautious policy of the Soviets in the people's democracies during this period.

The Stalinist Transformation Period, 1949–1953

The period of 1949 to 1953 represented a dramatic turn for the worse in church-state relations. The Stalinization process, directed by the Soviet Union and implemented by the respective local Communist leaderships, resulted in consolidation of the Communists' hold on power and the economic transformation along Soviet lines. In the GDR the process followed familiar lines. The SED was transformed from a fusion workers' party into a Leninist "party of a new type."[13] Former Social Democrats and others advocating a "special German path to socialism," such as Anton Ackermann, were either purged as Titoists or forced to recant their ideas. Democratic centralism and the ban on factions became the guiding principles of the SED. Non-Communist parties experienced *Gleichschaltung* and became transmission belts of the SED. Industry was nationalized, except for small enterprises, and central planning was instituted to direct the economic mechanism. Collectivization, though accomplished for the most part during the late 1950s, was initiated during this period. The forerunner of the National People's Army, the barracked people's police, was created. Finally, during this period the GDR assumed the Stalinist position on foreign policy, namely

[13]For discussions of the Stalinization process, see Childs, pp. 20–30; Weber, *Kleine Geschichte*, pp. 40–66; Staritz, pp. 155–92; McCauley, pp. 42–63.

a dichotomous view of the world divided into capitalist and socialist camps and a strengthening of bilateral ties to the Soviet Union. On the question of German unity, however, the GDR maintained its formal commitment to German reunification, in line with the Soviets' own ambiguity on the issue.[14]

Stalinization entailed heightened ideological struggle against the churches and religion. Despite the protections granted by the 1949 Constitution—including freedom of religious belief and conscience, the right to the undisturbed exercise of religion, the status of churches as bodies of public law, and the right of churches to collect church taxes and give religious instruction in schools—the church saw its traditional privileges attacked in what aptly can be described as a *Kirchenkampf*.[15] Religious instruction in the schools became nearly impossible, despite the constitutional provision protecting it. Church publications were curtailed due to alleged paper shortages. State subsidies to the churches were cut back and impounded. Compensation agreements covering state use of church land went unfulfilled. Church meetings were hindered by the refusal of local authorities to provide the necessary support services. Church diaconical institutions were confiscated by the state in many cases. The state promulgated an ordinance requiring the notification of state authorities for many church activities.

This period also saw a heightened emphasis on scientific atheism and Marxist-Leninist ideology in general, particularly with respect to the youth.[16] Religious belief was grounds for expulsion from the SED and most clergy who had been SPD members were now forced to leave the party. As early as 1950, the party declared its intention of "transmitting the progressive results of science, especially Soviet science, on the basis of Marxism-Leninism." This entailed the introduction of Marxism-Leninism in the university curriculum and infusing the ideology in all school subjects, by using politically reliable teachers. Many Christian teachers and students were either removed from their positions or denied access to higher education.

[14]Griffith, pp. 53–65, discounts the seriousness of Soviet proposals by Stalin and his successors; Childs, pp. 42–46, credits them with sincerity rooted in concern over West German rearmament. See also Weber, *Kleine Geschichte*, pp. 83–85 and Melvin Croan, "The Development of GDR Political Relations with the USSR," in *GDR Foreign Policy* (1982), ed. Schulz et al., pp. 188–92.

[15]Koch, *Staat und Kirche*, p. 39f; Solberg pp. 84–157.

[16]Daehn, pp. 35–37.

The most dramatic confrontations in this period surrounded the church youth work in the Youth Parishes and Evangelical Student Parishes.[17] The party youth organization, the Free German Youth (FDJ) organized disruptions of their meetings; the state security forces arrested numerous pastors active in the churches' youth work, claiming that church youth groups were "illegal organizations" in the service of Western intelligence services. State actions threatened to bring church youth work to a standstill.

This second period of Stalinist transformation not only occasioned heightened attacks on the institutional church and individual Christians but also saw greater church criticism of the political-economic measures of the regime.[18] The administrative measures and pressure employed in the drive to collectivize agriculture led to considerable opposition among farmers, which manifested itself in efforts by the church to limit the excesses of the state in this process. Similarly the church sought via private diplomacy and public statements to modify the coercive nature of the state's socialization of industry. The church became increasingly critical of the changes in the educational system that aimed to make affirmation of Marxism-Leninism a requirement for advancement in secondary school and the university.[19] Finally the churches disagreed with the regime over the tightening of restrictions covering inter-German travel and the measures aimed at sealing and securing the border areas.[20] With the exception of Bishop Moritz Mitzenheim of Thuringia, church leaders refused to participate in the state-sponsored People's Congress movement, which was the front organization allegedly supportive of a reunified Germany. Thus the social-economic changes internally and the growing alienation between the Germanies led the churches to criticize the regime, albeit modestly.

Notwithstanding these attacks on the traditional privileges of the churches and the heightened ideological pressure on youth, the repression of the churches was relatively mild, reflecting the fact that the Stalinization process was less severe in the GDR than elsewhere in the Eastern Europe.[21] In contrast to the Soviet Union, no churches or

[17]Solberg, pp. 138–49.
[18]Daehn, p. 27. For example, Bishop Mueller of Saxony-Magdeburg sent a letter to pastors comparing collectivization to Soviet policy in the 1930s and urging opposition to class struggle by parish members, especially farmers, reprinted in *KJ* 1953, pp. 174–77.
[19]Daehn, pp. 37–39.
[20]Solberg, pp. 127–30.
[21]Hanhardt, pp. 46–50. For discussions of the historical development of church-state relations in other bloc states, see Bociurkiw and Strong; Trevor Beeson, *Discretion and Valour:*

seminaries were closed in the GDR. Unlike dramatic cases in Hungary, Poland, and Czechoslovakia, church leaders were not removed from office or imprisoned. The churches retained institutional integrity and relative internal autonomy. Indeed the state continued to educate pastors in the theological sections at the state universities, hardly consistent with a strict policy of separation of the church from the social sphere.

For its part, the churches were less critical of the regime than in other Communist states. In contrast to the Catholic churches in Poland and Hungary, the East German Protestant churches did not advocate political opposition to the regime. Nor did the churches give a pledge of loyalty to the regime. The churches' noncommittal stance resulted not so much from political neutrality, but from the view widespread in the churches that the GDR was a provisional entity and would be replaced by a liberal democratic, unified Germany. The Soviets, ironically, lent support to this impression of provisionality, seeking to brake West German integration into the Western alliance by holding open the prospect of German reunification.

The character of Stalinist transformation in the GDR was to have a significant effect on future church-state relations. The relative mildness of the high Stalinist period left the autonomy and integrity of the Protestant churches more intact than in other Soviet bloc states, with the exception of Poland.[22] Moreover, the experience left less bitterness between the regime and the churches. The GDR churches were not emasculated as some Protestant and Orthodox churches were in other East European states; nor did they have a Stalinist victim, such as Cardinal Mindszenty in Hungary, to burden future attempts at reconciliation with the regime.

INCOMPLETE DE-STALINIZATION AND CONTINUED CHURCH-STATE CONFLICT, 1953–1958

Just as the Stalinist transformation in the GDR was milder than most in Eastern Europe, so too the de-Stalinization process in the GDR

Religious Conditions in Russia and Eastern Europe (1982). On Poland in this period, see Bogdan Szajkowski, *Next to God . . . Poland* (New York: St. Martin's, 1983), pp. 9–19.

[22]A descriptive comparison among churches in the bloc on a number of dimensions—social, legal, economic, and political—is found in Giovanni Barbarini, et al., *Kirchen im Sozialismus* (Frankfurt: Verlag Otto Lembeck, 1977), pp. 29–56.

was implemented to a much lesser extent than in many other states in the bloc.[23] Ulbricht proved astute at exploiting the factions in the Kremlin following the death of Stalin, as well as the Soviets' fear of instability in Eastern Europe, to maintain himself in power and avoid anything more than superficial changes in policy. Indeed the transformation of society along socialist lines continued practically unabated from 1953 to 1958, with continued deterioration of the relationship with the church.

It is ironic, then, that the first aftershock of the New Course pursued by the Kremlin following the death of Stalin should have been felt in the GDR. The worsening of economic conditions and living standards, as well as the increasing repression in 1952 and 1953 led to concessions by the regime in June 1953, with the exception of the increased work norms. The resulting workers' uprising on June 17, 1953, was crushed only with the help of Soviet troops.[24] The uprising had contradictory consequences: on the one hand, the economic policy was moderated and the norm increases were rescinded; on the other, Ulbricht used the Soviets' fear of instability to crush his political opposition. Advocates of greater flexibility on the German question (for example, Wilhelm Zaisser and Rudolf Herrnstadt) or of workers' rights to strike (for example, Justice Minister Fechner) were purged from the party. The Stalinist political transformation continued unabated—as reflected in acclamatory elections, an emasculated parliament, and *Gleichschaltung* of the bloc parties.

The acceleration of de-Stalinization in the wake of Khrushchev's secret speech in February 1956 likewise left the GDR relatively unaffected.[25] Ulbricht was apparently caught by surprise by the speech, since he had continued to invoke the teachings of Stalin in early 1956. Unlike other bloc states, the GDR was reluctant to engage in a thoroughgoing debate regarding the "excesses" of Stalin. Ulbricht very elliptically distanced himself from Stalin by admitting that "Stalin was not a classical thinker" and criticizing the cult of personality and methods of terror. Some opponents of Ulbricht, such as Franz Dahlem and Anton Acker-

---

[23]Regarding political developments in this period, see Childs, pp. 36–57; Weber, *Kleine Geschichte*, pp. 71–94; Hanhardt, pp. 67–71; McCauley, pp. 67–92.

[24]Weber, *Kleine Geschichte*, pp. 80–82; Childs, pp. 31–42; Arnulf Baring, *Uprising in East Germany: June 17, 1953* (Ithaca: Cornell University Press, 1972).

[25]See Weber, *Kleine Geschichte*, pp. 87–94.

mann, were rehabilitated, but Zaisser and Herrnstadt were pointedly excepted from this process. There was no discussion of political excesses or economic distortions in the GDR. Indeed, Ulbricht skillfully took advantage of the Kremlin's anxiety following the instability in Poland and Hungary in 1956 to press forward with nationalization of industry and completion of collectivization, as well as the repression of dissent among intellectuals (e.g., Ernst Bloch and the Harich group) and opposition within the SED (e.g., Karl Schirdewan and Ernst Wollweber, accused of being revisionists). Despite Ulbricht's success at maintaining power and limiting political and economic liberalization and possible instability, he was unable to achieve greater popular legitimacy for the regime. Indeed, the massive emigration from the GDR—1.4 million from 1949 to 1956—reflected the extensive popular dissatisfaction, but also contributed to Ulbricht's ability to avoid serious de-Stalinization.

For the church the half-hearted and incomplete de-Stalinization in this period resulted in continued conflict with the state. To be sure, the buildup of internal discontent and the Soviet pressure led to a temporary easing of tensions in the context of the June 1953 uprising, marked by a summit between Minister President Otto Grotewohl and the East Conference of the Church Leadership of the EKD on June 10, 1953.[26] In the communiqué from this meeting, the state pledged to "guarantee the church's existence according to the provisions of the constitution of the GDR"; and the church agreed to "avoid unconstitutional attacks and influences on the political and economic life." Moreover, the state pledged to "clarify" questions regarding the church's youth parishes and said that any students expelled from the college-track high schools and universities would be readmitted. The state also agreed to ease conditions for religious instruction in the schools, restore state subsidies to the churches, and release those church employees who had been interned by the state. In a related development, the FDJ Chairman, Erich Honecker, conceded the validity of the church's view that "the youth and student parishes are not organizations, but rather a collection of young Christians in the framework of the church." By most accounts the state made good on its promises on these concrete issues.

[26]Koch, *Staat und Kirche*, pp. 48–53; Solberg, pp. 150–72; Daehn, pp. 47–50; Guenter Kohler, ed. *Pontifex nicht Partisan: Kirche und Staat in der DDR von 1949 bis 1958: Dokumente aus der Arbeit des Bevollmaechtigten des Rates der EKD bei der Regierung der DDR Propst D. Heinrich Gruber* (1974), pp. 111–72.

However, the relaxation proved to be temporary as the state soon began to unilaterally abrogate the constitutional rights of the churches and to intensify its efforts at propagating scientific atheism. By late 1954 the state engaged the church in a new round of ideological conflict with the reintroduction of the youth consecration ceremony, or *Jugendweihe*, after abolishing it in 1950.[27] This ceremony, administered at the age of fourteen, has roots in the workers' movement and was atheistic in nature and aimed at undercutting the churches' confirmation ceremonies. The state claimed that its new version of the *Jugendweihe* was not atheistic and was a voluntary act by youth. The churches responded, on various occasions and in various manners, that the new ceremony was hardly voluntary since school officials were obligated to encourage participation in it. Moreover, the text used, *Weltall-Erde-Mensch,* clearly propounded a materialist view of the world, according to church analyses. As a result, the churches took an extremely firm line, maintaining that the decision regarding confirmation versus *Jugendweihe* was a question of belief, not political loyalty, and prevented those taking the *Jugendweihe* from being confirmed in the church.

A further problem arose regarding the youth parishes. Despite its concession that these were activities of the churches, the state moved in some cases to forbid meetings of these groups on a regional or national level.[28] This new interference in the church's youth work provoked protests from various church leaders, including Bishop Moritz Mitzenheim.

The state also undertook administrative actions designed to undercut the churches' public presence and institutional viability. The Benjamin Order, issued in February 1956 by Hilda Benjamin, minister of justice, effectively eliminated the constitutional provision guaranteeing public-legal organizations, including the churches, the right to use state tax lists for purposes of levying member contributions.[29] The order left the churches with no official information regarding the incomes of parishioners and no legal recourse in the event of nonpayment of church taxes. The consequences of this flagrant violation of the constitution were grave for the financial viability of the churches.

---

[27]Daehn, pp. 53–55, 67–69; Solberg, pp. 182–201.
[28]Daehn, p. 51.
[29]Koch, *Staat und Kirche,* pp. 53–56; Solberg, pp. 207–8; Kurt Rommel, "Religion und Kirche in sozialistischen Staat der DDR" (Ph.D. diss., Institut fuer Recht, Politik, und Gesellschaft der sozialistischen Staaten, Universitaet Kiel, 1975), pp. 78, 92, 94.

In 1958 another administrative action of the regime resulted in a reduction of the churches' constitutional status. The Ministry of Peoples' Education in the so-called Lange Order limited the right of religious instruction in the schools.[30] Such instruction was permitted only for those under fourteen years of age and only following a two-hour pause after the end of the regular school day, allegedly to protect the children from exhaustion. Moreover, the school director was given the power to choose the instructor. Needless to say, this administrative action greatly eroded the independence of the churches and caused a drop in the number of students receiving such instruction.

Finally, in 1958 Ulbricht heightened the campaign of ideological indoctrination by introducing his "Ten Commandments of Socialist Morality."[31] These commandments, adopted by the SED in 1958, but designed to set a standard for the citizenry as a whole, called for commitment to workers' solidarity; the defense of the workers' and peasants' power and the work discipline; and respect for socialist property and the family, among others. Like the *Jugendweihe* and other *ersatz* rites such as socialist name-giving, marriage, and burial ceremonies, Ulbricht's commandments seemed to be an obvious attempt to compete with and displace the church's own traditions.[32] Pressure on individuals to formally leave the church also increased, with dramatic impact on church adherence.

The intensification of conflict between church and state on the domestic level was increasingly overshadowed by conflict on the level of interGerman relations. For the next decade, the GDR's attempts to demarcate itself from West Germany and establish itself internationally were to dominate the relationship with the churches. The 1950s saw the two Germanies grow further apart and gain greater sovereignty at the expense of hoped-for reunification.[33] The FRG gained full sovereignty in the contexts of rearmament, NATO, and the EEC. Failing to prevent this development, with its overtures at the conference of foreign ministers in Berlin in 1954, the Soviet Union granted the GDR diplomatic recognition and partial sovereignty. By 1955 Khrushchev had taken a signifi-

---

[30]Koch, *Staat und Kirche*, pp. 53–56; Solberg, pp. 250–51.
[31]Koch, *Staat und Kirche*, pp. 56–57; Daehn, p. 69.
[32]Solberg, pp. 246–50, 258–61.
[33]Weber, *Kleine Geschichte*, pp. 83–85; Siegfried Kupper, "Political Relations with the FRG," in Schulz et al., pp. 265–74.

cant step on the road to consolidation of the GDR by proclaiming the "two-state theory" and assuring the GDR that reunification was only possible under the protection of the "socialist accomplishments of the GDR." Incorporation of the GDR into the Warsaw Pact and creation of the standing army, the National People's Army, was soon accomplished. The reintegration of the FRG into the international system and its increasingly key role in Western defense strategy, especially as a base for nuclear weapons, greatly strained the inter-German relationship and allowed the GDR to accuse the FRG of betraying the commitment to a reunified Germany.

It is not surprising that this increasing political divergence should have a deleterious effect on the GDR's relationship with the all-German churches, in particular the EKD. The West German churches had long given assistance in various forms to the "brother churches" in the East. For example, already in 1949 "sister parish" arrangements were developed. In the early 1950s numerous pastors from the FRG moved to the GDR to help alleviate the growing shortage of pastors there, and salary reductions were begun in West German churches to increase the compensation for church workers in the GDR. All of these actions, of course, worked against the state's efforts to limit the church's influence.

The state began to accuse the church of representing an extension of the West German church and working to undermine the stability of the GDR.[34] The state implicated the youth parishes in the uprising of June 17, 1953. The interior minister, Karl Maron, attacked the church in 1956, accusing it of working with the CDU/CSU forces in the GDR. The state accused the church of being involved in espionage under the guise of its railway mission activities. However, prior to 1955 the state had been relatively restrained in its attacks on ties to the West because the churches' inter-German ties offered the state a means of influencing the debate in West Germany and because the GDR enjoyed only a tenuous status in the Soviets' foreign policy. With the Soviets' greater commitment to the existence of the GDR and the growing consolidation of the GDR's status internationally, these church ties to the EKD became less attractive to the regime and indeed came to be viewed as liabilities.[35]

In this context of consolidation, the 1958 signing of the Military

[34]Daehn, p. 60; Solberg, pp. 202–10.
[35]Solberg, pp. 172–81.

Chaplaincy Agreement between the West German Army and the EKD triggered increased state attacks on the EKD.[36] The EKD legally delimited the agreement to only its West German member churches, and the East German member churches offered to sign a similar agreement with the East German regime, but the state rejected it. Although the agreement protected the church from interference by the West German military in the selection of chaplains, the GDR nonetheless alleged that the EKD was now legally tied to the FRG and the West German military.

Even before the announcement of the Military Chaplaincy Agreement, the increasing self-assertion of the GDR led the state to demand that the churches issue a declaration of loyalty. SED Central Committee Secretariat member Dr. Paul Wandel called for church-state discussions but not as two equal partners. "There must come in the church at some point a declaration, from which is evident that the church has a proper relationship toward the state."[37]

The shifting domestic and international context did indeed lead the churches to give a declaration of loyalty to the GDR, albeit one that was less than total and did not reflect a unified position of the churches. Already, at the 1956 EKD synod, a leading churchman from the GDR called for the church to free itself from its ties to a specific social order.[38] Hoping to obtain such a declaration from the church, the state agreed again to meet with a "representative" delegation of the church in 1958. The churches hoped that, as in 1953, such a meeting would ease the increasing tension with the state.

In the communiqué resulting from the July 1958 meeting, the church made several political concessions.[39] The church dropped its charge that the state had violated the constitution. For its part, the state merely affirmed the general provisions of freedom of faith and conscience. In an effort to deflect the state's criticism of the West German Military Chaplaincy Agreement, the church representatives declared that the churches in the GDR were not bound by the agreement. Moreover, the church gave an indirect vote of confidence in the state's foreign policy, claiming that "with the means available to it, the church serves peace between

[36]Daehn, pp. 64–67.
[37]Ibid., p. 61; Solberg, pp. 212–23.
[38]General Superintendent Guenter Jacob, quoted in Daehn, p. 62; Solberg, pp. 216–17.
[39]Koch, *Staat und Kirche*, pp. 56–65; Koehler, pp. 187–98; Daehn, pp. 70–75; Solberg, pp. 262–66.

peoples and thus agrees with the efforts for peace of the GDR and its government." Finally, in the most definitive statement yet of the church's position, the representatives proclaimed that "they respect the development of socialism and contribute to the peaceful construction of the life of the people." In return for these declarations, the church received the state's pledge to check complaints regarding the educational system and "clarification" of outstanding problems.

The 1958 communiqué engendered intense debate in the churches, both East and West, and led to criticism of Mitzenheim's concessions to the state. In retrospect, it can be seen as a markstone on the way to the church's self-definition as a "church within socialism." The church recognized that constitutional guarantees were unreliable at best. Although the formulation "respecting socialism" is a half-hearted one, it nonetheless reflected a major step from earlier positions the church had taken. The composition of the church delegation, led by Bishops Mitzenheim and Krummacher, reinforced this impression that the churches had accepted the GDR and begun to distance themselves from the EKD.

Unfortunately for the church, the 1958 communiqué led to little amelioration of the various conflicts with the state.[40] The disagreements over hindrances of religious instruction and the *Jugendweihe* continued unaffected by the state's pledges.

However, in terms of the *procedural* dimension of the relationship, the meeting marked a major shift in the state's policy.[41] Prior to this point, the GDR had often criticized the EKD, but had conducted business with its representatives, both East and West. Henceforth, the state would refuse to deal with duly elected leaders of the EKD from West Germany or West Berlin. In fact it would cease dealing with the EKD's emissary to the GDR, Provost Heinrich Grueber, who had long enjoyed a good working relationship with the state. This freezing out of the EKD was reflected in the composition of the delegation meeting with the state in 1958: neither Bishop Dibelius of Berlin-Brandenburg nor Grueber was present. Moreover, the state henceforth would deal primarily with the individual Landeskirche leaderships, granting the ever-more-progressive Bishop Mitzenheim special privileged status. This procedural shift reflected a substantive shift on the state's part. With the growing divergence of the two Germanies and the increasing consolida-

---

[40]Daehn, p. 74.
[41]Ibid., p. 71; Solberg, pp. 255–57, 276–77.

tion of the GDR's status in Soviet policy, the GDR sought increasingly to demarcate itself from the FRG. In the case of the churches, this meant increasing pressure on the all-German church institutions.

The churches' relations with the new order in East Germany exhibited considerable conflict from 1945 to 1958, but were, by and large, better than those in most other Soviet bloc states. The antifascist-democratic period, as in other bloc states, saw a relatively mild policy by the regime toward the churches. The Stalinist period, though characterized by harsher treatment of the churches, was nonetheless milder than most bloc states and left the institutional church largely autonomous and intact. The de-Stalinization process in the GDR was incomplete and consequently tension between the church and state continued. By 1958, however, the process of consolidation of the GDR was under way, and the ties to the FRG, which had previously been accepted by the state and were secondary to domestic conflicts in the state's policy, became the primary issue in the relationship with the churches. Thus, the churches' strong ties to West Germany, in particular in the form of the EKD, came under increasing state pressure in the 1960s, even as the regime began to extend new ideological overtures to Christians using the new "progressive" profile of Mitzenheim. These contrary tendencies will be the subject of the following chapter.

4 The EKD Split and Formation of the Kirchenbund, 1958–1969

The 1958 communiqué signaled a new phase of the Kirchenpolitik. The 1949 to 1958 period had been one in which the regime's socialist transformation goals had dictated curtailment of the rights of churches and Christians, although this process had been relaxed periodically and never had been as severe as in other Communist states. After 1958 the goal of breaking ties with the FRG became overriding in the state's policy. To be sure, pressure on the churches and Christians did not cease. Indeed emphasis on scientific atheism in the SED increased.[1] But the state selectively sought conciliation with "progressive" church leaders, to exert pressure for separation from the EKD. This eventually proved successful by 1969 with the formation of the Kirchenbund, although the separation was hardly a clean one.

In terms of the general political climate in the period, 1958 to 1969 saw a shift from continued Stalinization to socioeconomic consolidation, as well as a shift toward delimitation with respect to the FRG, particularly when the FRG made overtures to the GDR. Initially, with his political opposition largely crushed, Ulbricht heightened efforts at Stalinist transformation.[2] Collectivization was pressed to conclusion: the portion of collectivized land doubled in one year alone, from 45

---

[1] For the first time in the GDR a chair in scientific atheism was established at the university in Jena in 1966. It was occupied by Olof Klohr, whose sociological study of secularization was designated for use by the party cadres. See his *Religion and Atheismus Heute* (1966).

[2] Weber, *Kleine Geschichte*, pp. 94–104.

percent in 1959 to 84 percent in 1960. Ulbricht succeeded in concentrating power in his hands and developed a personality cult around himself. The mass organizations increased in size at the expense of the bloc parties. Socialist universities were proclaimed; socialist realism became the dominant force in the cultural policy.

Due in no small part to this harsher line, social discontent reached a new high, manifested in unprecedented numbers emigrating to the West.[3] The hemorrhage led ineluctably to Khrushchev's Berlin ultimatum in 1958 and the erection of the Berlin Wall in 1961, which ushered in a period of consolidation. New efforts at de-Stalinization were undertaken. Modest economic reforms in the form of the New Economic System of Guidance and Planning were begun in 1963. Higher education opportunities were increased. A more flexible position was articulated regarding allied social groups such as peasants.

Just as the regime sought greater internal legitimacy through more pragmatic policies, so too it sought international legitimacy, in this case via increased political and economic contacts outside the Soviet bloc and through Abgrenzung from the FRG.[4] The GDR won international recognition from certain Third World states, such as Egypt, and integration into the Soviet bloc proceeded apace, as manifested by the USSR-GDR Friendship Treaty in 1964. The GDR still maintained its official commitment to German unity, but it became less and less credible. The GDR proposed halfway measures, such as an exchange of newspapers with the FRG, which it then backed away from. This pattern was particularly evident from 1966 to 1969. Faced with the Grand Coalition's limited version of Ostpolitik, the GDR reacted allergically. The SPD-SED speaker exchange, proposed in 1966, led the SED to back off. The FRG's success in establishing bridgeheads in Eastern Europe led Ulbricht to turn up the anti-FRG rhetoric and to seek to limit all contacts between the Germanies after 1966.

Ulbricht also tightened policy in the economic and cultural areas.[5] The economic reforms were scaled back after 1965. Intellectual critics were accused of introducing "harmful tendencies" in cultural life. In place of these reforms, Ulbricht emphasized the building of the "developed social system of socialism." Science and management methods

[3]Ibid., pp. 102–4, 110–17; Kupper, in Schulz, pp. 274–84; Childs, pp. 59–65.
[4]Weber, *Kleine Geschichte*, pp. 127–29; Kupper, in Schulz, pp. 284–95; Childs, pp. 75–77.
[5]Weber, *Kleine Geschichte*, pp. 126–36; Childs, pp. 72–74.

would promote growth in socialism, which was now viewed as a relatively independent socioeconomic formation. Ulbricht's vaunted "socialist human community" would bring together various social groups to cooperate in this period.

"COMMON HUMANISTIC RESPONSIBILITY," SELECTIVE DIALOGUE, AND THE TWILIGHT OF THE ALL-GERMAN EKD

The 1958 meeting between Grotewohl, Mitzenheim, and Krummacher signaled a new period in the church-state relationship as well. In terms of state policy, this period was characterized by three features. First, the state intensified its efforts at Abgrenzung from the West German churches. As suggested by the protocol at the 1958 meeting, the state henceforth refused to deal directly with the EKD or its representatives. This extended to Dr. Kurt Scharf, president of the EKD Synod, who was refused reentry into the GDR section of the Berlin-Brandenburg Landeskirche following the construction of the Berlin Wall in 1961. The state justified this shocking action on the basis of his alleged "alliance with provocationist elements in Westberlin" and his role "symbolizing the Military Chaplaincy Agreement."[6]

Second, after 1958 the state increasingly emphasized the basis of cooperation between individual Christians and Marxists. This line took on programmatic character with Ulbricht's speech before the parliament on October 9, 1960, in which he stated, "Christianity and the humanistic goals of socialism are not contradictory." After the building of the wall in 1961, articulation of this "common humanistic responsibility of Marxists and Christians" became increasingly de rigueur in state pronouncements on the Kirchenpolitik.[7]

Despite its definitive nature, this declarative policy hardly reflected a major reversal in the regime's Leninist view of religion or the church. Ulbricht did not abandon the Marxian tenet that the socialist transfor-

---

[6]"ADN-Meldung ueber die Rueckkehr von Praeses Scharf nach Westberlin vom 1. September 1961," in Reinhard Henkys, ed., *Bund der Evangelischen Kirchen in der DDR: Dokumente zu seiner Entstehung* (1970), pp. 65–66.

[7]"Das Christentun und die humanistischen Ziele des Sozialismus sind keine Gegensaetze," in Henkys, *Bund der Kirchen*, p. 52.

mation would lead to the disappearance of the function or need for religion. At this point even the later Ulbrichtian modification of this analysis, namely that the scientific-technical revolution would lead to the disappearance of religion, was not yet evident. Nor did the pronouncement indicate a reprieve from state pressure to limit the churches' social presence and attractiveness. The new line emphasized cooperation with *Christians*, not with the churches. While tolerating the churches' role in the health care system, the state continued to strive to limit the church to religious ritual. The state continued to limit church attempts to adapt to social change, for example, outreach efforts to the new urban areas or by innovative church cultural activity designed to appeal to the youth.

Yet the new policy did represent part of a larger shift evident in the post-1961 GDR, namely the shift from mobilization and social transformation to consolidation. Under the rubric of *socialist human community*, the state appealed to various non-working-class groups in order to broaden the base of support for the building of socialism.[8] While not willing to see an expansion of the churches' role in society, the state moved away from the frontal assault on religion and the church that had characterized the GDR Kirchenpolitik between 1949 and 1958.

This consolidation was to be based in part on opposition to the alleged militarism of the FRG. In other words, the common ground with Christians was defined narrowly in terms of foreign affairs, namely the desire for peace. The logic of the state was clear, if not compelling: the common goal is peace; the threat to achieving this goal is the rebirth of revanchist militarism in West Germany; the midwife to this rebirth is the leading segment of the West German church.

Third, state policy in this period saw the continuation of the "selective dialogue" begun in 1958. The high points of this period were two meetings in the early 1960s, whose anniversaries were later to become vehicles for official pronouncements on the Kirchenpolitik. The first meeting brought together Ulbricht in his governmental capacity—namely chairman of the State Council, not as head of the SED—and Leipzig theology professor Emil Fuchs.[9] Fuchs, a liberal theologian, was Christian socialist in political orientation and reformist in his approach

---

[8]Federal Ministry of Inner-German Affairs, *DDR Handbuch*, p. 1173; C. Bradley Scharf, *Politics and Change in East Germany* (1984), pp. 132–33.

[9]"Sozialisten und Christen verbinden gemeinsame Ideale und Ziele," in Henkys, *Bund der Kirchen*, pp. 57–60, 65.

to internal church organization. The meeting was held on February 9, 1961, shortly before GDR participation in the EKD church congress was blocked and the wall ended travel between East and West Berlin. At this meeting, Fuchs presented a letter supportive of the GDR and signed by 32,000 theologians and church officers. On the ideological plane, while admitting differences in basic philosophy, they posited the basic consistency between socialism and Christianity's social and humanistic ideals (including its mandate for peace) and the ensuing need for cooperation in achieving these goals. On the organizational level, both sides blamed the leadership of the West German church for the collapse in state-EKD relations and attacked the upcoming Berlin church convention as a "provocation."

Similar themes of socialist humanism and Abgrenzung were sounded in the second meeting, the so-called Wartburg discussion between Ulbricht and Bishop Mitzenheim on August 18, 1964.[10] Unlike Fuchs, Mitzenheim was a conservative Lutheran in his theological orientation and restorationist regarding church organization.[11] But Mitzenheim construed the Lutheran Two Kingdoms Doctrine to justify active support for the state, in order to maintain the national church (*Volkskirche*) in Thuringia. The state, in turn, would increasingly use the aging conservative Mitzenheim to exert political pressure on the other Landeskirchen. Ulbricht posited the commonality of goals, conceding that people come to support socialism from various traditions and conceptions, and Mitzenheim concurred. From this mutual interest flowed the key formulation of the Ulbricht Kirchenpolitik: the "common humanistic responsibility of Christians and Marxists." In contrast with the Ulbricht-Fuchs meeting of 1961, the Ulbricht meeting with Mitzenheim made little mention of differences in basic philosophy. Instead, Mitzenheim assumed a traditional, Lutheran Two Kingdoms position, that "one should not make the city hall a church, nor the church a city hall." However, in concrete terms, he departed from a strict interpretation of this doctrine by endorsing treaties, disarmament, and peace as all flowing from the Gospel. Reflecting the internal tension generated by the wall, Ulbricht assumed a defensive posture, and attacks on the "NATO church" correspondingly receded into the background.

---

[10]"Unsere Gemeinsamkeit in der Wahrnehmung humanistische Verantwortung ist von grosser nationaler Bedeutung," in Henkys, *Bund der Kirchen*, pp. 72–75, 77–78, 80, 82–83.
[11]Brand, pp. 63–65; Solberg, p. 275.

Despite the increasing Abgrenzung campaign, both declaratory and in practice, the state continued to retain at least a formal all-German commitment. For example, in both meetings Ulbricht blamed not the populace and Christians of West Germany, whom he saw as peace-loving, but rather the leadership of the FRG and the West German churches, which he compared to the collaboration of the "German Christians" with Hitler.[12] A "firm unity in human responsibility" in the GDR, he argued, would assist the West Germans in fostering a policy of peace and understanding. Moreover, Fuchs used all-German formulations several times: a peace program was seen as necessary for the "national rebirth of Germany"; those equating anti-Communism and Christianity were "acting against the interests of the nation." Ulbricht also used all-German formulations, but left little doubt that he had a socialist united Germany in mind: "The future of all Germany belongs to peace and socialism." Thus in its church policy, as in its German policy generally, the state pursued an increasingly contradictory policy: continued commitment to a united Germany, albeit socialist, yet pressure for a division of the churches along inter-German lines.

In the context of the increasing permanence of the division of Germany and continued pressure on the churches, the state's new emphasis on "common humanistic responsibility of Christians and Marxists" and the willingness of the "progressives" to cooperate with the state led to new attempts in the church to define the role of Christians and the churches in the GDR. The vast majority of church leaders rejected the alleged "common humanistic responsibility," remaining either neutral or antagonistic toward the state. The former saw no necessary correlation between the ideals of Christianity and the organization of the economy along the lines of socialism or capitalism. The latter saw Communist rule in East Germany as largely a continuation of the repressive authoritarianism of the Third Reich. Its necessary corollary, *Kirchenkampf,* called for resistance by the church in the manner of the Confessing Church. The primary spokesman for the latter position was Bishop Dibelius, until 1966 Bishop of Berlin-Brandenburg and Chairman of the Council of the EKD. Although he had tried, along with Provost Grueber, to play the role of a bridge between the two Germanies, he became increasingly antagonistic toward the GDR in the late

[12]Henkys, *Bund der Kirchen,* pp. 58, 74, 80, 83.

1950s. In 1959 in his book *Obrigkeit* he argued that the strictures in Romans 13 regarding "obedience to Caesar" did not apply to the situation of Christians in the GDR.[13] He differentiated between a legal authority ordained by God and a totalitarian order not ordained by God. According to Dibelius, the absence of legal order in the GDR meant that it could claim no moral obligation from Christians, even on such matters as adherence to the traffic laws of the GDR.

This opposition by Dibelius drew considerable criticism and counterattempts to formulate a more positive position for Christians in the GDR. Dibelius' own Landeskirche distanced itself from his interpretation of Romans 13. Already in 1957 Johannes Hamel, a leading EKU theologian, had written in his publication "Christian in the GDR" that "even this authority, which is based on an ideology, cannot escape the imprint of God." Building on this, the EKU issued an advisory in 1959 that held that "our freedom in Christ allows us the readiness to live in these new social forms, so that we do not stubbornly oppose its implementation and do not cling to the previous patterns of ownership and occupation. It is necessary to cooperate willingly and actively also in new, unfamiliar, difficult forms which require sacrifice."[14]

The Lutherans in the VELKD were less sanguine about cooperating with Marxists, Mitzenheim's example notwithstanding. In its 1960 advisory, the VELKD recognized the GDR as God-given authority in the sense of Romans 13.[15] However, although Christians were thus required to meet civic responsibilities, political cooperation with the state was impossible "because the GDR cannot separate its atheistic worldview from its social-political goals." The atheistic state can only be "accepted and suffered, but not supported and promoted."

The Berlin Wall in 1961 shifted the center of gravity in the church debate toward the EKU position and away from the positions of Dibelius and the VELKD. This was manifested in the "Ten Articles of Freedom and Service of the Church" of the Eastern Conference of Church Leaderships (1963), namely the leaders of the GDR Landeskirchen.[16] It sought to aid Christians in avoiding the alternatives of

---

[13]Otto Dibelius, *Obrigkeit* (1963).

[14]Daehn, p. 89; The EKU advisory, "The Gospel and the Christian Life in the GDR," as cited in Hans-Juergen Roeder, "Kirche im Sozialismus," in Henkys (1982), p. 65.

[15]"The Christian in the GDR," as cited in ibid., p. 67.

[16]As cited in ibid., p. 68.

resignation and acclamation: "In the existing social conditions we must ascertain what God wants from us and to do good according to His will. We fall prey to a lack of faith if we assume that God has abandoned us in the existing conditions and thus begin to doubt, or if we interpret the historical and social circumstances as the direct gift of the will of God and accept them without reservation." Although carefully worded and balanced, it nonetheless reflected a considerable distancing from Dibelius and even a modest shift from the "respecting of socialism" of the 1958 communique.

Going even further in its acceptance of socialism was the Weissensee Study Group, a group of clergy centered in Berlin who were particularly critical of the national church tradition in Germany and of Dibelius in particular. In 1963 this group, which was to spawn future church leaders such as Bishop Albrecht Schoenherr, issued *Seven Theological Theses on the Freedom of the Church to Serve,* which maintained that "the belief in the Love of God makes man free to cooperate in this social order and to take on responsibility. Christians and non-Christians work together at the task of creating internally a human and just order and a lasting peace in the relations among peoples and states."[17]

These various attempts to redefine the role of Christians in socialism and the church's attitude toward the state were not sustained, however. Although this debate had resulted from the increasing permanence of the GDR in the late 1950s, such deliberations were relegated to a back burner in the face of increased state pressure to force organizational separation from the West German churches after 1966.

ABGRENZUNG AND THE CHURCHES' STANCE AT FUERSTENWALDE

The division between the East and West German churches was in fact more gradual than the tempo of the events in 1968 and 1969 would suggest. In the face of the increasing political constraints imposed by the GDR following the construction of the wall in 1961, the EKD made some practical accommodation, although it remained nominally unified. Precedent had been set by the Berlin-Brandenburg Landeskirche,

[17]From the Fifth and Seventh theses, in *KJ* 1964, pp. 196–97.

which in 1959 had legally transformed itself into an entity composed of two regions, both sharing a set of basic principles and a common bishop, yet with relatively independent synods, leadership, and administration.[18] The EKD too had adapted, though in organizational rather than legal terms. Since 1950 the Conference of Church Leaderships (GDR), often known as the Eastern Conference, had operated as an informal leadership group. After 1961 it became more formal: its chairman, Bishop Krummacher (Greifswald), served as spokesman for the GDR members on the Council of the EKD, and it became in reality the locus of decision on matters affecting the GDR churches. This shift of decisional competence to the GDR church leaders intensified after the mid-1960s, when FRG members of the EKD Council and church administration were barred from access to the GDR.[19] Although unified EKD Synod meetings had been prohibited from meeting on GDR territory since the mid-1950s, such meetings had been possible in East Berlin until 1961. When the wall made even an East Berlin meeting impossible, the EKD passed laws in March 1963 permitting regionally separate, though officially unified synods.

Political constraint on organizational activities was not the only, nor even perhaps the primary reason explaining the gradual process of division within the EKD. The intense process of social change taking place in the GDR led many East German church leaders to feel that the all-German EKD had become less relevant to the social context of the GDR churches. Many also felt that they were ignored by the West German majority in the EKD.[20] According to one observer, the problem was "not the browbeating of the GDR churches by the EKD, but rather the loss of relevance of the work of EKD organs in terms of its meaning not only for the churches in the GDR, but also for the whole EKD."[21] More than just relevance was at issue, however; many argued that since the consequences in the GDR of decisions of the EKD were not borne by West Germans, they could not responsibly make those decisions. Thus, due to differing social contexts and needs, as well as political con-

---

[18]"Die Regionalgesetze der Evangelischen Kirche in Berlin-Brandenburg," in Henkys, *Bund der Kirchen*, pp. 44–46.

[19]Based on discussion with informed sources.

[20]Interview with Dr. Johannes Althausen, Evangelical Church in Berlin-Brandenburg (East), November 1977. For example, an EKD study on agricultural problems seemed irrelevant to the collectivized agriculture in the GDR.

[21]Henkys, *Bund der Kirchen*, p. 18.

straints, the two sectors of the EKD began to grow apart even before the formal division in 1969.

Just as the split in the EKD was more gradual than the tempo of events would suggest, so too the state pressure for such a split escalated only gradually. While West Germany had pursued integration into the Western alliance and a "position of strength" vis-à-vis the East, the state and the USSR had found appeals to German unity, and hence German church unity, useful in pursuit of its foreign policy interests.[22]

However, affirmation of inter-German unity, including that of the churches, became more dangerous for the GDR when the FRG began to initiate tentative overtures toward the East in 1966. As a result, official attacks on the organizational unity of the EKD itself intensified. On May 1, 1966, *Neues Deutschland,* the SED organ, hinted obliquely at the embryonic new party line in maintaining that the normalization of state relations was a prerequisite for the normalization of interchurch relations.[23] Ulbricht himself sounded the state's message much more clearly in a September 1966 speech. Upon awarding Bishop Mitzenheim the Star of People's Friendship (in Silver), he concluded:

> In Germany there are numerous directions within the Church; I would even say, that there are numerous churches. There is one church which attends and spreads the principles of humanism in Christian respon-sibility. That is the church in the GDR. There is in West Germany a large number of Christians and ministers who are led by the idea of humanism, but next to them are bishops who have sworn themselves to the military church and to the policy . . . of the CDU (West). Thus in Germany basically a splintering in the circles of the church and Christianity has occurred.[24]

The CDU (East) followed with an even more ominous directive to the GDR churches. On February 9, 1967, at the yearly celebration of the Ulbricht-Fuchs meeting, Chairman Gerald Goetting described the EKD as a tool of West German foreign policy, the unity of which had become

---

[22]"Passierscheinverhandlungen wieder aufnehmen," *epd Landesdienst Berlin,* no. 70 (23 August 1966): p. 3. Spotts, pp. 237–68, describes the tendency among German Protestants in the 1950s to oppose military rearmament and integration into NATO.

[23]"Aus der Rede Walter Ulbrichts zum 20 Jahrestag der Gruendung der SED am 21. April 1966," in Henkys, *Bund der Kirchen,* p. 86.

[24]"Aus einer Ansprache Walter Ulbrichts anlaesslich der Verleihung des 'Sterns der Vol-kerfreundschaft' in Silber an den thueringischen Landesbischof Mitzenheim am 22. September 1966," in ibid., p. 89.

a "weapon in the Cold War against the GDR." Thus nine years after the Military Chaplaincy Agreement, he claimed that the "free and independent Evangelical Churches in the GDR cannot be mentioned in the same breath with the West German Evangelical Church which is bound to NATO through the Military Chaplaincy Agreement. Between the two extremes there is no institutional unity.[25]

Augmenting this diffuse public attack on the East German churches, the state privately attacked their ties to the EKD. The state criticized the election of Kurt Scharf as bishop of Berlin-Brandenburg in 1966 as a provocatory assertion of EKD unity and, given Scharf's close ties to the SPD, an indirect extension of the SPD's all-German conception. Some churchmen (e.g., General Superintendents Schoenherr and Jacob) were accused of having been manipulated by the EKD for this purpose.[26] The state attacked unorthodox cultural trends (e.g., jazz worship, as popularized in Karl-Marx Stadt) as inspired by the West German churches.[27] The 1965 Advisory on Pastoral Care of Military Draftees, a controversial piece, which advocated conscientious objection as preferable to military service and bore the imprint of the pacifist Bishop Johannes Jaenicke of Magdeburg, was subjected to harsh criticism by the state.[28] The landmark EKD memorandum in 1965, urging reevaluation of the FRG's stand concerning the Eastern territories and the Oder-Neisse boundary, was viewed by the GDR as an attempt to support the new CDU/SPD Ostpolitik and weaken the GDR internally. The GDR saw the memorandum and the Ostpolitik as guided by the principle of a "third way" (i.e., "ideological softening" of the GDR and mutual accommodation) and sought to counteract the influence of such thinking in church leadership circles.[29]

---

[25]"Aus einem Referat Gerald Gottings auf einer kirchenpolitischen Tagung der CDU (Ost) in Jena am 9. Februar 1967," in ibid., pp. 89–90.

[26]CDU archives, 1966.

[27]CDU archives, 3 August 1966.

[28]Regarding the Heidelberg Theses, see Guenther Heipp and Hans Ruecker, *Christen und Obrigkeit in geteilten Deutschland* (Hamburg: Herbert Reich Evangelischer Verlag, 1962). The Eastern Conference's Tract on Pastoral Care of Military Draftees, "On the Peace Service of the Church," from 3 November 1965, can be found in *epd Dokumentation*, no. 16 (27 March 1975): pp. 26–40.

[29]To the CDU the root cause of this alleged West German influence on the East German churches was their increasing financial dependence on the FRG. Subsidies from the West German churches cover approximately one quarter to one third of the budget of the GDR Landeskirchen. See CDU archives, 8 September 1966; CDU archives, 1966.

The escalation of state demands evoked immediate response by the GDR churches.[30] Meeting under intense state pressure in Fuersten-walde, outside Berlin, the 1967 Eastern regional synod of the EKD rejected the state's attacks.[31] Bishop Krummacher, Chairman of the Eastern Conference, rejected the state's demands, maintaining that the Gospel of Christ had given an impulse for the church to transcend borders and that the unity of the EKD served as an example to other churches of the primacy of ecumenicism over secular cleavages.[32] Krum-macher disputed the state's position that the sociopolitical environment binds the Gospel; EKD unity was no longer merely an institutional question but one of common creed.

In a statement that came to be known as the Fuerstenwalde declara-tion, the synod also rejected the state's demands. First, it maintained that separation from the EKD was required only in the case of false teaching or disobedience to God, which was not the case in the EKD. Second, the declaration maintained that there were good reasons to maintain organizational unity: the churches' guilt in the Third Reich, acknowledged in the Stuttgart Confession of 1945, and responsibility toward history and the German people in this regard; the imperative of the ecumenical movement; and the need to uphold human contacts between the two Germanies.[33]

The churches' position at Fuerstenwalde was not unified, however. The "progressive" Thuringian Landeskirche pressed for separation by refusing previously agreed Thuringian nominations for the EKD Coun-cil and the Presidium of the EKD Synod and proposing to regionalize the EKD synod and council. While rejecting the Thuringian proposal for an immediate regionalization, the synod did pass a law permitting such a regionalization, if found necessary by the EKD Council. As if to com-pensate for their reaffirmation of inter-German ties, the Eastern Con-ference bowed to state preference, vetoing the otherwise clear choice of

[30]For the responses of Bishops Fraenkel and Jaenicke, as well as that of Church President Mueller, see Henkys, *Bund der Kirchen*, pp. 90–95.

[31]The state pressured the GDR section of the EKD Synod to meet in Fuerstenwalde to prevent West German church representatives from direct contact with the synod, although contact was maintained by a complicated courier system.

[32]Excerpts from Krummacher's report to the synod, as found in Henkys, *Bund der Kirchen*, p. 96.

[33]"Erklaerung der in Fuerstenwalde versammelten Mitglieder der EKD-Synode vom 5. April 1967," in ibid., pp. 99–101.

politically conservative Lutheran Bishop Lilje (Hannover) as the new chairman of the EKD Council.[34]

To be sure, the Fuerstenwalde Declaration itself was not entirely unambiguous regarding unity. In the final section, it maintained: "We must mutually agree that we are obligated to serve in the part of Germany in which we live. That requires of all churches in the EKD that they always take the others into consideration in their decisions." Thus, despite the support for the EKD, Fuerstenwalde did provide proponents of separation with certain arguments.[35]

Notwithstanding this nuanced position of the church, the state reaction to it was immediate and predictably negative. In a rare personal attack, *Neues Deutschland* accused Bishop Krummacher of being used by the West German "military church."[36] His formula of a "border-transcending impulse of the church" was seen as "Bonn's revanchism in theological garb." Indignantly the paper pointed out that Krummacher was bishop of Greifswald, not of Pomerania (the term for the Landeskirche, which before 1945 had included areas now part of Poland). The SED tied the churches to the SPD, quoting Herbert Wehner, SPD minister for inter-German relations, that "on the German question, in the longer term the church will be able to do much which remains impossible in the political realm because of its own legal formalism." In a novel ideological twist, the SED maintained that since "Christianity, as is known, is much older than capitalism and of course older than imperialism, the highest stage of capitalist development, it can therefore not be a vital necessity for Christianity to bind itself to the progress and decay of imperialism." The Seventh Party Congress of the SED in 1967 also accused certain East German church leaders of ignoring the alleged majority of Christians and clergy who supported the SED's peace policy.[37]

The state's ire was vented on both bishops and the church activities. Bishops Krummacher and Noth were excluded from ecumenical meetings and denied invitations to the CDU party congress in 1968, despite

[34]CDU archives, 1967.
[35]Henkys, *Bund der Kirchen*, p. 20.
[36]"Kommentar des 'Neuen Deutschland' zur EKD-Synode vom 8. April 1967," in ibid., pp. 102–4.
[37]"Aus dem Bericht des Zentralkommittees an den VII Parteitag der SED, April 1967," in ibid., p. 105.

receiving invitations in 1964.[38] This slide into disfavor was particularly drastic in the case of Krummacher, who had previously enjoyed relatively good relations with the state. Already in 1966 the state revoked the license of the GDR edition of the official bulletin of the EKD. Soon state censors made it practically impossible to mention the EKD in church publications except in negative terms.[39] Moreover, meetings with West German churches were hindered. For example, synod meetings were forced out of Berlin in order to preclude West German participation. In the case of events that offered the possibility of inter-German contact, such as the celebration of the 450th anniversary of the Reformation in 1967, the state acted either to prohibit the events or to deny visas for West Germans.[40]

The writing was on the wall, and certain church organizations began to draw the conclusion even before 1969. For example, the Evangelical Student Parishes in Germany abandoned its all-German structure in May 1967. Likewise the diaconical organizations, more pragmatic than the churches per se, moved prior to 1969 to adapt to the reality of two German states. But with Fuerstenwalde, the churches responded to the state pressure with a seemingly firm *nein*. Within a year, however, the churches' position began to weaken in response to the new constitutional reality.

THE NEW CONSTITUTION

The immediate factor that intervened and weakened the churches' stance on EKD unity was the formulation and approval in 1968 of a new GDR constitution to replace the one dating from 1949.[41]

[38]For example, visas were denied them for the General Assembly of the WCC in Uppsala, 1968. "Lutherans Named to Key World Council Positions," *LWF Information*, no. 30 (23 July 1968): p. 3; Friedrich Krummacher, *Ruf zur Entscheidung;* CDU archives, 16 August 1968.

[39]EPS documents, 15 January 1968, pp. 2–4.

[40]A meeting of the LWF general assembly planned for the GDR and an East Berlin church congress were canceled. Based on discussions with informed sources. "Ostberliner Kirchentagstreffen abgesagt," *epd Landesdienst Berlin*, no. 109 (12 September 1968): p. 1. "Kirchengemeinde unter politischer Kontrolle," *SDZ*, 13 February 1968; *FR*, 20 June 1968; "Ost-Berlin verbietet Kirchentagstreffen," *FAZ*, 12 September 1968; "Pankower Einflussnahme auf Kirche," *Der Tagesspiegel*, 22 November 1967.

[41]Interview with Bishop Werner Krusche (Saxony-Magdeburg), May 30, 1979.

The SED justified a new constitution as necessary to consolidate the current stage of socialism and lay the groundwork for the transition to the next stage, namely Ulbricht's "developed social system of socialism." The other, unstated reason was the state's need to reformulate its position on the national question in the face of the incipient Ostpolitik of the CDU/SPD coalition.[42]

Comparisons with the 1949 constitution suggest that the first draft threatened to weaken the churches' role in several respects. First, the draft removed the special mention of religion in the clause guaranteeing equal rights to citizens, setting religion on a par with other "professed basic philosophies." Second, by eliminating "guarantees" of specific church activities (e.g., freedom of conscience and religious practice, the right of religious instruction, religious service and care, and church expression on vital issues) and mandating the churches to "order and execute their activities in agreement with the constitutional and legal dictates of the GDR," the draft constitution seemed to codify the constriction of church activities beyond the cultic.[43] Third, although the draft retained all-German phraseology and goals, the independence and permanence of the GDR was stressed. Ulbricht maintained that "our new constitution will make clear to those who still do not understand: the socialist GDR is not provisional."[44]

Finally, and most importantly, the state interpreted Article 38.1 of the new constitution—"The churches shall order their affairs according to the laws of the GDR"—as requiring organizational separation from the West German churches, especially after Bishop Mitzenheim's statement at a citizens meeting in Weimar that "state borders also form the borders of the possibilities of church organizations."[45] Already, a new law in January 1968 requiring registration and state approval of organizations

---

[42]*Volkskammer* speech by Walter Ulbricht of December 1, 1967, calling for a People's Commission to draw up a new constitution, cited in Koch, *Staat und Kirche*, pp. 82–85.

[43]"Aus einem Entwurf der DDR-Verfassung vom 31. Januar 1968," in Henkys, *Bund der Kirchen*, p. 106. See also "Aus dem Bericht Walter Ulbrichts zum Verfassungentwurf der DDR vor der Volkskammer am 31. Januar 1968," in ibid., p. 107. EPS documents, 15 January 1968, pp. 2–4.

[44]Mueller-Roemer, p. 14; Koch, *Staat und Kirche*, p. 87.

[45]"Aus dem Referat des Parteivorsitzenden Gerald Goetting vor dem Hauptvorstand der CDU (Ost) am 8. Februar 1968," "Landesbischof Mitzenheim auf einer Buergervertreterkonferenz in Weimar am 29.2. 1968, mit Antwort Walter Ulbrichts," in Henkys, *Bund der Kirchen*, pp. 106–7, 110–11, 116.

that were members of international organizations had left the unregistered GDR churches' ties to the EKD in doubt.[46]

Although Ulbricht ruled out any feedback from the churches, the bishops responded to the draft constitution in the so-called letter from Lehnin. Signed by all except Mitzenheim, this letter petitioned the state to restore the specific references to freedom of belief and conscience and the rights of the church. By focusing on the rights of Christians and the churches and leaving unaddressed the key issue of the legality of all-German institutions, the bishops began to retreat from their position at Fuerstenwalde.[47]

Although most individual church leaders concurred in this official church position of seeking changes or compromises in the draft, but not rejecting it entirely, "progressives" went even further.[48] For example, Krummacher, seeking to redeem himself for Fuerstenwalde in the eyes of the state, called for the international recognition of the postwar borders and of the GDR. Moreover, he placed the GDR churches in a "community of belief transcending state borders." Although this formulation distanced him from the Mitzenheim position, it also relativized the inter-German church ties, thus marking a retreat from his Fuerstenwalde stance, which had placed EKD unity on the plane of confessional belief. Krummacher also indicated his intention to vote in the constitutional referendum. Even though issued after the bishops had initially failed in their attempts at reaching a common position, Krummacher's stands were made without consulting the other bishops and displeased many in the church. Although the state gave widespread publicity to his position, both his public and private conciliatory gestures failed to end his persona-non-grata status with the state.

The role of Mitzenheim in the constitutional debate indicated the widening gap between the "progressives" and other church leaders. Not only did Mitzenheim not sign the bishops' letter, but he lent public support to the constitution. Contradicting the bishops' letter, he claimed

[46]EPS documents, 20 January 1968, p. 2.

[47]See "Brief evangelischer Bischoefe zum Verfassungsentwurf," in *Bund der Kirchen*, p. 112–14.

[48]CDU archives, 20 March 1968; CDU archives, 1968; EPS documents, 16 March 1968, p. 2; "Aus einer Stellungnahme von Bischof Krummacher zum Verfassungsentwurf im 'Evangelischen Nachrichtendienst in der DDR' vom 14. Februar 1968," in Henkys, *Bund der Kirchen*, pp. 111–12.

that the constitution guaranteed the legal rights of individuals and the churches.[49] Although he later claimed to have supported the letter, by propounding the principle that state borders determine church borders, Mitzenheim widened further the breach with the other church leaders over EKD unity. Many wished to prevent such "progressive" deviations from further weakening the church's position vis-à-vis the state.

Defections from the bishops' low-key, domestic-oriented strategy occurred at the other end of the churches' political spectrum as well.[50] Many, particularly in the EKU, opposed the constitution outright—for example, the EKU Church Chancellory head Franz-Reinhold Hildebrandt, EKU Synod President Lothar Kreyssig, and Dr. Johannes Hamel, a prominent theologian. Hildebrandt was particularly vocal, claiming for the EKD and EKU a "bridge-function between the East and West of our fatherland." Hamel, who was to play a major role in the debate surrounding the Kirchenbund, criticized the bishops for not questioning the entire constitution, starting with Article 1.

Bishop Fraenkel and his Goerlitz Landeskirche also predictably affirmed EKD unity. He criticized the draft for undercutting the rights of individual citizens, asked for freedom of conscience for those unable to acquiesce to the absolute demands of socialism, and requested an open referendum by all Germans to determine constitutional structure. Despite their vocalness, the critics of the constitution were limited in their forum (primarily Saxony-Magdeburg, Goerlitz, and the EKU), their power in the church hierarchy (with the exceptions of Fraenkel and Hildebrandt), and their content (focusing primarily on the issue of EKD unity, attacking the constitution per se only in Goerlitz).

Despite Ulbricht's earlier brusque rejection of input by the churches, the final draft contained revisions that reflected the state's sensitivity to the churches' official position and the written proposals from thousands of individual Christians. The equal-rights guarantee was extended to specifically cover "religious confession" in addition to "basic philosophy." The state could not, of course, admit this partial accommodation to the bishops' position, but justified the revisions on the basis of "the people's discussions, and Bishop Mitzenheim's contribution," thereby

---

[49]"Aus einem Interview der 'Neuen Zeit' mit Landesbischof Mitzenheim vom 4.2, 1968," in Henkys, *Bund der Kirchen*, pp. 109–10.
[50]CDU archives, 1968; CDU archives, 22 March 1968; CDU archives, 17 March 1968.

reinforcing its Mitzenheim strategy.[51] Ironically, the final formulation actually contradicted Mitzenheim's preference: it equated religious confession with other basic philosophies, as desired by the bishops, whereas Mitzenheim had maintained that convictions of faith are not questions of basic philosophy since they are directed by the word of God.[52]

On the question of legal guarantees of church activity in such areas as education and finances, the bishops fared less well. The state determined that the specific guarantees in the 1949 constitution would not be included in the new constitution. According to the report of the People's Commission, "the constitution gives the churches and religious communities a legal basis for the unhindered exercise of its spiritual and community activity, which concurs with the political interest and moral perception of the believing citizens."[53] The state's desire to eliminate these rights proved overriding. Even more damaging than the loss of these specified legal rights was the inclusion of the clause: "Details may be regulated through agreements." The state viewed this as a positive substitution for the previous rights, allowing it to negotiate agreements with the church on a pragmatic, ad hoc basis.[54] Unsettling to the church, however, was the possibility that such agreements might be proffered selectively and on an unfavorable basis.

The bishops' approach of constructive criticism of the constitution was thus a mixed one. The state appeared to give ground on the freedom-of-belief clause but held firm in eliminating rights of the churches. The state's decision to compromise, like its decision to retain a rhetorical commitment to the German nation, was informed by its desire to gain a show of support for the GDR. The state was clearly concerned that the April 1968 referendum on the proposed constitution—a rare occurrence in Soviet bloc states, namely an issue with a real chance to vote no—might result in a major expression of discontent. It thus sought to defuse potentially dangerous issues that might fuel such an expression of discontent by Christians.

---

[51]Rommel too inaccurately attributes this change to the influence of Thuringia and Mitzenheim. See Rommel, pp. 51–52.

[52]NZ, 31 March 1968.

[53]"Bericht der Kommission zur Ausarbeitung einer sozialistischen Verfassung ueber die Ergebnisse der Volksaussprache," in Klaus Sorgenicht et al., 1:171.

[54]Discussion with Dr. Herbert Trebs (CDU), member of the People's Constitution Commission, June 1979.

The results of the referendum did, to a certain extent, bear out the state's fears. Only 94.5 percent of the eligible voters approved the new constitution (91 percent in East Berlin itself), somewhat below the usual 98–99 percent approval rate in elections. However, it is not clear that this falloff can be laid at the doors of the church. All bishops voted in the referendum—in contrast with the 1967 communal elections, in which only six of eight voted—and the 90 percent turnout of the clergy contrasted dramatically with normal election turnout of approximately 60 percent at that time. Predictably, the Thuringian clergy voted in greater numbers than those of other Landeskirchen.[55] This higher-than-normal turnout may have contributed to the reduced percentage of ayes. However, the clergy did not boycott the vote en masse, which indicates that the state's compromises were effective in avoiding this worst of all scenarios in a mobilization effort.

The deliberations surrounding the new constitution represented a watershed for the churches. While not accepting the status quo in the GDR, the church accepted the goals of socialism in an attempt to influence the means toward their realization.[56] This reflected the growing influence of Schoenherr, who was to play a major role in the future deliberations. However, it became increasingly clear to them that the state was firmly intent on the Abgrenzung of the GDR churches from the West German churches and that these continuing organizational ties impeded dealing with the state.

But it also became clearer than ever to them that Bishop Mitzenheim's behavior weakened their position with the state. To be sure, the 1949 guarantees of the church's specific rights had been honored more in the breach than in the practice, and it is doubtful that Mitzenheim had cost them the battle over these constitutional articles. However, the churches had retained a considerable social presence. Now, given the state's strategy to differentiate among the Landeskirchen and Mitzenheim's willingness to accommodate it, the new constitution's vague offer to negotiate specific agreements raised the specter of selective agreements with individual, "progressive" Landeskirchen, particularly Thuringia, at the expense of the others.[57] The state did not hesitate to demonstrate

[55]CDU archives, 16 April 1968.

[56]The bishops' letter did not reflect an acceptance of the economic and political status quo, as maintained by Daehn, p. 107.

[57]One commentator sees the new constitution as an improvement in the church's position. See Hans Reis, "Konkordat und Kirchenvertrag in der Staatsverfassung," *Jahrbuch des oef-*

the rewards for such accommodation, citing the reduction of travel barriers for pensioners and the introduction of alternative, nonmilitary service as the fruits of Mitzenheim's good relationship with the state. This fear of separate agreements with the state and the sense of efficacy resulting from the bishops' letter—provide the context for the churches' reconsideration of its Fuerstenwalde position on EKD unity.

FORMATION OF THE FEDERATION OF EVANGELICAL CHURCHES IN THE GDR

By the spring of 1968 the church leadership widely believed that some adaptation to the new situation was necessary. However, in this fluid situation, views differed regarding what specific actions should be taken and what the state would find acceptable. Over the following year, the churches' proposals and plans changed considerably; the Federation of Evangelical Churches in the GDR took shape only as the result of a rather long, ad hoc process.[58]

Initially most church leaders—in particular Krummacher, chairman of the Eastern Conference and member of the EKD Council—hoped to simply regionalize the organs of the EKD on the basis of the Fuerstenwalde church law, thus obtaining independent decision-making power while retaining the organizational unity of the EKD. Some—for example, Krummacher and Noth—favored designating these regionalized organs the "Evangelical Church(es) in the GDR." The EKD Council reluctantly approved this regionalization—without, however, adopting the designation "Evangelical Church(es) in the GDR." The Eastern conference further sought to defuse the situation by replacing Krummacher, too closely identified with Fuerstenwalde, with the low-profile Bishop Beste as chairman in 1968.

It soon became clear that the state considered this insufficient. It

---

fentlichen Rechts 18 (1968), p. 375. Most scholars, however, concur that the constitution represented a weakening of the church's legal status. See Rommel, pp. 57–58; Siegfried Mampel, *Die Verfassung der sowjetischen Besatzungszone Deutschlands* (1966), p. 743f; Jens Hacker, "Korrekturen am Verfassungsentwurf," *DA* 1 (April 1968): 104; Dietrich Mueller-Roemer, "Die Grundrechte im neuen mitteldeutschen Verfassungsrecht," *Der Staat* 7 (1968): 320.

[58]This discussion of the formation of the Kirchenbund is based largely on discussion with Reinhard Henkys and Bishops Schoenherr, Braecklein, Krusche, Fraenkel, and Beste, among others.

rejected a regionalization as superficial and refused on principle to deal with the four GDR members of the EKD Council on the grounds that they were elected by the whole synod, not just the Eastern region. Some in the churches also viewed the church's response as inadequate. In particular, Schoenherr proposed the founding of a new organization, authorized by the Landeskirchen, rather than the EKD, and based on the Eastern Conference. By late May 1968 support for this view had grown to the point where the churches formed two commissions: a Structure Commission, mandated to propose new forms of organization for the eight GDR Landeskirchen, and a Negotiation Commission, mandated to conduct any negotiations with the state.

The formation of the Structure Commission under Schoenherr's chairmanship proved to be a turning point; the fact that its mandate derived from the Eastern Conference, and not the EKD Council, reflected the fact that the initiative in the process had shifted from the EKD Council and Chancellory to the Eastern Conference and the GDR Landeskirchen, in effect from Krummacher to Schoenherr. Not only was the Western region of the EKD thus closed out of formal participation in the commission's deliberations, but regionalization of the EKD ceased to be an option, given the commission's publicly stated goal of building a new organization. Indeed the questions faced by the commission were framed differently: What was to be the organizational relationship among the churches in the GDR? (Namely, were the Landeskirchen to become the basic unit of organization or was some form of central or federative church organization to be formed, and if so, with what powers?) What was to be their relationship to the EKD? (Namely, was membership in the EKD necessarily terminated by the formation of an independent GDR federation? Were the GDR churches to remain members of the EKD—either officially or tacitly—retain only a spiritual bond, or break completely?)

Throughout its deliberations, the Structure Commission by and large avoided the question of explicitly defining the residual ties to the EKD. Most church leaders seemed to believe that a resolution along the lines of the so-called twin church theory was possible—the existence of two parallel organizations—a solution that assumed latent membership in the EKD and continued activity of EKD organs in the GDR. Schoenherr seemed to support this position, maintaining that the independent organization of the GDR churches "means no rejection of the churches in the

EKD with which we are together in the community of the EKD."[59] However, leading elements in the commission feared jeopardizing the entire structural effort by prematurely making a definitive interpretation. Thus in the August 1968 draft charter of the incipient Kirchenbund, the clause dealing with the relationship to the EKD was deliberately vague: "In co-responsibility for all of Evangelical Christianity in Germany the Federation participates through its organs in all decisions which affect all Evangelical churches in Germany."[60]

Forces associated with the East German components of various EKD bodies, such as the EKD Synod and Chancellory, were alarmed at the vagueness of the "EKD-clause" in the draft charter and the minimalist characterization of the ties to the EKD. Meeting in Halle in October 1968 for consultation, the GDR members of the EKD synod sought to brake the Structure Commission's movement toward total separation, recommending that the Council of the EKD study the proposed charter of any new federation so that it could be introduced without giving up the community of the EKD.[61] They also sought terminological changes in the draft charter to distinguish the institutions of the proposed federation from the regional institutions of the EKD. Similarly, the EKD Chancellory in the GDR, referring to the Halle recommendation in a letter to the Landeskirchen, sought to make the Structure Commission responsible to the EKD Council, rather than the Eastern Conference, and thereby reassert the role of the EKD Council and Chancellory in the deliberations.[62]

Opposition to the Structure Commission's proposed charter also arose from the other direction, namely Thuringia and the state. While recognizing a "special relationship" with the West German churches, Thuringia echoed the state's attacks on the twin church theory on the grounds that any organization authorized by the EKD would be "flawed from birth." Thuringia demanded a clarification of the proposed federation's relationship to the EKD and objected to using the EKD charter as a legal basis for the new federation. Like the state, it rejected the attempt by the EKD Chancellory (East) to reassert the role of the EKD, insisting

[59]Schoenherr, to the Berlin-Brandenburg (East) Regional Synod in November 1968, as reported in *Die Welt*, 4 November 1968, p. 7.

[60]EPC archives, 3 September 1968.

[61]"Beschluss der EKD-Synodalen aus der DDR auf einer Informationstagung in Halle vom 4. Oktober 1968," in Henkys, *Bund der Kirchen*, p. 122.

[62]CDU archives, 1 November 1968.

that sole authority for the Structural Commission rested with the Landeskirchen and the Eastern Conference.

The state, too, criticized any compromise that might leave an ambiguous situation.[63] At the February 1969 CDU meeting, Seigewasser attacked "the minority of churchmen who zig-zag between the fronts, attempting to deny the consequences flowing from the existence of two German states and seeking to uphold the ties to the West German EKD. . . . A middle way is out of the question." In a veiled reference to the struggle between the EKD Chancellory and the Eastern Conference, he attacked "the structural-political manipulations whereby the long-due separation of the Landeskirchen from the EKD is to be circumvented."[64] Already in late 1968 the state began to demand privately that the EKD bodies in the GDR be disbanded and that GDR citizens lay down their offices in the EKD. Moreover, it insisted that all Landeskirchen change their church laws to replace "EKD" references with "Kirchenbund." The "progressive" Pfarrerbund made these demands publicly in late February 1969.[65]

By January 1969 the twin church theory was dead. Without accepting Thuringia's minimalist approach to relations with the EKD, the Landeskirchen, with the exception of Goerlitz, had rejected parallel EKD-Kirchenbund organizations in the GDR. Even Krummacher and other East German members of the EKD Council who favored the twin church theory, were forced to abandon this position in the face of the sentiment in the Landeskirchen. Schoenherr, in an interview on January 15, 1969, codified this consensus within the church leadership. He maintained that the organs of the EKD could no longer exercise their responsibility over the churches in the GDR. According to Schoenherr: "Church agencies must serve the witness of the church. When they can no longer do this, they must be changed. The witness of the church takes priority over its form of organization."[66] The contrast with the Fuerstenwalde Declaration is striking. Fuerstenwalde had rejected the argu-

[63]NZ, 31 October 1968.

[64]"Aus einem Referat des DDR-Staatssekretaers fuer Kirchenfragen . . . ," in Henkys, *Bund der Kirchen*, p. 142.

[65]"Aus einem Referat vom Propst Dietrich Scheidung . . . ," in ibid., p. 146. CDU archives, 3 April 1970; CDU archives, 5 June 1969; CDU archives, 24 January 1969.

[66]"Aus einem Interview des Evangelischen Nachrichtendienstes in der DDR mit dem Vorsitzenden der Strukturkommission, Bischofsamtsverwalter D. Albrecht Schoenherr, vom 15. Januar 1969," in Henkys, *Bund der Kirchen*, pp. 132, 134.

ment that differing societies dictated separate churches on the grounds that it elevated the social order over service to Christ; now separation was accepted on the grounds that only thereby could service be furthered. Although Fuerstenwalde contained some ambiguity, the pragmatism of Schoenherr contrasts starkly with the defiance of Krummacher and the synod of less than two years earlier.[67]

The churches sought to compensate for these concessions to the state by strengthening the "EKD-clause" in the charter. On the one hand, in the final draft the emphasis on co-determination was weakened to read: "in the responsibility for this community, the Federation accepts, in partner-like freedom, tasks which all Evangelical churches in the GDR and the FRG have in common." On the other hand, the final draft of the clause also spoke of "confessing the special community of Evangelical Christianity in Germany," thus giving the ties to the EKD doctrinal character.

This formulation of the "EKD-clause" came under intense attack from Thuringia. At the March 5, 1969, meeting of the Eastern Conference, which approved the Structure Commission's final draft of the charter and sent it to the Landeskirchen for ratification, the Thuringian representatives sought first to strike the article entirely, then to rewrite it so as to limit the special community with the West German churches to certain specific areas of cooperation (e.g., hymnals and Bible translations).[68] Both Thuringian proposals were rejected overwhelmingly by the Eastern Conference. Given the fruitlessness of these efforts, Gerhard Lotz, Mitzenheim's lieutenant, inspired the May 1969 Thuringian synod to mandate its representatives to the first synod of the new Kirchenbund to press for a clarification of the interpretation and application of the "EKD-clause," known officially as Article 4.4.

Thuringia also continued to diverge from the other Landeskirchen by acquiescing to the state's other demands. Already at its May 1969 synod, Thuringia revoked its mandate for its representatives to the EKD synod. Other Landeskirchen and Schoenherr himself balked at this

---

[67]Ibid., p. 20; Daehn, pp. 207–8.

[68]NZ, 11 May 1969; Henkys stresses the political benefits expected by Thuringia from this stance in "Partnerschaft als Ausdruck kirchlicher Gemeinschaft. Zur Geschichte des Bundes der Evangelischen Kirchen in der DDR," in *Kirche in diesen Jahren: Ein Bericht*, ed. Karl Immer(1971), p. 72. "Ergebnis der Thueringischen Landessynode . . . ," in Henkys, *Bund der Kirchen*, pp. 157–58.

precipitous unilateral step, choosing to end such mandates jointly after the formation of the Kirchenbund.[69] Acting at its synod on December 7, 1969, Thuringia also eliminated reference to the EKD in its constitution, thus forcing the hand of the Kirchenbund which, aware of Thuringia's intentions, voted to request such action of all Landeskirchen to retain the appearance of unity.[70] With respect to the four GDR members of the EKD Council, however, Thuringia could not take unilateral action since it had foregone election to a position on the council in 1967, and the GDR members, including Krummacher and Noth, refused to lay down their offices until the Kirchenbund was in place in September 1969.

The delay in making the Structure Commission's recommendations public allowed Schoenherr time to mobilize support for his compromise proposals, not an easy task in a period in which the relationship with the state had become even more polarized. In Saxony-Dresden, for example, the abrupt razing of the University Church in Leipzig resulted in numerous arrests and tension with the authorities. The Warsaw Pact invasion of Czechoslovakia in August 1968 also strained the relationship, manifested in numerous protests by pastors and parishioners, numerous arrests, and the Chancel Declaration of the Berlin-Brandenburg Church leadership, which criticized the GDR's actions and expressed solidarity with the Czechs.[71] On the other hand, Bishop Mitzenheim's attendance as the sole bishop at the CDU's Party Congress in October 1968 further underlined his accommodation to the state.

Ironically, however, this increasing polarization aided Schoenherr in obtaining approval of his compromise conception. The main priority of a large number of the church elite, especially Krummacher, was the reining in of Mitzenheim, whose "Thuringian Way" and favored position with the state had become ever more troublesome. This political disunity among the churches was further compounded by a rather

[69]"Beschluesse und Erklaerungen zur EKD vom 14. September 1969," in Henkys, *Bund der Kirchen,* pp. 166–67.

[70]Thuringia justified this move on the grounds that election of a new bishop required the elimination of the EKD's legal role in this process. All Landeskirchen followed this request except Mecklenburg, whose 1922 Constitution contained no reference to the EKD. See EPS documents, 21 January 1970, and EPC archives, 15 December 1969.

[71]The church leadership in Berlin-Brandenburg (East), alone among the GDR Landeskirchen, protested the invasion in a chancel statement read by most pastors. Several vicars were jailed for circulating letters to the Czech embassy. See "Die Kirchen in der DDR und Militaeraktion gegen die CSSR," *epd Gruener Dienst,* no. 33 (19 September 1968): pp. 22–23.

unexpected decision in December 1968 by the three GDR member churches in the VELKD. Saxony-Dresden, Thuringia, and Mecklenburg formed their own Lutheran confessional organization in the GDR, the United Evangelical Lutheran Churches in the GDR, or VELKDDR.[72] This demonstration of Lutheran confessionalism and unilateralism rankled the remaining ecumenically oriented Union Landeskirchen and lent credibility to Schoenherr's argument that an umbrella organization, a federation, was necessary to avoid continued erosion along political and confessional lines.

A large segment of the group favoring greater church unification in the GDR, particularly in the EKU hierarchy and the Landeskirchen of Berlin-Brandenburg and Saxony-Magdeburg, was at the same time adamantly opposed to separation from the EKD. For many, such as Hamel, EKD unity had become a question of creed; most, however, feared that separation from the EKD would foreordain separation from the Western portions of the EKU and Berlin-Brandenburg as well.[73] The Lutherans' formation of the VELKDDR tended to justify these fears; it became a model that the state used to pressure the remaining churches to "clarify their organizational status." The precipitous decision of the Lutherans narrowed considerably the room for maneuver of the other churches. Without the stronger doctrinal tone and reference to "special community" in the reformulated Article 4.4, the EKU Landeskirchen would have balked at separation from the EKD.[74] But Thuringia was likely to have blocked the formation of the federation if still stronger language was used. This point was not lost on either Schoenherr and others advocating more coordination of the churches. Thus, to build a unified church front vis-à-vis the state, they were forced to accept compromise on the issue of relations with the EKD.

At the other pole, Mitzenheim, reflecting the state's increasing drive for Abgrenzung from the FRG, was primarily interested in the greatest possible reduction of the formal ties with the EKD, without eliminating the specific informal and monetary ties. Schoenherr argued to Thuringia that Article 4.4 was preferable to Krummacher's stronger formulation

---

[72]EPS documents, 18 December 1968, p. 4.

[73]Indeed, in November 1968, Schoenherr's own Berlin-Brandenburg (East) synod had rejected his request for a synodal committee to deal with the GDR-wide structural question, thus indicating its suspicions of separation from the EKD. CDU archives, 1 November 1968.

[74]Based on discussion with Bishops Krusche and Schoenherr.

("community with the churches with which we are united in the EKD") and that without Article 4.4 the whole undertaking might be vetoed by such Landeskirchen as Berlin-Brandenburg and Saxony-Magdeburg.[75] Schoenherr also argued to Thuringia, as well as other Lutherans, that the EKU would balk at leaving the EKD without replacing it with some form of corresponding umbrella organization and that the VELKDDR would protect Lutheran confessional interests from the larger Union Landeskirchen. The unequivocal defeat of its attempt to weaken Article 4.4 convinced Thuringia that half a loaf was better than none.

Thus the constellation for compromise was present; each group, to maximize one value, gave ground on a lesser value. To gain cohesiveness among the GDR churches (and thereby reduce the probability of Mitzenheimian schisms), the EKU Landeskirchen accepted separation from the EKD; to gain organizational separation from the EKD, Thuringia concurred in the formation of the Kirchenbund. The constellation itself derived from the asymmetry in priorities; the urgency to bargain and seek resolution stemmed from the polarization of the groupings. This polarization, embodied in the figures of Mitzenheim and Krummacher, allowed Schoenherr to play the role of mediator and thereby derive considerable influence in the new Kirchenbund.

In addition to marshaling support among the GDR churches, the proponents of the Kirchenbund needed to gain the approval of the EKD. Legally, it was not clear that the GDR churches could simply secede from the EKD. Politically, it would certainly be more difficult for the new Kirchenbund if the EKD did not approve, especially if the EKD should treat the GDR churches as members-in-absentia, reserving positions for them in the EKD Council and Synod. Economically, EKD disapproval would be disastrous for the GDR churches if the EKD should withdraw its sizable subsidy.

EKD rejection of separation was certainly a possibility. Strong opposition to the move existed, especially in the Western portions of the EKU and Berlin-Brandenburg. Indeed, as in the East, it was initially thought that the Eastern Landeskirchen would remain tacit members of the EKD.[76] Yet with some exceptions, the EKD accepted the moves of the GDR churches and honored their request not to disturb their delib-

[75]EPC archives, 1968, p. 13; EPC archives, 15 November 1968.
[76]For example, Bishops Woelber and Dietzfelbinger in *LWF Information*, no. 34 (16 August 1968): p. 5. EPS documents, 4 June 1969, p. 7.

erations with public pronouncements affirming inter-German church unity.

Several factors seem to have played a role in gaining EKD acquiescence toward the new Kirchenbund. First, the election of Bishop Dietzfelbinger, a conservative Lutheran from Bavaria, as EKD Council chairman in 1967 proved auspicious. Coming after years of socially and politically vocal EKD Council chairmen, he represented the more conservative Lutheran wing of the EKD, which had felt as constrained by the ties with and consideration for the more social brothers in the East, as had those in the East by their ties with the West.[77] Dietzfelbinger's endorsement in January 1969 of the founding of the Kirchenbund— "regrettable, yet necessary"—was instrumental in the development of the EKD's response, not to mention the debate within the GDR churches themselves.[78]

Perhaps even more crucial to this process was Bishop Scharf (Berlin-Brandenburg), though for the exactly opposite reason—his social activism and strong ties to the churches in the GDR, rooted in the activist theological tradition and organizational ties of the Union churches. Like West German political leaders, he initially hoped to preserve the border-transcending character of the EKD. The mounting East German pressure on the GDR churches for separation caused him to modify this position.[79] Schoenherr's long personal friendship with Scharf no doubt helped him convince Scharf of the necessity of the move.

Finally, the inclusion of the Article 4.4 in the charter of the new Kirchenbund convinced West German church leaders that ties with the GDR churches would be maintained, despite organizational separation. The GDR churches assured the EKD of their intentions to flesh out the framework of the "special community."

After the crucial approval by the Eastern regional synod of the EKD

[77]Based on discussion with former Bishop Kurt Scharf.

[78]"Erklaerung des Ratsvorsitzenden der EKD, Landesbischof Dietzfelbinger (Muenchen), zum Schoenherr-Interview am 20. Januar 1969," in Henkys, *Bund der Kirchen,* p. 134.

[79]Scharf's commitment to German reunification can be seen in his endorsement of confederation in the letter exchange with Bishop Jaenicke, found in "Der Wortlaut des Briefswechsels zwischen D. Scharf und D. Jaenicke," *epd Landesdienst Berlin,* no. 35 (16 March 1967): pp. 3–6. In the face of the GDR's heightened Abgrenzung campaign, he sought to decouple the all-German church organizations from the political arena. See Gisela Helwig, "Absage an die EKD auf dem Erfurter CDU-Parteitag," *DA* 1, no. 8 (November 1968): p. 884, and "An die Einheit festhalten," *Der Abend,* 4 November 1968. In the end Scharf came to support the formation of the Kirchenbund. See his interview in *Der Spiegel* 23, no. 52 (22 December 1969): p. 12f.

on March 5, 1969, one hurdle remained: approval by each individual Landeskirche. Opposition to separation was stronger on the Landeskirche level than within the church hierarchy. The approval of the Kirchenbund by the EKD regional synod (East) helped to overcome some of this opposition in the Landeskirchen and to mobilize support from the EKD per se. Also, the state's lobbying effort against Article 4.4 led many who were otherwise skeptical of the new Kirchenbund to vote for it.[80] At their synodal meetings in spring 1969, every Landeskirche, from "progressive" Thuringia to "reactionary" Goerlitz, approved the new Kirchenbund. Ironically, strongest opposition to it arose in Schoenherr's own synod in Berlin-Brandenburg (East). Given its special situation and ties to West Berlin, it narrowly approved the Kirchenbund. Representatives of each Landeskirche thereupon signed the charter, formally known as the Basic Order, on June 10, 1969, and the Kirchenbund became a reality.

The years 1958 to 1969 saw the church-state relationship dominated increasingly by the issue of Abgrenzung from West Germany, particularly in the period after 1966. The state used a tactic of selective dialogue with certain "progressive" churchmen to promote the separation of the churches along East-West lines and to advance its new ideological stance of cooperation based on the alleged "common humanistic responsibility of Marxists and Christians." This new stance did not, however, represent a modification of the state's basic ideological conflict with religion or its attempts to curtail the churches' role in society. Although the churches rejected separation from the EKD at their Fuerstenwalde synod in 1967, the promulgation of a new constitution in 1968 and increased state pressure led to a shift in the churches' position. In a compromise between the "progressives" and the advocates of EKD unity, the GDR churches reversed this stance in 1969, separating formally from the EKD and creating an independent Kirchenbund.

The formation of the Kirchenbund and separation from the EKD was a reaction to state pressure, essentially defensive in nature. The churches were reluctant; they delayed the separation and sought to defuse the situation by personnel changes and regionalization plans. Moreover,

[80]EPS documents, 31 March 1969, pp. 3–5; EPS documents, 21 April 1969, pp. 2–3; EPS documents, 8 May 1969, pp. 2–4.

the separation was only partial, since the new Kirchenbund affirmed a special relationship with the EKD and the EKU and Berlin-Brandenburg remained nominally all-German, a situation that dominated the relations with the state in the period to be discussed in chapter 5. Contributing to the urgency of the situation was the new constitution, which opened up the real possibility of agreements between the state and the individual Landeskirchen. Although perhaps some of the principals had a conception of future development, the formation of the Kirchenbund resulted less from a positive consensus than from an uneasy coalition of very divergent interests in a polarized setting, skillfully brought together by Schoenherr. Overcoming the state's suspicion of remaining ties with the West German churches and articulating a positive conception of the Kirchenbund's future in the socialist GDR were tasks that remained for the Kirchenbund in the years ahead.

5 Nonrecognition of the Kirchenbund, 1969–1971

Viewed in retrospect, the formation of the Kirchenbund in June 1969 represents a watershed in the postwar relationship between church and state in the GDR. The separation was a precondition for the rapprochement that later developed. However this separation and eventual rapprochement must be viewed as a process rather than as the result of a finite event. Indeed, the state's initial response to the Kirchenbund reflected an ambivalent, wait-and-see attitude.

During the formation of the Kirchenbund, the state gave tentative indications of its approval. In February 1969, Seigewasser matter-of-factly acknowledged the churches' restructuring process:

> With interest and satisfaction we view the growth of those forces in the churches, which are drawing from the constitution the conclusions that are reasonable for the existence of churches in socialism and reflect the recognition of realities. We are seeing internal church efforts toward organizational independence of the Landeskirchen in the GDR.[1]

But this tentative endorsement was coupled with demands for clear organizational and political/intellectual separation from the EKD.

After the formal founding of the Kirchenbund, state spokesmen addressed it only fleetingly and primarily in agitatorial terms. For exam-

---

[1] "Aus dem Referat des DDR-Staatssekretaers . . . ," and "Aus dem Referat von Gerald Goetting . . . ," in Henkys, *Bund der Kirchen*, pp. 142, 144.

ple, in August 1969 Seigewasser obliquely commended the formation of
the Kirchenbund as a response to socialist reality:

> ... church circles through their own experience recognize the reality of
> actual relations and cooperate increasingly in our socialist human com-
> munity. . . . On the basis of this recognition [i.e., the contrary social
> development in the two German states] and our socialist constitutional
> reality grew the idea of the creation of the Federation of Evangelical
> Churches in the GDR.[2]

In a major address on the Kirchenpolitik in September 1969, Politburo
member Hermann Matern pointedly failed to mention the Kirchenbund, indicating merely that since the Seventh SED Party Congress, "the
development of relations between state and church have continued to
take an advantageous course for us."[3]

The state's nonrecognition of the new Kirchenbund extended to questions of protocol as well. Custom called for the state to receive officially
a newly elected bishop or church leadership body. However, the state
refused to meet officially with the Executive Board, although it did meet
with several of its members unofficially. The state also refused to grant
the Kirchenbund an organ for official notices. It even refused to conduct
business by mail with the new Kirchenbund, accepting only correspondence using the stationery of its predecessor, the Conference of GDR
Church Leaderships.[4]

This limbo status of the Kirchenbund—unofficial contacts with the
state, yet absence of formal relations—continued for almost two years.
Not until February 1971 did the state officially recognize the Kirchenbund. Several factors explain the state's delay: the continuing inter-
German church ties, the uncertainty of the internal political direction of
the Kirchenbund, the state's ambivalence regarding the GDR churches'
ecumenical relations, and the Landeskirche-oriented strategy of the
state.

---

[2]"Aus dem Referat des Staatssekretaers Hans Seigewasser," in *Auf dem Wege der sozialistischen Menschengemeinschaft: Eine Sammlung von Dokumenten zur Buendnispolitik und
Kirchenpolitik 1967–70,* ed. Guenter Wirth (1971), pp. 250–51.

[3]Herman Matern, *Unser gemeinsamer Weg zur sozialistischen Menschengemeinschaft*
(1969), p. 12.

[4]Schoenherr, Stolpe, and Braecklein were received unofficially by Seigewasser in September
1969. Daehn, p. 106. Discussion with Walter Pabst, formerly a member of the Kirchenbund
Secretariat.

REMAINING INTER-GERMAN CHURCH TIES

The primary factor in the state's nonrecognition of the Kirchenbund was clearly the remaining inter-German ties: the Kirchenbund-
EKD relationship, the Evangelical Church of the Union (EKU), and the
Berlin-Brandenburg Landeskirche. The state suspected that the Kirchenbund represented only a pro forma separation, designed to disguise
continuing West German influence and to deflect state criticism of the
still all-German EKU and Berlin-Brandenburg.[5]

Despite the formal separation from the EKD, the state feared that
Article 4.4 of the Kirchenbund Basic Order, affirming the "special community" with the West German churches, would allow continued inter-
German church ties. It permitted various interpretations, ranging from
the merely rhetorical to that of actual coordination of church policy.
Moreover, the competence of the Joint Consultation Group established
by the Kirchenbund and the EKD was quite open-ended. Much thus
depended on the substance that the leadership of the Kirchenbund gave
these procedural commitments.

Not wishing to jeopardize the formation of the Kirchenbund, the
state did not openly attack Article 4.4 until August 1969, just prior to its
first synod. Earlier, the state had employed the "Thuringian card" in an
unsuccessful effort to eliminate or modify the article. Once the Kirchenbund was a reality, the state became bolder in its demands.

Not surprisingly, the actors in the state's attack revealed differences of
approach, useful in the state's strategy. Strongest in its criticism was the
Pfarrerbund, which called for the outright *rejection* of the article. As
early as March 1969, it accused the churches of using Article 4.4 to
"uphold the old bonds with the EKD in modified form" and demanded
that they "overcome the ballast of the EKD not just institutionally, but
also intellectually and spiritually." Theologically, the Pfarrerbund's justification was subtle and not without appeal to many in the GDR
churches: "liberation prepares the way for inner renewal."[6] In contrast,
"progressive" churchmen, led by Humboldt University theology pro-

---

[5]EPS documents, 28 November 1969, pp. 10–11; EPC archives, 22 November 1969,
"Geheimgehaltener Beschluss"; EPC archives, 22 November 1969, "Protokollauszug."
[6]"Schreiben des Bundes Evangelischer Pfarrer an alle Bischoefe in der DDR," *KJ* 1969,
pp. 272–73. Walter Feurich, "Zum Kirchenbund," *Glaube und Gewissen* 15 (September
1969): 171–72.

fessor Hanfried Mueller, petitioned the synod demanding only *changes* in Article 4.4 and an explicit rejection of the churches' position at Fuerstenwalde.[7] The CDU also called for revision of the article in accordance with the mandate which the Thuringian synod had given to its representatives at the Kirchenbund synod.[8] Not surprisingly, the criticism of Seigewasser, expressed both publicly and privately, proved the most moderate in tone. Seigewasser spoke not of rejecting or revising Article 4.4 but of *reinterpreting* it.[9] He called for the creation of "clear and unmistakable relationships," claiming that the Kirchenbund can only "fulfill its tasks if it separates itself organizationally, legally, and intellectually completely from all ties to the EKD." In Seigewasser's view, many in the EKD did not realize that the GDR's "socialist society is a stable and final social and political reality" for the GDR churches, and "many previous interpretations of Article 4.4 of the Basic Order of the Kirchenbund reveal that many leading church office holders have also not made this realization."

The different emphases of the Pfarrerbund, CDU, and governmental officials regarding Article 4.4 reflected not simply state orchestration, but real differences of policy toward the Kirchenbund. However, the state permitted these differences because they served the state's interest: just as playing the "Thuringian card" exerted pressure on the other Landeskirchen, so the harsher attacks of the Pfarrerbund and the CDU gave the state's pronouncements on Article 4.4 the appearance of relative moderation, thus making the churches more amenable to compromise. Eventually, however, as it sought conciliation with the church, the state would act to curtail these differences.

Confronted with these external pressures, the synod of the Kirchenbund dealt with issues of organizational transition and Article 4.4 at its first session, held behind closed doors on September 10, 1969. On organizational transition, the state had sought the termination of EKD offices and responsibilities by Landeskirchen initiatives *prior to the*

[7]EPS documents, 26 September 1969, pp. 2–8.

[8]Both a meeting of Working Group on Church Questions of the Secretariat of the Main Executive Board of the CDU (reported in *NZ*, 4 September 1969) and *Neue Zeit* (editorial, 10 September 1969) took this position.

[9]Wirth, *Auf dem Wege der sozialistischen Menschengemeinschaft*, p. 252; CDU archives, 5 June 1969; CDU archives, 26 June 1969; CDU archives, 24 January 1969. Seigewasser indicated to Schoenherr that the Kirchenbund "would only be interesting when every tie to the EKD was clearly ended."

Kirchenbund synod meeting, as Thuringia had done in May 1969.[10] However, in an early success of coordination within the Kirchenbund framework, the churches effected this transfer of authority only *after* the organs of the Kirchenbund were in place and as a result of *joint* action by the GDR members of the EKD Synod. Though largely symbolic, this contributed to the legitimacy of the Kirchenbund and undercut the state's interpretation of the new organization as a "revolutionary act" by the GDR Landeskirchen.

The synod was less successful in articulating a defense of Article 4.4 against state criticism. The concluding address by president-elect of the synod, Ingo Braecklein of Thuringia, represented the Kirchenbund's official position. The address reflected the Kirchenbund's effort to stand firm on Article 4.4 in the face of the more extreme demands of the Pfarrerbund and the CDU, but at the same time to defuse the state's concern over a broad interpretation of the article by specifying the areas of community. Braecklein maintained that "because of language, history, and confession, we Germans of Evangelical belief are in a different community from those churches of the same confession on the ecumenical level." Yet in specifying these ties, he provided a relatively narrow interpretation of Article 4.4, emphasizing the "community of service, belief, and theological work, which links us with the churches in the other German state."[11] He thereby sought to minimize Seigewasser's demand for an "intellectual separation" from the EKD.

The state was apparently satisfied by Braecklein's distinction between spiritual and intellectual ties and his limitation of the "special community" to things spiritual. Both *Neues Deutschland* and *Neue Zeit* reported the synod perfunctorily without polemic.[12] The state was also pleased when the Kirchenbund leadership, its hand forced by Thuringia, requested in late 1969 that the Landeskirchen replace all references to the "EKD" in their constitutions with references to the "Kirchenbund."

But at the same time, the state continued its wait-and-see stance toward the Kirchenbund, pending the interpretations given to Article

[10]CDU archives, 5 June 1969.

[11]"Aus dem Schlusswort des Praeses . . . ," Henkys, *Bund der Kirchen*, pp. 167–68.

[12]*ND*, 17 September 1969; *NZ*, 17, 18, and 20 September 1969; EPC archives, 26 September 1969. The state did not protest Braecklein's publication of his comments in the West, although the CDU apparently did criticize this action. Moreover, *Neue Zeit* sought inaccurately to characterize Braecklein's comments in terms of the narrow formulation of the spring 1969 Thuringian synod.

4.4 by the Landeskirchen. The fall 1969 and spring 1970 synods of the Landeskirchen revealed that the narrow Braecklein interpretation found broad acceptance, openly or tacitly, in most Landeskirchen, with Saxony-Magdeburg and Goerlitz remaining the exceptions.[13] Most synods either did not address the issue or reaffirmed the Kirchenbund's position on it. As will be discussed, Berlin-Brandenburg (East) was preoccupied at its spring 1970 synod with its response to state pressure to separate from the West Berlin church and thus gave Article 4.4 scant attention. However, the state found reason for concern in the broader interpretations of Saxony-Magdeburg and Goerlitz. Bishop Krusche of Magdeburg emphasized the importance of "pragmatic manifestations" of Article 4.4. Similarly, Goerlitz Bishop Fraenkel sought to widen Article 4.4 beyond ecumenical ties and "spiritual community" to include a "bodily community," which the Kirchenbund "seeks to realize in the form of a cooperation of organizationally free and legally independent partners."

Complicating the state's calculations further was the role of the West German churches. The GDR insisted that the EKD officially acknowledge that its jurisdiction ended at the Elbe and change its all-German name "Evangelical Church in Germany," to preclude tacit membership of the GDR churches in the EKD.[14] Disconcerting to the state were statements by leading West German churchmen supportive of continued unity. The president of the EKD Synod, Johannes Beckmann, claimed that the community between the churches could not be equated to that in the ecumenical community. Citing the doctrinal question involved, he adamantly opposed changing the name of the EKD, since "it should not concede that it wants to be the Evangelical Church for all Germany."[15] Bishop Scharf (Berlin-Brandenburg)—citing a resolution of the World

---

[13]Synods in Saxony-Dresden, Greifswald, and Mecklenburg left Article 4.4 largely unaddressed. "Aus dem Bericht von Bischof Dr. Werner Krusche . . . ," in Henkys, *Bund der Kirchen,* p. 175; the Goerlitz position is found in an article by Fraenkel, reprinted in *epd Dokumentation,* no. 13 (26 March 1970): pp. 29–31. Review of the Anhalt, Greifswald, Saxony-Dresden, and Saxony-Magdeburg synods is found in CDU archives, 1970, "Einschaetzung der evangelischen Herbstsynoden 1969"; review of the Berlin-Brandenburg synod is found in CDU archives, 3 April 1970; Mecklenburg's position is discussed in CDU archives, 1970, "Einschaetzung der evangelischen Fruehjahrssynoden 1970."

[14]NZ, 25 June 1970; CDU archives, 1970, "Einschaetzung der evangelischen Fruehjahrssynoden 1970."

[15]"Gespraech mit dem Praeses . . . Beckmann," *epd Dokumentation,* no. 11 (24 February 1969): pp. 4–5.

Council of Churches opposing "Christian communities being forced by the state for nationalistic goals, to unify or to break apart for political reasons"—made highly publicized statements supporting the unity of Evangelical Christianity in Germany.[16]

In the first official EKD response to the new Kirchenbund, the EKD Council declared, following the September 1969 Kirchenbund synod, that it "respected the decisions taken by the churches in the GDR." But it underscored that "the shared responsibility for witness and service remains" and held in abeyance any further EKD response until the next EKD synod in spring 1970.[17]

Like the Kirchenbund synod, the May 1970 EKD Synod sought to strike a posture of compromise, ratifying realities but going no further.[18] The synod officially limited the validity of the constitution to the Western church areas and ceased to describe itself as the Western Regional Synod. In addition, it moved to fill vacant synod seats of the GDR churches, thus defusing the criticism that it was holding the seats open as part of Bonn's strategy of eventual reunification. However, the GDR's hopes for more far-reaching changes proved misplaced. The EKD synod reconfirmed the EKD's commitment to Article 4.4 and rejected changing the constitution or the name of the EKD. Nor did it act to fill the vacant GDR seats on the EKD Council until 1971.[19]

The Brandt government's new overtures in the Ostpolitik in late 1969 lent urgency to the state's campaign against all remaining inter-German ties, including the Kirchenbund's ties to the EKD. In February 1970 Goetting opened a new round in this campaign, demanding of the churches "a conscious new orientation, in order to overcome all

[16]"Aus dem Rechenschaftsbericht von Bischof Scharf . . . ," *KJ* 1970, pp. 251–53; "Ist die Einheit nur noch ein Mythos?," *Der Spiegel* 23 (22 December 1969): 32–34.

[17]"Erklaerung des Rates der Evangelischen Kirche in Deutschland . . . ," in Henkys, *Bund der Kirchen*, pp. 171–73.

[18]Some, for example, the retiring synod president, Dr. Puttfarcken; Bishop Meyer of Luebeck; and newly elected Synod President Raiser, supported changing the name to avoid the misunderstanding that the EKD sought to speak for all of Germany. Others argued on the basis of tradition, as well as the all-German names still extant (e.g., SPD, SED), for retention of the name "EKD." The EKD Chancellory argued for the status quo on legal grounds, viewing the formation of the Kirchenbund formation as a revolutionary act. In the end the synod decided to defer the issue for later consideration of church constitutional reform, apparently due to the even balance on this question in the synodal committee. See "Interview des Deutschlandfunks mit Prof. Ludwig Raiser," *KJ* 1970, p. 247. For the declaration and resolution of the synod, see "Erklaerung der Synode," in Henkys, *Bund der Kirchen*, pp. 204–5; EPC archives, 5 January 1970.

[19]*NZ*, 17 May 1970; *BS*, 14 February 1971.

political-ideological tendencies which . . . are misused for Bonn's so-called 'new Ostpolitik.' "[20] Goetting sought to relativize the "spiritual community" between the Kirchenbund and EKD by placing it on the same plane with general ecumenical relations.

As the fall 1970 Kirchenbund synod approached, the state's campaign against Article 4.4 increasingly focused on the alleged abuse of Article 4.4 by the West German churches in order to maintain a "crypto-organizational unity, not simply spiritual community."[21] Again the CDU organ, *Neue Zeit,* led the assault, criticizing the EKD synod's failure to change its name and to fill the vacant GDR seats on the EKD Council. The state viewed the EKD's stance as an ecclesiastical variant of Bonn's all-German conception and blamed in particular Bishop Scharf. Moreover, it accused Scharf of giving Berlin-Brandenburg unity "an important function in the realization and practicing of Article 4.4" and using church unity "to overcome the political borders in the East of Europe."[22] The state demanded that the Kirchenbund synod in fall 1970 clearly reject this alleged West German interpretation.

The Kirchenbund synod, caught in the crossfire between the state, on the one hand, and several of its own Landeskirchen and certain elements within the West German churches, on the other, tried to find a middle course. In his report to the synod, Chairman Schoenherr implicitly rejected Goetting's call for "new orientation," maintaining that the formation of the Kirchenbund reflected the increasingly different conditions of church service in the two Germanies rather than a political or ideological statement.[23] However, in politically tactful terms, he underscored the genuineness of the break with the EKD. Taking a cue from Goetting, he appeared to equate inter-German church ties with ecumenical ties—"We live together with the Christians in the FRG and the whole ecumenical movement in a community of belief"—and sought to

---

[20]"Aus einem Referat Gerald Goettings . . . am 9. Februar 1970 in Leipzig," in Henkys, *Bund der Kirchen,* pp. 194–95.

[21]"Selbstbewusste Haltung," *Kirche und Mann,* August 1970, p. 6; *NZ,* 25 June 1970.

[22]*NZ,* 17 May, 24 June, 28 June 1970. The West German Evangelical Press Service did not report these statements, quoting only Scharf's rejection of a split in Berlin-Brandenburg as "ecumenically anachronistic and also politically wrong," given the atmosphere of detente, and recording his disappointment and satisfaction, respectively, with the results of the EKD synod and the EKU/Berlin-Brandenburg synods on the question of inter-German church relations. See "Die Atmosphaere ist entspannt," *epd Landesdienst Berlin,* no. 79 (24 June 1970): p. 1.

[23]"Bericht der KKL . . . ," "Beschluss auf Antrag des Berichtsausschusses," and "Schluss-wort des Synodalpraeses . . . ," *epd Dokumentation,* no. 28 (13 July 1970): pp. 4, 9, 12–14.

give substance to the narrow spiritual interpretation of Article 4.4, citing theological discussions with the EKD since 1969 on the politically uncontroversial topic of a revision of Luther's translation of the New Testament. Also, in what must be seen as a mild rebuke of the EKD Synod, the Executive Committee of the Kirchenbund indirectly endorsed a name change by the EKD.[24] Thus, although the synod did not revise Article 4.4, by relativizing the special community with the EKD in ecumenical terms and emphasizing a limited interpretation of Article 4.4, it repudiated the broader interpretations of some West Germans and some GDR Landeskirchen, including some earlier statements of Schoenherr himself.

The state was basically satisfied with the outcome of the synod, despite the Kirchenbund's failure to revise Article 4.4. In effect claiming victory, the official media hailed the aspects of the synod that underscored the independence of the Kirchenbund and ignored those emphasizing continued community.[25] *Neue Zeit* interpreted the Kirchenbund's statements as a rebuttal to Scharf.

This positive treatment of the synod's outcome did not, however, reflect merely another exercise of distortion by the state media; it also represented a shift in the state's expectations of the Kirchenbund on this issue. Despite its renewed *public* campaign against Article 4.4, including intense lobbying of synod members by local committees of the National Front, the state realized *privately* that the Kirchenbund was unlikely to alter Article 4.4 and that the most that could be hoped for was a more favorable interpretation.[26] To be sure, the jousting on this issue did not end with the fall 1970 Kirchenbund synod, nor even with February 1971 recognition of the Kirchenbund. For example, "progressive" elements associated with the Pfarrerbund and the CDU again introduced proposals to change Article 4.4 at the June 1971 Kirchenbund synod. But by mid-1970 the state had concluded that the Kirchenbund was unlikely to alter or reinterpret Article 4.4. The narrowing and relativizing of Article 4.4 by the Kirchenbund, particularly by Schoenherr, represented a partial, though largely rhetorical victory for the state. The

---

[24]The Kirchenbund wished the EKD's study committee "success in the efforts to find a name which eliminates as much as possible misinterpretations of the community remaining between us."

[25]*ND*, 30 June 1970; *NZ*, 30 June and 4 July 1970.

[26]EPS documents, 25 June 1970, pp. 2–3.

finessing of the issue by the Kirchenbund and the slow process of separation by the EKU and the Berlin-Brandenburg Landeskirche led the state to turn its attention to these other still-all-German church organizations.

Organizational division of the Evangelical Church of the Union (EKU) along East-West German lines proved a more complicated problem for the state than division of the EKD, for several reasons. First and most important, unlike the EKD, the EKU was in fact a church, not simply a loose umbrella organization. The member Landeskirchen claimed not only a common history and tradition, bound up with the growth of Prussian power, but also a common creed. Second, in terms of political orientation, the EKU Landeskirchen were more leftist than the Lutheran Landeskirchen, a bias revealed in the rearmament debates in the FRG in the 1950s and one not lost upon the GDR leadership. Thus the state's charge of "NATO-bound military churches" was less credible vis-à-vis the EKU. Moreover, unlike the situation in the EKD, the internal balance of power in the EKU lay in the GDR region. Hence with a division of the EKU, the state risked losing a potential channel of influence in the FRG. Third, the heritage of Confessing Church opposition to the Third Reich was stronger in the EKU churches, leading to a greater polarization of views than in the EKD as a whole. This heritage led some EKU leaders to be more critical of the regime, others to be more cooperative with the antifascist successor state, the GDR.

Following the erection of the Berlin Wall in 1961, the EKU had attempted, with varying success, to continue functioning as a unified entity.[27] A 1963 decree had permitted separate synod meetings as long as these met simultaneously and considered identical agendas. Although the executive body, the EKU Council, had continued to meet as one body in East Berlin, the denial of visas to President Beckmann and the West Berlin members had forced it to designate proxies in order to conduct business constitutionally. The EKU constitution remained valid for both areas. The chancellory, which handled the day-to-day business, had opened a branch office in West Berlin for the Western churches, but had retained its headquarters in East Berlin.

Interestingly enough, the EKU responded before other all-German church organizations to the state pressure for division associated with

[27]EPS documents, 17 October 1968, p. 1.

the 1968 GDR constitution. Hoping to ease the pressure, the council passed an ordinance in 1968 providing for independent regional synods if necessary.[28] These regional synods could pass differing resolutions; however, changes in the constitution of the EKU required joint concurrence. With this concession the EKU sought to uphold the fiction of a unified synod and to avoid regionalization of the council.

These limited moves by the EKU did not satisfy the state, however, which in 1968 was bent on total separation of the two Germanies. However, though the state was interested in a split in the EKU, it placed a greater priority on the EKD and Berlin-Brandenburg and focused its primary efforts there. Even in his major address on the subject in August 1969, Seigewasser saved his heaviest salvos for the Kirchenbund-EKD relationship, mentioning almost as an afterthought that the renunciation of all positions and offices of the EKD in the GDR "applies logically for the EKU and its offices also."[29]

By early 1970, however, the state became more strident in its criticism of the EKU, for several reasons. First, as indicated earlier, the state was relatively satisfied with the Kirchenbund's handling of Article 4.4 and the transitional arrangements. Thus the state could shift its focus to the EKU and Berlin-Brandenburg. Second, since state pressure on the churches increased prior to synod meetings and since the EKU synod had not met since spring 1968, state pressure was bound to increase as the May 1970 synod approached. Finally, it became clear that the EKU would not follow the example set by the Kirchenbund and the VELKDDR in making a clear organizational break from its West German component. Thus the July 1969 election of Bishop Fraenkel, a vocal critic of the state, to the chairmanship of the EKU Council constituted a major setback for the state. Also, the fall 1969 synod of the large and impor-

---

[28]The ordinance was proposed by a committee, dominated by full-time church functionaries and including such ardent opponents of separation from the Western churches as EKU Chancellory (East) President Hildebrandt and Provost Ringhandt of East Berlin. EPC archives, 22 April 1968.

[29]In its broadly worded emphasis on separation of the Landeskirchen in its February 10, 1969, statements, the state implicitly demanded a resolution of the EKU question as well. "Aus dem Referat des DDR-Staatsekretaers," "Aus dem Referat von Gerald Goetting," and "Aus einer Rede . . . ," in Henkys, *Bund der Kirchen*, pp. 142, 144, 159–61. Henkys confirms Seigewasser's lower priority on EKU division, as opposed to Berlin-Brandenburg division. EPC archives, 26 September 1969.

tant Magdeburg Landeskirche led the state to perceive its new bishop, Werner Krusche, as a defender of EKU unity.[30]

The state's fears were borne out. At its February 1970 meeting, the council of the EKU narrowly rejected total separation and voted to implement the 1968 regional ordinance with minor modifications.[31] The EKU Synod was thus regionalized along East-West lines, but the EKU Council remained all-German. Moreover, in March 1970, Fraenkel openly rejected a division of the EKU, arguing that doctrinal discussions between the EKU and VELKDDR, begun in December 1969, presumed the continued existence of the EKU.[32] Moreover, he maintained that a division of the EKU would mean its effective dissolution, since an EKU (West) consisting of only two Landeskirchen, in addition to West Berlin, would be a "pure fiction."

The state responded with a barrage of criticism throughout spring 1970. As in the case of the Kirchenbund, the state orchestrated various forces—the National Front, left-leaning theologians, the CDU, and the Pfarrerbund—in an effort to exert influence on the deliberations of the upcoming synod.[33] The state's efforts focused primarily on the Berlin-Brandenburg and Saxony-Magdeburg Landeskirchen, in which opposition to separation was strongest.

The state spokesmen employed primarily two, rather contradictory approaches. Goetting, for example, linked the resolution of the EKU question to the state's relationship with the Kirchenbund, seeking to use the EKU churches' commitment to the viability of the Kirchenbund to

[30]Early pressure on the EKU occurred privately, as recorded in CDU archives, 26 July 1969; CDU archives, 1970, "Einschaetzung der evangelischen Herbstsynoden 1969." Seigewasser, in discussions with Stolpe, labeled Fraenkel's election a "provocation" and insisted a change in the EKU was "unavoidable."

[31]CDU archives, 1970, "Einschaetzung der evangelischen Fruehjahrssynoden"; EPS documents, 10 February 1970, pp. 1f. The ordinance is found in "Regionalordnung der EKU . . . ," *KJ* 1970, p. 269.

[32]"Aus dem Bericht Bischof Fraenkels . . . ," *epd Dokumentation*, no. 23 (8 June 1970): p. 27.

[33]For discussion of the campaign of the National Front, proregime theologians, and the Pfarrerbund, see Goeckel, "Detente," pp. 136–38. Also Carl Ordnung, speaking before the Working Group "Christian Circles" of the Magdeburg Regional Committee of the National Front, reported in *NZ*, 15 May 1970; the Working Group "Christian Circles" of the Potsdam Regional Committee of the National Front, reported in *NZ*, 22 May 1970; *NZ*, 17 and 23 May 1970; and Eberhard Klages, "Klare Markierung," *Evangelisches Pfarrerblatt*, no. 5 (May 1970): pp. 113–14.

pressure them to break their ties to the EKU (West). At the February 1970 CDU meeting, in addition to his familiar call for a "consequent new orientation" based on the 1968 Constitution, Goetting argued that if the EKU did not make organizational changes, it would "burden the efforts of the Kirchenbund and the Evangelical Landeskirchen, whose leaders were, for the most part, concerned with the development of a trusting relationship with the socialist state."[34]

In contrast, Seigewasser argued for division of the EKU by appealing to EKU tradition, especially its Confessing Church heritage. Addressing the left-leaning Weissensee Study Group, Seigewasser maintained that "it is not a matter of disbanding of the EKU, but rather of continuing the positive traditions of the Evangelical Union by constituting an independent EKU in the GDR."[35] In this view he was supported by a letter-writing campaign organized by Humboldt University theologian Hanfried Mueller and the left-leaning Weissensee Study Group led by him.[36] Seigewasser's emphasis on EKU tradition was an attempt to counter the argumentation by some opponents of EKU division that sacrificing the unity of the EKU prior to full church unification in the Kirchenbund would result in the loss of the Confessing Church heritage.[37]

By using these rather contradictory lines of argument, appealing to ecumenical Kirchenbund unity as well as particularistic EKU tradition, the state was acting tactically to mobilize a broader base of support for separation from the West German EKU. But Seigewasser's emphasis on EKU tradition also reflected the state's strategic thinking at this point. Although the state desired a division along East-West lines, it feared that a total dissolution of the EKU might strengthen the Kirchenbund and preferred to retain the EKU as a counterbalance to the Kirchenbund.

The May 1970 EKU synod, which dealt with the issue, was the scene

[34]"Aus einem Referat Gerald Goettings . . . ," in Henkys, Bund der Kirchen, p. 192; "Aus der Rede Gerald Goettings . . . ," in Wirth, Auf dem Wege der sozialistischen Menschengemeinschaft, pp. 293–94.

[35]To be sure, Seigewasser spoke only of a general "clarification process" at the February 1970 CDU meeting. See "Grusswort des Staatssekretaers . . . ," in Wirth, Auf dem Wege der sozialistischen Menschengemeinschaft, p. 288; NZ, 23 April and 1 May 1970.

[36]Mueller's view supporting a radical separation of the worldly and spiritual kingdoms is found in his Der Christ in Kirche und Staat, Hefte aus Burgscheidungen no. 4 (1958), pp. 12–13.

[37]This was the view shared by such EKU leaders as Bishop Fraenkel, Johannes Hamel, and EKU President Hildebrandt, among others.

of intense disagreement, contrary to some interpretations.[38] The forces favoring retention of inter-German EKU unity were, as expected, led by Bishop Fraenkel. In his capacity as chairman of the EKU Council, he gave a ringing defense of EKU unity in his report to the synod.[39] Ironically, like Seigewasser, he called upon the liberal activist heritage of the Confessing Church and the postwar EKU, a "spiritual experience" that distinguished it from the EKD and made the Kirchenbund's example irrelevant for the EKU. For the state, this heritage required a new orientation to the socialist environment; for Fraenkel it meant holding onto a unified structure to promote inter-German reconciliation. He also rejected the state's argument that the EKU was hindering the development of the Kirchenbund and touted the political significance of the East German majority in the EKU. Fraenkel's argumentation was designed to justify the council's earlier, limited moves toward separation and its proposed synod resolution, which affirmed that "we hold fast to the unity of the EKU."[40]

Against Fraenkel and much of the EKU "establishment" were the four remaining bishops who favored greater moves toward separation from the EKU (West).[41] As had long been expected, the most vocal proponents of separation were Bishop Krummacher of Greifswald and Church President Mueller of Anhalt, their volte-face regarding separation from the West German churches now complete. Arguing along the lines of Goetting, they maintained that EKU unity crippled the develop-

[38]Daehn, pp. 104–5, 233. Despite access to excellent source material, Daehn offers an incomplete and, in part, inaccurate account of the EKU division. First, he claims that the state did not call for EKU separation publicly in 1969 and 1970, whereas Seigewasser (August 1969) and Matern (September 1969) spoke to the EKU question. Second, his view that the 1970 EKU synod underscored unity does not do justice to the clear shift away from the Fraenkel position at this synod. Third, he does not register the decline in the state's polemic vis-à-vis the EKU after 1972, nor the state's ambivalence regarding the division of the EKU. Finally, he ignores the commitment to a "brotherly relationship" and the "necessity to consult" in the Magdeburg resolutions of 1972, an inter-German commitment much more concrete than the Kirchenbund's.

[39]"Aus dem Bericht Bischof Fraenkels," *epd Dokumentation*, no. 23 (8 June 1970): pp. 28–35.

[40]Synod President Kreyssig wrote synod members, urging them not to accept the existence of two German states fatalistically. See Goeckel, "Detente," p. 139; EPC archives, 1970; CDU archives, 1970, "Einschaetzung der evangelischen Fruehjahrssynoden 1970"; and "EKU-Synode tagte in Magdeburg," *Evangelischer Nachrichtendienst* 23, no. 21 (27 May 1970): pp. 2–4.

[41]More extensive discussion of the debate can be found in Goeckel, "Detente," pp. 139–40. NZ, 6 June 1970; EPS documents, 5 May 1970, p. 5; CDU archives, "Einschaetzung der evangelischen Fruehjahrssynoden 1970."

ment of the Kirchenbund. Given his tenuous position in the Kirchenbund and his own Landeskirche, Bishop Schoenherr was more indirect
in refuting Fraenkel, referring to the dialectic of the unity in belief and
the diversity in structure as justification for greater separation.

Despite their strength in the council and chancellory, the forces favoring the status quo suffered a defeat in the deliberations of the synod.[42]
The council's strongly worded resolution supporting unity—"We hold
fast to the unity of the EKU"—was replaced by a more ambiguous one:
"The EKU shall be upheld and not given up." The new version shrewdly
left unclear whether it affirmed the EKU's inter-German unity or the
EKU's distinctiveness from the Lutherans, resulting not surprisingly in a
number of different interpretations of the synod's action.[43] The synod
also sought to curtail the influence of the EKU Council and Chancellory,
setting up a committee to submit proposals for an independent EKU in
the GDR and making the committee responsible to the synod and not
the EKU Council.

Yet the synod hardly represented total victory for the state. It rejected
an immediate break with the Western section, the state's preferred
scenario. Moreover, the state failed in its attempt to speed up the
machinery in the EKU decision process; the synod refused to call a
special session of the synod in 1971 to consider the committee's proposals for separation.

Despite the incompleteness of the EKU's moves in 1970, the state had
assurance of movement toward separation from the Western region of
the EKU. The forces favoring a restructuring of the EKU were clearly
ascendant. To be sure, deliberations were too halting and uncertain to

[42]Opponents to separation included EKU Council members Fraenkel, Hamel, Pietz, and
Kreyssig. "Beschluesse der Regionalsynode . . . ," *epd Dokumentation*, no. 23 (6 June 1970):
p. 35. This latter wording reflected the counterproposal of Consistory President Kupas (Potsdam), Pastor Langhoff (Brandenburg), Joachim Franke (Potsdam), and Professor Mueller
(Berlin).

[43]The CDU interpreted it to mean the "specific theological tradition of the Evangelical
Union within the Kirchenbund" (*NZ*, 26 May 1970). The churches' own press service interpreted this statement in terms of the "special heritage of the EKU for the future way of the
church," i.e., referring to inter-confessional negotiations. See "EKU-Synode tagte in Magdeburg," *Evangelischer Nachrichtendienst* 23, no. 21 (27 May 1970): pp. 2–4. Henkys, on the
other hand, emphasized the East-West aspect, seeing it as affirming not so much the organizational unity, but rather the maintenance of "spiritual-theological substance" of the EKU, in
"Die Substance soll erhalten werden," *epd Ausgabe fuer kirchliche Presse*, no. 21 (27 May
1970): pp. 1–2. In an indication of the statement's lack of clarity, the synod president of the
EKU (West) regional synod in June 1970 interpreted it as a "yes to the continued existence of
the EKU, not just its Basic Articles" ("Aus dem Bericht . . . ," *KJ* 1970, p. 279).

suit the state.[44] It continued to pressure the EKU using administrative measures. For example, the state denied visas to all EKU representatives to the 1970 Lutheran World Federation meeting in Evian, France, except for those from Greifswald who by then enjoyed the state's favor; all VELKDDR representatives, on the other hand, were granted visas. However, the formation of the synodal committee and its all-GDR composition seemed to offer promise that, contrary to Fraenkel's conception, both the council and the synod of the EKU would be divided along inter-German lines.[45] Moreover, the state was more alarmed than the CDU at the political ramifications that a more unified Kirchenbund increasingly portended. Since the EKU's existence might brake these centralizing tendencies, the state was more tolerant of the EKU's hesitating moves.

In addition to the EKD and the EKU, the state pressed for a division in the Landeskirche Berlin-Brandenburg. Reflecting the postwar political division of Berlin, this Landeskirche consisted of a Western section (West Berlin) and an Eastern section (East Berlin and the surrounding rural area known earlier as the Mark Brandenburg). This church had not remained unaffected by the Cold War confrontation that had plagued the city as a whole. Indeed, the most heated battles on all aspects of inter-German church unity and, for that matter, on all questions regarding church-state relations had been fought in Berlin-Brandenburg.

It is ironic that Berlin-Brandenburg should have been particularly subject to polemic since Berlin-Brandenburg had long accommodated new political realities. In the 1950s, Scharf, then a provost, recognized the possibility of a total closure of access between the Eastern and Western sectors of the city and founded parallel institutions in East Berlin: a branch chancellory and a second seminary, the *Sprachenkonvikt*. Finally, an emergency regulation dating from 1959 permitted the formation of regional synods and church leaderships and the appointment of a bishop's administrator for the Eastern sector; with the building of the Berlin Wall in 1961, this provision was implemented.[46]

---

[44]*NZ*, 26 May and 6 June 1970. The Kirchenbund resolution, "that also the Synod of the EKU endorses and supports the process of growing together of the churches in the GDR," was interpreted by *Neue Zeit* as a preference for a split in the EKU. *Neue Zeit* argued that "so long as its standing committees are 'all-German' in composition, the EKU forfeits any possibility of bringing its activities into the Kirchenbund." See *NZ*, 11 July 1970.

[45]CDU archives, 13 July 1970; "Zusammensetzung des Ausschusses zur Vorbereitung der Verfassungsreform," *KJ*, 1970, p. 278.

[46]"Die Regionalgesetze der Evangelische Kirche in Berlin-Brandenburg," in Henkys, *Bund der Kirchen*, pp. 44–46.

Heightening this irony is the fact that prior to 1969 the state had tacitly accepted the regionalization. Seigewasser had maintained a relatively good relationship with the first bishop's administrator, Guenther Jacob. Even as late as 1967, meeting with Schoenherr, the new bishop's administrator, Seigewasser expressed the hope "that Berlin-Brandenburg will conduct its affairs without interference from Westberlin."[47] Despite its ambiguity, Seigewasser's comment cannot be interpreted as a demand for a total break. In fact, the state's stance on Berlin-Brandenburg paralleled the GDR's ambivalent stance on the Berlin question prior to the Ostpolitik; it sought to delimit itself from West Germany; yet in the form of the so-called three state theory, it posited the separate status of West Berlin from the FRG and tacitly hoped to incorporate West Berlin into the GDR eventually.[48]

The state, curiously, seemed more interested in the division of Berlin-Brandenburg than of the EKU, for several reasons. Unlike the EKU, the locus of power in Berlin-Brandenburg lay in the West, not the GDR. Moreover, Berlin-Brandenburg was less effective than the EKU as a counterbalance to the feared centralistic tendencies in the Kirchenbund. Finally, its bishop, Kurt Scharf, successor to Dibelius, was a potent symbol of German unity. Despite his earlier accommodations to political realities. Scharf was deeply committed to the unity of the Landeskirche, the EKD, and Germany. He saw a responsibility for the churches to work peacefully against the division of Germany. Thus in 1967 he had endorsed Ulbricht's 1966 proposal for a confederation of the two Germanies.[49] With the onset of the Ostpolitik, the state would no longer tolerate such an all-German stance.

Thus the state's relative tolerance of Berlin-Brandenburg's all-German status disappeared, although it initially used private contacts and administrative means to express this.[50] Already, with the election of Scharf as bishop in 1966, relations with the Landeskirche had chilled. Following Goetting's attack on the EKD in 1967, the border authorities began to interfere with the church's couriers and made simultaneous synods impossible.

[47]ND, 17 January 1967.
[48]See Hans-Heinrich Mahnke, "Das Hauptstadtproblem," in Drei Jahrzehnte Aussenpolitik der DDR, eds. Hans-Adolf Jacobsen et al. (1979), p. 111f.
[49]Der Tagesspiegel, 16 March 1967.
[50]CDU archives, 24 April 1969; EPS documents, 21 April 1969, p. 3.

However, like the EKU, Berlin-Brandenburg was subject to little public agitation prior to late 1969 because obtaining approval of the Kirchenbund and favorable interpretation of Article 4.4 was more crucial to the state. A public polemic against Berlin-Brandenburg unity prior to the May 1969 synod, at which the Kirchenbund was ratified, might have resulted in rejection of the Kirchenbund by Berlin-Brandenburg, thus jeopardizing the founding of the Kirchenbund and separation from the EKD. Despite its misgivings concerning the Kirchenbund, the state did not wish to risk jeopardizing its formation.

Moreover, the state had a larger axe to grind, namely Berlin-Brandenburg's opposition to the GDR's participation in the Warsaw Pact intervention in Czechoslovakia. The church leadership condemned the action in the form of a pronouncement read in all pulpits on September 8, 1968. The state meted out harsh punishment for this political deviation: after August 1968 new theology students, pastors, and even Schoenherr himself were denied permission to reside in Berlin; the church congress planned for late September 1968 was canceled by the magistrate of East Berlin; official and private discussions between church leaders and the state came to a standstill.[51]

Several factors made the deliberations regarding division of Berlin-Brandenburg particularly difficult and painful. First, the church, too, had been affected by the special character of the situation itself—the physical proximity, the human and cultural ties, the tradition—that made the East-West confrontation most poignant and real in Berlin. A division between the East and West German churches was bound to be more wrenching in Berlin than elsewhere.

Second, the person and role of Kurt Scharf contributed to the problem of further regionalization. With his engaging and pastoral personality, his record of opposition to Hitler while in the Confessing Church, and his years of service in the East, Scharf was revered by almost all in the Landeskirche, even many "progressives" in the East. Moreover, he attracted great sympathy as provost when he was denied reentry to East Berlin after the wall was built. But Scharf's role also complicated the process. After 1961 he was elected chairman of the council of the EKD and, in these dual roles, became a target for both sides. On the one hand,

---

[51]EPC archives, 1968, pp. 14–15. "Auszuege aus dem Bericht der regional Kirchenleitung Ost der Evangelischen Kirche in Berlin-Brandenburg . . . ," *epd Dokumentation*, no. 13 (26 March 1970): p. 20.

he was anathema to conservative West German churchmen because of his liberal political views—for example, his opposition to the Vietnam War. On the other hand, he remained a convenient target for the GDR's polemic against the EKD, even after giving up the chairmanship of the EKD Council in 1967, and the object of particular personal antipathy by Seigewasser. As a result, Scharf was elected bishop in 1966 by an unlikely coalition of liberal churchmen in West Berlin and conservative churchmen in the East, those in the East seeing in the election a symbolic act of German unity.[52]

Finally, Scharf's dual roles were mirrored in Schoenherr. As the head of both the GDR-based Kirchenbund and the Eastern portion of still all-German Berlin-Brandenburg, Schoenherr embodied the incongruity between these two organizations. This duality not only confronted Schoenherr with situations of conflicting loyalties, but also foreordained an interdependence between the Kirchenbund and Berlin-Brandenburg in terms of the state's policy. Of course, this interdependence could operate to either the advantage or disadvantage of the inter-German unity of Berlin-Brandenburg.

This increasing incongruity had arisen already at the May 1969 synod called to ratify the Kirchenbund, but the church leadership sought to avoid confronting it. The margin of support for the new Kirchenbund in Berlin-Brandenburg was extremely slim. To avoid having to obtain a two-thirds majority and to avoid raising the issue of implications for the unity of Berlin-Brandenburg, the church leadership ruled that approval of the new Kirchenbund did not constitute a change in the Basic Order and hence required only a simple majority.[53] Beyond these internal parliamentary aspects, Schoenherr, as guiding force behind the Kirchenbund, had another reason for this position, namely a desire to establish the viability of the Kirchenbund. A change in the Basic Order would require West Berlin's approval, in effect making the formation of the Kirchenbund dependent on West Berlin approval and compromising the credibility of the Kirchenbund with the state.

[52]Ironically the conservatives also were instrumental in rebuffing Jacob's attempt to upgrade the bishop's administrator position and replacing him with Schoenherr. Based on discussion with Superintendents Steinlein and Furian, Berlin-Brandenburg.

[53]"Progressives" hoped to force the linkage to the Kirchenbund by arguing that the change did affect the Basic Order, but the state backed off from supporting them. For example, no petitions or resolutions were submitted by "progressives" and Prof. Mueller, leading agitator in the past, was quite low-key, both indications of the state's caution. See Goeckel, "Detente," p. 151; EPC archives, no date, "Bedarf die Zustimmung"; "Schoenherr Referat," *epd Dokumentation*, no. 25 (12 May 1969): p. 15.

The church leadership sought unsuccessfully to exploit Schoenherr's dual roles in order to gain advantage for the Berlin-Brandenburg Landeskirche from his leading role in the Kirchenbund.[54] For example, prior to the selection of the first Kirchenbund chairman in September 1969, the leadership sought to gain official residence for Schoenherr in Berlin by suggesting that he was unwilling to lead the Kirchenbund without such a residence. The state refused, insisting that Schoenherr become bishop of the GDR-based Landeskirche first. Another indication of the state's intransigence was its rejection of a "Bengsch solution" for Berlin-Brandenburg.[55] This refers to the status enjoyed by the Catholic church in Berlin under former Cardinal Bengsch. A resident of East Berlin and citizen of the GDR, Cardinal Bengsch headed a Catholic diocese encompassing both East and West Berlin and was granted limited visiting rights to West Berlin. Although the state accepted such a solution for the Catholic church, it rejected the Protestants' proposal for such an arrangement following Scharf's retirement in 1972.

As in the case of the EKU, the state's public campaign against Berlin-Brandenburg unity intensified after the Kirchenbund became a reality. In his August 1969 speech, Seigewasser demanded a "clear decision regarding the complete independence in leadership and structure" from "the special political entity of Westberlin," arguing that continued unity was inconsistent with Berlin-Brandenburg's endorsement of the Kirchenbund.[56] Likewise, in September 1969 Matern called for "full organizational and legal church independence of the Landeskirchen of the GDR from the West German and Westberlin churches." In typically cryptic style, he referred to the "failed attempts by the enemy to misuse the churches in the GDR in actions supporting the counter-revolution," admitting obliquely the problems with Berlin-Brandenburg over Czechoslovakia.

In late 1969 the state's campaign against Berlin-Brandenburg unity intensified, focusing increasingly on Bishop Scharf. Scharf had argued at the West Berlin synod in December 1969 that Berlin-Brandenburg played a special role in maintaining the "special community of German

[54]CDU archives, 5 June 1969; CDU archives, 24 July 1969.
[55]CDU archives, 26 July 1969. Klemens Richter, "Die vatikanische Ostpolitik und die DDR," *DA* 12 (July 1979): 746.
[56]Henkys, *Bund der Kirchen*, p. 161; Matern (1969), pp. 12–13. Visas for bishops to attend the LWF Executive Committee meeting in Denmark in November 1969 were denied. Schoenherr was refused an appointment with Seigewasser until March 1970, coincidentally the month of the Berlin-Brandenburg (East) synod. EPC archives, no date, "Kein Termin."

Christianity" pledged by the Kirchenbund in Article 4.4, and that this spiritual community must take corporeal expression. Scharf endorsed strategic compromises, such as regional variations in the Basic Order and designation of Schoenherr as bishop, but did so to "hold onto our special community."[57]

The CDU's rebuff of Scharf's proposals revealed that the state was not inclined to accept these partial measures. *Neue Zeit* attacked Scharf's views as reflecting "close cooperation with the goal-setting of Bonn's Deutschlandpolitik," and Goetting went so far as to accuse Scharf of using Berlin-Brandenburg as a "base for the West German military church."[58] Scharf's proposed compromises were rejected as a "blueprint for continued veto power from Westberlin." According to the CDU, the unity of Berlin-Brandenburg implied the continued membership of the Eastern region in the EKD and left West Berlin incompetent to represent the Eastern region in ecumenical relations. Scharf attempted to blunt the state's attacks on him by narrowing and softening his position regarding unity, giving the Eastern region greater room for maneuver. But the vehemence of the state's attacks on Scharf and its lobbying of church leaders signaled that incremental measures were inadequate.[59]

In the Eastern region itself, approaches to the problem varied. Some advocated doing nothing, in hopes of waiting out the storm; others pushed for clear and total separation. Some proposed a "Bengsch solution"; others favored practical or legal measures aimed at incrementally increasing the prerogatives of the church leadership or synod, while retaining the 1959 regional order. With the Thuringian/Kirchenbund decision to replace references to the EKD in the Landeskirche constitutions, doing nothing ceased to be an option. This forced the question of Berlin-Brandenburg's incongruous legal status, since such a change in Berlin-Brandenburg's constitution required approval by both regions. The assumption under which the Eastern region had entered the Kirchenbund—that ratification required only a simple majority because no

---

[57]"Aus dem Rechenschaftsbericht von Bischof Scharf . . . ," *KJ* 1970, p. 251; "epd-Interview mit Bischof D. Kurt Scharf vom 19. Februar 1970," in Henkys, *Bund der Kirchen,* p. 198.

[58]*NZ,* 22 December 1969; "Aus einem Referat Gerald Goettings," in Henkys, *Bund der Kirchen,* pp. 192, 196.

[59]The title of "bishop" for Schoenherr was rejected as tokenism in *NZ,* 6 March 1970. For example, the Working Group "Christian Circles" of Potsdam Regional Committee of the National Front, reported in *NZ,* 5 February and 1 March 1970; the Weissensee Study Group, reported in *NZ,* 5 and 8 March 1970; the Pfarrerbund, reported in *NZ,* 6 March 1970.

changes in the Landeskirche constitution were necessary—no longer held. The linkage with the Kirchenbund thus left the Eastern region facing a dilemma, either to take actions resulting in looser legal ties with West Berlin or risk further isolation and impair the viability of the Kirchenbund.

Schoenherr sought to find a middle way between total separation and continued unity. He was more committed to the viability of the Kirchenbund and church service in its social context than to inter-German church unity, but he sought to limit such separation to incremental steps toward regional autonomy.[60] Under his guidance the church leadership recommended in January 1970 that the synod vote to permit regional variations in the constitution, to change the constitution to confirm Berlin-Brandenburg's membership in the Kirchenbund, and to bequeath the title "bishop" on Schoenherr. He also requested that the synod authorize a study of a new bishop election law, thus hinting at even further incremental steps toward separation.

But Schoenherr balanced his support for equality and independence for the Eastern region with criticism of the state's campaign against Scharf. He inveighed against "the atmosphere-poisoning newspaper polemic against our Westberlin brothers and especially against our brother Bishop D. Scharf."[61] In addition, Schoenherr directly criticized the state's limitations on access to Berlin for himself, pastors, and students.

The synod debate of the church leadership's proposals for incremental regionalization was polarized and acrimonious. Conservative forces opposed to separation accused the church leadership of "playing a game of double-talk" and rejected designation of Schoenherr as bishop, claiming that a "sign of affinity" with the West Berlin region was required, not merely the assertion of spiritual community. On the other side, those favoring a complete break, led by de Maiziere (CDU) and Professor Hanfried Mueller, dismissed the church leadership's proposals as inadequate, claiming that Schoenherr could not claim the bishop's title since he had never been elected to that office.[62]

---

[60]EPS documents, 21 January 1970, pp. 1–2; EPS documents, 18 March 1970, pp. 4–6.

[61]"Auszuege aus dem Bericht . . . ," *epd Dokumentation*, no. 13 (26 March 1970): pp. 19–20.

[62]Pastor Mueller and Pastor Knecht, quoted in *DW*, 9 March 1970; De Maiziere quoted in "Fuer und gegen die Kirchentrennung," *epd Landesdienst Berlin*, no. 28 (10 March 1970): pp. 1–2; Hartmut Bunke, "Bald zwei Berliner Landeskirchen," *Die Liberale Zeitung*, 3 April 1970; Goeckel, "Detente," p. 161.

Despite the assaults from right and left, the synod followed the church leadership's middle-of-the-road approach. Proposals from the conservatives to deny the title to Schoenherr and to send a telegram of loyalty to Scharf were rejected or altered.[63] The synod also opted for quiet diplomacy regarding residency permits for East Berlin. The left, on the other hand, realizing that it enjoyed little support among members of the synod, eventually endorsed the church leadership's proposals in the final vote. Despite the polarized debate, all of the resolutions proposed by the church leadership in its report were approved by large majorities.[64] The synod was thus able to declare that its membership in the EKD had ended and to change the wording of the Basic Order accordingly. It also issued a declaration of the independent exercise of responsibility by the organs of each region, including the bishop's functions. Finally, the synod formed a working group to study the constitution, the Regional Order, and the bishop election law—which was to report to the synod within three years.

The results of the synod reflected the attempt of the church leadership and the synod members to balance two competing goals: the desire to avoid the appearance of rejecting the community with the West Berlin church, especially as embodied in Bishop Scharf, and the felt need to assert the independence of the Eastern region. In marked contrast to the situation of the EKD, the special location of Berlin and, more importantly, the border-transcending personal loyalty to Scharf made a complete break unthinkable to most in the Eastern region at that time. Thus Schoenherr defended Scharf against the state's polemic and the church leadership avoided a repudiation of his 1966 election by timing any changes in the bishop question to occur after Scharf's retirement in 1972.[65] On the other hand, Schoenherr's phraseology, the informal awarding of the title of bishop to Schoenherr, and the formation of the committee to study the bishop question all relativized the role of Scharf and reflected moves toward a separate bishopric for the Eastern region.

In mobilizing support for its actions, the church leadership benefited from the role of both Scharf and Goetting.[66] By emphasizing Scharf's

---

[63]The Knecht resolution is referred to in *DW*, 11 March 1970. The synod's resolutions are found in "Beschluesse der Regionalsynode Ost vom 10. 3.1970," *KJ* 1970, pp. 259–60.

[64]"Beschluesse der Regionalsynode . . . ," in Henkys, *Bund der Kirchen*, pp. 198–200.

[65]Henkys points out that a synodal resolution addressing Schoenherr as bishop would have represented a de facto rescinding of its 1966 decision for Scharf. See *DAS*, 22 March 1970.

[66]CDU archives, 26 January 1970; CDU archives, 23 February 1970.

supposed intransigence on the separation issue and the strong support for him in the synod, the church leadership was able to cast its incremental decisions in a positive light to the state. By the same token, Goetting's hard-line position allowed the church leadership to assume a defiant posture, defending Scharf and rejecting total separation, useful in justifying its moves toward regionalization to both the Western region and the grass roots at home.

Although the synod did not bring the complete separation that the state had demanded, the state reacted favorably to the synod's actions. For example, the CDU hailed the synod's resolutions as "aiming at the complete organizational separation from the Westberlin church."[67] To be sure, the state would have preferred that the synod change the Basic Order unilaterally, rather than following the current Basic Order and making its change dependent upon the approval of the June 1970 Western regional synod. Nevertheless, the state was pleased that the synod did not merely reinterpret the references to the EKD, but acted to eliminate them. Moreover, the rejection and/or softening of conservative resolutions, the wide margin of support for the church leadership's proposals, and the retirement of certain conservative leaders identified with the EKD were greeted by the state.[68]

Other than the perception of the limited maneuverability available to the church leadership and the real moves toward separation by the synod, two additional factors explain the state's positive response. First, the state hoped to use the results of Berlin-Brandenburg for leverage on the upcoming May 1970 EKU synod, which was deliberating the same issue of inter-German organization.[69] Second, it represents an early manifestation of the state's reorientation of its Kirchenpolitik from the Landeskirche level to the Kirchenbund level, from Mitzenheim to Schoenherr, a development that will be reviewed in greater depth in the next chapter.

The Eastern synod's resolution allowing independent regional changes in the constitution still required the approval of the Western synod in order to take force. Meeting in June 1970, the Western synod

---

[67]NZ, 12 and 14 March 1970.
[68]Ibid. CDU archives, 1970, "Einschaetzung der evangelischen Herbstsynoden 1969"; CDU archives, 1970, "Einschaetzung der evangelischen Fruehjahrssynoden 1970."
[69]This linkage is made in NZ, 12 and 14 March 1970; EPS documents, 18 March 1970, pp. 4–6.

gave its approval, acting favorably upon Scharf's recommendation.[70] At the same time it affirmed that the Berlin-Brandenburg Church "observes in partner-like freedom in its two regional synods the special community of the Berlin-Brandenburg Church and remains intact as the Church in Berlin-Brandenburg." In his report to the synod, Scharf stressed the example to be set by Berlin-Brandenburg in realizing Article 4.4's "special community" and maintaining the EKU's unity.

With this approval by the Western region, attention shifted to the deliberations of the committee mandated to review the bishop question. Although its deliberations were drawn out so that its report would coincide with Scharf's retirement in 1972, its support for a separate bishop's office for the Eastern region soon became clear.[71] Although the state toyed with engaging "progressive" synod members to speed the process, it chose to remain patient on the issue and by late 1970 became reconciled to the partial separation in Berlin-Brandenburg, as revealed by the relative absence of public polemic on the issue thereafter.

In the case of each of these inter-German church organizations, one sees during this period organizational accommodation to state pressure for Abgrenzung. In the case of the Kirchenbund it took the form of organizational independence; in the cases of the EKU and Berlin-Brandenburg, it took the form of greater regional autonomy. Church-state conflict continued over the nature and extent of the remaining ties, leading the state to withhold recognition from the Kirchenbund in order to press for greater Abgrenzung. With the Kirchenbund's narrowing of its interpretation of Article 4.4, the process of regionalization in the EKU and Berlin-Brandenburg, and the greater realism on the part of the state, the context for an overture to the Kirchenbund was laid by late 1970.

THE INTERNAL POLITICAL DEVELOPMENT OF THE KIRCHENBUND

A second explanation for the state's nonrecognition of the Kirchenbund was the state's concern over the internal political develop-

[70]"Aus dem von Bischof D. Kurt Scharf erstatteten Rechenschaftsbericht," "Kirchengesetz ueber die Aenderung der Grundordnung durch die Regionalsynoden von 20. Juni 1970," and "Beschluss zur Gemeinschaft der Berlin-Brandenburg Kirche," *epd Dokumentation,* no. 28 (13 July 1970): pp. 19–20.
[71]"Tagung der Regionalsynode Ost, 7.–11. Mai 1971," *KJ* 1971, pp. 333–35.

ment of the Kirchenbund. The state was uncertain of the role the Kirchenbund would seek in GDR society and political life: of the social presence it would seek, of the stance it would take on major issues, and of the response it would make to the problems of individual Christians in a Marxist-Leninist society.

Like other Marxist-Leninist systems, the GDR had sought to arrogate control of all spheres of public life.[72] As chapter 3 indicated, the state had largely eliminated the churches' presence in the education system in the 1950s and sought where possible to reduce its not insubstantial presence in the areas of social welfare and culture. Even church-owned theological seminaries, particularly in Berlin, were sometimes pressured. Moreover, in an effort to gain greater influence over the clergy, the state had made curriculum and personnel changes in the state universities' theological departments. Some areas of church social service (e.g., hospitals) seemed to have gained the state's acceptance; however, in other areas (e.g., kindergartens and summer youth camps), the state sought to reduce the churches' presence by means of regulations or competition from state-run social services.[73] In the area of cultural activities, the picture was much the same. Some church activities were tolerated and even fostered as part of the "cultural inheritance" of the GDR (e.g., the St. Thomas Choirboys and organ concerts of Bach); other cultural activities remained taboo (e.g., jazz worship, certain topics of the Evangelical academies, and retreats for youth) or were rebuffed as attempts to expand the churches' cultural sphere (e.g., performances by members of state orchestras in church concerts).[74]

In addition to limiting the churches' social presence, the state sought the churches' support on social and political issues, including foreign policy. When the church expressed dissent, the state preferred that it not be done openly but in private discussions with state officials. The churches had pledged to "respect the development of socialism" but had

[72]"The church shall if possible remain limited to cult status," quoted in CDU archives, 3 June 1969.

[73]The capacity of church hospitals has remained roughly constant. State kindergartens have competed with the church kindergartens, which decreased in number in the 1950s. Based on discussion with Ernst Petzold, former director of Home Mission and Church Relief Agency, and Bishop Schoenherr.

[74]An official work on the cultural policy mentions religious aspects (e.g., maintaining the legacy of Luther, activities of church choirs) without references to their institutional basis in the church. The Ministry of Culture is allocated sole responsibility for the cultural policy. See Hans Koch, *Cultural Policy in the German Democratic Republic* (Paris: UNESCO Press, 1975), pp. 30, 40, 45–49. See also EPC archives, 1968, pp. 13–14.

withheld the total, uncritical engagement desired by the state. Nor had they shied away from expressing public criticism, as the bishops' proposed changes in the 1968 draft constitution indicated. With the exception of Mitzenheim's endorsement of GDR foreign policy and Berlin-Brandenburg's criticism of the intervention in Czechoslovakia, the churches had treated non-German foreign policy issues with public silence and private criticism. On issues relating to the treatment of Christians, the churches had not limited themselves to quiet diplomacy, using both public synods and private discussions with the state to criticize the youth dedication ceremony, the problems in staging youth retreats, and the discrimination of Christians.

In all these areas—the churches' social presence, the social and political positions taken by the churches, and church grass-roots grievances—the state feared that the churches would test the strength of their new-found unity by seeking to expand their social presence or by becoming more vocal on political issues and Christians' grievances. This fear was made more real by the contradictory nature of the forces that converged to form the Kirchenbund, a coalition that included both those who saw the Kirchenbund as a means of reining in "progressives," such as Mitzenheim, and those who saw it as a means of freeing the churches' criticisms from the state's charge of West German manipulation.

In this new and uncertain structural situation, state recognition of the Kirchenbund depended on the answers to the questions posed by Kurt Huettner, a leading SED policymaker: "what is the Kirchenbund now politically and who has the power there?" Until 1971 the state's answers indicated that, in Huettner's words, "the majority of the church leaders had not found their place in the socialist society."[75]

The question of power in the Kirchenbund centered on the selection of the chairman of the Executive Board and the general secretary of the Secretariat. Would they represent the numerically weak, "progressive" Mitzenheim group; the numerically strong, politically abstinent Lutheran wing; or the numerically strong, politically engaged Union churches? Various factors precluded certain bishops from serious consideration for the chairmanship: Fraenkel was too critical, Mitzenheim was not critical

---

[75]Kurt Huettner, SED Central Committee Secretariat, quoted in CDU archives, 30 June 1970.

enough and too old; Krusche of Saxony-Magdeburg was too unknown; the small size of his Anhalt Landeskirche disqualified Mueller. Krummacher, still persona non grata to the state, was also not viable. As head of the powerful Saxony-Dresden Landeskirche, Noth would have been a logical candidate, but he had assumed a standoffish stance regarding the Kirchenbund; the state was probably unenthusiastic about him, given his former membership on the EKD Council and his often critical stance in private vis-à-vis the state. The remaining and, in fact, leading candidates for the chairmanship were Beste, bishop of Mecklenburg and former chairman of the Eastern Conference of Church Leaderships, and Schoenherr, head of the Structure Committee and architect of the Kirchenbund as well as head of Berlin-Brandenburg's Eastern region. Beste, a conservative Lutheran, had largely abstained from politics, with the exception of his support for land reform in 1946 and his participation in the People's Congress movement.[76]

The state was also ambivalent about Schoenherr, a politically engaged yet critical Union churchman. His ties with the West German churches, especially Berlin-Brandenburg, and his handling of the Berlin-Brandenburg statement on Czechoslovakia had caused friction with the state.[77] However, though he did not hesitate to protest discrimination against Christians in the education system, he was generally circumspect in such protest. Also, his prior membership in the "progressive" Weissensee Study Group and the Prague Christian Peace Conference, his unofficial activity in certain National Front events, and his primarily leftist political orientation served him in good stead with the state.[78] Thus the state favored his selection as chairman, although, as noted earlier, it was unwilling to compromise on the issue of Berlin-Brandenburg to strengthen his position. The state anticipated a reasonable relationship with Schoenherr via his protege, Manfred Stolpe, who was selected general secretary and with whom the state had enjoyed a good working relationship.

[76]CDU archives, 30 June 1969; Matern, p. 25.

[77]CDU archives, 6 January 1969; CDU archives, 3 June 1969.

[78]Schoenherr met every year with the authorities in the district of Frankfurt/Oder, condemning, for example, the Vietnam War and endorsing CPC work in 1967. See EPC archives, 5 January 1967. Also based on discussion with Professor Trebs, Humboldt University, Berlin, GDR. CDU archives, 6 January 1969. Stolpe was prepared in principle to attend the ceremonies commemorating the Wartburg meeting planned for August 19, 1969, according to CDU archives, 24 July 1969. Consistory President Kupas and Stolpe attended the National Front symposium on November 10, 1970.

Although these personnel selections seemed to bode well for the Kirchenbund's relationship with the state, there still remained the question of what policies they would pursue. And even if they should propound policies acceptable to the state, would they be able to consolidate their positions within the Kirchenbund in order to translate these policies into the official Kirchenbund position? Though it tended to view the Kirchenbund as structurally analogous to the centralized SED, the state realized that the power of these new leaders would be limited by the need to garner support from other members of the twenty-five-member Conference of Church Leaderships or the five-member Executive Board. Moreover, the anomaly of Schoenherr's position was apparent to the state: paradoxically, his position was probably more secure within the Kirchenbund, due to his role as a tactful consensus-builder, than in his own Landeskirche, in which he faced strong opposition. Should he fail to effect the separation from the Western region or to win election as the new bishop in 1972, the Kirchenbund might be left in the hands of those more critical of the state.

The state, deciding not to leave this process to chance, proffered "guidance" to the Kirchenbund in this "internal church clarification process."[79] In his February 1970 address, Goetting indicated that organizational separation from the West German churches must be accompanied by a "conscious new orientation" and spelled out three manifestations of this "new orientation" expected of churches.

1. The churches should "let the socialist constitution guide their work in all social aspects" (in other words, delimit themselves from the West German churches).

2. "The churches, in the GDR and ecumenically, should support the efforts of the forces of peace in the world and make a contribution to a real European peace order" (in other words, work for the international legal recognition of the sovereignty and equal status of the GDR and the inviolability of the post-1945 borders, including lobbying the West German churches in this respect).

3. The churches should express "solidarity with all peoples in anti-imperialistic struggle" (in other words, lend moral and material support

[79]"Aus einem Leitartikel der 'Neuen Zeit' vom 20. September 1969," in Henkys, *Bund der Kirchen*, pp. 171–72.

for Soviet-sponsored national liberation struggles, especially in Vietnam and the Middle East).

The CDU also extended this desired "new orientation" to the domestic question of the churches' relationship to the "construction of socialism." The CDU expected an "intellectual new orientation" that focused on the churches' immediate environment of socialism, seeking to make itself more relevant to society.[80] Required for this relevance and understanding of socialism, according to the CDU's Goetting, was participation in the society. He praised the "numerous pastors and theologians active in the National Front and serving as elected officials at all levels." "New orientation" also entailed theological Abgrenzung from modern Western theology. In the CDU's view, there was no need for the churches in "our socialist society to adhere to the ecclesiastical-theological developments in late capitalism."[81] As might be expected given its role in theological education, the CDU placed more emphasis than the state on internal change in the church.

Although the state endorsed these internal church changes, it clearly gave higher priority to the directly political aspects of "new orientation," particularly the goals of Abgrenzung, recognition of the European status quo, and support for national liberation struggles. The state was concerned to dampen the euphoria sweeping the GDR populace in the wake of the Brandt initiatives of 1969. Until now the GDR had only reluctantly and partially supported the Soviet's negotiations with the FRG and sought to avoid serious discussions with the FRG by insisting that recognition of the GDR under international law and a European security conference to guarantee the inviolability of post-1945 borders be preconditions of negotiations.[82] The state sought not only to win the churches' endorsement of these goals, it sought to counter positions, such as the mission of reconciliation propounded by Bishop Krusche, that it interpreted as variations of convergence theory or "social demo-

---

[80]"Aus einem Referat Gerald Goettings," in Henkys, *Bund der Kirchen*, pp. 194–95. See also the theological address by Prof. Hans-Hinrich Jenssen in *NZ*, 28 February 1970.

[81]The appearance of Dr. Dorothea Soelle, controversial West German theologian, at an event of the Evangelical Academy in East Berlin in late 1969 caused obvious consternation in certain official circles and may have been the immediate cause of this attack.

[82]See, for example, Kupper in Jacobsen et al., pp. 435–38.

cratism" and saw as reflecting and contributing to the popular expectations of Ostpolitik.

In its early years, the Kirchenbund, under the leadership of Schoenherr, pursued policies that created the basis for cooperation between the state and the Kirchenbund. Despite the barrage of state criticism of Article 4.4, the 1970 synod sent several conciliatory signals.[83]

The synod indicated a new focus on GDR society and receptiveness to social and political participation. Schoenherr, in his report to the synod, endorsed in general terms social engagement and relevance of the church, rejecting the political abstinence often espoused by Lutherans. The Kirchenbund synod affirmed this view, indicating that "the Federation will have to prove itself as a witness and service community of churches in the socialist society of the GDR." This oft-repeated slogan represented not only another assertion of independence from the EKD, but also a positive response to the CDU's call for "new orientation" focusing on GDR society. Furthermore, the synod agreed that this GDR-focused social engagement included cooperation with Marxists. In his report Schoenherr cited the 1947 Darmstadt Declaration of the Confessing Church and the churches' guilt for failing to cooperate with Marxists in opposing the Third Reich:

> We erred, when we overlooked that the economic materialism of Marxism should have reminded the church concerning the task and promise of the Christian community for the life and society in the here and now. We have failed to make the concerns of the poor and disenfranchised into our concern as Christians, according to the Gospel of the coming Kingdom of God.

While this exercise in mea culpa was hardly remarkable in postwar Germany or in the GDR churches, Schoenherr used it to make an overture to the state. Finally, the synod attempted to allay the state's suspicions that the churches would seek to use their new-found unity to assert and expand their presence in society. The synod couched its social responsibility in terms of service to others, not in terms of maintenance of the church. According to Schoenherr: "the church . . . cannot and wishes not to claim the old privileges. It only asks to be able to serve its

---

[83] All citations of Schoenherr from "Bericht der KKL . . ." and "Beschluss auf Antrag des Berichtsausschusses," *epd Dokumentation*, no. 28 (13 July 1970): pp. 3, 7, 11, 12.

God unhindered. As church of the crucified Christ it is called not to rule, but to serve."

On concrete issues in the relationship with the state, the synod was also quite diplomatic. It did raise problems regarding ecumenical contacts and import of Western theological literature, but these were rather mild frictions. Other, more contentious issues, such as education discrimination and problems regarding alternative military service, were avoided at the synod. Although this downplaying of disagreements with the state is in part attributable to the synod's preoccupation with the creation of internal machinery for the Kirchenbund, it also reflected an attempt to win the state's confidence.

In addition, Schoenherr, as the key figure in the church-state relationship, assumed a conciliatory posture generally during this period. He obliquely endorsed GDR membership in the United Nations and opposed U.S. and Israeli policy in Vietnam and the Middle East, respectively.[84] In a regional CDU newspaper, he hailed the World Council of Churches' support for liberation movements in southern Africa as a "sign of solidarity" in the context of an "elementary problem of the dignity of mankind."[85] By making these statements in regional rather than national forums, Schoenherr could claim that he was not speaking authoritatively for the Kirchenbund; however, they did demonstrate policy positions congruous with the state's desired "new orientation." Although maintaining some distance from the National Front himself, Schoenherr did not object to members of the Berlin-Brandenburg Church Leadership participating in its activities. Through Stolpe he maintained a close working relationship with the state authorities and the CDU.[86]

Thus, while not echoing every aspect of the state's desired "new orientation," especially those touted by the CDU regarding the internal character of the church, Schoenherr and the Kirchenbund did pursue a policy that demonstrated a receptiveness, both theoretically and in practice, to cooperation with the state, particularly at the lower levels.

---

[84]*ND*, 14 January 1970. *Neues Deutschland*'s straightforward reporting of this rather indirect endorsement of UN membership for the GDR was exaggerated by *Neue Zeit* to mean an endorsement of international recognition of the GDR. This reveals again the CDU's more agitational role, especially in terms of popular identification with the GDR as a political community.

[85]The Schoenherr article is reprinted in *KJ*, 1970, pp. 197–99.

[86]CDU archives, 6 January 1969; CDU archives, 24 July 1969.

By February 1971 this policy had allayed some of the state's initial fears and uncertainty regarding the direction of the Kirchenbund.

ECUMENICAL RELATIONS OF
THE GDR CHURCHES

Another reason for the initial reluctance of the state to recognize the Kirchenbund officially was the problematic nature of the international relations of the GDR churches. Paradoxically, this issue was later to become one of the chief factors promoting the state's normalization of relations with the Kirchenbund. The state's policy toward these relations was, of course, in part a function of its perception of the churches' remaining inter-German ties and their internal political development. Yet because the state had considerable control over the extent of these international relations and because they more directly affected the foreign policy interests of the state, the state's treatment of these relations demonstrated the state's dilemmas and the role played by its foreign policy in its shift regarding the Kirchenbund.

As noted in chapter 2, prior to the separation from the West German church organizations, most of these international ties were handled administratively by all-German bodies. For example, the East German member churches' relations with the World Council of Churches (WCC) and the Lutheran World Federation (LWF) were handled by committees and administered in the EKD headquarters in Hannover, although GDR citizens had been proportionately represented in the all-German representation in these bodies. Although nominally handled in Hannover, ecumenical exchanges were in practice processed in the EKD's branch office in East Berlin. This was necessary to facilitate the acquisition of travel visas from the GDR Ministry of Foreign Affairs. Travel visas were granted on a case-by-case basis by this ministry, in coordination with the state secretary for church questions and local government officials. This dual system made it possible for the state to manage the sometimes-conflicting levels of the Kirchenpolitik: the national Kirchenpolitik, involving especially the GDR's foreign policy goals, and the local Kirchenpolitik, focusing on goals of political stability and mobilization. Naturally, this dual system increased the uncertainty involved in the churches' ecumenical relations and made some centralization of the churches' ecumenical operations unavoidable.

With the increasing primacy of Abgrenzung in the state's policy in the late 1960s, the all-German nature of these international church ties made them increasingly untenable. Bishops with positions in the EKD, such as Noth and Krummacher, were prevented from fulfilling their international ecumenical responsibilities. Holding international church meetings in the GDR became impossible, as indicated by the state's reversal of its approval of church plans to hold the 1970 LWF General Assembly in Weimar.[87]

The application of this ban on ecumenical travel was hardly uniform, however.[88] For example, Thuringia, with its special place in the state's Kirchenpolitik, was relatively unaffected. Some church leaders, such as Bishops Schoenherr and Beste, were generally allowed to travel because of their relative political circumspection and potential leadership roles in the new Kirchenbund. Other bishops, such as Noth and Krusche, less politic on both inter-German and domestic political matters, were virtually prohibited from ecumenical travel.

However, the formation of the Kirchenbund and the end of all EKD functions in the GDR confronted the state with a new dilemma. On the one hand, ecumenical participation by the GDR churches continued to carry certain drawbacks, such as probable encounters with West German church leaders and the participation of representatives of the still all-German EKU and Berlin-Brandenburg. Moreover, the churches would probably seek the ecumenical participation of certain GDR church leaders who were persona non grata in the state's eyes. On the other hand, such participation brought definite advantages from the state's perspective, as articulated by a leading CDU spokesman.[89] In this

---

[87]According to one source, this cancellation stemmed from the state's refusal to guarantee visas to all reporters covering the assembly. Certainly the state feared the presence of West Germans in general, in particular at a forum featuring Bishop Krummacher. Seigewasser cited the West German claim of sole representation of Germany as the reason for the cancellation. See Juergen Jeziorowski, "Gesandt in die Welt," in *Kirche vor der Herausforderung der Zukunft*, ed. Juergen Jeziorowski (Stuttgart: Kreuz Verlag, 1970), pp. 9–10.

[88]For example, the Thuringian member of the LWF Executive Committee, Dr. Schanze, received a visa for its 1968 meeting, the same meeting for which Krummacher had been denied one, according to *LWF Information*, no. 38 (28 August 1968): p. 4. Beste and Schoenherr traveled to Geneva for ecumenical meetings in 1968 and 1969, even while inter-German organizational questions remained unresolved. Bishop Noth was not allowed to attend the 1969 WCC Central Committee meeting since he was still a member of the EKD Council. See *LWF Information*, no. 51 (14 November 1968): p. 7; "Blake warnte vor Karikaturen des Christentums," *epd Zentralausgabe*, no. 184 (13 August 1969): p. 2. No West German representatives were permitted to attend the installation of Krusche as bishop, according to "New Bishop Consecrated in East German Church," *LWF Information*, no. 50 (4 November 1968): p. 6.

[89]NZ, 7 October 1970.

view, independent GDR participation in these international ecumenical organizations, like GDR participation in other INGOs, would promote the international recognition of the GDR and erode the effect of the FRG's Hallstein Doctrine. It would also help to develop a sense of GDR consciousness among the GDR representatives to these organizations. Finally, such participation would help foster alliance with "progressive" forces, especially in capitalist lands.

Evidently the state found that these benefits of ecumenical contacts outweighed the costs. The general ban on international travel was loosened considerably after the formation of the Kirchenbund. The fact that this occurred *before* the state's recognition of the Kirchenbund reveals the importance that the state placed on this international presence of the churches.

Nonetheless, the state sought to minimize the costs of these increased ecumenical contacts. Multilateral conferences provided the greatest increase in international status and the easiest opportunity to limit the costs; the state could selectively deny visas to proposed delegates and still likely enjoy the international prestige from the GDR's participation. On the other hand, bilateral exchanges gave the churches greater bargaining power, since they could threaten to postpone the exchange.

The first test of the state's response to this dilemma came in late 1969 and involved Kirchenbund participation in the World Council of Churches. In November 1969 the WCC invited representatives of the Kirchenbund to Geneva to negotiate the termination of the EKD's responsibility for the representation of the eight GDR churches and the transfer of this responsibility to the Kirchenbund.[90] A delegation composed of Chairman Schoenherr, Deputy Chairman Noth, and President Braecklein was scheduled to travel in December 1969, but the visit was canceled at the last minute when the state refused a visa to Bishop Noth. Although Noth was no longer a member of the EKD Council, he remained barred from travel by the state for domestic political reasons: the incarceration of his son for aiding an escape attempt, Noth's bitter criticism of the state's harsh three-and-one-half-year sentence, and Noth's uncompromising opposition to the youth dedication ceremony and other policies of the GDR. Thus, the GDR, seeking to foster its international standing without sacrificing the goals of its domestic Kir-

---

[90]"Protokoll ueber eine Vereinbarung mit dem Oekumenischen Rat in Genf ueber die Mitgliedschaft der Kirchen in der DDR," *KJ* 1970, pp. 298–99.

chenpolitik, granted visas to only Schoenherr and Braecklein. The Kirchenbund, pursuing a policy of canceling an exchange if a significant member of the delegation was refused a visa, called the state's bluff and tabled the trip to Geneva. Faced with a choice between its goals, the state conceded and allowed Noth to travel with the delegation to Geneva in late January 1970.[91] The status-conscious state soon found itself making another unpleasant concession: to end the Kirchenbund's financial dependence on the EKD for its contribution to the WCC, the state approved an allocation of hard currency for this purpose.[92]

The ties of the GDR member churches with the LWF seemed to come under less fire than those with the WCC, probably because the EKD had not been directly involved and because the timely split from the VELKD by the three Lutheran Landeskirchen in December 1968 removed considerable pressure from their ties with the LWF. By 1968 the GDR member churches had already set up a GDR National Committee to handle these ties. Yet because the LWF enjoys less international visibility and has a greater preponderance of West German churches than the WCC, the state has preferred the latter as an international forum.

Church participation in the LWF also confronted the state with the dilemma of conflicting international and domestic policy. Bishop Krummacher's leading role in the EKD and his support for it at the Fuerstenwalde synod in 1967 had led the state to interfere with his activity in the LWF Executive Committee, of which he was a member. However, the state's desire for international recognition, in conjunction with Krummacher's dramatic turnaround on the issue of EKD unity and relinquishing of his post on the EKD Council, led to his rehabilitation, as manifested in the state's gradual lifting of its travel ban.[93] In the first Kirchenbund-era test, Krummacher was denied a visa to the December 1969 LWF Executive Committee meeting in Denmark. However, the

[91]*Der Tagesspiegel,* 29 January 1970; *FAZ,* 18 and 22 December 1969; discussion with Lothar Teichman, member of the church leadership, 1969–1977, and Ralph Zorn, former LWF representative in West Berlin.

[92]*FAZ,* 18 February 1970; "Oekumenischer Rat erwartet deutsche Hilfe aus Finanznot," *epd Zentralausgabe,* no. 33 (14 February 1970); "Bericht der KKL . . . ," *epd Dokumentation,* no. 34 (19 July 1971): p. 9.

[93]For example, in Matern's references to the National Committee for a Free Germany, the Soviet-sponsored organization of anti-Nazi Germans in exile, at no point was Krummacher's important role mentioned. Also, Bishop Beste and Mecklenburg received inordinate praise and attention (in terms of the 1946 land reform and the early postwar People's Congress movement), another indication of neighboring Bishop Krummacher's persona non grata status. See Matern, pp. 21–22, 25.

state did permit him to travel to Sweden and participate indirectly via courier, a sign of loosening restrictions. This was confirmed in 1970 by the state's approval of the participation of a GDR delegation, headed by Krummacher, at a meeting of Scandinavian and German churches in Sweden in 1970.[94] Although no longer burdened by the ballast from Krummacher, church participation in the LWF continued to be affected negatively by the remaining inter-German unity of the EKU. In the case of the LWF General Assembly in 1970, the state denied visas to ten of the thirty-six GDR delegates, all members of EKU Landeskirchen or youth still subject to military service.[95] The only EKU churchmen allowed to attend were those from Krummacher's Greifswald Landeskirche. Again the state sought to avoid sacrificing its other goals to its goal of GDR participation in international church organizations. In this case the state triumphed: the churches protested the action, but given the immutability of the assembly, decided to attend with the truncated delegation.

Though the state was most interested in fostering international ecumenical activity because of the desired demonstration effect on Western churches, it also closely watched the content and context of this participation to measure the internal development of the GDR churches and to determine the attractiveness of various international ecumenical organizations in terms of the state's "new orientation" goals.

As the more visible and universal organization, the WCC was certainly more important in terms of the GDR's main goal, achieving international recognition. However, the LWF also proved hospitable in this regard. At its General Assembly in Evian, France (July 1970), the LWF called for universal membership in the United Nations, citing specifically the FRG and the GDR, and endorsed a proposed European security conference, two initiatives that the GDR supported in attempts

---

[94]"LWF Executives Open Assembly Discussions" and "DDR Churchmen Refused Permission to Attend LWF Executive Meeting," *LWF Information*, no. 54 (10 December 1969): pp. 5, 8; "Nordisch-Deutscher Konvent tagte in Leipzig," *Evangelischer Nachrichtendienst* 23 (9 September 1970): 6; EPS documents, 28 November 1969. Huettner indicated that "the reasons for the previous negation of Bishop Krummacher have been eliminated with his behavior at the synod," a reference to his shift on Article 4.4, according to CDU archives, 24 September 1969. Krummacher endorsed the WTO's Budapest appeal. See CDU archives, 6 August 1969.

[95]CDU archives, 26 July 1969; CDU archives, 13 July 1970.

to blunt the FRG's Ostpolitik.[96] The animated discussion of the political situation and human rights in Brazil, original site for the assembly until criticism forced the LWF to move it to France, found the GDR representatives taking an active part. The state applauded this as a breakthrough in terms of the LWF's social engagement and the GDR's participation.[97]

In terms of the goals of "new orientation," particularly support of "progressive" forces in the West, the WCC also provided a favorable forum for GDR participation, due in particular to the opportunity provided by its Program to Combat Racism (PCR).[98] The PCR, approved by the WCC in August 1969, included a special fund primarily for liberation movements in southern Africa, which proved quite controversial among some member churches. The GDR churches supported the PCR from its inception.[99] Dr. Johannes Althausen and Elisabeth Adler, both politically active Berliners and delegates to the WCC meeting authorizing the PCR, became visibly identified with the Program. Student parishes and the umbrella Ecumenical Youth Service in Berlin pressed for official church support for the program. In December 1970 the Kirchenbund's Conference of Church Leaderships expressed its support for the PCR, including the special fund, and announced a special collection for the PCR within the framework of the yearly Bread for the World collections. The Kirchenbund underscored its commitment by undertaking a study on the racism problem and by raising 1 million marks for the PCR in 1971.

---

[96]*Evian 1970: Offizieller Bericht der Fuenften Vollversammlung des Lutherischen Weltbundes* (1970), pp. 143–45. The Conference of European Churches was even more hospitable to GDR interests. See "KEK fuer Anerkennung des Status Quo in Europa," *epd Zentralausgabe*, no. 230 (6 October 1967): p. 1.

[97]CDU archives, 1 August 1970; CDU archives, 1 October 1970.

[98]An overview of the PCR can be found in Elisabeth Adler, *A Small Beginning: An Assessment of the First Five Years of the Program to Combat Racism* (1974).

[99]"Evangelische Kritik aus der DDR an westdeutscher Rassismus-Diskussion," *epd Landesdienst Berlin*, no. 155 (8 December 1970): p. 6; "Konferenz der Kirchenleitung tagte," *KJ* 1970, p. 287; "DDR Kirchenbund unterstuetzt einstimmig das Anti-Rassismus Programm . . . ," *epd Dokumentation*, no. 10 (15 February 1971): pp. 19–20; Schoenherr's support is found in his "Die Menschwerdung Gottes ruft zum Dienst am Ganzen," *KJ* 1970, p. 199. Paul Verner greeted the Kirchenbund's profile on the PCR issue, in his "Gemeinsam auf dem guten Weg des Friedens und des Sozialismus," in *Christen und Marxisten in gemeinsamer Verantwortung,* ed. Paul Verner and Gerald Goetting (1971), p. 36. See "Information zum Antirassismus Program des Oekumenischen Rates der Kirchen," nos. 1–11, mimeographed (Berlin, GDR: Bund der Evangelischen Kirchen in der DDR).

The Kirchenbund's support for the PCR risked misinterpretation as opportunistic support for the state's foreign policy and a demonstration of the desired "new orientation." Some Landeskirchen—in particular, Saxony-Dresden and Goerlitz—feared that the grass roots would draw these conclusions and showed less enthusiasm for the PCR.[100] The Kirchenbund sought to correct this misinterpretation by stressing the church's true motivation. Reiterating the WCC position, it argued that force was always a second-best alternative to reconciliation by negotiation. It justified the PCR on the basis that "racism is an open denial of Christian belief" and that "overcoming it is today a model case for the full realization of general human rights." Couching the program in terms of human rights reflected the thinking of Schoenherr and represented a clear rejection of the state's interpretation of racism as a function of capitalist imperialism. However, this did not prevent the CDU from employing it in its Abgrenzung rhetoric, contrasting the Kirchenbund's support for the PCR with the opposition to it in the West German churches.[101]

Bilateral international relations of the GDR churches also proved useful in the state's quest for international recognition. For example, the state approved the beginning of a reciprocal exchange between the Kirchenbund and the British Council of Churches, despite Britain's status as a capitalist member of NATO, since it offered an opportunity to offset Bonn's Ostpolitik by establishing international ties with Western allies of Bonn. The Kirchenbund also expressed a strong interest in establishing relations with churches in socialist states and reported limited exchanges with the Polish churches.[102] In another show of identification with the GDR, the Kirchenbund delegations began in 1969 to travel to meetings in Western countries without first obtaining the approval of the Allied Travel Board in West Berlin.[103]

[100]Based on discussion with Lothar Teichmann, synod member, Superintendent Steinlein (Berlin-Brandenburg), and Bishop Fraenkel.

[101]*NZ,* 3 March 1971. The EKD opposed the special funds grants to liberation movements and boycott of corporations in southern Africa, favoring instead funding for specific projects. See Hudson, pp. 106–28, for a discussion of the PCR.

[102]"Bericht der KKL," *epd Dokumentation,* no. 28 (13 July 1970): p. 11.

[103]This agency was set up by the Western powers to handle the Western travel of citizens of the GDR, whose passports were not recognized by the West, and thus it rankled the GDR as it sought to break out of its isolated world status. See Kupper, in Jacobsen et al., p. 428. At the same time, the lack of diplomatic relations with Western countries was used as an excuse for rejecting GDR ecumenical travel in many cases, the argument being "the GDR cannot protect you in those countries." Thus the church was in a double bind.

The drawbacks feared by the state from the international activity of the GDR churches in this period did in fact materialize, although the state attempted to minimize the costs in terms of its goals of inter-German Abgrenzung and domestic control. For example, East German church leaders consulted with West Germans at the large LWF General Assembly in Evian and the meeting of Scandinavian-German churches in Sweden in August 1970. The state accused Scharf of using these international meetings, arguing that "since the signing of the treaty between the USSR and FRG, the attempt is clear to expand the so-called inter-German contacts."[104] Despite the founding of the Kirchenbund, the state continued to forbid ecumenical travel to the FRG, even by church leaders in the good graces of the state. As a result, to avoid conflict with the state, international church organizations rarely scheduled ecumenical meetings in the FRG during this period.[105] Moreover, in some cases the state did not allow its lust for international status to override the goals of its domestic Kirchenpolitik. For example, it imposed ecumenical travel bans on Krusche and Fraenkel, to be discussed later.[106] This minimization of the costs from international activity proved easiest in the case of multilateral conferences, for which the state could selectively deny visas and still enjoy the international prestige from the church's participation; it was more difficult in the case of bilateral exchanges, which the churches could threaten to postpone.

In most cases, however, the state reluctantly paid the price. The general ban on international ecumenical travel was loosened considerably after the formation of the Kirchenbund. The fact that this opening occurred prior to the state's recognition of the Kirchenbund demonstrates the importance that the state placed on these international ties. Raison d'etat argued for this independent international participation by the GDR churches; the context and content of the churches' activity from 1969 to 1971 offered promise. International participation also offered the state leverage in promoting its desired "new orientation" by using ecumenical resolutions to prod the GDR churches. For example, Seigewasser was quick to use the "ecumenical debate of basic questions, such as peace, security, racism, disarmament, neocolonialism" to berate

---

[104]Fritz Flint, State Secretary's Office, quoted in CDU archives, 20 August 1970.
[105]For example, the Nordic-German Church Convention, even though including FRG churches, met primarily in the GDR and neutral Scandinavia.
[106]EPS documents, 25 June 1970, p. 3.

the GDR churches for their failure to take an official stand on the recognition of the GDR: "we have experienced synods and church conventions given over totally to internal church contemplation, without even once giving a glance outside to the world with its battles and concerns."[107]

The Soviets too were interested in ecumenical activity by the Kirchenbund. After permitting the Russian Orthodox Church to join the WCC in 1959, Soviet interest increased in the late 1960s with the WCC's tilt toward leftist, Third World causes.[108] To foster and consolidate this leftist-activist shift in the WCC, the Soviets sought greater coordination of the socialist bloc member churches there. In the case of the Kirchenbund, the state's nonrecognition of the Kirchenbund hindered this coordination.

Thus despite different priorities—the GDR interest in international recognition in order to derail Bonn's Ostpolitik, the Soviet interest in using international church bodies for its broader foreign policy objectives—both positions argued for support for greater international activity by the Kirchenbund. The churches' restructuring of the basis of their international ecumenical activity and their positions in international organizations—given the state's drive for international status—helped erode the state's ambivalence regarding the Kirchenbund by 1971.

The State's Move from a Landeskirche Strategy to a Kirchenbund Strategy

Finally, the state recognition of the Kirchenbund reflected a shift in the strategy of its Kirchenpolitik, necessitated by the changed structural situation that the formation of the Kirchenbund brought about. Previously this strategy had been one based on differentiation among the Landeskirchen. After mid-1969, two factors called this strategy into question: the growing unification of the church and the reduced opportunities for the state to pursue a policy of differentiation favoring one Landeskirche over another.

[107]NZ, 12 November 1970.
[108]Fletcher discusses the Russian Orthodox Church's rapprochement with the ecumenical movement (pp. 120–21), Soviet motives (pp. 125–29), and the PCR (pp. 131–34). Matern, pp. 51–64.

Church Unification Efforts

One development that altered the structural situation facing the state was the movement toward greater church unification in the GDR. The years 1969 to 1971 saw renewed efforts to bridge what were considered archaic confessional and organizational divisions. This development in the GDR was part of a larger international phenomenon. The ecumenical movement worldwide gained increased momentum in the 1960s. On the European level, doctrinal discussions between Lutheran and Reformed churches began in Leuenberg, Switzerland. Since its founding, the EKD had strived toward unity.

The particular situation in the GDR seemed especially conducive to this long-term goal. The confessional situation offered more promise than elsewhere: the vast majority of congregations were Lutheran; the few Reformed congregations enjoyed protection. Moreover, the Lutheran-Reformed confessional differences had blurred since the 1930s as Reformed-influenced, Barthian thought increasingly influenced Lutheran theology. To the individual parishioner, the Reformed-Lutheran doctrinal differences and the Union-Lutheran organizational differences were anachronistic. An Erfurter could reasonably ask why he, from Thuringia, should for church purposes be considered subject to the distant, "Prussian" Union church of Saxony-Magdeburg. The arrangement of such anachronistic Landeskirche boundaries and a multitude of other internal reforms had been largely deferred out of fear of the impact on the ties with the EKD. Many hoped that the formation of the Kirchenbund would facilitate these reforms. Some reforms were a matter of sheer financial necessity: the shrinking income of the GDR churches dictated more efficiency and less overlap in the churches' bureaucracy. Finally, confronted with a centrally planned, centrally controlled Soviet-type state, the GDR churches were more likely to seek a unified stance than would churches in a liberal democracy.

One factor that facilitated this process of church unification was the increase in the Kirchenbund's powers and areas of responsibility during this period. From its inception the Kirchenbund represented an attempt to embody the community already realized among the GDR churches and to foster further growth in that community. In January 1969, as chairman of the Structure Committee, Schoenherr emphasized the

theme of church unity in the formation of the Kirchenbund.[109] He cited
the progress toward greater church unity on matters such as baptism
and shared communion, as codified in the Basic Order of the proposed
Kirchenbund. However, Schoenherr was careful to disavow the concept
of a centralized "super-church," a development feared especially by
many Lutherans and smaller Landeskirchen, not to mention the state, at
least at that point. "Such a super-church would necessarily degenerate
into a church of bureaucrats, as evidenced by the negative role played by
the churches in the Kirchenkampf in the Thirties," he emphasized.
Church unity would result from an incremental process in Schoenherr's
view. Despite this verbal circumspection, he intended that the Kirchenbund should provide a legal basis for coordinated strategy toward the
state.

The structure of the new Kirchenbund represented a modest centralization over previous bodies, despite its federal basis of organization.
The resolutions of the synod and the statutes of the Conference of
Church Leaderships could be rejected by the individual Landeskirchen.
But Church Leadership resolutions required only a simple majority,
rather than the unanimity required of its predecessor, the Eastern Conference.

However, more important to church unification than the powers of
the Kirchenbund were the areas of responsibility that it acquired. To be
sure, the areas of competence that the Basic Order explicitly gives the
Kirchenbund are few, though not insignificant. The Basic Order gives
the Kirchenbund explicit competence over the areas of mission and
service agencies and ecumenical relations of the member churches. Yet
the Basic Order implies wider competence, allowing the Kirchenbund to
acquire functions with the agreement of the Landeskirchen (Article 6) or
for Landeskirchen to cede functions to the Kirchenbund (Article 7).

Even before the Kirchenbund's first synod, the VELKDDR acted to
realize these implied powers by delegating responsibilities to the Kirchenbund.[110] Smarting from charges that its abrupt decision to constitute the VELKDDR in December 1968 had reinforced confessional differences and inhibited the potential for church unification, the VELKDDR

---

[109]"Aus einem Interview . . ." and "Ordnung des Bundes der Evangelischen Kirchen in der
DDR," in Henkys, *Bund der Kirchen,* pp. 127–34, 33–34.
[110]"Bekenntnis und Kirchengemeinschaft," *epd Zentralausgabe,* no. 157 (12 July 1969):
pp. 4–5.

delegated the area of publications to the Kirchenbund, later adding the areas of ecumenical relations, missions, parish life, and the Catholic Church Working Group.[111] However, reflecting the Lutherans' traditional concern for doctrinal questions, the synod also proposed binding doctrinal discussions with the EKU, maintaining that "church community is possible only by agreement of the bases of proclamation of the Gospel."

The September 1969 synod of the Kirchenbund sought to foster this momentum on church unification, using incremental steps.[112] It called on member churches and the VELKDDR and EKU to delegate functions to the Kirchenbund. It also created two commissions, for ecumenical affairs and education, two areas least divisive among the churches, but also areas of greatest interface with the state. The synod did not define the Kirchenbund's responsibilities any more explicitly, awaiting the response of the VELKDDR and EKU. This inaction reflected not only incremental caution, but also the conflict between the Synod, which advocated strong independent commissions for the Kirchenbund, and the Conference of Church Leaderships, which wished to retard this centralizing tendency.[113]

The Union Landeskirchen in the EKU were less enthusiastic about church unification. The proposals for ceding competence to the Kirchenbund confronted the EKU with a dilemma: from its union conception the EKU was particularly receptive to church unification; but any moves toward cooperation within the framework of the Kirchenbund would necessarily threaten the EKU's all-German status. The EKU Council, reflecting the influence of Chairman Fraenkel and Consistory President Hildebrandt, greeted with official silence the proposals for ceding competence to the Kirchenbund. Although both the EKU Council and Synod showed greater interest by mid-1970, the asymmetry between the VELKDDR and EKU in this matter was unmistakable.[114]

---

[111]"Verlautbarung des Sekretariats . . . vom 16. Maerz 1970," in Henkys, *Bund der Kirchen*, pp. 100–102.

[112]"Richtlinienbeschluss des Bundessynode," in ibid., pp. 164–65.

[113]EPS documents, 26 September 1969, pp. 3–5; EPS documents, 28 November 1969, p. 11.

[114]The synod's resolution supporting church unification is found in "Beschluesse der Regionalsynode Ost der EKU," *epd Dokumentation*, no. 23 (8 June 1970): p. 35. The EKU Council's offer is reported in "Bericht der Konferenz . . ." *epd Dokumentation*, no. 28 (13 July 1970): p. 7. "Auszuege aus der Berichterstattung des ena," *epd Dokumentation*, no. 41 (17 October 1970): pp. 58–60.

Individual Landeskirchen responded somewhat more positively. For example, Bishop Krusche endorsed the development of full church community, but argued that the EKU be retained pending the formation of the necessary organs of this new community. He rejected the state's allegation that the EKU hindered church unification, arguing that "attempts at influence from outside could only hinder the practical cooperation among the churches."[115] Already at its May 1969 synod approving the Kirchenbund, Berlin-Brandenburg (East) endorsed widening the responsibility of the Kirchenbund to avoid overlap, without mentioning the role of the EKU in this process.[116]

Despite the EKU's reluctance, incremental progress toward greater church integration was achieved during this period. In November 1969 the Conference of Church Leaderships issued guidelines for the work of the Kirchenbund commissions.[117] In them it gave a key coordinating role to the general secretary of the Secretariat. However, responding to EKU concerns, as well as suspicions of the state regarding a "centralized super-church," the conference decided against adding more commissions in March 1970.[118] By late 1970 a Joint Preparation Group, with paritative representation from the Kirchenbund, VELKDDR, and EKU (East), was formed to deal with the delegation of competence to the Kirchenbund.[119] The parity with the VELKDDR reduced the EKU's fear of the effects of simply ceding areas to the Kirchenbund and offered a defense against the state's demand for clear separation, since such participation presumed the continued existence of the EKU. The Kirchenbund also scored a victory by gaining the agreement of the Landeskirchen to consult on important new church laws and to defer to the Kirchenbund on the controversial question of baptism.[120]

Parallel to this organizational centralization and expansion of Kirchenbund function was the development of doctrinal discussions that offered the promise of a common theology for further church unifica-

---

[115]"Aus dem Bericht von Bischof Dr. Werner Krusche . . . ," in Henkys, *Bund der Kirchen*, pp. 177–78.

[116]"Beschluesse der Regionalsynode Ost . . . ," *KJ* 1969, p. 281.

[117]"Verlautbarung des Sekretariats . . . ," in Henkys, *Bund der Kirchen*, pp. 183–86.

[118]"Entscheidung ueber Kommissionen und Ausschuesse des Bundes," *KJ* 1970, pp. 285–86.

[119]"Konferenz der Kirchenleitung tagte," *KJ* 1970, p. 287.

[120]"Bericht der KKL," *epd Dokumentation*, no. 28 (13 July 1970): p. 7; "Koordinierungsaufgaben fuer den DDR-Kirchenbund," *epd Landesdienst Berlin*, no. 116 (29 September 1970): p. 6.

tion. These discussions predated the founding of the Kirchenbund.[121] However, they took on added relevance with the July 1969 proposal by the VELKDDR for doctrinal discussions with the EKU. The more conservative Lutheran elements, such as Bishops Beste and Mitzenheim, saw dialogue as a means of braking the growth of a super-church on the EKU model, or at least of assuring that the incremental growth of such a church be based on Lutheran theology.[122] More liberal Lutherans viewed it as a means of fostering church unification by eliminating the long-outdated confessional disputes.

The EKU accepted the offer immediately, but for mixed reasons.[123] Some, for example Krusche, sought to eliminate the doctrinal differences. Others, however, for example Fraenkel and Hildebrandt, hoped to use the discussions to prevent the dissolution of the all-German EKU, since the discussions presumed the continued existence and negotiating capacity of the EKU. Their motive was thus similar to the motive for not conceding competence to the Kirchenbund—they would undertake only such actions which would not erode the EKU as an institution, to avoid tampering with its all-German status. Parity between the EKU and VELKDDR in the discussions did not, however, resolve the further question of Western participation. The EKU (East) insisted upon permanent Western representation, which the VELKDDR rejected. They compromised by agreeing to Western participation on an ad hoc basis.[124]

The Kirchenbund responded to the doctrinal discussions with restraint, stressing theological goals of shared communion and pulpit access, but Schoenherr and other Kirchenbund officials clearly saw them as instrumental in building a viable Kirchenbund.[125] Not only was the EKU's all-German status added ballast in the relationship with the state, it inhibited cooperation within the Kirchenbund. In his efforts to remove this obstacle by moving the EKU toward a satisfactory resolution of this inter-German issue, Schoenherr was aided by the VELKDDR's offer to delegate responsibilities to the Kirchenbund and by the doctrinal

---

[121]"Lutheran-Reformed Study Session Set," *LWF Information*, no. 30 (23 July 1968): p. 6; "Lutheran-Reformed Talks See Closer Fellowship," *LWF Information*, no. 18 (14 April 1969): p. 3.
[122]"Bischof Beste: Dienst der Kirche von Belastungen freihalten," *epd Zentralausgabe*, no. 282 (6 December 1968): p. 7.
[123]"Aus dem Bericht Bischof Fraenkels vor der Magdeburger Regionalsynode der EKU," *epd Dokumentation*, no. 23 (8 June 1970): p. 32; EPS documents, 3 October 1969, p. 1.
[124]Ibid.
[125]"Bericht der KKL," *epd Dokumentation*, no. 28 (13 July 1970): p. 8.

discussions proposed by the VELKDDR: they highlighted the contradictions in the EKU's status. Thus it is not surprising that he should praise the Lutheran's "will for community and the mutual trust as expressed by the resolutions of the 1969 Lutheran general synod" and implicitly admonish the EKU by omission.[126]

By late 1970, though the EKU remained all-German, the Kirchenbund had become viable. In its structure and powers, it had effected a certain centralization. Though the scope of its responsibility had been initially limited, it had grown considerably with VELKDDR and, eventually, EKU cooperation in its commission work. The doctrinal discussions offered the potential of a common theological basis for further cooperation. This process of church unification caused the state to take the Kirchenbund seriously and contributed to its reconsideration of its Landeskirchen-based Kirchenpolitik strategy.

The Demise of the Landeskirche-based Kirchenpolitik

The formation of the Kirchenbund and its development over time changed the church structure facing the state and left the state unsettled. Until 1969 its Kirchenpolitik had operated in a relatively decentralized structural context: eight separate and independent Landeskirchen, with very diverse traditions; two confessional church bodies, also with differences of belief and tradition; and the EKD, which in practical terms had ceased to be a negotiating partner for the GDR in 1958. Facing this structure, the state had sought to play one Landeskirche against the other. This was most obvious in the state's use of Thuringia against the other Landeskirchen. But it was also evident to a lesser extent in the state's alternating swings between Mecklenburg and Greifswald. Corollary to this differentiation by Landeskirche was a Kirchenpolitik executed bureaucratically by district councils and their specialists on church questions. Of course, the conception and direction for the painting originated in Berlin; but the brush was wielded by the district officials. Some used broader strokes than others: some districts pursued a milder policy (e.g., Dresden, Erfurt, Frankfurt/Oder, Suhl), others a

---

[126]"Auszuege aus der Berichterstattung des ena," *epd Dokumentation*, no. 41 (17 October 1970): p. 59.

harsher policy (e.g., Rostock, Karl-Marx-Stadt, Leipzig). This district-based implementation of policy enabled the state to vary the Kirchenpo-litik not only *among* Landeskirchen but, in the case of large Landes-kirchen, *within* the Landeskirche (e.g., Saxony-Dresden, in which it differed among Karl-Marx-Stadt, Leipzig, and Dresden).[127]

The state had been satisfied, for the most part, with the results of this approach. Internal deliberations indicate that the SED was convinced that "this orientation on the Landeskirchen has proven itself and led to an increasing differentiation, within and between individual churches. Through this process the progressive forces in the individual churches have been strengthened also." Moreover, certain segments of the state had a vested interest in it: the district-level authorities, for whom it meant more decisional room, however limited, than a centrally imple-mented strategy would allow; and the CDU, which was represented at most district-level meetings with the churches and was particularly identified with the *Mitzenheimpolitik* (the core of the Landeskirche strategy). As much as international and internal church factors, the bureaucratic standard operating procedures of the Landeskirche strat-egy, and the vested interests behind it, were responsible for the initial nonrecognition of the Kirchenbund.[128]

For tactical purposes the state did modify its line somewhat during the formation and approval process of the Kirchenbund in early 1969. Both Seigewasser's February 1969 address and the CDU's contribution to the March 1969 Congress of the National Front avoided a previously standard argument that, in failing to separate from the West German churches, the church leaders lagged behind the parishes in terms of "state consciousness."[129] The state sought to avoid offending church leaders at a time when their approval of the proposed Kirchenbund hung in the balance. In a similar departure, the CDU contribution

[127]For example, conflict over issues such as jazz worship made for a worse church-state relationship in Karl-Marx-Stadt, as described in *Echo der Zeit,* 28 August 1966, and *Der Tagesspiegel,* 22 November 1967.

[128]As early as the first draft of the theses for the twentieth anniversary of the GDR, the CDU registered its opposition to a centralistic super-church, viewing the Landeskirchen as the only legitimate representation of the church parishes. The SED, however, struck this in the final draft. The first draft, written by Heikisch (CDU) sometime in 1968, is found in CDU archives, 13 November 1968. After discussion with Naumann of the Central Committee of the SED on 11 December 1968, Heikisch dropped the attack on a potential super-church. The SED evaluation is found in CDU archives, 18 April 1969.

[129]The main political speech by Professor Jensson, in CDU archives, 21–23 April 1969.

quoted Schoenherr's January 15, 1969, endorsement of Mitzenheim's formula—"State borders build the limits of church organizational possibilities"—but without attributing it to Schoenherr, an obvious attempt to avoid identifying him with Mitzenheim and thereby compromising his credibility in his own Berlin-Brandenburg (East) Synod.

However, despite these tactical bows to the Kirchenbund and its leaders in early 1969, the state retained its Mitzenheimpolitik. Throughout 1969 the state used the Thuringian's "vanguard status" to push for clear separation from the West German churches.[130] In the conception of the SED, it was necessary "that the Thuringian synod retain a special profile and become a vote of confidence in Bishop Mitzenheim. Thereby the criticism against Article 4.4 must be clear, despite the general approval of the draft Basic Order." Gerhard Lotz, the leading legal adviser to Mitzenheim, attempted to sabotage Article 4.4 at the March 1969 meetings of the Eastern Conference. The May 1969 Thuringian synod issued a narrow interpretation of Article 4.4 and removed its mandate to its EKD Synod representatives, in contrast to the transition procedure followed in other Landeskirchen. The Thuringian delegates to the first synod of the Kirchenbund opposed any verbal ties with the EKD, and the November 1969 Thuringian synod removed unilaterally all references to the EKD from its church constitution, forcing the Kirchenbund's hand on this matter, as noted earlier.

Just as early 1969 marked the zenith of Ulbricht's stature, so the National Front congress in March 1969 was probably the high-water mark of the Mitzenheimpolitik. Mitzenheim's speech was quite polemical and extremely supportive of the GDR's foreign policy, condemning the "expansionist efforts of Israel, the sectarian anarchy of China, the revanchist imperialist powers' designs in Europe, and the global policeman USA's repression in Vietnam."[131] Mitzenheim received top billing at the congress both in terms of protocol and substance: he was a member of the congress's presidium and the main address on the Kirchenpolitik repeated Mitzenheim's earlier admonishment to the churches—

---

[130]Regarding Lotz's opposition to Article 4.4, see CDU archives, 11 May 1969. *DA* 3, no. 1 (January 1970): p. 105, indicates the changes in Thuringia's constitution. The SED's conception is found in CDU archives, 18 April 1969.

[131]"Ansprache von Landesbischof D. Dr. Mitzenheim auf dem Kongress der National Front des demokratischen Deutschlands," in Wirth et al., eds., pp. 225–26.

"in structuring their service realize they are churches for the citizens of a socialist state."[132]

The authoritative pronouncement on the Kirchenpolitik by Hermann Matern, member of the SED Politburo, in September 1969 reveals that the state intended to continue this Landeskirche strategy.[133] He referred primarily to the Landeskirchen, "in whose competence the process [of independence from the West German churches] alone lies." He addressed the Kirchenbund only fleetingly and in agitatorial terms. Also his praise of Bishop Beste and the Mecklenburg Landeskirche and his failure to mention the disgraced Bishop Krummacher reveal a continuation of this differentiation strategy.

Similarly, one can see this intent in Seigewasser's major address in August 1969. Unlike Matern, he did refer to the Kirchenbund, but always used the misappellation "*Bund der evangelischen Landeskirchen in der DDR,*" thus again underscoring the Landeskirche element. That the state intended to continue dealing with the churches primarily on the level of the district was clear in Seigewasser's reference to "the positive development of the relations of the evangelical Landeskirchen in the GDR to the state organs, *especially to the councils of the district*" (emphasis added).[134]

But it became more difficult to pursue this strategy as Thuringia became increasingly less inclined to play the game. Even while Mitzenheim was bishop, there were indications of a shift in Thuringia's previously pliant attitude. Despite the propagandistic profile of Mitzenheim at the congress of the National Front in March 1969, he gave an early sign of independence by declining the state's offer of election, along with Lotz, to the National Council of the National Front.[135] In another intimation of a shift, Mitzenheim predicted continued contacts on the Landeskirche-district level, but indicated his support for the Kirchenbund's negotiating role by maintaining that "basic questions which affect all Landeskirchen would be negotiated by the common

---

[132]Nationale Front des demokratischen Deutschland, *Kongress der Nationalen Front des Demokratischen Deutschland, Berlin, 21/22 Maerz 1969, Protokoll* (1969), 1:193.

[133]Matern, pp. 13, 21, 25.

[134]Wirth et al., eds., p. 253.

[135]State approval of Mitzenheim's candidacy for the National Council is indicated in CDU archives, 5 February 1969. Between early February and mid-March, Mitzenheim rejected the offer.

legitimate representatives with the state."[136] The Kirchenbund leadership cleverly helped to erode the special Thuringian relationship with the state by scheduling the visit of WCC officials to East Berlin for early February 1970, thus giving Mitzenheim cause to pass up his traditional participation in the CDU's February festivity.

Part of the erosion in the special Thuringian relationship with the state resulted also from the Thuringian Synod's new assertiveness toward Mitzenheim and his rather authoritarian style. This made itself apparent in the rebellious actions of the spring 1969 Thuringian synod, which in important respects did not run according to the plans of Mitzenheim and Lotz.[137] Although recommending that the first synod of the Kirchenbund consider the narrow interpretation of Article 4.4, the synod took this position *after* rejecting Lotz's proposal to unilaterally place a narrow interpretation on the article. The synod also approved a motion granting female pastors equal status with male pastors, despite the long-standing opposition of Mitzenheim. Finally, in a response to Mitzenheim's increased propaganda supportive of the state, the synod seriously considered a proposal to set guidelines for the bishop's public positions.

Reacting to this criticism from his own Landeskirche, Mitzenheim himself became somewhat more critical of the state. In late 1969, he wrote to Seigewasser complaining about the discrimination against and insults toward Christian children in the school system and threatened to go to Ulbricht if necessary.[138] These problems also occasioned his veiled admonishment in his greetings to the CDU's February 1970 meeting: today it is necessary to put into practice this basic recognition (of constitutionally guaranteed equal rights for Christians) and to let it become the decisive maxim for the solution of individual cases. In the same statement, his justification for supporting international recognition for the GDR—"in order to arrive at new forms of inter-state interaction (*Verkehr*), also with the Federal Republic"—was ambiguous and almost suggestive of increased inter-German contacts, certainly not a hard-line Abgrenzung position.[139] Finally, Thuringia coop-

---

[136]*NZ*, 11 May 1969.
[137]EPS documents, 14 May 1969, pp. 5–7.
[138]CDU archives, 5 December 1969.
[139]"Gruessschreiben von Landesbischof D. Dr. Mitzenheim," *KJ* 1970, p. 208. CDU archives, 23 January 1970; CDU archives, 7 September 1970; CDU archives, 17 September 1970.

erated with Saxony-Magdeburg in a joint church convention, despite state pressure to limit its ties with this more outspokenly critical Landeskirche.

This shift toward a more independent Thuringian line accelerated under Braecklein, Mitzenheim's successor. Even before his election as bishop in May 1970, Braecklein had hewn a different line than Mitzenheim. As senior administrator for theology, he had been overshadowed by Mitzenheim and Lotz in terms of the relationship with the state. However, as Mitzenheim's pace slowed in his later years, Braecklein had effectively carried out the functions of bishop. As a result, his succession as bishop had been a foregone conclusion. With his participation in the building of the Kirchenbund and his defense of the Basic Order (including Article 4.4) at the Thuringian synod of May 1969, the state began to question his desirability as a successor to Mitzenheim and sought to promote the candidacy of Dr. Walter Saft, professor at the Preaching Seminar.[140] However, the state realized that Saft's chances were practically nil in the face of Braecklein's popularity. As a result, the state found itself less able to influence key decisions of the Thuringian Landeskirche.

This independent line became even more clear after Braecklein's election and Lotz's accommodation to the fact. It was manifested most starkly in the shift in Thuringia's stance regarding Article 4.4: in 1969 it advocated a narrow interpretation, in 1970 it gave merely tacit support for the proposals to reexamine Article 4.4. As president of the synod, Braecklein opted for and worked in support of the viability of the Kirchenbund. In his address at his installation as bishop and in his August 1969 interview with *Neue Zeit,* Braecklein revealed that the Thuringia's relationship with the state would be reconsidered. The state saw Braecklein representing a "programmatic line on the order of the rightist SPD conception" and sought, again unsuccessfully, to bring in Saft as Braecklein's successor as senior administrator.[141] Clearly, in 1969 and 1970, Thuringia executed a turn away from its close alignment with the state's Kirchenpolitik and toward inter-church cooperation in the Kirchenbund. This forced the state to reconsider its Landeskirche-based strategy.

---

[140]CDU archives, 3 June 1969; CDU archives, 23 January 1970; CDU archives, 7 September 1970.
[141]CDU archives, 30 June 1970.

Already in 1969, the state revealed a parallel questioning of the previous relationship with Thuringia. For example, Seigewasser's address of August 1969, despite its emphasis on the Landeskirchen and nonrecognition of the Kirchenbund, clearly downplayed Mitzenheim and his "vanguard role" in the Kirchenpolitik.[142] The first draft of this speech praised "especially Thuringia" for "adapting to the reality of socialism"; the final version praised "church circles" for "recognizing the real relationships." Seigewasser praised Mitzenheim's role "that has encouraged his fellow church officials to travel the way of reason and trustful coexistence," wording much more modest than the first draft entailed, in effect placing him on a par with other church leaders. In other passages in which Mitzenheim's special profile would clearly have been the order of the day in earlier addresses, Seigewasser referred only to "church circles."

Matern's September 1969 speech reveals a similar devaluation of Mitzenheim.[143] Mitzenheim's participation in the People's Congress movement remained unmentioned; the Wartburg discussion received very little consideration; Mitzenheim's formula regarding the constitution was ignored. In fact, in the section dealing with the organizational independence of the GDR churches from the West German churches, no mention was made of Thuringia at all, much less a pathbreaking role. The devaluation of Thuringia's profile extended to Braecklein in 1970: the district authorities in Erfurt delayed meeting with the new bishop and the official media implicated him in its 1970 attacks on Article 4.4.[144]

Thus parallel to Thuringia's increasingly independent stance, the state began to distance itself from Thuringia, although it stopped short of embracing the Kirchenbund. Rather than discard its Landeskirche strategy as the new Thuringian line became clear, the state sought to cast Anhalt in the role previously played by Thuringia. The opportunity for this presented itself with the retirement of Church President Mueller in late 1970. The state's relationship with Mueller had been a mixed one. He had sent a scathing letter to Goetting protesting Goetting's attack on the EKD in 1967; yet he had come to support the division and a narrow

---

[142]"Aus dem Referat," in Wirth, *Auf dem Wege der sozialistischen Menschengemeinschaft,* pp. 249–50; CDU archives, 19 August 1969.

[143]Matern, pp. 12–14, 25, 26.

[144]NZ, 25 June 1970; EPS documents, 24 November 1970, pp. 6–7.

interpretation of Article 4.4. In the case of the EKU, he vehemently attacked the Fraenkel position and supported total separation.[145] He publicly endorsed a European security conference, yet spoke in politically subtle terms of an "honorable coexistence—next to each other and toward each other" of both German states. The state had favored him with considerable foreign travel. But his support of closer cooperation with the Landeskirche of Saxony-Magdeburg met with the disfavor of the state, which sought to discourage any contacts with Krusche in particular and with Magdeburg in general.[146] Such contacts and cooperation could lead to the merger of the two churches, a proposal often bandied about in church circles. If realized, such a merger would run counter to the decentralized, Landeskirche-based church structure which the state desired to retain.

Yet Anhalt held promise for the state. Its pastors participated in the local National Front activities at relatively high rates.[147] Pastor Eberhard Natho seemed a promising candidate for succeeding the retiring Mueller as church president. One of the younger generation of church leaders, Natho placed greater emphasis on the churches' role in socialist society. He had publicly endorsed the development of socialism and peace, including the recognition of the GDR and UN membership, and underscored Anhalt's independence, thereby distancing himself from Krusche and Mueller. As a representative in the city legislature in Dessau, he had enjoyed close contacts with the state, particularly with the CDU. In fact, shortly before his selection as new church president, he traveled to the Soviet Union as the guest of the CDU.

The state clearly favored Natho for the church presidency over the other contender, Dr. Gottfried Forck, then head of the Brandenburg Preaching Seminar and later bishop of Berlin-Brandenburg. The state had not found Forck particularly to its liking in Brandenburg. For agitational purposes, however, the state argued that Forck's candidacy was an attempt by Krusche to dominate Anhalt, and it worked behind

[145]"Briefwechsel zwischen dem anhaltischen Kirchenpraesident D. Martin Mueller und dem Vorsitzenden der CDU (Ost), Gerald Goetting," in Henkys, *Bund der Kirchen*, p. 94; NZ, 6 June 1970. CDU archives, 1970, "Einschaetzung der evangelischen Herbstsynoden 1969."

[146]"Kirchliche Neugliederung in Sachsen-Anhalt geplant," *epd Zentralausgabe*, no. 229 (23 November 1970): p. 4.

[147]According to CDU archives, 6 August 1969, 10–15% of all Anhalt pastors and 40–50% of the congregation members participated in these activities, higher than in other Landeskirchen. *ND*, 17 December 1970; CDU archives, 16 October 1970.

the scenes to discredit Forck politically. Although the effect of this campaign should not be minimized, Anhalt's provincialism was probably the more decisive factor, since Forck, unlike Natho, came from outside the Landeskirche. The outsider Forck was defeated and Natho was elected church president by a wide margin.[148]

Despite Anhalt's promise, however, it could not play the role of Thuringia. It was too small and weak financially to be a model for the other Landeskirchen. Moreover, in the context of the Kirchenbund, it was too small to influence policy, or even to buck it effectively. Thus the state realized, perhaps even before starting, that an "Anhalt Way" was not a viable strategic option.

The state continued its differentiation strategy in other Landeskirchen as well. In the northern districts of the GDR, Bishop Beste and Mecklenburg enjoyed the state's attentions during the period of Krummacher's taboo status. However, Krummacher endeared himself to the state again with his support for recognition of the GDR and the Budapest Appeal for a European security conference, as well as for his support for the narrow interpretation of Article 4.4 and separation from the EKU (West).[149] As noted earlier, Krummacher's rehabilitation was reflected in renewed international travel. Like Anhalt, however, Greifswald was too small to fill the shoes of Thuringia, and the state's alternation between these two Landeskirchen in the northern GDR retained only regional significance.

In contrast with these Landeskirchen, the picture in other Landeskirchen was far from rosy from the state's perspective. For example, church-state relations in Goerlitz were particularly acrimonious. Bishop Fraenkel, a veteran of the Kirchenkampf under Hitler, had long offered direct criticism of the state and society in the GDR. To be sure, he did bow to political realities in some instances: he supported forming the Kirchenbund and changing the name of the Landeskirche from revisionist-laden Silesia to Goerlitz—both in the face of strong opposition within his Landeskirche. But on inter-German issues, his positions were strongly at odds with those of the state: he interpreted Article 4.4 in terms of a "corporeal community" and maintained that "the goal of this article is guided by a possible reunification of both parts of Germany."

[148]CDU archives, 26 November 1970.

[149]In spring 1969 at a meeting with state officials, Krummacher endorsed publicly the WTO's Budapest Appeal for a European security conference. See NZ, 3 April 1969. CDU archives, 21 April 1969.

He staunchly held to EKU unity and, hailing the Brandt-Stoph meetings in Erfurt and Kassel, demanded an inter-German dialog "which remains open for new perceptions and new ways." On domestic matters he claimed a watchguard role for the church regardless of constitutional changes and criticized anew the youth dedication ceremony and discrimination against Christians in schools.[150] The state countered by discouraging Fraenkel's participation in joint church conventions and hindering logical contacts between Goerlitz and the Polish Protestant churches.[151]

The relationship between Saxony-Dresden and the state had also been strained for some time. Inter-German issues were particularly problematic here, due to Bishop Noth's membership on the EKD Council. Noth gave up his office only reluctantly. The 1969 Dresden synod approving the Kirchenbund could hardly have supported Article 4.4 more strongly, claiming that "the historical tie of Christians in Germany can no more be dissolved than the bond to Christ." The state's campaign against this resolution was unmatched at any other approval synod that spring.[152] Saxony-Dresden's interpretation of Article 4.4 clearly went beyond Thuringia's and most likely beyond Schoenherr's and Krusche's. The state admonished the Saxon leadership against "half-way measures."[153] On foreign policy matters, the Dresden Landeskirche had also taken controversial positions: Noth sent a pastoral letter following the invasion of Czechoslovakia; a synodal resolution demanded freedom of movement over the borders of the GDR.[154]

On domestic issues the Dresden Landeskirche had been equally as critical. Noth criticized strongly the effective prerequisite of a loyalty pledge to Marxism-Leninism and the state in order to study beyond the tenth grade, calling it a violation of the freedom of belief and conscience anchored in Article 20 of the Constitution. The synod demanded a viable conscientious objector status and affirmed Dresden's adamant condemnation of the youth dedication rite as atheistic and hate-producing.[155] The state responded negatively to this, rebuffing

---

[150]"Aus dem Bericht Bischof Fraenkels vor der Goerlitzer Synode am 4.4.1970," *epd Dokumentation*, no. 23 (8 June 1970): pp. 24, 26; CDU archives, 31 March 1969.

[151]EPS documents, 25 June 1970, p. 3; EPS documents, 21 September 1970, p. 3.

[152]CDU archives, 15–19 March 1969.

[153]CDU archives, 11 April 1969.

[154]EPC archives, 9 November 1968, p. 5.

[155]EPC archives, 1969; EPC archives, 1970; CDU archives, 1970, "Einschaetzung der evangelischen Herbstsynoden 1969."

church efforts to save the University Church in Leipzig from urban renewal in 1968 and prohibiting travel by Noth between 1968 and January 1970.[156]

Although Bishop Fraenkel was the bishop most critical of the state and Bishop Noth the most bitter towards the state, the state found Bishop Krusche of Saxony-Magdeburg the most threatening in the years 1969 to 1971. Although raised in Saxony-Dresden, he had received his theological education in West Germany, returning to the GDR in 1953 in response to a call to counter the shortage of pastors. Despite his Lutheran upbringing, he was strongly influenced by the Barthian call for Christian social engagement characteristic of the Union churches, thus yielding a democratic, immanent critique of socialism.

The Magdeburg Landeskirche had long vocally criticized the state. Dr. Johannes Hamel and EKU Chancellory President Hildebrandt had both criticized the new constitution and strongly opposed separation from the EKD and EKU (West). Bishop Jaenicke, Krusche's predecessor, had had a mixed relationship with the state: he criticized the FRG's Hallstein Doctrine and any EKD equivalent; yet he raised the hackles of the state with his criticism of its treatment of conscientious objectors.[157]

Elected bishop in spring 1968, Krusche was initially rather nonpolitical. He supported the Kirchenbund, but rejected Mitzenheim's legalistic justification in favor of Schoenherr's service-oriented explanation. His interpretation of Article 4.4—opposing a verbal interpretation in favor of a "pragmatic clarification of its meaning"—was not as strong as Fraenkel's or Noth's, but was much broader than that of other church leaders.[158] His position on EKU unity was rather unclear and certainly less-than-optimal as far as the state was concerned.[159]

---

[156]"Leipziger Universitaetskirche gesprengt," *epd Zentralausgabe*, no. 124 (30 May 1968): p. 1.

[157]Hildebrandt is quoted by the CDU: "It is a reality that we stand in a larger community, which has been built between East and West of our fatherland, and whose clear expression is the EKD and EKU. The churches in the EKD have a bridge function between East and West." See CDU archives, 22 March 1968. The Jaenicke-Scharf exchange on the question of the *Alleinvertretungsanspruch* and the churches is described in "Der Wortlaut des Briefwechsels zwischen D. Scharf and D. Jaenicke," *epd Landesdienst Berlin*, no. 35 (16 March 1967): pp. 3–6. Jaenicke's stand on conscientious objector status is revealed in "Zweifel an der Gemeinsamkeiten von Christen und Marxisten . . . ," *epd Zentralausgabe*, no. 68 (21 March 1967): p. 3.

[158]"Erklaerung der Synode . . ." and "Aus dem Bericht von Bischof Dr. Werner Krusche . . . ," in Henkys, *Bund der Kirchen*, pp. 149–50, 175.

[159]"Auszuege aus einem Bericht der Magdeburgischen Kirchenleitung vom 6.11.1970," *epd Dokumentation*, no. 10 (15 February 1971): pp. 4–5.

More thorny, however, was Krusche's stance regarding the domestic issues of contention with the state.[160] Regarding the state's Kirchenpolitik, he maintained "that though one cannot speak of a forceful attack on the church, nonetheless the church increasingly has been pushed out of the public sphere and its work has been constricted." He rejected the claim of exclusive validity of Marxism-Leninism in the educational system, charged that those opting for unarmed service were being used by the state on military projects, and criticized the state's denial of worship space in new urban areas.

In content, this critique varied little from those of Berlin-Brandenburg, Dresden, Gorlitz—and even from certain expressions of Greifswald and the "new Thuringia." What made it a particular anathema to the state was Krusche's political approach and his view of the churches' role in socialism. Krusche's criticisms were not those of a traditional, "reactionary" head of a "bourgeois church," but rather those of a future-oriented bishop, interested in the reform not only of the church but of the society. Although he accepted the socioeconomic basis of socialism, Krusche saw the churches' role in terms of cooperating to improve the "real existing socialism" along the lines of a democratic socialism. For example, he criticized the lack of free elections and argued for greater democratic freedoms.[161]

Such a position—accepting socialism in order to change it—immediately set off alarm bells in the SED, obsessed as it was since August 1968 with eliminating the reformist virus of the Prague Spring and increasingly paranoid of "social democratic tendencies" with the SPD's rise to power in the FRG. The state viewed the Magdeburg Landeskirche as "only giving declarations of loyalty in order to concurrently gain a platform for critical remarks," seeing it as "fixated on the positions of the West German EKD." After April 1969 the state and the CDU broke off discussions with Krusche on the district level and barred him from foreign travel.[162] By refusing logistical support, the state sought unsuccessfully to discourage the cooperation between other Landeskirchen and Magdeburg in the planning of joint church conventions in 1970. The state also sought to curb Krusche's influence with the theological

---

[160]"Bericht von Bischof Krusche . . . ," *KJ* 1969, pp. 167–72.
[161]CDU archives, 15 December 1970.
[162]CDU archives, 3 June 1969; CDU archives, 28 June 1970; CDU archives, 23 December 1969; EPS documents, 5 November 1970, pp. 2–4.

faculty in Halle by recruiting new members from the "progressive" Berlin faculty.

The conflict with Krusche intensified in the fall of 1970 with his pronouncements regarding reconciliation.[163] Krusche described the churches' role in a world of "increasing mutual interdependence" as one of the "service of reconciliation." Qualifying this somewhat, he indicated that "reconciliation does not eliminate the conflicts, but does remove their hostility." This service of reconciliation extended to the Kirchenbund which, after the formative period, "must make its witness concrete," and to individual Christians also. He encouraged Christians to participate in the realization of social goals and in "open discussion of all problems of life." Krusche also expressed criticism of the treatment of Christians in schools and in unarmed military service. But it was his concept of reconciliation and the churches' role in its realization that most rankled the ideological and Abgrenzung-oriented state.

The state wasted no time in responding, lashing out in private discussion and public polemic. In a frontal assault, Carl Ordnung (CDU) labeled Krusche's ideas "examples of convergence theory and social democratism."[164] Ordnung limited reconciliation to the relationship between God and man; peace, in his view, was a question of political reason and insight. Divergence and polarization, rather than global interdependence, was the "essential characteristic of our epoch, valid for the church as well." "Service to peace is today the fight against imperialism, not the reconciliation with it," he maintained. Ordnung's personal attack on Krusche caused a wave of indignation in the churches, leading to an exchange of letters and rebuttals, including an unpublished defense of Krusche by Schoenherr.[165]

The attack on Krusche and "social democratism" in the churches was part of a larger SED campaign emphasizing internal Abgrenzung in the face of the West German Ostpolitik. This included rejecting not only any alleged "social democratic" tendencies, but also so-called "non-

[163]The following discussion quotes from "Auszuege aus einem Bericht . . . ," *epd Dokumentation*, no. 10 (15 February 1971): pp. 1–10.

[164]NZ, 19 December 1970; an acrimonious meeting between Krusche and state representatives is recorded in CDU archives, 15 December 1970.

[165]Schoenherr sent a letter on December 28, 1970, to the editor of *Neue Zeit*, defending Krusche. While the CDU Archive does not contain a copy of this letter, it does possess Ordnung's reply to Schoenherr. Needless to say, *Neue Zeit* did not publish the Schoenherr letter.

scientific, emotional" responses, whether to Brandt and the Moscow Treaty or to the protests of the New Left in the West. Thus, the CDU underscored the primacy of reason and the necessity of planning, arguing that "nothing truly socialist develops spontaneously."[166]

In all three cases—Goerlitz, Saxony-Dresden, and Saxony-Magdeburg—the state faced criticism. In tiny Goerlitz the bark was bigger than the bite. In Saxony-Dresden the state expected the situation to change with a successor to the aging Noth. But in the case of Saxony-Magdeburg, the state faced a young, visionary bishop in a large, important Landeskirche. Despite the eager-yet-inadequate replacement in Anhalt, the straying of Thuringia left the state's Landeskirche-based strategy somewhat wanting in its ability to influence these critical Landeskirchen. In this context the Kirchenbund began to appear ever more attractive.

Moreover, the state was attracted by the potential political influence of the Kirchenbund over the clergy. On numerous issues, the Kirchenbund leadership was more "progressive" than the grass-roots clergy and could be useful in influencing them.[167] Regarding the church conventions in 1970, for example, SED policymakers observed that "one could reach agreement with the officials in the church rather quickly, but that 'second fiddles' often attempted . . . to misuse the church conventions by ignoring the agreements, not even fearing to embarrass church leaders." Moreover, given the low level of clergy participation in political organizations (by the state's own estimate, no more than 15 percent were active in the National Front activities and only about a hundred were elected representatives at some level of government), Schoenherr's relative openness to National Front participation offered the possibility of promoting greater clergy political participation.

Thus these three factors—the reduced possibilities of pursuing its Landeskirche-based differentiation, the rise of problems in certain Landeskirchen (particularly in Magdeburg), and the rather more "progressive" stance of the Kirchenbund—led the state to shift in the direction of

[166]EPC archives, December 1970. Ordnung's views reflected closely SED directives to fight ideas of convergence, revisionism, etc. in CDU archives, 5 November 1970.

[167]The SED observation is found in CDU archives, 5 November 1970. According to CDU archives, 11 August 1969, 60% of the pastors in the GDR showed moderate support mixed with criticism of the GDR and 20% rejected the GDR totally. Fifteen percent "pledge allegiance to the GDR as a socialist Fatherland and prove it with their participation," according to CDU archives, no date, "Zum Beitrag."

a Kirchenbund-based strategy. The first suggestions of this were noted in the state's argument that the continued all-German status of the EKU and Berlin-Brandenburg hindered church unification and burdened the Kirchenbund's relationship with the state.[168] This argument assumed the existence of the Kirchenbund and the desirability of its growth toward an unified church. Thus, it would appear that the state's goal of inter-German Abgrenzung in the church took priority over its desire to retain a decentralized church organizational structure.

Yet the state's policy during this period was contradictory. The state, and the CDU in particular, clearly did not relish the idea of an unified super-church. The state perceived aspects of centralization in the new Kirchenbund: the majoritarian principle in the church leadership procedures, the delegation of competence to the Kirchenbund, the joint EKU-VELKDDR commissions, and the doctrinal discussions. The state sought to counteract this trend, which it felt the Kirchenbund leadership promoted.[169] Typically, the CDU and Pfarrerbund sounded the warnings against centralization more loudly than the state. The head of the Pfarrerbund, for example, charged that the churches were pursuing not "new orientation," but merely new structure, designed to retain their social and political status at the expense of a congregation-based democratization.[170] The inconsistency of the state's position became most obvious in the case of the EKU: the state promoted EKU separation from the West on the basis of church unification, yet sought to retain the EKU as a counterbalance to the Kirchenbund by hailing the positive traditions of the EKU.[171]

Yet, despite its opposition to the centralization of the Kirchenbund and its reluctance to abandon its Landeskirche strategy, the state realized not only that the Kirchenbund was a reality, but that it could be useful in achieving the state's goals of Abgrenzung and domestic politi-

---

[168]"Aus einem Referat Gerald Goettings . . . am 9. Februar 1970 in Leipzig," in Henkys, *Bund der Kirchen*, p. 192; *NZ*, 6 June 1970.

[169]CDU archives, 1970, "Einschaetzung der evangelischen Herbstsynoden," indicates that both Schoenherr and Noth favored overcoming Landeskirche provincialism; CDU archives, 30 June 1970.

[170]*NZ*, 6 December 1969 and 28 June 1970. Already in early 1969 the state registered its displeasure with the prospect of the new Kirchenbund, as indicated in "Neue Struktur," *Glaube und Gewissen* 15 (April 1969): 63.

[171]*NZ*, 23 April, 1 and 26 May 1970. Other observers make this point as well: *Rheinische Post*, 4 May 1970; Reinhard Henkys in a broadcast of the Westdeutscher Rundfunk, 25 April 1970, Evangelical Press Center, West Berlin.

cal stability. Schoenherr and the Kirchenbund had already proved effective in steering the EKU and Berlin-Brandenburg toward greater independence from their Western components.[172] Schoenherr sought to use this stance on the issue of inter-German church ties to build greater credibility with the state for the Kirchenbund and himself. In its ecumenical relations and in its domestic line, the Kirchenbund had proved itself. With the increasing Soviet pressure on the GDR to respond more positively toward the FRG's Ostpolitik, the GDR sought to bargain with the FRG from a stronger position by achieving greater international recognition prior to such negotiations. Abgrenzung and independent participation in international ecumenical organizations by the churches promoted this goal. But the state also hoped to use the Kirchenbund to influence the clergy and the more critical Landeskirchen, especially Saxony-Magdeburg.[173] To this end the state sought to increase the credibility and influence of Schoenherr and the Kirchenbund. Therein lies the motivation for the recognition of the Kirchenbund by the state in February 1971. Measured by the state's standards of domestic and international "new orientation," the Kirchenbund had developed positively and had become more attractive as a means of restraining dissent in the church, whereas a Landeskirche-based strategy was becoming less viable.

[172]An indication of Schoenherr's role is revealed in the advice of his adviser, Stolpe, to the CDU: "Help could be given by the CDU meeting on February 9 if we make clear maximal demands of the EKU and Berlin-Brandenburg, but be ready to accept that only minimal solutions would initially result." CDU archives, 26 January 1970.

[173]Insight into the SED's changing conception is its plan to "achieve a constructive influence on the loyal majority of the church leadership of the Kirchenbund and create the preconditions for normal relations. Through this understanding a stronger isolation of the ever more active rightist forces should concurrently be achieved." CDU archives, 30 June 1970.

6 From Recognition to Limited Rapprochement, 1971–1972

The years 1971 and 1972 were transitional ones in the church-state relationship. For the reasons developed in chapter 5—the international and internal developments in the church, the narrowing prospects for a continued Landeskirche-oriented strategy—the state proceeded to recognize the Kirchenbund in February 1971. It continued to press for Abgrenzung from the West German churches, particularly through its campaign for ideological vigilance in the face of the successful West German Ostpolitik. However, the period saw the state reconcile itself to a less-than-total separation from the West German church ties. The declining conflict associated with this inter-German dimension of the relationship was, however, accompanied by increasing tension over domestic dimensions. As a result, the promise of Ulbricht's overture to the churches in 1971 was not realized in the early period of the Honecker era.

State Recognition of the Kirchenbund, February 1971

The timing of the state's overture toward the Kirchenbund is significant in terms of the analysis of the postwar Kirchenpolitik of the GDR: the transition period of 1971–1972 reveals considerable continuity between Ulbricht and Honecker in their policies toward the church. The overture, timed to coincide with the tenth anniversary of the Ulbricht-Fuchs meeting, had been planned since mid-1970, well before the demise of Ulbricht. Though the policy of rapprochement came to be associated with Honecker, the credit for the initial shift belongs to Ulbricht. Moreover, the assumption of power by Honecker in May 1971 brought no immediate breakthrough in relations with the church.

The state's initiative consisted of two stages: Politburo member Paul Verner and CDU Chairman Gerald Goetting gave major addresses on February 8, 1971, and State Secretary Seigewasser met with the Executive Board of the Kirchenbund on February 24, 1971.[1] The addresses of both Verner and Goetting sounded the typical Ulbrichtian themes of the humanistic concerns linking Christianity to socialism and the need for the churches to support the "all-around strengthening of the GDR."

Not surprisingly, both speakers were preoccupied overwhelmingly with issues related to Abgrenzung. Verner reiterated the state's insistence on a narrow interpretation of Article 4.4 and set the EKD-Kirchenbund relationship on a par with other ecumenical relations. Employing inflammatory language similar to that prior to Fuerstenwalde 1967, Goetting disclaimed "any possible form of 'special community' between the NATO-bound West German and Berlin (West) church leaderships and the independent Landeskirchen in the GDR." Both speakers demanded the complete division of the still all-German EKU and Berlin-Brandenburg. However, Verner devoted considerably more attention to the EKU question than to the Berlin-Brandenburg one, reflecting the state's relative satisfaction with the latter's direction and Schoenherr's role in this process.

The "all-around strengthening of the GDR" also entailed support for key foreign policy positions of the GDR. Thus, Verner lauded church leaders who had endorsed a European security conference, diplomatic recognition, and UN membership for the GDR and called for further such support in ecumenical forums. Despite the inconsistency with his call for Abgrenzung, Goetting urged that GDR church circles, "in ecumenical responsibility," encourage West German Christians and churches to support *Bundestag* ratification of the pending Eastern

---

[1]Verner and Goetting speeches appear in *epd Dokumentation*, no. 14 (15 March 1971): pp. 1–24.

treaties. Apparently some ecumenical relations remained more equal than others.[2]

Directly related to these inter-German and international concerns were fears of internal ideological erosion resulting from the detente with the FRG. Goetting characterized the SPD's Ostpolitik as "imperialistic," "a new version of the Hallstein Doctrine." In a formulation echoing Ulbricht in his attempts to brake the Soviets' moves toward detente, Goetting argued that this SPD policy was designed to "weaken the alliance of the Soviet Union with other states in the socialist community."

This ideological appeal served as the basis for repeated calls for "theological Abgrenzung" from so-called imperialistic theories that relativized the difference between East and West. Conceptions such as "technological society," "post-industrial society," and "pluralistic society" that allegedly deny or mask this contradiction were attacked as "variations of convergence theory." "New orientation" on the part of the churches precluded "standing between the fronts of capitalism and socialism, as well as in 'critical distance' to our state." These attacks were aimed particularly at Bishop Krusche. The rebuff of a "bridge-function" for the churches or "critical distance" vis-à-vis the state was a direct response to Krusche's positions, discussed in chapter 5. Indeed, following the Magdeburg synod at which Krusche articulated these views, the state modified its preliminary conceptions of the February 8 addresses in order to sharpen the attacks on his ideas.[3] Notwithstanding Verner's claim—"unlike the Prussian and fascist experiences, a 'socialization' of the Christian teaching has not, and will not, occur"—the state continued to set limits to the acceptable conceptualization of the church's proper role.

Verner hinted at the possible rewards available to the church from a "good and lasting relationship" with the state, suggesting that it would "make possible the resolution of certain practical issues and serve the ecumenical interests of the GDR churches." Clearly the state conceived the relationship with the Kirchenbund in terms of a tradeoff: in exchange for church support of the GDR in international forums and the churches' self-restraint regarding criticism of GDR domestic policy, the

[2]CDU archives, 15 December 1970.
[3]CDU archives, 8 October 1970; CDU archives, 10 November 1970.

state offered practical concessions, as envisioned in Article 39.2 of the constitution. However, Verner clearly limited the issues subject to resolution. He effectively dismissed the issues of discrimination against Christians in education and career and questions of military service from the agenda for negotiations. In what has since become de rigueur for any church-state agreement, Verner underscored the immutability of the differences in worldview between Marxism and Christianity.

In addition to the substantive significance of these authoritative speeches—"all-around strengthening of the GDR," demands for "theological Abgrenzung," offers of practical agreements—the February overture was designed to represent a tacit recognition of the Kirchenbund. However, the exchange of recognition was marred by the refusal of the church representatives to attend the event following a bureaucratic snafu over the invitations. Early CDU plans had called for a greeting by Schoenherr and participation limited to a few select bishops, thus representing a continuation of the Landeskirche strategy. When the Secretariat of the SED Central Committee decided in December 1970 to make an overture to the Kirchenbund, plans were changed to include the entire Executive Board and all bishops, with the exceptions of Fraenkel and Krusche. This broader invitation was disputed by higher-level officials in the SED Secretariat, however, with the result that the state invited selected bishops and only part of the Executive Board. This move backfired when the invitees exercised solidarity with those excluded and refused to attend.[4] Apparently the state was more interested than the churches themselves in formal recognition of the Kirchenbund, since the state thereupon invited the Executive Board to an official meeting that made official the recognition of the Kirchenbund implied in Verner's address: henceforth the state would deal directly with the duly elected church leadership.

The debate regarding the invitees to the February event points up another significance of the state's overture, namely the demotion of the CDU in the state's planning. The state's desire to increase its influence in the Kirchenbund by recognizing it implied direct church-state negotiations, at the expense of the CDU's role as mediator of the state's policy.

[4]*BS,* 7 March 1971; CDU archives, 10 November 1970; CDU archives, 13 November 1970; CDU archives, 17 December 1970; CDU archives, 11 January 1971; CDU archives, 12 January 1971; CDU archives, 9 February 1971.

Fearing this development, the CDU had already sought unsuccessfully to shore up its position in 1970 by garnering Verner as the main speaker for its February 1970 gala. Gaining Verner in February 1971 represented a Pyrrhic victory for the CDU, however; in a move to entice participation by the Kirchenbund, the state broadened the sponsorship to include the National Front and the state secretary's office, thus effectively diluting the CDU's leading role.[5] The fiasco surrounding the churches' refusal to attend embarrassed the state initially; the Kirchenbund meeting with Seigewasser shifted this embarrassment to the CDU.

The follow-up meetings to the meeting of the Executive Board with Seigewasser also confirm trends in the state's strategy.[6] The CDU's demotion is revealed in the absence of Goetting at the initial meeting with the Executive Board; only after numerous state meetings with the various Landeskirchen did Goetting meet with the Executive Board. The successive meetings in the state's diplomatic initiative confirmed that, despite the overture to the Kirchenbund, it continued to differentiate among the Landeskirchen, in some cases (e.g., Krusche) delegating low-level officials, in others (e.g., Fraenkel, Noth) failing to meet with critical church leaders.[7] Goetting's meeting with Bishop Braecklein suggests the CDU's continued special relationship with Thuringia.

In the Kirchenbund's official response to the Verner/Seigewasser initiative, Schoenherr sought to establish as much common ground with the state as possible, while diplomatically expressing subtle criticism.[8] Thus, he joined with Verner in underscoring the immutable differences in basic philosophy, but expressed the hope that the "Marxist partner could view the actions of Christians as unsuspicious and helpful." Indicating that "the church will oppose all attempts to discriminate against this state," he reiterated the churches' support for international recognition, UN membership for the GDR, and a European security conference. Citing the Kirchenbund's support for the WCC's Program to Combat Racism, he underscored the importance to the churches of

[5]CDU archives, 11 January 1971.

[6]Regarding the meeting with the Executive Board, see *NZ*, 25 and 27 February 1971, and *epd Zentralausgabe*, no. 56 (20 March 1971): p. 6. Regarding the other church-state meetings, see *NZ*, 4, 5, 16, 20, 25, 30, and 31 March 1971 and 29 May 1971.

[7]Neither Bishop Noth nor President Johannes, chief administrator, were present at the Saxony-Dresden meeting, according to *NZ*, 25 February 1971.

[8]The Schoenherr address is found in *epd Dokumentation*, no. 16 (29 March 1971): pp. 43–47.

working ecumenically for "goals which lie in the interests of peace between all peoples and achievement of general human rights."

Schoenherr balanced these positions with subtle criticism. He rejected the total Abgrenzung from the West German churches demanded again by Verner and Goetting, arguing that Article 4.4 was not informed by an all-German political conception. On domestic matters, Schoenherr praised the state's guarantee of freedom of conscience and belief, of equal rights, and of military service without weapons. But he used this praise as a vehicle to criticize the educational and career discrimination against Christians choosing unarmed military service. Viewing the panoply of church life, "from individual evangelization to church conventions," as based on the congregation rather than the church organization, Schoenherr put the state on notice that the church would not be reduced to mere ritual, as apparently desired by the state.

Despite his criticism Schoenherr interpreted the state's overture as the "arrival of a new stage" in the church-state relationship, one in which "problems which affect all eight churches in common will be discussed directly between the central state organs and those of the Kirchenbund," a view that the synod of the Kirchenbund affirmed.[9] In allowing the text of the somewhat critical Schoenherr address to be publicized by the East German Evangelical Press Agency, the state seemed to confirm that it was serious about negotiations and a new relationship with the church.

The reactions of other church leaders to the state's overture were varied, some more acclamatory than Schoenherr, some more critical. On the one hand, leaders that tilted toward the regime, such as Krummacher and Natho, used their meetings with state officials to underscore the "change in consciousness" in the relationship and to endorse GDR foreign policy positions on such issues as the Vietnam War and a European security conference.[10]

On the other hand, others were more critical of the state in their meetings with officials. For example, further demonstrating the new stance of Thuringia, Bishop Braecklein demanded "equal chances for

[9]"Bericht der KKL . . . ," *epd Dokumentation*, no. 34 (19 July 1971): pp. 4 and 15 regarding the Events Ordinance, p. 17 regarding problems in education, and "Beschluss der Synode . . . ," p. 19.

[10]NZ, 5 March 1971; *Evangelische Nachrichtendienst* 24 (10 March 1971): 11; NZ, 19 May 1971.

Christians in education, occupation, and advancement possibilities"
and "equal worth in the responsibility and cooperation in the state and
public life with other citizens."[11] Moreover, in a reference to state
reluctance to provide support services for church retreats and church
congresses, he demanded "equal priority with other users of the needs of
public life."

The outsiders in the state's Kirchenpolitik, such as Bishops Krusche
and Fraenkel, were predictably the least sanguine. At its meeting with
the state, the Magdeburg Church Leadership rejected Verner's demand
for "the all-around strengthening of the GDR" and scored his demand
for partisanship as a "socializing" of the church's important social
responsibility.[12] Proclaiming the church's independence of class struggle, the church leaders rejected the state's demonization of the West and
urged that the GDR be more forthcoming toward Brandt's Ostpolitik.
They rejected a statement supporting European security and recognition of the GDR, deferring to Schoenherr's statements in this regard.
The acrimonious character of the meeting and the church's displeasure
with the CDU's recent polemic against Krusche led the Magdeburg
Church Leadership to refuse even a perfunctory statement in the official
state media regarding the meeting. Fraenkel too was critical of the
state's initiative, emphasizing the ideological differences in the relationship more than Magdeburg.[13]

Despite the strong declaratory positions taken by Verner and Schoenherr, both sides expressed an interest in negotiating agreements and
these were expected imminently. To be sure, the bargaining positions
seemed far apart. The state desired unconditional support of socialism, internationally and domestically, and greater control of "deviant"
church leaders and church activities such as youth work, theological
schools, and student work. Speaking for the Kirchenbund, Schoenherr
desired state recognition of the churches' social presence (namely, an
end to attempts to restrict them to purely cultic status) and of the
churches' right to represent their members in problems with the state
(namely, an end to discrimination against Christians).[14]

---

[11]The Braecklein meeting is discussed in "Gleiche Chancen fuer Christen in der DDR
gefoerdert," *epd Zentralausgabe*, no. 56 (20 March 1971): p. 6.
[12]CDU archives, 29 March 1971.
[13]*KJ* 1971, pp. 250–53; *SDZ*, 20 April 1971.
[14]"Gegen Diskriminierung der DDR, fuer Gleichberechtigung der Christen," *epd Landesdienst Berlin*, no. 41 (25 March 1971): p. 4.

Despite the high expectations that the recognition of the Kirchenbund would lead to pragmatic negotiations, the concrete results were meager for the churches. First, the state did make changes in its media policy that reflected increased attention to the Kirchenbund. Responding to longstanding requests of the Kirchenbund, the state in June 1971 granted it a publication license for an official information bulletin, the *Mitteilungsblatt der Bund der Evangelischen Kirchen in der DDR.*[15] The state also merged its two official agitational publications, the *Evangelisches Pfarrerblatt* and *Glauben und Gewissen,* into one new journal, *Standpunkt,* that was designed to focus on the Kirchenbund and compete more effectively with the churches' journal, *Die Zeichen der Zeit.*[16]

Second, the state permitted further ecumenical activity by the Kirchenbund. In June 1971, the state approved hard currency allocations to the Kirchenbund to cover its contributions to the WCC and LWF ($25,000 each).[17] Ecumenical contacts were fostered, such as the first-time visit by the entire Executive Board to Geneva in March 1972 and short-term work assignments in Geneva by GDR church officials.[18] Even Bishop Krusche, though politically in jeopardy, was permitted to travel on ecumenical business.[19]

The state's concessions, though not inconsequential, were narrow in focus. The approval of the *Mitteilungsblatt* was designed to increase the credibility of the Kirchenbund, both at home and abroad. The increased ecumenical contacts were designed, in large part, for foreign consumption. Both moves benefited the church elite, particularly the Kirchenbund leadership in Berlin. The possibilities for negotiations and agreements on broader issues of mutual interest, as provided in the 1968 constitution and promised by the state in its February initiative, remained unexplored in 1971 and 1972. Schoenherr expressed the disappointment of the churches with this situation in his report to the July 1971 synod of the Kirchenbund.

[15]"Bericht der KKL," *epd Dokumentation,* no. 34 (19 July 1971): p. 7; CDU archives, 30 June 1971.
[16]CDU archives, 23 July 1971; EPS documents, 25 June 1970, p. 5.
[17]"Bericht der KKL . . . ," *epd Dokumentation,* no. 34 (19 July 1971): p. 9; CDU archives, 30 June 1971; EPS documents, 16 July 1971, p. 2.
[18]"DDR Kirchenvertreter zu Tagungen des LWB in Genf," *Evangelische Nachrichtendienst* 24 (21 April 1971): 3; "Bericht der KKL . . . ," *epd Dokumentation,* no. 25 (12 June 1973): p. 16; "International Seminar opens in Strasbourg," *LWF Information,* no. 42 (15 September 1971): p. 3.
[19]"Anfaenge einer 'Theologie in sechs Kontinenten,'" *Evangelische Nachrichtendienst* 24 (8 September 1971): 9–10.

There are several reasons for the state's failure to carry through on its initial offer to negotiate, some related to the Honecker succession, others related to the tactics and longer-term strategy of the regime.

The most important reason for the postponement of the rapprochement with the Kirchenbund was the replacement of Ulbricht as first secretary of the SED by Honecker in May 1971. This succession was dictated by the Soviets and resulted largely from Ulbricht's intransigence on the issue of Ostpolitik.[20] Indications of the pending fall of Ulbricht can even be found in Verner's speech, namely the relative absence of references to "socialist human community," Ulbricht's pet slogan.[21] The resolution of the succession resulted in greater GDR receptiveness to the Ostpolitik under Honecker. However, in other policy areas, including the church policy, the succession resulted in inertia and mixed signals.

At the Eighth SED Party Congress in May 1971, Honecker's silence on the Kirchenpolitik and the absence of references to the "common humanistic responsibility of Marxists and Christians" portended a lower priority for the Kirchenpolitik in general. To compensate for the increased exposure to the West that Ostpolitik entailed, Honecker generally increased the emphasis on ideological vigilance: the leading role of the working class (not simply its party); the new conception of the nation as the "socialist nation," as opposed to the earlier formulation of the "socialist state of the German nation"; and the development of "socialist personality" based on "socialist consciousness," rather than less-ideological "socialist state consciousness." This heightened emphasis on ideology by Honecker may have been motivated by fear of ideological infection and a desire to distinguish himself from Ulbricht, but it had negative effects on individual Christians and the churches.[22] Not surprisingly it resulted in a freeze on rapprochement with the

---

[20]A. James McAdams, *East Germany and Detente* (1985), pp. 110–15; Griffith, pp. 200–206.

[21]Paul Verner, "Vereint auf dem guten Weg des Friedens und Sozialismus," *epd Dokumentation*, no. 14 (15 March 1971): pp. 2–13.

[22]Analyses of the impact of the Eighth Party Congress of the SED on the Kirchenpolitik can be found in Reinhard Henkys, "Bedeutsame Schweigen," *epd Zentralausgabe*, no. 123 (28 June 1971); Erwin Wilkins, "Die Kirchen in der Deutschen Demokratischen Republik," *KJ* 1971, p. 228; Reinhard Henkys, "Kapitalistisches Ueberbleibsel: Kirchenpolitik nach dem letzten SED-Parteitag," *Evangelisches Kommentar* 5 (April 1971): 215–18. The new approach to the national question was codified in the revision of the GDR constitution in 1974, in which all references to Germany and the German nation were dropped. See "Nationalfrage," Federal Ministry for Inner-German Affairs, *DDR-Handbuch*, p. 1118.

Kirchenbund and, in fact, increased attempts to control the danger of ideological contamination that the church posed.

Even in the absence of a succession in May 1971, however, the long-term strategy of the state precluded a major rapprochement with the church. The initiative of February 1971 did not represent a change in the state's long-term goal of reducing the churches to mere ritual on a par with the churches in most Soviet bloc states.[23] As Schoenherr noted, this goal clashed with the churches' own self-conception. Negotiations with the church would certainly raise issues affecting this goal; official recognition of the churches' role in society would publicly contradict it. Willing to tolerate the contradiction privately, but not to legitimize it publicly, the state sought to avoid definitive negotiation of the issues.

Another reason for the reluctance to negotiate was differences in organizational interests that the SED leadership tolerated. The Kirchenpolitik, while officially the bailiwick of the state secretary for church questions and the corresponding bureau in the SED Central Committee Secretariat, is affected by other bureaucracies as well. These bureaucracies include the Ministry of Education, the Ministry of Technical and Higher Education, the Ministry of the Interior, and the National People's Army. These bureaucracies may not only resist a new policy of rapprochement, but may pursue policies counter to such rapprochement. There seems little doubt, especially in the context of intensifying ideological Abgrenzung, that these bureaucracies were more hard-line than the State Secretary's Office. Yet, since democratic centralism subjected them to the SED Politburo and Secretariat, this inconsistent pattern across bureaucracies did not stem from random bureaucratic differences, but rather from either conscious design by the SED leadership or the inability of the leadership to reach a consensus. Given the nature of the succession—dictated by the Soviets and rooted in foreign policy differences—the former is more likely to have been the case.

Finally, the state had tactical reasons to limit the rapprochement with the churches. It lay in the state's interest to prolong this process in order to gain as much leverage as possible over the churches.

To focus solely on the impact of the Honecker succession would be to exaggerate its importance in the Kirchenpolitik. In the short term, the previous sources of tension did not disappear and the concessions to the

---

[23]Daehn, p. 106.

churches remained meager. Indeed, the state conceptualized its spring 1971 opening to the Kirchenbund as a means of ameliorating these sources of tension by dampening criticism from the churches.

ABGRENZUNG IN THE CONTEXT OF THE OSTPOLITIK

Although it remained at the top of the church-state agenda, the issue of the East German churches' ties to the West German churches declined as a source of tension during 1971 and 1972. Even as the GDR church organizations moved to defuse the issue in various ways, Abgrenzung from the West German churches became less urgent for the state. With the increased receptiveness of Honecker to the Ostpolitik, the GDR no longer found it propitious to continue its polemic against remaining inter-German church ties. Indeed, given East German church activity on the issue of peace, the state found such ties generally useful in promoting West German approval of the Eastern treaties.

In the case of the Kirchenbund, the moderation in the official demands for Abgrenzung was signaled only indirectly. Prior to the July 1971 synod of the Kirchenbund, the CDU and the Pfarrerbund again proposed a reformulation of Article 4.4, which, if approved, would have replaced the "special community of Evangelical Christianity in Germany" with the "spiritual community of world Christianity."[24]

The state, however, brought considerably less enthusiasm to this enterprise than the CDU and the Pfarrerbund. The routine National Front meeting prior to the synod addressed primarily the domestic role of the churches and Christians; only one speech specifically touted Abgrenzung from the EKD.[25] The absence of any pronouncements by Seigewasser and any official efforts to lobby individual synod members on behalf of the CDU's proposal further indicated the state's softer line on Article 4.4.[26] Again, the harsh polemic of the CDU and related organizations allowed the state to assume a moderate posture for tactical purposes. It was more interested in a consolidation of the Kirchenbund synod behind Schoenherr's February stand, a development which

[24]*NZ*, 26 June 1971.
[25]*NZ*, 1 July 1971.
[26]EPS documents, 16 July 1971.

might have been undermined by continued intense polemic on Article 4.4.

The synod ignored the CDU's proposed alteration of Article 4.4 but continued to distance itself diplomatically from the EKD. In the church leadership's report to the synod, relations with the West German churches were discussed only briefly, primarily in terms of either spiritual matters or political issues, such as the Program to Combat Racism, on which the Kirchenbund disagreed with the EKD.[27] On the symbolic level, for the first time the Kirchenbund synod did not exchange greetings with the EKD synod.[28] The now-famous phrase coined by Schoenherr at the synod—"church within socialism, not separated from it, nor in opposition to it"—implied at a minimum an orientation on the GDR as the environment of the churches.

Likewise, the Kirchenbund's increasingly independent profile on the level of ecumenical relations contributed to building an identity separate from the EKD. In January 1971 the independent membership of the GDR churches under Kirchenbund jurisdiction was finalized.[29] The Kirchenbund also reinforced its divergence from the EKD on the issue of the Antiracism Program by raising large sums for the program, sending the head of the churches' relief organization to Tanzania to meet with members of Frelimo, the liberation movement in Mozambique, and commissioning documents and materials to increase understanding in the churches.[30] By referring to "intense discussions in the West German churches" and citing West German support for Portuguese colonial regimes, the Kirchenbund also nurtured the state's interpretation of the Kirchenbund's action.[31]

At the same time the Kirchenbund moved to increase its bilateral ties with churches in both West and East. The exchanges with the British Council of Churches (November 1970), the Swiss Federation of Evan-

---

[27]"Bericht der KKL . . . ," *epd Dokumentation*, no. 34 (19 July 1971): p. 9.

[28]The 1972 report of the Conference of Church Leaderships devoted even less attention to relations with the West German churches. See "Bericht der KKL . . . ," *epd Dokumentation*, no. 30 (17 July 1972): p. 31.

[29]*FAZ*, 18 and 22 January 1971; "Tagung des Oekumenischen Zentralausschusses beendet," *Evangelischer Nachrichtendienst* 24 (27 January 1971): 1.

[30]"Wortlaut des Schreibens . . . ," *epd Dokumentation*, no. 10 (15 February 1971): p. 20; "West German Synod Backs WCC on Race," *LWF Information*, no. 10 (March 1971): pp. 5–6; "Bericht der KKL . . . ," *epd Dokumentation*, no. 34 (19 July 1971): p. 11.

[31]"Berichte in Addis Abeba," *Evangelischer Nachrichtendienst* 24 (3 February 1971): 11–13; *NZ*, 9 June 1971.

gelical Churches (March 1972), and the French Federation of Protestant Churches (October 1972) showed the Kirchenbund's determination to maintain contacts with Western churches in the face of the attenuation of ties with the EKD.[32] At the same time, the Kirchenbund shrewdly sought to develop ties to churches in the socialist bloc. In addition to the continuing exchange with the Polish Ecumenical Council, new contacts with the Bulgarian Orthodox Church and the Russian Orthodox Church were undertaken. In the context of Honecker's increased emphasis on socialist integration and unbreakable alliance with the Soviet Union, these contacts redounded to the churches' credit with the state.

The state realized these auspicious actions by the Kirchenbund belied the fact that Abgrenzung was rejected in certain Landeskirchen and by the vast majority of the clergy.[33] Bishop Krusche, for example, practiced "special relations" by meeting with leaders of the West German Landeskirche Hesse-Nassau, a meeting the state denounced as "illegal."[34] Bishop Fraenkel reminded the GDR of the existence of one German nation, despite its division into two states.[35] Even Bishop Krummacher rejected Abgrenzung, asserting that "Jesus is not the God of only the socialist world."[36]

This failure of "socialist state consciousness" notwithstanding, the state reduced its Abgrenzung rhetoric vis-à-vis the Kirchenbund after mid-1971, coincident with GDR acquiescence to Soviet negotiation on the Berlin question.[37] The reporting of the July 1971 synod dramatically reflected this shift.[38] Initially the CDU organ *Neue Zeit* highlighted the steps toward Abgrenzung supposedly taken by the Kirchenbund and charged West German and West Berlin church leaders with

---

[32]Based on reports of the Conference of Church Leaderships to the synod in 1971, in *epd Dokumentation*, no. 34 (19 July 1971): pp. 11–12, and 1972, in *epd Dokumentation*, no. 30 (17 July 1972): pp. 30–31.

[33]A CDU study of pastors in 13 *Bezirke* found that only 27% supported *Abgrenzung;* the remainder rejected it completely or in part. See CDU archives, 1 November 1971.

[34]CDU archives, 3 August 1971; CDU archives, 14 June 1971.

[35]"Fraenkel fuer gemeinsames kirchliches Votum zur Sicherheitskonferenz," *epd Zentralausgabe,* no. 77 (21 April 1971): p. 4.

[36]Reinhard Henkys, "Zehn Jahre nach dem Ulbricht-Fuchs-Gespraech," *epd Zentralausgabe,* no. 27 (8 February 1971): p. 6.

[37]Griffith, pp. 184, 200–209; F. Stephen Larrabee, "The Politics of Reconciliation: Soviet Policy towards West Germany, 1964–1972" (Ph.D. diss., Columbia University, 1978), pp. 248–310.

[38]NZ, 10 and 21 July and 7 August 1971; Sepp Schelz, "Loyal, aber doch kritisch! Der Ertrag von Eisenach," *Lutherisches Monatsheft* 10 (August 1971): 377.

seeking to force an "opposition role" on the GDR churches. However, the SED upbraided the CDU for its overzealous reporting, and a later analysis in *Neue Zeit* concentrated on praising the Bishop Rathke's endorsement of social engagement during the synod, leaving Abgrenzung pointedly unmentioned.

Nineteen seventy-two saw a further reduction in the state's efforts toward Abgrenzung by the Kirchenbund. With the travel agreements between the FRG and the GDR in late 1971, it became difficult to hinder unofficial contacts, and they flourished. But the state gradually loosened restraints on official contacts with West German church leaders in this period. For the first time, an official representative of the EKD, albeit the pro-Ostpolitik Bishop Heintze, was permitted to attend a Kirchenbund synod in July 1972. In contrast to its earlier polemics against such meetings, the GDR media left the EKD's October 1972 synod in West Berlin relatively unscathed.[39]

The treatment of the EKU demonstrated how dramatic the shift in the state's policy on continuing inter-German church ties was by 1972. Throughout 1971 the state, in Verner's authoritative address and private discussions with the churches, continued to press the EKU for division in the EKU and hampered EKU participation in ecumenical activities and all-German EKU Council meetings.[40] Prior to the 1972 synod of the EKU, the Weissensee Study Group and *Neue Zeit* again called for separation, invoking familiar arguments: the examples of the VELKDDR and in particular Berlin-Brandenburg (East), which had just voted to create a separate bishop's office; the potential ecumenical profile of the EKU; and the burden of the all-German EKU on the process of church unification in the GDR.[41]

But the 1972 campaign was markedly milder than that at the last EKU Synod in 1970, indicating the shift in the position of both the state

[39]*NZ*, 18 February 1971. This article accused the EKD of political motives in meeting in West Berlin, thereby seeking to pressure the Berlin-Brandenburg (East) Landeskirche toward separation from the West Berlin region. Compare with *NZ*, 19 October 1972. In CDU archives, 18 October 1972, the *Neue Zeit* polemicist, Eberhard Klages, indicated that he toned his article down to a minimal criticism of the West Berlin location of the EKD synod and its "anachronistic" title, with the approval of SED Secretariat staff member, Kurt Huettner.

[40]"Bericht des EKU-Ratsvorsitzenden Bischof . . . ," *epd Dokumentation*, no. 20 (15 May 1972): p. 13. CDU archives, 14 April 1971; CDU archives, 25 May 1971; EPS documents, 19 February 1971, pp. 1–2; EPS documents, 19 February 1971, p. 2; *FAZ*, 21 April 1972.

[41]*NZ*, 22 January and 21 April 1972; "Weissenseer Arbeitskreis zur EKU Synode," *Evangelische Nachrichtendienst* 25 (12 April 1972): 5–6.

and the EKU on the issue. The state ceased to employ its traditional forums—the February CDU event and attacks by Seigewasser—to articulate its demands on the churches. Moreover, realizing that the hardline "progressive" forces led by Hanfried Mueller had become polarizing and lacked credibility, the state shifted its support to the more credible efforts of moderate forces in the synod. Finally, the state modified its 1970 rhetoric, dropping the idea of a "specific EKU tradition" and the charges that the EKU (West) was historically "unprogressive" and tied to Bonn's all-German conception.

The EKU also acted to defuse the issue by undertaking measures of separation beyond those envisioned by the EKU hierarchy in 1970, a result of the retirement of strong proponents of unity and the shift in opinion in the synod.[42] The choice facing the synod in 1972 turned on the issue of regionalizing the EKU Council. Reflecting the influence of prominent church leaders supporting unity, the regionalization committee recommended the regionalization of the synod, but retention of a unified council, essentially Bishop Fraenkel's position in 1970.[43] Moderates proposed retaining formal unity of the EKU, but regionalization of all institutions, including the council. The Kirchenbund Secretariat and leadership clearly lined up in favor of the proposal for more extensive regionalization.[44] The key to the decisive victory of the more extensive regionalization proposal, however, was the tactical shift by Fraenkel, chairman of the EKU Council. In marked contrast to his opposition in 1970, Fraenkel supported regionalization in his report to the 1972 synod, now agreeing with the "wish of the state that those who are responsible for the leadership of a church also be members of this state."[45]

Despite the more extensive regionalization that resulted in 1972, the EKU Synod's actions represented only a partial separation from the Western region, making it much less autonomous than the Kirchen-

[42]"Neuer Praesident der EKU-Kanzlei in Ost-Berlin," *epd Zentralausgabe* (24 January 1972).

[43]This committee was set up by the 1970 EKU-East regional synod to review the EKU's inter-German structure. Though predominantly composed of GDR citizens, it included four representatives delegated by the 1970 EKU-West regional synod. *Potsdamer Kirche*, 14 May 1972.

[44]Eberhard Klages, "Organtrennung und Divergenz," *Evangelisches Pfarrerblatt*, no. 6 (June 1972): p. 165; CDU archives, 9 May 1972.

[45]The following discussion of Fraenkel's report is based on "Bericht des EKU . . . ," *epd Dokumentation*, no. 20 (15 May 1972).

bund.[46] In terms more strongly inter-German than Article 4.4 of the Kirchenbund, the EKU spoke of the *"brotherly* community" in the EKU (emphasis added), mandating the regionalized councils to pursue "common deliberations." Such consultations on a wide-range of subjects began almost immediately and constituted a de facto continuation of the unity of the EKU council. The inclusion of this clause, as well as the influence of Fraenkel, led the EKU (West) to support regionalization, after having strongly opposed such action earlier.

This less-than-total separation would have evoked condemnation from the state even a few months earlier. But the official response to the synod was remarkably positive, particularly when compared with the response to Article 4.4 in 1969.[47] The state heralded the new regionalization as the "organizational-legal independence of the EKU leadership organs" and interpreted the obligation for consultation as an "exchange of opinions, as on the ecumenical level between churches of similar confession, not as a binding voice in the other region's affairs." The state conferred legitimacy on the regionalized EKU by meeting with its new president and even facilitated the visits of West German EKU leaders who favored the Eastern treaties.[48]

In the case of Berlin-Brandenburg, the state also reduced its Abgrenzung demands and settled for a second-best solution to the inter-German question. Despite the earlier movement toward regionalization, reaching an acceptable resolution in Berlin-Brandenburg proved more difficult than with the EKU.

Several factors introduced new uncertainties in this process. Opposition to regionalization remained strong in the Eastern Regional Synod, particularly over the sensitive issue of a dual bishopric. The synod's Guidelines Committee had reached a consensus in favor of separate

---

[46]The EKU resolutions are found in ibid., p. 2. For a review of the resolutions and the ensuing inter-regional cooperation see "Der Weg der Evangelischen Kirche der Union," *epd Dokumentation*, no. 29 (18 June 1974): pp. 46–51. Daehn, pp. 104–5, ignores these important components of the Magdeburg resolutions.

[47]NZ, 25 and 29 April 1972; Eberhard Klages, "Organtrennung und Divergenz," *Evangelisches Pfarrerblatt*, no. 6 (June 1972): p. 165.

[48]Based on discussion with Senior Administrators Groscurth and Heidungsfeld (EKU-West Chancellory), 23 January 1979. For example, the state granted visas for the EKU-East Synod to Synod President Wilm (EKU-West) and Synod President Immer (Rhineland Landeskirche), both supporters of the treaties. In contrast, it rejected a visa for a VELKD guest at the fall 1972 VELKDDR synod. "EKU and Kirchenbund verabschiedet Bischof Krummacher," *epd Landesdienst Berlin*, no. 68 (14 June 1972): p. 1; "Closer Ties Urged among DDR Churches," *LWF Information*, no. 44 (3 November 1972): p. 6.

bishops, but disagreement remained over whether this should be timed to coincide with Scharf's retirement in 1972. Second, a change in the bishop's office required the approval of the West Berlin Regional Synod, which might reject a second bishop for theological or political reasons. Third, the Verner/Seigewasser overture led some to anticipate a reprieve from the state's drive for organizational Abgrenzung in Berlin-Brandenburg. Finally, both regional synods expected to benefit from the East-West negotiations over the German question, in particular the advent and conclusion of Four Power talks on the status of Berlin. Anticipating access to East Berlin for Bishop Scharf, some rejected a second bishop or hoped to delay a decision.[49]

Complicating the situation still more were Schoenherr's dual roles—head of the Kirchenbund as well as Berlin-Brandenburg (East)—which affected deliberations in contradictory ways. On the one hand, the synod came under increasing pressure to eliminate the gap between Schoenherr's nominal rank as "bishop's administrator" and his actual responsibilities as leading spokesman for the GDR churches. The increase in his stature following the state's recognition of the Kirchenbund heightened this embarrassment. Moreover, Berlin-Brandenburg (East) doubtless found it painful to be accused of hindering the development of the Kirchenbund by maintaining its links with West Berlin. On the other hand, the state found itself with less leverage on the issue as a result of its developing Kirchenbund strategy and Schoenherr's key role in it. Schoenherr's correspondingly greater leverage led the state to accept a compromise in order to avoid risking total defeat on the Berlin-Brandenburg issue, and thereby Schoenherr's demise.

As in the case of the EKU, the state continued to press the Berlin-Brandenburg church for separation in 1971, moving to squelch the rising expectations in the wake of the February 1971 initiative and the breakthroughs in the Ostpolitik.[50] Seigewasser warned colorfully that "so much china had been smashed in Berlin-Brandenburg in the last twenty years, that it is no longer justifiable." *Neue Zeit* blamed Scharf for striking the language in a CEC resolution calling for the normalization of the status of "Westberlin," arguing that the Eastern region was being misrepresented in ecumenical organizations.

The May 1971 Eastern regional synod approved the recommenda-

[49]CDU archives, 14 April 1971.
[50]CDU archives, 14 April 1971; NZ, 7 and 8 May 1971.

tions of the Guidelines Committee set up at the 1970 regional synod.[51] These called for changes in the constitution of the Landeskirche at the 1972 synod and election of a separate bishops in 1973, after the retirement of Scharf. The synod also approved its recommendation to change the constitution to limit membership of the Eastern region to the Kirchenbund only. The synod rejected the proposals of "progressives" to delimit the Landeskirche to only the GDR parishes, as well as the proposals of "conservatives" to delay the election of a second bishop. However, the West Berlin church and the broader political context threatened to derail the timetable of the Eastern region. The West Berlin synod delayed taking legally binding action until 1972.[52] More importantly, the signing of the Four Power Agreement on Berlin on September 3, 1971, threatened to stall or reverse the trend toward separation. In November, for example, Bishop Scharf expressed hopes that the agreement would yield ecumenical possibilities for West Berlin. The GDR interpreted this as hesitation on the issue of separation.[53] Schoenherr sought to reassure the state that the Four Power Agreement would not affect the move toward two bishops.[54]

In this context, the state moderated its policies in late 1971 in an attempt to shore up Schoenherr's embattled position and strengthen the Eastern region's resolve.[55] The state finally granted him a residence permit for East Berlin, dropping its earlier precondition that he be elevated to bishop first. The media refrained from hard-line demands prior to the 1972 synod and the state muzzled the "progressives" who had been demanding the promulgation of a new constitution for the Eastern region. In order not to harm Schoenherr's chances for election to the new bishopric, the official media avoided positive statements regarding him. The moderated official line paid off. The March 1972 Eastern regional synod followed the agreed-upon timetable, voting to

---

[51]"Die Tagung der Berlin-Brandenburg Synode," *Evangelischer Nachrichtendienst* 24 (19 May 1971): 4–5.

[52]*KJ* 1971, pp. 333, 335–39.

[53]"D. Scharf setzt Hoffnung auf Berlin Verhandlung," *epd Landesdienst Berlin*, no. 141 (20 November 1971): p. 2; CDU archives, 1971, "Einschaetzung."

[54]CDU archives, 3 November 1971.

[55]"Bericht der KKL . . . ," *epd Dokumentation*, no. 30 (17 July 1972): p. 32. *NZ*, 21 March 1972 reported merely the expectations of district-level CDU meetings that the Berlin-Brandenburg synod "would solve the bishop question in agreement with realities." Other examples of the media polemic included *NZ*, 24 March 1972, and "Termintreue," *Evangelisches Pfarrerblatt*, no. 3 (March 1972): p. 81. CDU archives, 20 October 1972; *NZ*, 31 October 1972.

change the church law to create a separate bishop's office, but making this decision contingent upon the approval of the Western regional synod.[56]

Despite the fact that the West Berlin church hierarchy, including Scharf, supported the two-bishop solution, the Western synod refused to have its hand forced.[57] In cooperation with the defeated "conservatives" in the Eastern regional synod, a significant group in the Western synod sought to use the improved East-West political climate to delay the election of a second bishop. The synod thus voted to respect the decision to establish an Eastern regional bishop, but, falling one vote short of the two-thirds necessary, denied passage of the church law concerning election procedures. Thus the synod refused to limit Scharf's jurisdiction. By calling the Eastern synod's bluff, the Western region confronted it with unpalatable alternatives: electing a bishop without prior approval by the Western region, thereby endangering the unity of the Landeskirche; or deferring the election, thereby incurring the state's wrath.

The Eastern synod, in turn, called the Western synod's bluff by proceeding with the election of its own bishop at the November 1972 synod. The church leadership sought to garner support from the "conservatives" for the election of a second bishop by seeking unsuccessfully to recruit one as a candidate for bishop.[58] Schoenherr also obtained the endorsement of Fraenkel and did not spare the state criticism on issues of discrimination of Christians. Despite this attempt to build a consensus, Schoenherr barely squeaked through to victory on the third ballot. Approximately one-third of the synod abstained on all three ballots; in fact only through the erosion of support for the alternate straw candidates did Schoenherr obtain the two-thirds majority necessary. By stressing the continuing unity of the Landeskirche in his acceptance speech and making his assumption of office contingent upon the approval of the Western regional synod, Schoenherr sought to mollify

[56]"Kirchengesetz ueber das Bischofsamt . . ." and "Kirchengesetz zur 11. Aenderung der Grundordnung . . ." in *Mitteilungsblatt* . . . , no. 4 (5 September 1972): pp. 58, 63–64.
[57]"Briefwechsel zwischen den regionalen Kirchenleitungen" and "Aus dem Bericht von Bischof D. Scharf . . . ," *KJ* 1972, pp. 366, 369–70.
[58]"Drei Kandidaten fuer die Bischofswahl in Ost-Berlin," *epd Zentralausgabe*, no. 212 (1 November 1972): p. 1; "Tiefe Beunruhung ueber staatliche Politik auf den Bildungssektor," *epd Landesdienst Berlin*, no. 134 (6 November 1972): p. 2; "Schoenherr: Freude ueber Erleichterungen durch Verkehrsvertrag," *epd Zentralausgabe*, no. 215 (6 November 1972): p. 2. CDU archives, 20 October 1972.

the opposition to the dual-bishop solution. But he also issued a warning that Western failure to approve "may gravely endanger that which one wants to uphold, i.e. the unity of the Berlin-Brandenburg Landes-kirche."[59]

The Western synod now found its own bluff called and the unity of the Landeskirche severely tested. Schoenherr's comments failed to appease his opponents in the Eastern synod, who appealed to the Western region to reject the election. Nonetheless, this East-West Berlin coalition was unable to prevent the Western regional synod from finally approving the dual bishopric in November 1972. Thus, the stalemate was resolved: the Eastern region received its own bishop, but the unity of the Landes-kirche, though severely tested, remained intact.[60]

The state, given the intense opposition in Berlin-Brandenburg and the accelerating pace of the Ostpolitik, welcomed this resolution. Of course, it was incensed at the inter-German oppositional coalition and suspected that a Brandtian conception was afoot in the Eastern church leadership. Had it faced this incomplete separation a little over a year earlier, the state would have attacked it; by November 1972 it was grateful for even this partial step of Abgrenzung.

Each of these cases—the Kirchenbund, the EKU, and Berlin-Branden-burg—reveals the impact of the shift of the GDR's policy toward inter-German relations after late 1971. To be sure, the further moves toward inter-German separation that these organizations made during this pe-riod helped to defuse the issue for the state. However, the state's accep-tance of the partial separations in the EKU and Berlin-Brandenburg is testimony to the extent of the change in state policy under Honecker. Moreover, the facilitation of inter-German contacts by the Kirchen-bund, and particularly by the pro-Ostpolitik EKU, in 1972 indicates that not only was the state more willing to tolerate these remaining inter-German ties, but also that it saw them as useful in gaining ap-proval of the Eastern treaties, then pending Bundestag ratification.

In addition to easing the state's objections to inter-German church ties, the shift in the GDR response to West German Ostpolitik also led

---

[59]*KJ* 1972, pp. 377–80; "Erster Bischof der Ostregion betont Willen zur Zusammenarbeit," *epd Landesdienst Berlin*, no. 134 (6 November 1972): p. 4.

[60]"Eine Kirche auch bei zwei Bischoefen," *epd Landesdienst Berlin*, no. 139 (15 November 1972): p. 2; "West-Berliner Synode beschloss Bischofsgesetz," *epd Landesdienst Berlin*, no. 144 (19 November 1972): p. 4.

the state to be more receptive to the churches' stance regarding the Ostpolitik and European security. Ironically, after years of having criticized church pronouncements on inter-German relations, the state now found itself supporting such pronouncements in its effort to gain West German approval of the Eastern treaties and the convening of a European security conference. The state also came to value the greater credibility of international ecumenical organizations, such as the WCC and LWF, and during its peace offensive in 1972, the state promoted the Kirchenbund's participation.

For the churches, taking public positions on the issue of peace was easier than on other issues. Peace was a goal all agreed with, and the burden of World War II and desire for reconciliation by Germans operated to make such positions popular. However, the state's continual invocation of the issue led the church to seek to avoid charges of opportunism by citing international ecumenical organizations where possible.

During its consolidation, the Kirchenbund expressed support on the issue of peace only in general terms. The 1970 Kirchenbund synod supported the "German obligation for peace and social justice."[61] Speaking for the Kirchenbund leadership at the February 1971 meeting with Seigewasser, Schoenherr decried "all attempts to discriminate against this state" and endorsed UN membership for the GDR.[62] The 1971 Kirchenbund synod moved beyond this stance by endorsing a European security conference, carefully citing the statements of international bodies, such as the Conference of European Churches, thus allaying the state's fears that the synod would lag behind the church leadership and the central church bureaucracy.[63]

Of course, individual church leaders were bolder in their foreign policy expressions. Bishop Krummacher and Church President Natho, for example, continued to support a European security conference in official organs, such as *Neue Zeit*.[64] Again proving more outspoken

[61]"Bericht der KKL . . . ," *epd Dokumentation*, no. 28 (13 July 1970): p. 12.
[62]"Ansprache Bischof D. Schoenherrs . . . ," *epd Dokumentation*, no. 16 (29 March 1971): p. 13.
[63]NZ, 30 June 1971; "Bericht der KKL . . . ," *epd Dokumentation*, no. 34 (19 July 1971): pp. 15, 20–21.
[64]Bishop Krummacher, "Ruf, der uns unmittelbar angeht," NZ, 29 December 1971. The Kirchenbund bureaucracy used its informational effort on world poverty in 1971 to urge full membership of the GDR in all UN organs involved in development programs. See "Im Aufbruch gegen die Weltarmut," *Die Zeichen der Zeit* 25 (September 1971): 336–45.

than the Kirchenbund as a whole, Schoenherr endorsed the Eastern treaties in 1971.[65] Schoenherr's position contrasted considerably not only with the official silence of the Kirchenbund, but also with the cautious and partial support of the EKD for the treaties. However, despite the state's official support for the treaties, it is doubtful that these expressions won Schoenherr much goodwill with the state prior to late 1971. The private lobbying of some church leaders for a GDR more forthcoming toward the Brandt Ostpolitik certainly won none either.[66]

By late 1971, parallel to the state's greater acceptance of inter-German church ties, the state began to encourage the churches' engagement on behalf of the Eastern treaties and European security. The first indication of the state's interest in greater cooperation with the churches on peace questions came in a letter by Professor Stefan Doernburg, general secretary of the GDR Committee for European Security, to the participants of the CDU's February 1972 conference on European security.[67] Doernburg indicated that the effort to gain the support of West European public opinion for the European security conference was open to "all forces which advocate detente and cooperation in Europe, including representatives of various orientations and world views." He praised the "Christians *and their churches* in the GDR which have always advocated peace and cooperation" (emphasis added), including active work in the GDR Committee for European Security. Thus, the emphasis in this new official peace drive was on a broad-based coalition, including not simply atomized GDR Christians, but also the GDR churches.

The state's solicitousness of the churches' support on these issues extended to a precedent-setting church-state consultation on European security on March 1, 1972.[68] For the first time, the state deigned to discuss with official representatives of the churches a topic not directly

---

[65]Schoenherr endorsed them as "an end to an especially painful chapter of European history." See Albrecht Schoenherr, "Die Menschwerdung Gottes . . . ," *Neuer Weg*, 25 December 1970, reprinted in *KJ* 1970, p. 198; *SDZ*, 19 November 1971.

[66]Bishop Krusche's efforts are discussed in CDU archives, 29 March 1971.

[67]CDU archives, 11 February 1972; CDU archives, 24 February 1972; CDU archives, 29 February 1972, "Brief Goettings an Bischof Albrecht Schoenherr"; CDU archives, 29 February 1972, "Brief Goettings an Alfred Kardinal Bengsch." With the exception of Bengsch, Goetting solicited declarations of support for a European security conference. The dating of these letters reveals the continued priority in the Kirchenpolitik strategy given the minor, as opposed to the major, churches.

[68]"Bericht der KKL . . . ," *epd Dokumentation*, no. 30 (17 July 1972): p. 31; CDU archives, 11 May 1972.

related to the churches' institutional interests. The state representatives, led by Dr. Harold Rose of the Ministry of Foreign Affairs and Dr. Doernburg, explained the GDR positions in unpolemical and relatively objective terms. The formal responses provided to the churches' queries indicated that the state was more interested in mobilizing the churches' support for GDR policy than in pursuing dialogue. Yet the meeting set a precedent for attributing to the churches a role in society beyond that of mere ritual, a precedent that would be reinforced by later such informational meetings.

The church representatives at the meeting balanced support for the European Security Conference with veiled criticism of the GDR. Speaking for the Kirchenbund, Schoenherr emphasized the churches' past support for such a conference, citing statements in ecumenical forums and GDR synods. He conceded that priority should be given to questions of peace and security, including inviolable borders, over those of improvements in human rights and contacts. However, he made clear that the relations with the FRG should not be those of "cold existence," but of "good neighbors." Moreover, Schoenherr and the other Kirchenbund representatives did not hesitate to make circumspect reference to the continuing problems for Christians in the GDR. Thus the Kirchenbund attempted to make the linkage between the international Kirchenpolitik and the domestic Kirchenpolitik, between the church's status as an ecumenical actor and the church's status as a collection of individual Christians.

During the spring of 1972, the church responded positively to the state's overture, expressing its support for the European security conference and the Eastern treaties. The church leadership voted to send an observer to the Brussels Forum on European Security, an ad hoc peace meeting subject to considerable Soviet influence. It issued a pronouncement in Geneva in which the Kirchenbund advocated that the GDR be granted the equal right to participate in the upcoming UN Conference on the Environment in Stockholm, but couched this position in pragmatic terms of functional cooperation.[69] Thus the Kirchenbund aided the GDR's efforts to enter the world community through the back door of functional international organizations.

[69]"Teilnahme der DDR an Umweltschutzkonferenz gefordert," *Evangelischer Nachrichtendienst* 25 (22 March 1972): 6; *NZ*, 14 March 1972. LWF General Secretary Appel and WCC General Secretary Blake endorsed this position also, thus indicating that the Kirchenbund's position had impact in Geneva. See *FAZ*, 22 March 1972, p. 4.

Moreover, various church leaders raised their voices in support of passage of the Eastern treaties by the Bundestag.[70] Using the language of Honecker, Schoenherr urged their ratification as a "precondition for a totally new phase of political 'living together' *as peaceful neighbors.*" Implicitly invoking the SPD political conception of "change through convergence," he pleaded that "the conditions of life of people in the GDR and the other European states are directly affected." As a harsh critic of the state, Fraenkel's first-time endorsement of the treaties and a European security conference at the April 1972 EKU (East) synod was even more heartening to the state. He rejected "adherence to legal positions which may not correspond to the necessity of world peace" and linked approval of the treaties with "negotiations between the GDR and the FRG in the interest of the solution of difficult human problems," thus articulating a Brandtian position linking detente with domestic change in the GDR.[71] During the Bundestag debate, General Superintendent Jacob sent a letter to Chancellor Brandt thanking him for his policy of negotiation and for the expected improvement of relations among people.[72]

These stands by the East German churches had a direct effect on the debate within the West German churches concerning the Eastern treaties.[73] Reflecting the West German Lutherans' stance, the EKD assumed a position of political neutrality, bordering on abstinence, toward the treaties. The declarations of support of the treaties by Schoenherr and the EKU (East) led the EKU (West) to endorse the treaties. The Jacob letter to Brandt was introduced by Brandt in the Bundestag debate to show support for the treaties among the GDR populace.

In 1971 and 1972 the state had shown for the first time a willingness to grant the churches a role regarding questions of peace, especially as they related to the FRG. As a result of the shift in foreign policy under Honecker, the goal now became West German ratification of the Eastern

---

[70]"Gespraech des EPD mit dem Vorsitzenden des Bundes . . . ," *epd Dokumentation*, no. 12 (20 March 1972): pp. 2–3.

[71]"Bericht des EKU-Vorsitzenden . . . ," *epd Dokumentation*, no. 20 (15 May 1972): pp. 18, 20.

[72]"Brief von Generalsuperindendent D. Dr. Guenter Jacob (Cottbus) an Bundeskanzler Willy Brandt zur Ostpolitik," *epd Dokumentation*, no. 26 (23 June 1972): p. 20.

[73]"Erklaerung zur Gegenwaertigen Auseinandersetzung ueber die Ostvertraege," "Erklaerung der 25," "Erklaerung Landesbischof D. Lohse," "Wort zu der Entscheidung ueber die Ostvertraege," and "Antwort der Leitende Bischof der VELKD D. Woelber (Hamburg) vom 30. Maerz 1972 auf die Erklaerung der 25," *KJ* 1972, pp. 123–25, 127–29, 134.

treaties and West German support for a European security conference. The state did not fail to engage the CDU in this campaign, as revealed by the CDU's increased inter-German diplomacy. But the state gave the leading role to the GDR churches, with their greater credibility in the West.[74] GDR officials may have been irked that the churches behaved more "progressively" abroad than at home. But they quietly accepted the churches' inter-German organizational ties and contacts with West German church leaders who until recently had been scurrilously attacked by the GDR media.[75] It is unlikely that the churches' activities were crucial in the Bundestag approval of the Eastern treaties. But the visibility of the church's inter-German ties and the state's shifting stance on the German question increased its receptiveness to these activities and would lead to long-term change in the church-state relationship.

DOMESTIC LIMITATIONS TO RAPPROCHEMENT

As a result of the greater congruence of views of the church and state regarding inter-German relations, this issue receded in salience and the question of the churches' domestic role moved increasingly to center stage. Within the church there were differing conceptions of the churches' proper role and the desirability of social-political participation by Christians and clergy. Moreover domestic issues continued to produce conflict with the state.

The Debate of the Church's Role in the GDR

The separation from the West German churches forced the churches to frame anew the question of their role in the domestic political system. The churches had expressed limited support for the system, pledging loyalty in 1953 and respecting the development of socialism in 1958, for example. They had also expressed considerable

[74]The churches' lobbying of the Bundestag on behalf of the Eastern treaties thus parallels the Soviets' own efforts to win the CDU (West) support for them. See Larrabee, pp. 322–62.

[75]Even the CDU came to endorse this "special community," albeit backhandedly, admonishing West German church leaders interested in "brotherly community" with GDR representatives to support European security and normal relations between the two German states. See "Fuer bruderliche Gemeinschaft zwischen der DDR und BRD," *epd Landesdienst Berlin*, no. 59 (23 May 1972): p. 4.

opposition to many of the domestic goals and changes of the regime. However, the assumption underlying these positions was that the regime was provisional and that the domestic rules of the game would look very different in a reunified Germany. The separation from the West German churches, however incomplete, represented the churches' admission of the bankruptcy of this assumption. The 1970s saw a lively debate regarding the proper relationship of the church to the state, fostered by the democratic nature of the churches internally. The East German churches had no shortage of role models of such relationships in other socialist states, including coopted churches in the USSR, Bulgaria, and Romania; oppositional churches in Poland and Czechoslovakia; and subservient churches in the case of various sects.

The state's view of the churches' proper role, articulated particularly by the CDU following its party congress in 1972, called for the "identification" of the churches with socialism as a consequence of its "new orientation."[76] In effect, the state desired a "church for socialism." That this desired political acclamation did not guarantee the churches ideological acceptance by the regime was indicated by the ambiguous statement by an official of the CDU that "the church is not a systemic factor, but on the other hand, should not be a foreign body in socialism."[77] Most in the church rejected the "identification with socialism" desired by the state and CDU. However, their views on the proper role of the church in the GDR varied considerably.

"Church within Socialism"   The most prominent perspective was articulated by Bishop Schoenherr. Schoenherr's statement at the 1971 synod of the Kirchenbund—"A witness and service community of churches in the GDR will have to consider carefully its place: in this given society, not separated from it, nor in opposition to it"—has framed the issue ever since, because it spawned the malleable concept of "church within socialism."[78] Schoenherr rejected a political ghettoization of the church by the state and the Lutheran tendency toward "internal emigration" by Christians from society. But he also rejected the extremes of both political opposition and a "church for socialism."

[76]"Entschliessung des 13. Parteitages der CDU," *Dokumente der CDU* 3 (1969–72): p. 320.
[77]CDU archives, 13 January 1971.
[78]Based on discussion with Bishop Schoenherr.

In this view, the social-economic system provided the context for the church, but its goal was not the promotion of socialism.

"Separation of the Two Kingdoms"   An alternative view, reflecting more traditional Lutheran deference to the state and political abstinence, was best articulated by Bishop Braecklein of Thuringia. Braecklein recognized the state as a God-given "force of order" and disclaimed any role of the church to "interfere in the tasks of the state and politics." Christians were called to give "positive loyalty" to the state. But he too rejected a "church for socialism," arguing that Lutherans cannot "endorse or demand a certain state form, certain social form, or certain economic structures as genuinely Christian."[79] For the most part, Braecklein's view was shared by his fellow Lutherans in Saxony-Dresden as well.

"Church for Others"/"Advocate for the Weak"   A third stream of thought saw the churches' proper role in helping individuals, especially those outside its traditional membership, who failed to measure up to the state's standard for "socialist personality." Rooted in Bonhoeffer's concept of a "church for others," this view found its most outspoken proponent in Bishop Rathke of Mecklenburg.[80] Although Lutheran, Rathke saw a socially active role for the church as a "proxy for those too weak, too slow or too afraid to stand up against injustice and inhumanity," focusing on alcoholics, writers, and political prisoners. Rathke was thus more explicit than Schoenherr regarding the churches' social role.

"Critical Solidarity"   A view widely represented in the Union churches called for the church to exercise "critical solidarity" with the GDR. Its advocates rejected both the total identification with socialism desired by the state and political neutrality. Coined by Bishop Krusche of Magdeburg and elaborated by his protege, Dr. Heino Falcke, "critical solidarity" implied social and political criticism by the churches, but within the context of a general approval of socialism.[81]

[79]Landesbischof Braecklein zum Bericht der Lutherischen Kirchenleitung," *epd Dokumentation*, no. 49 (15 October 1971): p. 20. "Gleiche Chancen fuer Christen in der DDR gefordert," *epd Zentralausgabe*, no. 56 (20 March 1971): p. 6.

[80]EPC archives, 1971.

[81]"Bericht der Kirchenleitung der Evangelische Kirche der Kirchenprovinz Sachsen . . . ," *KJ* 1971, pp. 365–66.

This position of "critical solidarity" was espoused most articulately by Dr. Heino Falcke, a protege of Bishop Krusche, in his address to the 1972 Kirchenbund synod.[82] In it he rejected the state's view that faith may provide the motivation but that socialism alone can provide the normative content for social action. But he also rejected an introverted, apolitical religion. To Falcke, Christians are freed by Christ to pursue *muendige Mitverantwortung* (mature coresponsibility): "We are free from the fixation on a self-concept of socialism that only leaves possible a total yes or total no. Christ liberates from the crippling alternative between opposition out of principle and uncritical cooptation, to one of concrete differentiated cooperation." Socialism exists under the promise of Christ, according to Falcke. As a result, even when disappointed, Christians "with engaged hope of an improved socialism" can remain active in society.

Falcke accompanies his general approach with specific proposals. While endorsing socialism in the Third World and distancing himself from liberal notions of pluralism, he addressed many taboo topics of GDR socialism. He discussed the existence of suffering in socialism, alienation in the workplace, and the pressure to perform. Advocating greater freedom and justice in general, like Krusche earlier, he called for greater openness and information in GDR society. He rejected Abgrenzung as an attempt to stabilize society internally by fostering distance from outsiders.

The emphasis of Krusche and Falcke on the churches' social mission contrasted with both Rathke's focus on helping individuals and Braecklein's political abstinence. It bears a kinship to Schoenherr's conception of "church within socialism," but is more socially critical.

"Guardian Office"   A final approach saw the church as a critical voice of conscience in relations with the state. Reflecting his experience during the Kirchenkampf under Hitler, its primary advocate, Bishop Fraenkel of Goerlitz, defended a God-given role of the church as guardian against abuse of power.[83] Employing a variant of Schoenherr's formulation, "church within socialism, but not under it, nor in its

---

[82]Dr. Heino Falcke, "Christus befreit—darum Kirche fuer Andere," *epd Dokumentation*, no. 30 (17 July 1972): p. 10.

[83]"Aus dem Bericht . . . ," *epd Dokumentation*, no. 23 (8 June 1970): p. 24; "Bericht des EKU-Ratsvorsitzenden Bischof D. Hans-Joachim Fraenkel . . . ," *epd Dokumentation*, no. 20 (15 May 1972): p. 15.

spirit," Fraenkel emphasized the unbridgeable philosophical chasm between church and state.

From the state's perspective, these viewpoints on the church's proper
role ranged from the inadequate to the dangerous. For example, it
found both Schoenherr's formulation "church within socialism" and
Braecklein's Lutheran passivity insufficient. Seigewasser directly criticized the "church within socialism" formula, arguing that the church
should make an affirmation (*Bekenntnis*) of socialism, as contained
in the church constitution of the Hungarian churches.[84] By arguing
that "peace and socialism are identical," the state sought to link the
churches' domestic direction to the growing agreement on foreign policy issues.[85] In Fraenkel's "guardian role" for the church, it saw a threat
to the leading role of the SED and thereby to its conception of socialism.

The state was especially agitated by the "critical solidarity" view
advocated by Krusche and Falcke, particularly Falcke's notion of "improved socialism." To the state, his call for greater freedom of information and exchange of opinions smacked of Prague Spring revisionism.
Aware of the tenor of his address, the state had tried unsuccessfully to
persuade him to revise it. After the address was given, state representatives met with Kirchenbund leaders late into the night, demanding
unsuccessfully that the address be struck completely from the record of
the synod.[86] The treatment of the synod in the official media also
revealed the state's negative reaction. The state media interpreted the
synod as a retreat from the 1971 synod. The state discredited Falcke's
advice on the improving of socialism as "modernization of bourgeois
positions with the help of revisionist vocabulary."[87]

Falcke's position did not go uncontested in the churches either. The
church leaders rejected the state's demand to excise the address from the
record but did distance themselves from it during the remainder of the
synod and limited its circulation among the parishes.[88] Some, such as

[84]CDU archives, 28 July 1971.

[85]The Seigewasser speech is dealt with in *Deutsche Zeitung—Christ und Welt*, 5 February
1971, p. 16, and *NZ*, 18 March 1971.

[86]*NZ*, 7 January 1971; CDU archives, 26 May 1972.

[87]*NZ*, 5 and 6 July 1972; *ND*, 5 July 1972; *NZ*, 9 July and 5 August 1972; Carl Ordnung,
"Ueber das spezifisch 'Christliche,'" *Standpunkt* 1 (January 1973): 5–6.

[88]"Bericht des Sekretariats des Kirchenbundes ueber die Aussprache zu den Hauptreferat,"
KJ 1971, pp. 292–93; "Die Tagung der Bundessynode," *Evangelischer Nachrichtendienst* 25
(5 July 1972): 15; "Beschluss des gemeinsamen Antrages der vier Arbeitsgruppen der Synode
zum Hauptthema," *epd Dokumentation*, no. 30 (17 July 1972): p. 19. By contrast, the 1971
synod materials had been widely circulated among the local parishes.

Thuringia and Mecklenburg, criticized Falcke's Barthianism on theological grounds; others distanced themselves on political grounds.[89]

Thus, the views regarding the proper domestic role of the churches in GDR society varied greatly, not only within the church but between church and state. It was to be expected that this divergence on the general philosophical level should lead to disagreements on the practical level as well and hamper the developing rapprochement.

The state's desired "identification" with GDR socialism also had its corresponding practical side, social and political engagement by Christians and clergy. The central issues of social engagement for Christians were participation in the youth dedication ceremony (*Jugendweihe*) and membership in the Free German Youth (FDJ), the SED's youth organization. The state viewed these as affirmations of loyalty to the state and socialism. The churches, on the other hand, had long opposed the *Jugendweihe* as atheistic in character and inconsistent with confirmation. Under the pressure of school authorities, participation in *Jugendweihe* became almost universal in the 1960s, and the churches' hard-line stance eroded. Although practice varied among the Landeskirchen and even among various superintendents within Landeskirchen, for the most part the churches abandoned the stance that taking the *Jugendweihe* precluded confirmation.[90] On similar grounds the churches had long rejected participation in the FDJ, but in practice they came to tolerate such participation.

The state also sought greater political engagement, namely, voting in elections by both Christians and pastors, and participation in the bodies of the National Front, the Pfarrerbund, and the CDU. The state followed particularly closely the voting participation by the clergy as an indicator of the churches' stance toward the state.[91] As table 6.1 indicates, in the 1960s, this voting participation had hovered around 60 percent, with participation in local elections somewhat greater than in parliamentary elections, probably due to the greater proximity to the

---

[89]The Thuringian view is found in "Unbewaeltigte Aufgabe," *Glaube und Gewissen* 18 (November 1972): 210–11. The Mecklenburg view is found in "Dresden 1972," *Mecklenburgische Kirchenzeitung*, 30 July 1972. Among those distancing themselves from Falcke were Gienke, Natho, and Stolpe. See CDU archives, 25 July 1972; CDU archives, 28 July 1972; CDU archives, 9 November 1972.

[90]Heinrich Frickel, "Stationen einer 20 Jaehrigen Entwicklung: Konfirmandenunterricht und Konfirmation in der DDR," and Gerhard Schmoltze, "Nach 20 Jahren: Jugendweihe in der DDR," *KiS* 1 (July 1975): 9–11, 18.

[91]CDU archives, 28 May 1974; CDU archives, 16 April 1968; CDU archives, 1971, "Information ueber die Herbstsynoden"; CDU archives, 1974.

Table 6.1. Lutheran clergy participation in GDR local and national elections (in percent)

District	1963 National Parliamentary	1965 Local Elections	1967 National Parliamentary	1968 National Constitutional Referendum	1970 Local Elections	1974 Local Elections
Rostock	79	84	75	75	83.6	93.6
Schwerin	70	73	65	96	95.0	88.4
Neubrandenburg	62	76	74	70	89.0	88.3
Potsdam	43	66	55	88	73.7	80.6
Frankfurt/Oder	32	46	43	80	77.0	79.8
Cottbus	38	51	47	92	68.8	66.2
Magdeburg	54	55	45	93	70.0	76.6
Halle	48	54	54	88	77.5	83.3
Erfurt	85	89	87	95	86.8	94.5
Gera	89	91	95	99	94.8	98.5
Suhl	95	97	94	99	96.8	97.8
Dresden	40	45	40	90	62.0	73.3
Leipzig	67	67	64	96	78.3	81.6
Karl-Marx-Stadt	36	51	43	91	58.2	61.0
Berlin	40	49	54	97	73.0	85.5
GDR TOTAL	58	65	60	90	78.4	81.8

Sources: CDU archives, 16 April 1968; CDU archives, 1974

voter of the candidates and issues in local elections than in parliamentary elections. The 1968 plebiscite on the new constitution, the first election since 1949 in which a political choice was possible, was a watershed. As a result of the greater public credibility of this election, 90 percent of the clergy voted. Thereafter, participation in the general elections also increased dramatically, to approximately 78 percent in the 1970 communal election and 82 percent in the 1974 communal election.

Table 6.1 also demonstrates considerable variation in voting across Landeskirchen. Despite the end of the separate "Thuringian Way" by Braecklein, civil administrative districts that Thuringia encompassed (Erfurt, Gera, and Suhl) enjoyed clergy voting participation levels in the mid-90 percent range, making unavoidable the conclusion that voting participation was actively encouraged by the Thuringian church leadership. By the same token, Gorlitz (Cottbus district) and Saxony-Dresden (Dresden, Karl-Marx-Stadt districts), registered participation levels considerably below the GDR average, doubtless reflecting the reserved stance of Bishops Fraenkel and Noth vis-à-vis the state. The other Landeskirchen fell between these two extremes: Mecklenburg (Schwerin, Rostock districts) and Greifswald (Rostock, Neubrandenburg, Frankfurt/Oder) fell in the 80 percent range; Berlin-Brandenburg (Berlin, Potsdam, Frankfurt/Oder), Saxony-Magdeburg (Magdeburg, Halle, Leipzig), and Anhalt (Halle) in the 70 percent range.

Even more revealing than this ranking of the Landeskirchen is the relative shift among them since the mid-1960s elections. The greatest increases were found in Berlin-Brandenburg, Mecklenburg, Saxony-Magdeburg, and to a lesser extent, Saxony-Dresden. Participation levels in Thuringia, Greifswald, and Gorlitz, on the other hand, altered little.

These variations by Landeskirche and by time period reveal that, despite the overall increase in participation, political participation by clergy in voting remained a function of Landeskirche tradition and the attitude of the respective bishop. Landeskirchen that traditionally had been either "progressive" or politically abstinent remained so; those that traditionally had a less extreme profile, such as Berlin-Brandenburg, Mecklenburg, and Saxony-Magdeburg, saw disproportionately large increases in participation, largely as a result of the favorable attitude of their new bishops (Schoenherr, Rathke, Krusche, respectively) toward political participation.

Political participation by the clergy in forms other than voting remained considerably lower. Despite Bishop Krummacher's active participation in the National Front and Schoenherr's openness to such activity, participation by clergy in the activities of the National Front remained low, not exceeding 20–30 percent of the total Evangelical clergy.[92] Membership in the CDU hovered around two hundred, approximately 4 percent of the clergy. Participation in the Pfarrerbund did not exceed one hundred.

Thus, the trends in social and political participation by the churches were mixed. The increase in voting participation by clergy seemed to bode well for the developing rapprochement. The variation by Landeskirche remained substantial, but the greater openness of the Kirchenbund leadership to participation reinforced the Kirchenbund strategy by the state. Participation in mass organizations and the CDU, on the other hand, remained low, despite the greater openness of the Kirchenbund to such activity.[93]

Domestic Issues of Conflict

Discrimination in Education   The domestic issue that most hampered the church-state rapprochement (and has remained most intractable) was discrimination against Christian youth in the education system. Despite constitutional guarantees of freedom of belief and conscience and of equal access to education, such protections did not extend to the process of admission to the college preparatory high school, the *Erweiterte Oberschule* (EOS). Admission to this school in the eighth grade was a necessary and in most cases a sufficient condition for direct, full-time study at the university. This already extremely selective process became even tighter in the late 1960s and early 1970s, bringing into greater play the questions of participation in *Jugendweihe* and the FDJ, especially since the *Jugendweihe* also occurred in the eighth grade.

It confronted Christian families with difficult ethical dilemmas. With the increasing participation in the *Jugendweihe* and the FDJ, failure to

---

[92]CDU archives, 1 November 1971; CDU archives, 1974.

[93]Adalbert Moeller, "Die Gesellschaftliche Verantwortung des Christen im Sozialismus," *Umschau '74: Evangelische Christen in der DDR—Zwischenbilanz in 40 Streiflichtern* (Berlin, GDR: Evangelische Verlagsanstalt, 1974), pp. 219–27.

engage in these political activities became more conspicuous. Not wish-ing to harm their children's chances, Christian parents often let the children themselves decide whether to participate in the activities, or even encouraged their children to participate in them. As the residual of nonparticipants became ever smaller, it became increasingly concen-trated with children of pastors. Already discriminated against because of their status as children of intelligentsia, they now faced discrimina-tion for a second reason.

For the state the issue posed a difficult decision as well, a familiar clash of ideology and economic rationality. On the one hand, the party's eschatological ideology continually prodded it to foster the develop-ment toward communism, which included the disappearance of reli-gion. Yet on the other hand, economic rationality argued for a more meritocratic educational system, with which discrimination based on religious attachment was obviously inconsistent. Political prudence called for holding dissatisfaction among Christians to a minimum with-out yielding them key positions in society that might erode the party's control.

The conflict over the education system, though long a problem, be-came more acute after Honecker's assumption of power in May 1971. Earlier, in its drive for universal participation in the *Jugendweihe* and FDJ, the state had underscored their reconcilability with confirmation. Now in some decisions on admissions to the EOS, it began to treat them as irreconcilable, forcing parents to choose between confirmation and the state activities.[94] Moreover, the incidence of harassment of Chris-tian children in the classroom rose in 1971. The state began to forbid participation by pastors and their wives in the *Elternaktiv,* a parent-teacher association, fearing that they might serve as a local forum to criticize treatment of Christians in the education system.[95] Even CDU

[94]The restrictive higher education policy was signaled by the "Directive on Application Procedure, Selection, and Admission to On-Campus Study at Universities and College Admis-sion Regulations," 1 July 1971, *Gesetzblatt der DDR,* pt. 2, 1971, p. 486. Pressure at school on catechism participants is reported in "State Pressures Parents on Confirmation Classes," *LWF Information,* no. 34 (28 July 1971): p. 3. The bishops' letter to superintendents also deals with the problem, as found in "Schreiben des Bischofskonvent . . . ," *KJ* 1971, pp. 243–45. "Konzentration ist noetig," *KiS,* no. 2 (1973): p. 31. This tightening of the ideological screws in the education system particularly affected Thuringia and the fortress of the *Volkskirche* (national church), the *Erzgebirge* region in Saxony-Dresden. See CDU archives, 1 November 1971; CDU archives, 13 December 1971; CDU archives, 28 December 1971.

[95]Reinhard Henkys, "Hoehere Bildung nur fuer Atheisten?," *KJ* 1971, pp. 246–47; CDU archives, 17 December 1970.

parents were only allowed to participate on an ad hoc, case-by-case basis.

A major reason for the increased conflict was the heightened emphasis on ideology in the early Honecker reign, particularly propounded at the Eighth SED Party Congress in June 1971.[96] The Ministry for Higher and Technical Education issued an executive order on July 1, 1971, which emphasized the "active cooperation in the development of the socialist society" and the "preparedness for active defense of socialism" as preconditions for postsecondary study. The FDJ leadership was given a major role in evaluating the political qualifications of students.

In addition, the constraints of higher education policy served as a contextual factor in explaining the increased conflict.[97] In the early 1970s the state sought to reduce admissions to the overexpanded higher education system, a process that necessarily entailed cutbacks in the EOS as well. However, Christians bore a disproportionate share of these cutbacks. Whether due to educators seeking the simplest means of weeding out students or to ideological fervor on their part, the effect remained discrimination.

The churches' response prior to 1971 had been measured, a mix of public and private criticism.[98] Preoccupied with internal matters, the Kirchenbund had largely ignored the issue at its early synods. Schoenherr raised the issue discreetly at his meeting with Seigewasser and certain Landeskirchen, such as Magdeburg, Thuringia, and Mecklenburg had criticized the state in meetings with state officials.

The increasing discrimination in mid-1971 led the churches to become increasingly vociferous.[99] It became apparent that certain Landeskirchen—Mecklenburg and Thuringia, in particular—were being subjected to harsher treatment. In addition, discrimination was more widespread in certain districts—such as Rostock, Schwerin, Leipzig,

[96]Karl Barto, "Werden die DDR-Hochschulen fuer politische Passivisten unzugaenglich?" reprinted in *KJ* 1971, pp. 245–46.

[97]Hans-Peter Schaefer, "Chancengleichheit und Begabtenfoerderung in der DDR," *DA* 10 (August 1977): 318–28.

[98]"Gleiche Chancen fuer Christen in der DDR gefordert," *epd Zentralausgabe*, no. 56 (20 March 1971): p. 6; "Schoenherr gefordert," *epd Zentralausgabe*, no. 90 (10 May 1971): p. 2; CDU archives, 29 March 1971. In April 1971, the newly elected bishop of Mecklenburg, Dr. Heinrich Rathke, relayed his synod's protest of discrimination in a letter to the parish church councils, urging them to take grievances to the local authorities. See CDU archives, 14 April 1971.

[99]CDU archives, 29 March 1971.

Frankfurt/Oder, Magdeburg, Suhl, and Gera—than in others, such as Dresden and Cottbus. In Mecklenburg, the Rostock district authorities placed a cap of 20 percent on the proportion of Christians in the EOS and exerted direct pressure on catechism instructees, leading to a 90 percent drop in catechism classes. Reflecting the seriousness of the situation in Thuringia, Braecklein forged ahead with the Thuringian study documenting educational discrimination, despite state attempts to defuse individual cases and to dissuade him.[100] Although less critical church leaders such as Krummacher and Natho downplayed the issue, their synods often heatedly discussed the worsening situation.[101]

As on other issues, Magdeburg proved to be much more outspoken. Bishop Krusche inveighed against the "second-class status" of Christian citizens and described the situation in Kirchenkampf terms.[102] The fall 1971 synod of the Magdeburg Landeskirche reinforced Krusche's blunt criticism and urged those affected to invoke the constitution and the UN Declaration on Human Rights.[103] At the same time it counseled Christians "not to sell their birthright for a serving of lentil stew" but to accept the suffering and hold fast to their beliefs.

Attempting to walk a middle way, the Kirchenbund exercised criticism in a diplomatic fashion, endorsing the use of quiet diplomacy with the regime. The church leadership noted the increased ideological emphasis in the admission to the EOS and asked that the "effective social activity of students be considered, even if it does not occur in the forms which are offered by the society."[104] The synod itself seconded the church leadership's concern, but deferred to the church leadership and Schoenherr to seek a resolution to the problem via quiet diplomacy. Planners for the synod considered the idea of a "white book" detailing cases of discrimination, but rejected it as impolitic.

[100]CDU archives, 1 July 1971; CDU archives, 26 October 1971; CDU archives, 13 December 1971.

[101]EPC archives, 28 October 1971; EPC archives, 4–7 November 1971. "Die Tagung der Saechsischen Landessynode," *Evangelischer Nachrichtendienst* 24 (10 November 1971): p. 8. "Herbsttagung der anhaltischen Landessynode," *Evangelischer Nachrichtendienst* 24 (17 November 1971): p. 10. The CDU's coverage of the fall synods can be found in CDU archives, 1971, "Information ueber die Herbstsynoden"; CDU archives, 16 November 1971; CDU archives, 2 November 1971; CDU archives, 15 November 1971.

[102]CDU archives, 26 October 1971; CDU archives, 5 November 1971; CDU archives, 13 April 1972.

[103]"Bericht der Kirchenleitung . . . ," *KJ* 1971, pp. 242–43; CDU archives, 15 November 1971.

[104]"Bericht der KKL . . . ," *epd Dokumentation*, no. 34 (19 July 1971): p. 17.

In addition to political criticism, some of the Landeskirchen attempted to deal with the problem by delaying confirmation until the ninth or tenth grade, thus relieving the zero-sum character of the Jugendweihe-confirmation decision.[105] However, no uniform internal policy on confirmation was realized by the churches, since some, particularly in Saxony-Dresden, did not wish to give even tacit approval to the *Jugendweihe*.

Initially the state proved unreceptive to any diplomacy, quiet or otherwise. It rejected the idea that the church might represent aggrieved parents, acting like a grass-roots-oriented interest group representing the concerns of its "constituency." Such a status for the church would jeopardize a key ideological tenet, the party's claim to total power in the society. The state even denied the existence of a problem, claiming that problems in admission to the EOS derived not from one's decision to be confirmed, but from one's failure to affirm loyalty to the GDR via participation in the *Jugendweihe* and the FDJ. Insults to Christian children were dismissed as the actions of sectarians.[106]

However, the accuracy of the churches' charges and the extent of such discrimination were confirmed by the private diplomacy undertaken by the CDU on the issue. Publicly the CDU leadership mimicked the official line. However, individual CDU members, such as CDU members of the Greifswald synod in fall 1971, spoke out against the increasing discrimination. Gerhard Lotz, a leading official in the Thuringian church, complained that "on the mountaintops the sun is still shining, but in the valleys it is damn dark."[107] Finally, the CDU leadership sought out discussions with state authorities responsible for the *Jugendweihe* and the FDJ, as well as with the military.[108] The officials reassured the CDU that participation in confirmation and even nonparticipation in *Jugendweihe* did not, by itself, constitute grounds for EOS rejection. Yet it left little doubt that it considered *Jugendweihe* participation a legitimate criterion in making EOS decisions. In addition, it sought to assuage CDU fears that support for the *Jugendweihe* was not a prerequisite for

---

[105]"Konzentration ist noetig," *KiS* 1 (December 1973): 33.

[106]CDU archives, 28 July 1971; CDU archives, 13 April 1972.

[107]CDU archives, 16 November 1971; CDU archives, 5 November 1971; Lotz quoted in CDU archives, 13 April 1972.

[108]Werner Wuenschmann, member of the CDU Secretariat, met in early 1972 with representatives of the Central Commission for the *Jugendweihe*, according to CDU archives, 1972; CDU archives, 13 April 1972.

participation in the *Elternaktivs*. Likewise, the FDJ leadership assured the CDU that Christians could be elected to leading positions in the FDJ. Although the CDU's actions were clearly designed to defend the interests of its often opportunistic membership, they nonetheless reflected the seriousness of the general problem of discrimination against Christians.

Despite its initial rebuff to the church, the state did give some ground on the issue by late 1971 and early 1972.[109] The state began to admit that a problem existed—explaining it, however, not as systematic discrimination but as the result of necessary cutbacks in the higher education system. The state suggested that if discrimination had occurred, it stemmed not from ideological reasons but from political ones, such as the failure of clergy to vote.[110] In addition, the state cynically sought to defuse the churches' criticism by according improved treatment to children of clergy.[111] Also—at a December 1971 meeting with Schoenherr, Braecklein, and Stolpe—Seigewasser assured the church leaders that the state's policy had not changed since February 1971 and agreed to consider such cases that could not be resolved at the district level.[112] This did yield concrete results, as Seigewasser's office did manage to reverse the decisions on admission to the EOS in certain cases.[113]

This represented, at best, a partial victory for the church. The state appeared to grant the church officials the right to represent the grievances of Christians. However, such representation did not extend to the source of the problems, the ideologically oriented Ministry of Education, but would be mediated by the district and/or central state authorities charged with the responsibility for the Kirchenpolitik. Thus any redress would remain circuitous and partial, subject to bureaucratic pathologies and the general winds of the Kirchenpolitik. Moreover, the state seemed bent on limiting the object of this "lobbying" to the

[109]That the state secretary's office was aware of discrimination in education is indicated in CDU archives, 22 October 1971.

[110]Goetting: "A pastor who takes pride in never having voted can hardly expect the relevant representatives of the education system to leave such a fact unnoticed." CDU archives, 3 November 1971.

[111]Fifty to 80% of applications by children of clergy for EOS admission were approved in 1971. Such children were already overrepresented in the EOS, given their relative numbers in the population, it was argued. CDU archives, 28 December 1971.

[112]The extensive materials collected by Thuringia served as the basis for this meeting. "Schreiben des Bischofskonvent . . . ," *KJ* 1971, p. 244. CDU archives, 13 December 1971.

[113]CDU archives, 13 April 1972.

children of clergy. The post hoc disposition of nonclergy cases did little to ameliorate the effects of the generalized atmosphere of intimidation and mistrust.[114]

Throughout 1972 the Kirchenbund continued its approach of quiet diplomacy. In synod statements and letters to parishioners, its leadership sought to reassure the grass roots that it was taking action. Yet it sought to avoid public statements at home or abroad that might have exacerbated the conflict.

The state clearly preferred this approach of private dialogue and negotiation to one of open confrontation. The state sought to make the rewards of dialogue—the opportunity for the church to petition for redress in particular cases and for changes in broader policy—contingent upon the avoidance of critical public statements by the churches.[115] But the state proved unwilling to go beyond the resolution of individual cases in these private negotiations, continuing to see the problem in terms of sectarian actions. Since most Christian parents were intimidated from taking their protest to the church officials, the churches were able to expose only a small fraction of individual cases of discrimination, thus appearing to vindicate the state's position. Even regarding the churches' role in the individual cases, the state continued to follow a contradictory pattern: some state representatives granted the church the right to speak for Christian parents; others continued to deny it.

Military Service   Another problem affecting church-state relations stemmed from the role of the military. The burden of World War II and the tradition of German militarism had led many, especially Christian youth, to reject military values. This trend clashed with the GDR's increasing emphasis on the necessity of military preparedness. The introduction of the *Bausoldat* option in 1964 somewhat ameliorated conflict with the church in this area. But friction increased again with the onset of the Ostpolitik, as the GDR sought to shore up popular military resolve in the face of the understandable softening of attitudes in a period of relaxation of tensions.[116]

---

[114]*KJ* 1971, pp. 243–45.

[115]CDU archives, 13 April 1972.

[116]Thus, for example, the civil defense system, linking enterprise- and neighborhood-based units with the military, was reorganized and consolidated in 1970, according to "Zivilverteidigung," Federal Ministry of Inner-German Affairs, *DDR-Handbuch*, p. 1219.

Two dimensions of this issue created the friction in the relationship. First, discrimination in educational and career opportunities particularly affected those opting for *Bausoldat* status. Since relatively few opted for such status, the problem remained less visible than general discrimination in education. However, in 1970 the increased discrimination began to affect theology students at the state universities, heretofore a group relatively unaffected by such status. Beginning in that year, readiness to serve in the military was made a prerequisite for admission to study; current students were pressured to forego the *Bausoldat* service immediately or face exmatriculation.[117] Of course, this carried dire consequences for the church as an institution since it threatened the churches' capacity for pastoral replacement.

The second dimension of the problem involved the military nature of the *Bausoldat* projects.[118] Many rejected such work as inconsistent with their pacifist motivation and requested a transfer to health and social projects. The state refused their requests and sought to isolate them from other conscripts, hoping to limit the impact of this ideological concession.

The churches unsuccessfully protested state policy in this area. Numerous church leaders, in particular Bishop Krusche, raised the issue in meetings with the state. The Kirchenbund leadership asked the state not to "curtail the validity" of the *Bausoldat* option but rather to continue to practice this, for students also.[119] The state refused to respond to the church's requests. At the meeting with the CDU, the military representatives assured the CDU that indeed Christians could become officers, provided they possessed the correct "socialist state consciousness," hardly addressing the immediate concerns of the church regarding treatment of *Bausoldaten*.[120] Thus this issue, which affected not only individuals, but also the church's institutional interests, remained a point of conflict.

Theological Education   Another area of increasing conflict with the state was that of theological training. The churches' interest in

[117]CDU archives, 16 December 1970.
[118]CDU archives, 20 October 1971.
[119]"Bericht der KKL . . . ," *epd Dokumentation*, no. 34 (19 July 1971): p. 17.
[120]The Kirchenbund repeated its concerns at its 1972 synod. "Bericht der KKL . . . ," *epd Dokumentation*, no. 30 (17 July 1972): p. 30; CDU archives, 13 July 1972; CDU archives, 13 April 1972.

organizational maintenance and autonomy required recruitment and education of new pastors in sufficient numbers and independent of state influence. This became increasingly difficult in the late 1960s and early 1970s. The number of new theology students declined considerably and the output of new pastors failed to keep pace with the increasing numbers of pastors retiring. Moreover, the heretofore relatively un-politicized training of clergy at the state universities was threatened by the state's ideologically based reform of the universities, again part of a general increase in emphasis on ideology by the SED in the wake of the Ostpolitik.[121] Setting the tone for the application of this reform to theological education, Kurt Huettner, a leading SED policymaker main-tained that "the perspective of a theologian in the GDR is good as long as he stands for socialism and does not make late-bourgeois ideology part of the content of his doctrine."[122] This reform had several concrete effects on theology education, primarily at the state universities.

The main thrust of the reform was to better integrate university study and research with practice.[123] In the areas of theology, this meant greater emphasis on the *social* aspects in the theological curriculum, for example practical and systematic theology, ecumenical relations, and modern church history. Practicums and social engagement became part of the curriculum. The study of Marxism-Leninism (the so-called *Grundlagenstudium*), long-required of other students, now become mandatory for theology students as well. The state viewed the greater integration of pastors into social relations as a means of fostering "new orientation," namely greater support for socialism.

Complementing this new emphasis on social relevance, the state theology departments attempted to wean the students from their pre-vious dependence on Western theology, with its alleged pluralistic, "so-cial democratic" bias. Obtaining literature from the West, even from ecumenical organizations that were currently enjoying the favor of the state, became extremely difficult.[124] The CDU and theologians close to

---

[121]For a discussion of the Third Higher Education Reform, set in motion in 1967, see Marianne Usko, *Hochschulen in der DDR* (Berlin-West: Verlag Gebr. Holzapfel, 1974), pp. 7–29, and "Universitaeten und Hochschulen," Federal Ministry for Inner-German Affairs, *DDR-Handbuch*, pp. 1100–1108.

[122]Quoted in "Zukunftsaussichten von Theologiestudenten," *epd Landesdienst Berlin*, no. 34 (9 March 1971): p. 4.

[123]"Der 'Idealtheologe,'" *KiS* 2 (June 1976): 27–31.

[124]Even materials from Geneva for the Anti-Racism Program were confiscated. See CDU archives, 1 December 1971.

it recommended the formation of a commission for theological literature, which would promote the *"DDR-Spezifik"* in theology. A study of the "ideal pastor" conducted by the various theological faculties painted a picture of ideological conformity.[125]

The reform also sought to limit contacts between the state university theology departments and the churches' schools. Official contacts, such as lectures, which heretofore had been tolerated, became taboo by 1970. Despite its desire to reduce the length of study from five years to four, the state refused to transfer instruction in ancient languages to the church schools to achieve that goal.[126]

Not surprisingly, the reform aimed to increase political engagement and loyalty among students. FDJ work, previously practically dormant in the theology sections, was intensified by requiring membership for leadership positions.[127] Mandatory military training for students began in the fall of 1970. Admission to the university was made contingent upon a pledge to undergo thirty days of military training yearly. Those opting for *Bausoldat* status were not exempt from this requirement and were required to have completed service as *Bausoldat* before applying for the university.[128]

The threat of the reform to the church's institutional interest was immediate and real. Already the toll from the new military service requirement had been heavy: only 97 new students matriculated in 1970, compared with 123 in 1969, a drop of 21 percent in the first year of the new policy alone.[129] The continuation of such a trend would be crippling for the churches, already confronted with a shortage of pastors.

On the other hand, the policy also carried certain dangers for the state. Increased emphasis on "praxis" implied a certain interface with the churches, although they hardly represented the ideal socialist institution.[130] Moreover, the increased politicization of the university, especially the new policy on military service, threatened to drive stu-

[125]Hans-Hinrich Jenssen, "Nach zehn Jahren: DDR-Spezifik in der Theologie," *Evangelisches Pfarrerblatt,* no. 2 (February 1971): pp. 33–34; CDU archives, 3 April 1971; EPS documents, 29 January 1971, pp. 5–6.
[126]CDU archives, 16 December 1970.
[127]CDU archives, 16 December 1970; "Der 'Idealtheologe,'" *KiS* 2 (June 1976): 27–31.
[128]CDU archives, 28 October 1970.
[129]"840 Seminarians in East Germany," *LWF Information,* no. 39 (1 September 1971): p. 2.
[130]"Der Idealtheologe,'" *KiS* 2 (June 1976): 27–31.

dents away from the state universities into the churches' schools, thus defeating the very purpose of the new policies. As table 6.2 reveals, this was indeed the effect of the state's policies: the church schools' enrollment grew by 140 (52 percent) between 1970–1971 and 1974–1975, taking up the slack from the 103 student drop (20 percent) in enrollment in the state university departments in the same period. Enrollment in some state departments dropped by as much as two thirds from that projected. Parallel to this development was the increasing concentration of female theology students in the state departments as the male theology students opted for the church schools, thereby escaping the military service prerequisite.[131] Of course, the state could have closed the church schools, but that would have precipitated a Kirchenkampf that the state wished to avoid.

The churches' attempts to alter the state's new policies, particularly regarding military service, were to no avail.[132] To be sure, the state—realizing that the drop in matriculation and the increasing concentration of women in the state departments reduced its influence among the still male-dominated clergy—began to doubt the wisdom of its policy.[133] Yet by 1972 no amelioration of the problem was in sight.

Restrictions on the Churches' Public Meetings   Along with the educational discrimination issue, the greatest source of conflict in the church-state relationship involved the churches' right to assemble freely. In particular, the state challenged the status of certain cultural and recreational activities of the churches that lay outside the area of religious practice, narrowly defined. The status of such activities, especially retreats for youth, church congresses, and cultural activities such as organ concerts, had always been rather tenuous. Although the state had not used physical coercion against such activities since 1953, it had sought to hinder them by administrative means. These included such tactics as citing alleged health code violations or refusal to supply food and transportation to retreats and congresses.[134] Now these activities

---

[131]Based on discussion with Bishop Schoenherr.

[132]"Ansprache Bischof D. Schoenherrs beim Empfang des Vorstandes . . . ," *Evangelischer Nachrichtendienst* 24 (17 March 1971): 15; "Bericht der KKL . . . ," *epd Dokumentation*, no. 34 (19 July 1971): p. 16; "Bericht der KKL . . . ," *epd Dokumentation*, no. 30 (17 July 1972): p. 30; EPS documents, 5 November 1970, p. 4.

[133]CDU archives, 3 November 1972.

[134]EPS documents, 19 February 1971, p. 2.

Table 6.2. Enrollment of theology students in the GDR, 1965–1977

Year	State Sections	Churches' Seminaries	Churches' Preaching Schools	Total
1965	642			
1969	537			
1970	504	270	70	844
1971	469	——300——		769
1972	467			
1973	417	——330——		747
1974	401	410	74	885
1975	375	350	70	795
1976	371	410	75	856
1977	382	——530——		912

Sources: Although incomplete, these statistics are sufficient to show the general trend. Figures for the state sections are taken from the following volumes of the *Statistisches Jahrbuch der DDR,* hsgr. Staatlichen Zentralverwaltung fuer Statistik (Berlin: Staatsverlag der DDR): 1966, p. 477; 1971, p. 384; 1972, p. 394; 1973, p. 370; 1974, p. 370; 1975, p. 346; 1976, p. 348; 1977, p. 340; 1978, p. 302. Sources for the churches' own schools include for 1970, "840 evangelische Theologiestudenten in der DDR," *epd Landesdienst Berlin,* no. 104 (24 August 1971), p. 2; for 1971, "Etwa 770 Theologiestudenten in der DDR," *epd Landesdienst Berlin,* no. 21 (23 February 1972), p. 4; for 1973, *DDR, Material zur Politische Bildung,* ed. Be Ruys and Peter Heilmann (Berlin: Druckerei Hans J. Grundmann, 1973), p. 139; for 1974, "Theologiestudenten der DDR in Zahlen," *epd Landesdienst Berlin,* no. 161 (9 October 1975), p. 3; for 1975, *Kirche im Sozialismus,* no. 3 (July 1975), p. 30; for 1976, *Information des Bundes* . . . (April 1976); for 1977, "3000 Theologen in der DDR ausgebildet," *FAZ,* 15 December 1971, p. 4.

were subjected to a new attack in the form of the Council of Ministers' "Order on the Holding of Public Events" (*Veranstaltungsverordnung*). The order, approved November 26, 1970, threatened to restrict the churches' freedom of assembly in several ways.[135]

—With certain exceptions, all public events were to be announced to the local police. Exempt were church meetings "conducted by persons in full-time service of the churches and taking place in the rooms normally used by the churches." The order specifically itemized events—such as worship services, communions, and baptisms—that were considered valid religious activities. Religious activities were viewed narrowly;

[135]Based on "Verordnung ueber die Durchfuehrung von Veranstaltungen," *Gesetzblatt der DDR,* pt. 2, no. 10 (22 January 1971): pp. 69–71; CDU archives, 21 January 1972; EPS documents, 19 February 1971, p. 2.

numerous cultural- and leisure-oriented church activities were omitted from the list. Much depended on whether the state treated the list as exhaustive or merely suggestive.

—Outdoor events, even those on church property, and indoor dance events required approval by the appropriate police authorities. This affected particularly the parish youth group activities and regional church congresses.

—State approval was required for nonresidents of the GDR to appear at meetings. Thus, the churches would be held responsible for all foreigners appearing at any church activity, an obvious attempt to curtail contacts with the West German churches.

—Finally, the catch-all clauses mandated that "the events must uphold the principles and goals of the constitution of the GDR, the laws and other legal orders, and not damage public order and security." This granted the authorities considerable discretion in applying the order.

The most ominous aspect for the churches was that, for the first time, they would be required to report to the police. Previously the state had required notification and inspection for health and fire purposes. To be sure, the churches had *voluntarily* notified the local government officials regarding its youth retreats. But they had not been required to notify the police. Clearly the thrust of the state's policy was to limit the scope of church activity to that of ritual.

Initially, however, the churches' response was reserved. At the February 1971 meeting with the state, Schoenherr underscored the traditional emphasis on the laity among churches of the Reformation and rejected a church limited to ritual, but he did not mention the new order directly.[136] During the spring of 1971 the Landeskirchen also paid scant attention to the order, although both Fraenkel and Jacob, in the vein of Schoenherr, rejected any trend toward a church limited to ritual.[137] The churches' initial low-key response to the new order was due to uncertainty regarding the state's implementation of the order. The full impact of the order was not felt until the summer of 1971, when the events most affected, such as retreats, were scheduled. Moreover, the churches were

[136]"Ansprache Bischof D. Schoenherrs beim Empfang des Vorstandes," *Evangelischer Nachrichtendienst* 24 (17 March 1971).
[137]Fraenkel and Jacob in *KJ* 1971, pp. 223, 250–53. Schoenherr addressed the issue at the Berlin-Brandenburg Synod, in "Bericht der Kirchenleitung . . . ," *KJ* 1971, p. 237. The Executive Board of the Kirchenbund also raised it briefly at its meeting with Goetting in March 1971.

led to believe that the state's policy on notification by the churches had not been altered and that internal directives to that effect had been issued within the Ministry of the Interior.

Over time, however, it became clear that this was not the case. In practice, the list of activities exempt from notification proved more exhaustive than suggestive. Certain clearly religious events—such as synods and retreats of full-time church workers—though not listed, were treated as exempt from notification on a de facto basis by the police. However, for important cultural events—such as student retreats, exhibitions, and church concerts—notification was demanded. Gatherings involving more than one parish, such as church congresses, required permission. Sporting and dance events on church premises were forbidden outright.

The greatest impact of the new regulation occurred in youth retreats, church music events, and modern worship services. Seeking to reduce the churches' attractiveness to youth as an alternative for leisure time, the state, especially the FDJ, had long sought to inhibit youth retreats, excursions involving recreation and Bible study. Earlier the state had employed health and fire regulations and administrative measures to this end and had been considering an outright ban on such retreats.[138] Church concerts of organ and choral music also proved increasingly attractive to non-Christians. Until this point, the state had tolerated such concerts, but now it began to prevent publicly employed musicians from performing in them and to require police notification. Finally, the modern forms of worship, such as the well-known jazz services in Karl-Marx-Stadt, also threatened to challenge the FDJ's claim on the youth.

The churches' responses to the ordinance varied along familiar lines.[139] Thuringia, which had always notified the police regarding retreats, continued to do so; most other Landeskirchen refused and were fined, in some cases heavily, as in Saxony-Dresden. Some churches shifted their retreats to Thuringia to avoid trouble. Behind these differing responses lay not only political differences, but fundamental disagreement concerning what should be considered religious. Were church musical events a proclamation of the Gospel or not? What

---

[138]CDU archives, 17 June 1969.

[139]CDU archives, 28 March 1973. The fines were seldom paid, since the pastors' church-based bank accounts could not be garnisheed.

portion of a retreat must be devoted to Bible study in order to call it a Bible retreat? Saxony-Dresden and Saxony-Magdeburg, in particular, viewed the issue in absolute terms. Thuringia's position was encapsuled in Gerhard Lotz's retort that "a table prayer at a hunting banquet does not make it a religious event."

Despite these different responses and fundamental positions among the churches, the Kirchenbund was formally quite unified in rejecting the narrow interpretation of religious events reflected in the implementation of the ordinance. At its June 1971 meeting, the church leadership defended Bible retreats as "religious observances in the sense of the constitutionally-guaranteed exercise of religion." While thus rejecting police notification, it indicated that the current practice of notifying the civil authorities would be continued.[140] It charged that "the obligation to notify the police had covertly become an obligation to obtain permission" and asked for the state's assurances that the list of exempted events was meant to be suggestive, rather than exclusive.[141]

Despite this unified stance, the church leadership was hesitant to put the credibility of the church on the line, especially given the voices in the churches which urged acquiescence. Thus the Kirchenbund leadership sought to avoid public confrontation at the 1971 synod. For its part, the synod merely endorsed the church leadership's positions without strengthening them.[142]

The Kirchenbund sought a resolution of the conflict through quiet diplomacy, but several meetings with the state in 1972 proved futile. After numerous requests from the church, the state held two "informational meetings" with the church, in January and June 1972.[143] The church was soon disabused of whatever illusions it had that compro-

---

[140]"Beschluss der KKL . . . vom 26. Juni 1971," *epd Dokumentation*, no. 34 (19 July 1971): p. 23.

[141]"Bericht der KKL . . ." and "Beschluss der Synode . . . ," *epd Dokumentation*, no. 34 (19 July 1971): pp. 4, 19.

[142]Krusche again proved more vocal than other bishops and the Kirchenbund synod, condemning the order in his meetings with the CDU and his report to the Magdeburg synod. CDU archives, 15 November 1971; EPS documents, 16 July 1971; CDU archives, 3 August 1971.

[143]The Dresden church leadership, hard hit by fines, also haggled with Seigewasser, as reported in "Grundsatzaussprache Kirche-Staat in Leipzig," *epd Landesdienst Berlin*, no. 55 (10 May 1972): p. 3. Regarding the Kirchenbund-state meetings, see CDU archives, 21 January 1972. The first meeting was not authoritative in protocol terms, since the Kirchenbund Executive Committee and Seigewasser were represented by deputies; but the second meeting entailed the principals and was hence authoritative.

mise by the state was in the offing. The state representatives repeated the state's hard-line position and demanded the rescinding of the church leadership's June 1971 resolution. In his response, Schoenherr reiterated the church's opposition to a ritualized church and notification qua permission, as well as its hopes for internal bureaucratic directives. The second meeting reflected no significant change in positions and was likely timed to dampen increasing unrest at the upcoming Kirchenbund Synod by promising dialogue with the Executive Board.[144]

This tactic proved unsuccessful. The state's rigid enforcement of the ordinance, even in Thuringia, unified the churches' stance and the Kirchenbund intensified its protest even at the 1972 synod.[145] The church leadership's report stated bluntly: "We fail to see that the decision on what are religious observances can be left to the organs of the German People's Police. We are of the opinion that it is the business of the church to determine what is considered a religious observance."

The ordinance represented an attempt by the state to limit the scope and content of church activities to rituals performed in the church by church clerics. It was directed particularly at those activities aimed at modernizing the church, since they portended a new attractiveness for the church, particularly among youth, and were harder to oversee and control due to the spontaneity often involved. It is also to be explained by the state's renewed drive for Abgrenzung and ideological vigilance given new exposure to the West due to the Ostpolitik. In conjunction with the increased emphasis on socialist integration in the face of detente, the ordinance also reflected the Soviets' efforts to bring the GDR into closer alignment with other Soviet bloc states, which, with the exception of Poland, had limited the churches, for the most part, to ritualistic activity.[146] Finally, the ordinance reflected the inertia and bureaucratic interest of the Ministry of the Interior, which is responsible for the police.

Independence of Theology and Church Publication　A continuing source of tension derived from state infringement on the theological autonomy of the church in its communications. Notwithstanding Ver-

---

[144]Wolf-Dieter Zimmermann, "Nicht ohne kritische Distanz," *Lutherisches Monatsheft* 11 (August 1972): 399; CDU archives, 21 January 1972.
[145]"Bericht der KKL . . . ," *epd Dokumentation*, no. 30 (17 July 1972): pp. 21–22, 27.
[146]CDU archives, 23 July 1971.

ner's forswearance of "socialization of the church's doctrine," the CDU specifically attacked the work of certain West German theologians (e.g., Soelle, Moltmann) as revisionist and "theologically-disguised social democratic conceptions."[147] Moreover, certain specific Christian tenets came under fire, especially in broadcasts and books. For example, the concept of the sinful nature of man was rejected by the state as negating the optimistic basis of socialism. The state also criticized the churches' underemphasis on the role of wealth in one's alienation from God, arguing that only socialism provided the basis for the realization of the original concerns of Christianity. Such issues had long been the subject of controversy, both between the Ministry of Culture and the Evangelical Publishing House and between Radio GDR and the church officials responsible for the radio ministry over Radio GDR.[148] However, they took on new significance given the heightened emphasis on ideology and the "socialist personality" in 1971. Discussions with the state in 1971 and 1972 proved fruitless.[149]

The Abortion Issue   The legalization of abortion in early 1972 also led to church criticism of state policy. Despite Honecker's promotion of population growth to offset the effect of pre–Berlin Wall emigration and low birth rates, the GDR followed the lead of West Germany and Poland and liberalized its abortion laws. The state's preliminary soundings of public opinion revealed considerable opposition to the new measures among the Christian population, particularly among the clergy. Some supported the law, claiming it would simplify pastoral counseling; most, however, opposed the new law for ethical reasons.[150]

---

[147]NZ, 31 July and 12 October 1971; CDU archives, 8 November 1971.

[148]Beatrice Winter, "Zur Problematik der Mitarbeit der Evangelischen Kirche im Rundfunk der DDR in den Jahren 1946–1958" (dissertation, Free University of Berlin, 1979). "Bericht der KKL . . . ," *epd Dokumentation*, no. 30 (17 July 1972): p. 28. In part, the Kirchenbund's desire for greater ecumenical contact must be seen in this light: the Kirchenbund hoped to maintain greater theological autonomy by means of theological literature and publication licenses from Geneva. Such imports remained subject to stringent controls, according to EPC archives, 1 February 1970.

[149]See Arthur Hanhardt, Jr., "East Germany: From Goals to Realities . . . ," in *Political Socialization in Eastern Europe*, ed. Ivan Volgyes (New York: Praeger, 1975), pp. 66–69. For East German sources on the socialist personality, see Guenter Neuner, *Zur Theorie der sozialistischen Allgemeinbildung* (Berlin, GDR: Volk und Wissen Verlag, 1973), and Frank Adler et al., *Arbeiterklasse und Persoenlichkeit im Sozialismus* (Berlin, GDR: Dietz Verlag, 1977). See also *Bericht des Zentralkommittees an den VIII. Parteitag der SED* (Berlin, GDR: Dietz Verlag, 1971), p. 70, and Heinrich Frickel, "Stationen einer 20jaehrigen Entwicklung: Konfirmandenunterricht und Konfirmation in der DDR," *KiS* 1 (July 1975): 12.

[150]Opponents to abortion viewed it as violating the Fifth Commandment, as contributing to sexual laxness, as fostering indifference to children and inconsistent with the state's own

The CDU attempted unsuccessfully to mobilize support among Christians for the new law, arguing that the law would promote the equal rights and independence of women.[151] But, in addition, the CDU argued that Christians should apply situational ethics, rather than an absolute standard, since in scientific socialism "marriage and reproduction are no longer subject only to the laws of nature, but can be consciously structured to meet social goals."

On January 15, 1972, the eight bishops, reflecting the opposition in the church at large, issued a proclamation in which they roundly condemned abortion as the "killing of human life" and as counter to the Fifth Commandment.[152] Although viewing abortion as justifiable only in exceptional situations, they endorsed birth control as an alternative for women wishing to avoid pregnancy. While approving of the voluntary nature of the law, the bishops warned of the law's long-run effect—the "inescapable general apathy of the conscience with respect to the value of life."

One might expect the state to be incensed by the churches' criticism on an issue affecting not simply the churches' narrow interests, but society at large. However, the state itself was ambivalent regarding this policy change and tacitly greeted the ethical position of the churches.

This tacit acceptance of the bishops' criticism manifested itself in two unprecedented state actions. First, at a meeting with selected bishops, Seigewasser and a representative of the Ministry of Health explained the state's rationale and signaled the state's toleration of the church's dissent on this issue.[153] The state defended the law on pragmatic grounds—the need to limit illegal abortions and better plan the work schedules of women—and conceded that birth control remained preferable to abortion. The church representatives questioned the need for the new law, especially given the low population growth, and reiterated their ethical opposition, but they assured the state that they would respect it. They asked that the state respect the reservations of doctors opposed to performing abortions and urged that the quality and availability of the means of birth control be improved. Seigewasser indicated that total agreement on this issue was not expected.

---

family law, as ineffective in reducing criminal abortions, and as leaving doctors no room for individual decisions on the issue. See CDU archives, 29 December 1971.

[151]CDU archives, no date, "CDU Argumentationsthesen"; CDU archives, 10 January 1972.

[152]"Wort der Bischoefe der ev. Landeskirchen in der DDR vom 15. Januar 1972," *epd Dokumentation*, no. 6 (23 February 1972): pp. 84–85.

[153]CDU archives, 21 January 1972.

Second, for the first time in the GDR's history, members of the parliament were allowed to dissent publicly from a decision of the SED. Encountering resistance in its own ranks to the law, the CDU lobbied quietly to revise the draft law in order to place certain limits on the availability of abortion, to emphasize the doctor's obligation to counsel women seeking abortions, and to guarantee the rights of doctors to refuse to perform abortions on ethical grounds.[154] Although the SED rejected these proposed changes, it did permit CDU dissent in the June 1972 parliamentary vote on the new law: fourteen CDU members opposed it; eight others abstained. Goetting openly conceded the divisions within the CDU.[155]

The state's handling of the abortion issue should not be construed as an indication of general state acceptance of dissent. It does, however, reveal greater recognition on the part of the state that certain of its sometimes-contradictory interests may in fact be served by tolerating limited dissent by the church. In this respect, the managed disagreement over this issue represented a harbinger of the symbiotic relationship between church and state that later developed on the issue of peace.

Procedural Limitations of the Rapprochement with the Churches

In addition to the substantive areas of conflict discussed above, conflict of a procedural nature also demonstrated the limits of rapprochement. In its elite-level rapprochement, the state continued to differentiate among various Landeskirchen, though less so than before 1971. At the informational meeting with the church on European security, the state dealt with the Kirchenbund officially; however, the church delegation at the meeting regarding abortion was not representative of either the bishops or the Kirchenbund. The state continued to

[154]Schoenherr felt confident enough of the state's tacit toleration of this "dissent" to use his trip to Geneva in March 1972 to warn of the danger to society from the new law. Fraenkel indicated the lack of state disquiet at the churches' position. "Gespraech des EPD mit dem Vorsitzenden . . . ," *epd Dokumentation*, no. 12 (20 March 1972): p. 2; "Ein Wort zur oeffentlichen Verantwortung der Kirchen in der gegenwaertigen Situation," *epd Dokumentation*, no. 17 (10 April 1973): p. 44.

[155]"Orientierung zur Frage des Schwangerschaftsabbruches," *epd Dokumentation*, no. 19 (8 May 1982): p. 4; *NZ*, 20 February and 10 March 1972; "Durchfuehrungsbestimmungen zum Gesetz ueber die Unterbrechung der Schwangerschaft," *Gesetzblatt der DDR*, pt. 2, no. 12 (20 March 1972); CDU archives, no date, "Hinweise und Anregungen."

target its ire at certain bishops. For example, Fraenkel remained persona non grata due to his role in the EKU debate, though his policy switch on EKU unity in spring 1972 was greeted by the state. Krusche too remained in disfavor, due less to his earlier criticism of the political system of the GDR than for his condemnations of the Events Ordinance and educational discrimination.[156] Despite his relatively circumspect address at the 1971 Kirchenbund synod, Rathke was subject to a harsher treatment than other bishops, partly due to the state's antipathy toward his modernizing tendencies, particularly in the areas of urban ministries and youth church congresses. Thuringia posed an interesting case. The educational discrimination seems to have been more frequent there, although the friction over the Events Ordinance was considered less due to the Thuringian habit of reporting most events. The state appeared to be punishing Braecklein for his departure from Mitzenheim's policies.

The other Landeskirchen received relatively better treatment. The state continued to court the flirtatious Natho in Anhalt.[157] It greeted the election in Greifswald of Bishop Gienke, who followed in the relatively "progressive" line of Krummacher. The relationship with Saxony-Dresden remained conflict-ridden; however, the state took an active interest in the succession to retiring Bishop Noth and was pleased that the moderate Hempel defeated the conservative, pietistic forces supporting Dr. Voigt. Although often hewing a hard line in certain districts of Berlin-Brandenburg, the state sought for the most part to shore up Schoenherr's position in the Landeskirche in order to maintain stability in the Kirchenbund, which it viewed as more "progressive" than most of the Landeskirchen.[158]

Nineteen seventy-one and 1972 saw the recognition of the Kirchenbund by the state and appeared to open a new era in the church-state relationship. Following the Ulbricht succession and Honecker's consequent cooperation with Soviet detente policy, the state accepted and even promoted the churches' ties to the FRG and international organizations. As a natural consequence of this normalization, the church turned its attention to defining its domestic role as a "church within socialism."

[156]CDU archives, 28 December 1971.

[157]Natho, for his part, continued to endorse in *Neue Zeit* the participation in elections, to be sure in the context of the Christian role in society. See *NZ*, 7 November 1971 and 17 April 1974.

[158]CDU archives, 28 December 1971.

The wide range of viewpoints within the church on this question was demonstrated during the internal church controversy over Falcke's controversial espousal of "critical solidarity."

The state's response to Falcke's position of "accepting socialism in order to change it" revealed the limitations to this rapprochement during 1971 and 1972, however. The state refused to tolerate the church articulating an alternative vision of society and continued to differentiate among the Landeskirchen in its dealing with the churches. The rapprochement remained limited to interactions and concessions at the elite levels. Despite the reduced conflict over *Abgrenzung* on the international level and the tacit state acceptance of church dissent on abortion, areas of domestic conflict—the treatment of individual Christians, institutional interests of the church, and societal issues—continued to divide church and state. Attempts by the church to deepen the rapprochement at the levels of treatment of individual Christians and institutional interests resulted in, at best, marginal change in specific cases.

7 Deepening Rapprochement, 1973–1978

To the state, Falcke's criticism of the state and conception of "improved socialism" epitomized the dangers inherent in the new policy of detente with the FRG. Increased contact with the West might lead to ideological "contaminations," particularly of the Social Democratic variety so feared by the SED. Certain elements in the churches, who were subject in any case to greater political influences from the West, might experience rising expectations of liberalization in the GDR in the wake of detente. Not only was the state determined to limit this linkage of international relaxation and domestic change as much as possible, but it sought to limit the damage from whatever linkage did prove necessary. Forced by the Soviet Union to compromise on detente, the GDR sought to compensate for this weakening by shoring up ideologically. The oft-reiterated ideological justification for this contradictory policy was the alleged "dialectical unity of peaceful coexistence and Abgrenzung."[1]

The churches were caught between these two tendencies. On the one hand, with their network of inter-German ties, the churches were among the leading beneficiaries of detente. Yet at the grass roots, the churches were particularly subject to the increased emphasis on ideolog-

---

[1] Peter Jochen Winters, "Die Aussenpolitik der DDR," in *Handbuch der deutschen Aussenpolitik*, ed. Hans-Peter Schwarz (1975), pp. 805–6; Institut fuer Internationale Beziehungen an der Akademie fuer Staats- und Rechtswissenschaft der DDR, *Aussenpolitik der DDR— Fuer Sozialismus und Frieden*, especially p. 53.

ical purity and vigilance. This ideological shoring-up did not preclude a certain rapprochement with the church leadership; but until late 1972 it remained limited to superficial, Berlin-oriented gestures.

The period after 1972, however, saw a deepening of the rapprochement. With their ties to the West German churches and international organizations, the churches proved a litmus test of human rights in the GDR, particularly in the context of increasing attention paid to this issue at the CSCE. In addition to coping with this international exposure, limiting the damage from detente also entailed dampening the increasing criticism on the grassroots level in the democratically organized churches. These factors led the state to offer pragmatic agreements on several of the domestic issues of conflict with the churches in 1973 and 1974. For its part, the church continued the Schoenherr line of dialogue with the state and increasing participation in official activities, such as peace forums. However, the tension between rapprochement at the leadership level and ideological conflict on the grass roots led to increased criticism of the new relationship, culminating in the suicide protest of Pastor Oskar Bruesewitz in the town square in 1976. In the wake of the Bruesewitz affair, the state initiated a major overture to the Kirchenbund—the Honecker summit with the church leadership in March 1978, accompanied by significant concessions, largely of an institutional nature. These agreements not only helped ameliorate conflict with the church, but constituted a de facto recognition by the state of the legitimacy of the churches' social presence. But this period also revealed the long-term limitations to and problems in this rapprochement between church and state, problems that then continued to plague the relationship.

DETENTE AND THE INTER-GERMAN CHURCH RELATIONSHIP

As a result of the churches' decisions for separation and the acceleration of inter-German detente, the churches' inter-German relations continued to decline as a source of conflict with the state. Indeed, the remaining ties to West German churches became more of an advantage than a disadvantage.

In terms of the Kirchenbund, the acrimony over Abgrenzung from the

EKD and Article 4.4 disappeared.[2] The state ceased its agitation regarding "special community" affirmed in Article 4.4. For its part the Kirchenbund continued to downplay Article 4.4 in its synods, either leaving it unmentioned or interpreting it in terms of "normal bilateral relations."

Following the regionalization of the EKU in 1972, the state finally normalized relations with this body, although not to the degree enjoyed by the Kirchenbund. The regionalization and the replacement of critical leaders, such as Hildebrandt, president of the EKU Chancellory, and Fraenkel, chairman of the EKU Council (East), with less critical leaders facilitated the state's resumption of official contacts with the EKU.[3] But differences remained regarding the desirable level of contact between the two regions. The state demanded an end to the joint sessions of the two regional councils and balked at West German participation at EKU (East) regional synods.[4] But with the liberalized travel arrangements under detente, the state abandoned as futile its efforts to prevent Western participation.

As in the case of the EKU, the state came to accept the partial solution reached by Berlin-Brandenburg in 1972. To be sure, it protested that the churches' "two bishops, one church" theory violated the Basic Treaty and its recognition of postwar borders. The state took pains to limit the

[2]Sources indicating the state's shift include Georg Schaefer, "Standort und Engagement," *Standpunkt* 1 (January 1973): 10; Guenther Wirth, "Bemerkung zur Bilanz," *Standpunkt* 1 (April 1973): 86–88; Guenther Wirth, "Die Versuchung des Nationalismus," und "Zu Kernfragen des ideologischen Kampfes," *Standpunkt* 1 (May 1973): 115–17, 131–32; Guenther Wirth, "Ueber einen Erkundungsausflug," *Standpunkt* 1 (June 1973): 143. Internal CDU sources include CDU archives, 14 June 1973; CDU archives, 28 March 1973. For indications of the churches' affirmation of the special relationship with the West German churches, see "Bericht der KKL . . . ," *epd Dokumentation*, no. 25 (12 June 1973): p. 16; "Bericht der KKL . . . ," *epd Dokumentation*, no. 45 (19 November 1973): pp. 2–10; "Bericht der KKL . . . ," *epd Dokumentation*, no. 52 (11 November 1974): p. 18; *KiS* 4 (April 1978): 3. In certain settings some pronouncements went further than this. Braecklein, for example, spoke of "spiritual and intellectual bonds" with the West German churches, clearly beyond his 1969–70 formulations. The Kirchenbund prayer for the twenty-fifth anniversary of the GDR used an all-German formulation also. See "Ansprache von Landesbischof D. Ingo Braecklein," vor der Generalsynode der VELKDDR, *epd Dokumentation*, no. 30 (23 July 1973): p. 4; "Dank— Fuerbitte—Hoffnung," *Mecklenburgische Kirchenzeitung*, 29 September 1974, p. 2.

[3]"Taetigkeitsbericht der Kirchenkanzlei der EKU—Bereich DDR . . . ," *epd Dokumentation*, no. 29 (18 June 1974): pp. 5, 7, 19–24. Ecumenical ties involving the EKU were allowed to burgeon after 1972 also.

[4]The state opposed, but finally agreed to EKU (West) representation in the person of president of the synod Wilm (Bielefeld), according to "Die Tagung der EKU-Synod," *Evangelischer Nachrichtendienst* 27 (15 May 1974): 4; CDU archives, 13 September 1973; CDU archives, 26 April 1974.

West Berlin representation at the inauguration of Schoenherr as Eastern bishop in February 1973 and, ignoring the Four Power Agreement on Berlin, continued to deny the West Berlin bishop, Scharf, entry to the GDR.[5]

Nonetheless, the state mellowed on the issue following the inauguration of Schoenherr as bishop. CDU Chairman Goetting hailed this event as the "conclusion of a development." The state normalized the relationship with church officials in Berlin, granting residence permits in East Berlin for pastors and theology students again and dampening media polemics considerably.[6] While not giving up its goal of total separation, the state reconciled itself to working patiently with "progressives" in the Landeskirche to foster long-term, piecemeal changes, such as a new constitution for the Eastern region.

However, because of Berlin's broader political significance to the German question and the ambiguity of the Basic Treaty regarding Berlin's status, Berlin-Brandenburg could not escape the continued inter-German jousting over Berlin. For example, the GDR, employing its own particular interpretation of the Basic Treaty, resisted any attempts to strengthen West Berlin's status. Thus it exerted considerable pressure on the Kirchenbund to oppose the plans of the WCC to hold a meeting of its Central Committee in West Berlin in August 1974. Although the Kirchenbund representatives on this committee abstained on the issue, their interest in detente led the Soviets to override GDR opposition and to approve the meeting and Eastern participation in it.[7] Similarly, state efforts to promote separation via constitutional change in the Berlin-Brandenburg church met with little success.

In general the state pursued a rather contradictory policy, under-

---

[5]*NZ*, 13 February 1973; CDU archives, 29 January 1973; CDU archives, 22 March 1973. "Interview des Westdeutschen Rundfunks (Gottfried Vetter) mit Bischof Scharf am 31.12.72," Evangelical Press Center, West Berlin.

[6]In 1973 the official media was subdued and only Hanfried Mueller attacked the two-bishops solution. See *SDZ*, 14 February 1973, p. 7. Positive soundings toward the 1973 synod are found in Georg Schaefer, "Standort und Engagement," *Standpunkt* 1 (January 1973): 7–8. The first official meeting between the state and Landeskirche Church Leadership was held on 7 December 1973 at a meeting to weigh the results of the 1973 Moscow peace congress. "Bericht der Kirchenleitung . . . ," *epd Dokumentation*, no. 27 (4 June 1973): p. 35; "Aktuelle Uebersicht," *KiS* 1 (1974): 4.

[7]CDU archives, 20 September 1973; CDU archives, 27 August 1973; CDU archives, 13 September 1973. Ernst Stiller, "Weltkirchenrat 1974 zu Gast in Berlin," *Der Tagesspiegel*, 16 September 1973, p. 51. For the official reinterpretation of the significance of this meeting, see Carl Ordnung, "Oekumene in Westberlin," *Standpunkt* 2 (July 1974).

scoring the differences between the East and West German churches, particularly on international issues, yet permitting greater contact between them. For example, it criticized as "neo-colonialist" the EKD's stands on UNCTAD and development aid and contrasted the churches' positions on the antiracism program of the WCC.[8] Yet exchanges and travel between the churches were facilitated in ever-growing measure and at higher levels of protocol. The Kirchenbund and EKD were permitted to exchange official representatives to each other's synod, at modest rank in 1973, at the bishop level in 1974, and at the chairman level in 1977.[9] Even conservative anti-Communists, such as former Bishop Hans Lilje (Hannover), were granted access to the GDR.[10] By 1977 the state even allowed GDR participation in an EKD church congress in West Berlin.

Nonetheless, the state was still leery of substantive cooperation on social-political issues. For example, in 1974 the state opposed a proposed joint EKD-Kirchenbund position on the CSCE, leading the churches to drop the idea.[11] Nor was it ready for the churches' advocacy of inter-German contacts, as indicated by its rejection of church criticism of the GDR's hike in the minimum currency exchange for visiting West Germans.[12] Yet by 1977 the two churches became bold enough to issue a joint declaration on peace and detente, a harbinger of vari-

[8]Eberhard Klages, "Wie der 'stille Amerikaner'," *Standpunkt* 1 (May 1973): 117; *NZ*, 8 February 1973; Guenther Wirth, "Ein Seminar ueber Engagement? Ein Seminar des Engagements," *Standpunkt* 1 (September 1973): 234–35.

[9]Greetings of Senior Administrator Walter Pabst (June 1973), Synod President Wahrman (February 1974) and Bishop Gienke (November 1974) are found in *epd Dokumentation*, no. 24 (8 June 1973): pp. 75–79, *epd Dokumentation*, no. 5 (4 February 1974): pp. 33–35, and *epd Dokumentation*, no. 54 (18 November 1974): pp. 59–61. The presence of EKD Council member Prof. Wenzel Lohff and EKD Synod Speaker von Heyl at the May 1973 and November 1974 Kirchenbund synods is recorded in *epd Nachrichtenspiegel*, no. 23 (6 June 1973): p. 7a, and *epd Dokumentation*, no. 52 (11 November 1974), p. 19. No non-GDR citizens were invited to the October 1973 Kirchenbund synod, a constitutive meeting focusing largely on the organization of the new Synod and Kirchenbund leadership, according to *epd Dokumentation*, no. 5 (4 February 1974): p. 34. See also *KiS* 4 (February 1978): 9.

[10]The Lilje visit is recorded in "Hope Expressed for More East-West Church Contact," *LWF Information*, no. 29 (16 August 1973): p. 6. *NZ*, 23 June 1977; *KiS* 3 (October 1977): 5.

[11]Such a joint statement was first proposed by Fraenkel in 1971, according to "Fraenkel fuer gemeinsames kirchliches Votum zur Sicherheitskonferenz," *epd Zentralausgabe*, no. 77 (21 April 1971): p. 4, but proposed more seriously in the Kirchenbund in 1973. "Arbeitsbericht des Kirchenbundes . . ." *Mitteilungsblatt*, no. 1 (30 March 1973): p. 4. CDU archives, 15 May 1973.

[12]The EKU and Berlin-Brandenburg (East) both criticized the state action. See "Bericht des Vorsitzenden . . . Bischof D. Horst Gienke . . . ," *epd Dokumentation*, no. 29 (18 June 1974): p. 80, and "Bericht der Kirchenleitung . . . ," *epd Dokumentation*, no. 27 (4 June 1974): p. 38.

ous joint declarations during the worsening East-West relations after 1979.[13]

THE CHURCHES' INTERNATIONAL ACTIVITIES

The advantages of church participation in international ecumenical organizations began to fade during this period. Although the state was still quite interested in the international status that GDR participation in these organizations represented, this became less urgent after the GDR gained widespread international recognition and membership in the United Nations in 1973. Moreover, as such organizations began to confront sensitive political issues, such as human rights in the Soviet bloc, this participation threatened to become politically costly. In conjunction with the drive for socialist integration to prevent ideological erosion due to detente, these disadvantages led to heightened efforts of promote church ties with the other churches in the Soviet bloc.

Despite these drawbacks, the GDR continued to foster ties with international ecumenical organizations because they provided international status and opportunities for Abgrenzung from the West German churches. Indeed contacts increased dramatically: the numbers of GDR citizens able to travel to the West on ecumenical business roughly doubled each year after the founding of the Kirchenbund.[14] The state permitted major meetings of the LWF and the WCC to be held in the GDR in 1973 and 1974, respectively. Delighted by the EKD's criticism of him in the context of the antiracism program, the state accorded WCC Secretary General Philip Potter very high protocol on his visits to the GDR, including a meeting with chairman of the Council of Ministers Horst Sindermann.[15]

The churches continued to assume relatively "progressive" positions in these organizations on issues relating to the Third World. Figuring prominently in this, of course, was the continued disagreement with the EKD regarding the WCC's antiracism program. Despite internal crit-

---

[13]"Gemeinsame Erklaerung," *epd Dokumentation*, no. 5 (23 January 1978): p. 78.

[14]Discussion with Senior Administrator Walter Pabst, Kirchenbund.

[15]Potter was given favorable treatment in the GDR media. See for example, *ND*, 1 and 6 June 1973. Potter visits are reported in "Bericht der KKL . . . ," *epd Dokumentation*, no. 45 (19 November 1973): p. 7, and "Bericht der KKL . . . ," *epd Dokumentation*, no. 52 (11 November 1974): p. 14.

icism of the program and declining collections for it, the Kirchenbund Church Leadership issued calls for additional fundraising collections in 1973 and 1975.[16] Consultations with the EKD failed to resolve their differences over the issue, which were again manifested in divergent votes in the WCC Central Committee.[17] The VELKDDR expressed support for the black Lutheran churches in Namibia, even while the EKD was financially supporting the white Lutheran churches there. After the military coup in Chile in fall 1973, the churches expressed solidarity with the Chilean people and the Kirchenbund set up a fund for Chilean refugees.[18]

Although the Kirchenbund justified its continued support of these Third World causes on the basis of human rights, it added partisan anti-imperialistic nuances to its practical efforts. The churches' activities during the Tenth World Youth Festival in Berlin in August 1973 demonstrated this.[19] The state had initially opposed any church activities, fearing spontaneous manifestations of dissent at this massive rally, the first such event involving large numbers of foreign visitors since the new inter-German travel agreements took effect. However, the church used its various events—such as exhibits in churches, discussion groups, and general worship services—to express support for national liberation movements and downplay differences of Weltanschauung with the state. No incidents of protest developed and the church's pronouncements, more partisan than their official ones, heartened the state.[20]

[16]The Kirchenbund's affirmation of support is found in *Mitteilungsblatt . . .* , no. 2 (30 May 1973): pp. 18–22, and *Mitteilungsblatt . . .* , no. 1 (5 March 1975): p. 1. For criticism, see Bishop Hans-Joachim Fraenkel, "Die Freiheit des Christen zum Dienst in der Gesellschaft," *epd Dokumentation*, no. 19a (16 April 1974): p. 2.

[17]The Kirchenbund position on the PCR can be found in *KJ* 1974, pp. 478–81; the EKD position is found in "Stellungnahme des Rates . . . ," *epd Dokumentation*, no. 33 (15 July 1974): pp. 107f; the EKD-Kirchenbund consultation is referred to in "Bericht der KKL . . . ," *epd Dokumentation*, no. 52 (11 November 1974): p. 19; CDU archives, 26 August 1974.

[18]"Ansprache von Landesbischof D. Ingo Braecklein . . . ," *epd Dokumentation* no. 30 (23 July 1973): p. 5; Lukas de Vries, "Church and Political Situation in Namibia," *LWF Information*, no. 14 (24 April 1973): pp. 4–8. "Bericht der KKL . . . ," *epd Dokumentation*, no. 45 (19 November 1973): p. 6; "Bericht der KKL . . . ," *epd Dokumentation*, no. 52 (11 November 1974): p. 24; "Bericht des Vorsitzenden . . . Bischof D. Horst Gienke . . . ," *epd Dokumentation*, no. 29 (18 June 1974): p. 80; "Stellungnahme der Landessynoden zur Situation in Chile und in Nahen Ost," *KiS* 1 (December 1973): 38; EPC archives, March 1974, pp. 1–2; "Bericht der KKL . . . ," *epd Dokumentation*, no. 25 (12 June 1973): p. 5.

[19]"Bischof Schoenherr auf einem Gespraechsabend . . . ," *epd Dokumentation*, no. 45 (19 November 1973): pp. 22–23; CDU archives, 3 August 1973; CDU archives, 9 August 1973.

[20]CDU archives, 20 August 1973.

Despite this convergence of church and state positions on Third World issues generally, a major difference developed on the Middle East. The GDR had long refused to pay reparations to Israel for the victims of the Holocaust and severely criticized Israeli actions in the Middle East. Following the Yom Kippur War of 1973, the GDR voted in favor of a 1975 United Nations resolution condemning Zionism as racism. Despite their generalized support for national self-determination by Third World peoples, the churches felt a particular burden to seek atonement for the Holocaust and reconciliation with the Jewish people. The churches have sought to counteract the official GDR view that the roots of fascism have been eliminated in the GDR and that hence the GDR is absolved of guilt for the consequences of the Third Reich.[21] Thus, in contrast to the state's condemnation of Israeli "imperialism," the churches in 1973 called for a just peace guaranteeing the rights of all parties to a secure existence and rejected the use of force. In 1975 they rejected the equating of Zionism with racism, maintaining that "as Christians we see ourselves placed with the people of Israel in the history of God according to the witness of the Bible; in the past as Germans we rejected in a terrifying way the right of the Jewish people to exist." This divergence from state policy was reinforced in 1978 with the churches' focus on the fortieth anniversary of the Night of Broken Glass. Bishop Schoenherr was particularly concerned with correcting the GDR's distorted interpretation of the fascist inheritance and with the welfare of the Jewish people.

In addition to this substantive conflict, international ties entailed a number of other secondary conflicts between church and state. For example, they provided opportunities for GDR church representatives to practice their "special community" with the FRG churches. Par-

---

[21]"Bericht der KKL . . . ," *epd Dokumentation*, no. 25 (12 June 1973): p. 5, and "Bericht der Kirchenleitung der Evangelische Kirche in Berlin-Brandenburg (Ost) . . . ," *epd Dokumentation*, no. 27 (4 June 1974): p. 43. The 1974 synod of the VELKDDR did not address the Middle East situation and Gienke's report in the 1974 EKU synod was relatively weak. Curiously, Schoenherr was less favorable to the Palestinians than Dr. Peter Kirchner, head of the Jewish community in the GDR, who endorsed the "national rights of the Palestinian Arabs" in his return greetings to the Evangelical churches on 11 November 1973, as found in "Information aus der Arbeit des Kirchenbundes," mimeographed (Berlin, GDR: Sekretariat des Kirchenbundes 2501—1139/1973). Regarding the 1975 UN resolution on Zionism, see "Erklaerung der Leitenden Geistlichen der Gliedkirchen . . . zur Zionismusresolution vom 27. Nov. 1975," *epd Dokumentation*, no. 9 (23 February 1976): p. 22, and *KiS* 2 (February 1976): 3–4. Regarding the Night of Broken Glass, see "Beschluss," *epd Dokumentation*, no. 42–43 (9 October 1978): p. 33. Schoenherr spoke out against antisemitic manifestations in GDR society at the 1978 Kirchenbund synod. See *Der Tagesspiegel*, 26 September 1978.

ticularly prior to Scharf's retirement as bishop in 1976, these meetings rankled the state.[22]

Second, the state's domestic Kirchenpolitik continued to interfere periodically with the churches' international participation. Thus in some cases the state refused visas to certain individuals for reasons of the local Kirchenpolitik and thereby jeopardized the participation of an entire delegation.[23] Certain areas of ecumenical work, such as evangelization by fundamentalists, were more problematic than others from the state's perspective.[24] Despite the Kirchenbund's official policy of canceling an entire delegation if essential delegates are denied visas, as a practical matter, the state still retained considerable clout in using ecumenical travel as a lever in its domestic Kirchenpolitik.

Third, the state balked at the Kirchenbund's attempts to include more laity in international delegations.[25] Limiting travel to only full-time church personnel threatened to divide the church into two classes, those allowed to travel to the West and those not allowed, a situation inconsistent with the Lutheran conception of a priesthood of all believers. Thus the church would face a schism parallel to that in GDR society as a whole, namely between those with and those without access to Western currency. In addition to this theological motivation, the Kirchenbund leadership hoped that greater participation by laity in international ecumenical organizations would reinforce the church's credibility with the grass roots. The Kirchenbund's support for the antiracism program, for example, had met with much criticism and rejection among the laity, as indicated by the drastic drop in contributions to the special collections for this purpose.[26] The state too sought to increase grassroots

[22]"DDR-Kirchenbund nach Schweden eingeladen," *epd Landesdienst Berlin,* no. 132 (17 August 1973): p. 2; CDU archives, 28 September 1973.

[23]For example, when the state refused visas to some members of Kirchenbund delegations to France and Sweden, the Kirchenbund retaliated by canceling the entire delegations. The Gienke-led delegation of the Kirchenbund finally went to Sweden in May 1975, according to *KiS* 1 (July 1975): 3. CDU archives, 16 August 1974; CDU archives, 10 September 1974.

[24]For example, fearing the proselytization and "charismatic" character of fundamentalists, the state curtailed GDR participation in the Conference on World Mission and Evangelization in Bangkok (January 1973) and a conference of fundamentalists in Lausanne (1974). "Weltmissionskonferenz in Bangkok . . . ," *epd Landesdienst Berlin,* no. 1 (2 January 1973): p. 4, and discussions with Church Administrator Dr. Johannes Althausen.

[25]"Bericht der KKL . . . ," *epd Dokumentation,* no. 52 (11 November 1974): p. 27; "5 Jahre Kirchenbund—500 Jahre Landeskirchen. Interview . . . mit OKR Stolpe," *epd Dokumentation,* no. 36 (7 August 1974): p. 48.

[26]Ibid. "Bericht der KKL . . . ," *epd Dokumentation,* no. 25 (12 June 1973): p. 5; "Bericht der Kirchenleitung der Evangelische Kirche in Berlin-Brandenburg (Ost) . . . 1974," *epd Dokumentation,* no. 27 (4 June 1974): p. 31.

support for these stands. But travel visas for laity required the approval of their workplace supervisors, who usually feared the loss of the work time, or worse, a defection to the West. However, the state had little to fear from losing "superfluous" pastors to the West. Moreover, in pursuing its goal of a ritual-oriented church, the state had no interest in fostering more lay activity. Thus travel visas for laity remained rare.

Fourth, the organizational focus of the churches' international ecumenical activity, the WCC and LWF, became less attractive for the state as these organizations increasingly addressed issues of human rights in the Soviet bloc. As noted earlier, during the early period of the Ostpolitik, ecumenical organizations assumed positions useful to the Soviet strategy by calling for international recognition of the two Germanies and a European security conference, thereby helping to generate public pressure on the West to negotiate. However, with the treaties in place, the spotlight shifted to the *content* of the European security conference and, like the West European states, these international ecumenical organizations began to address the so-called Basket III issues of human rights and the free flow of people and information.[27] In addition to the CSCE debate, another factor for increased attention to human rights in these organizations was internal crisis, particularly in the WCC.[28] Some member churches criticized what they viewed as the World Council's social activism, support of armed liberation movements, and failure to criticize Soviet bloc repression of religion; some cut back financial contributions, leading to a fiscal crisis in the WCC. To restore the WCC's credibility, they favored placing the antiracism program in the framework of a broader WCC defense of human rights, including the Soviet bloc violations.[29]

[27]Robert Legvold, "The Problem of European Security," *Problems of Communism* 23 (January–February 1974): 13–33; J. F. Brown, "Soviet Policy in Eastern Europe and the Impact of Detente," and John Dornberg, "East Germany: The Special Case," in *East European Perspectives on European Security and Cooperation*, ed. Robert R. King and Robert W. Dean (New York: Praeger, 1974), pp. 1–16, 102–17.

[28]German fundamentalists were critical in *epd Dokumentation*, no. 21 (29 April 1974): pp. 1–45. Regarding the LWF, see "LWF President Discusses International Challenges," *LWF Information*, no. 27 (1 August 1973): p. 2; "LWF Leaders Express Christian Hopes for Security," *LWF Information*, no. 14 (3 April 1974): pp. 1–3.

[29]Although the EKD assumed a critical position in this debate, it continued to give financial support. See "Protokoll der gemeinsamen Sitzung des Rates der EKD und Stab der OeRK; 7 Juni 1974 in Genf," *epd Dokumentation*, no. 33 (15 July 1974): pp. 30–35; "Diskussionsbeitrag in Plenum von Dr. Weizsaecker am 15.8.," *epd Dokumentation*, no. 40 (2 September 1974): pp. 113–14.

Thus the general drive by the Soviets for greater socialist integration in the face of the dangers of detente and their particular defensiveness regarding the human rights debate in international ecumenical organizations combined to produce greater attempts by the Soviets to garner cooperation by the Kirchenbund with the churches in the Soviet bloc, both bilaterally and in ecumenical forums. In these efforts the Soviets found ready support from the GDR, in particular from the CDU.[30] The CDU media continually underscored the leading role on the Russian Orthodox Church and the Soviet Union in general.

The churches, on the other hand, were much less sanguine about the prospect of a "special community" with other churches in the bloc.[31] Rhetorically, the Kirchenbund stressed the special meaning of ties based on the common task in a socialist society. In reality, however, the GDR churches considered themselves "Western" by tradition. Moreover, they were skeptical of the credibility and independence of the churches, not only the Russian Orthodox Church, but also the other Protestant denominations in Eastern Europe. To be sure, there was some genuine interest in contacts with them, motivated in part by a desire to encourage their independence, in part by accommodation to the state's wishes and in part by ecumenical curiosity. Also, for Lutherans, the largely German minority churches in Rumania, Latvia, and Estonia held interest by virtue of national tradition.

The Kirchenbund's skepticism of socialist integration by the churches was borne out in contacts with other Soviet bloc states.[32] Political differences with the Hungarian churches emerged; theological discussions with the Russian Orthodox Church revealed little common ground. Ties with the churches in Czechoslovakia and especially in Poland were burdened by the national enmity of these peoples toward the Germans. Thus despite the Kirchenbund's rhetorical support for

---

[30]For a collection of positive articles on the churches in the Soviet bloc, see Gerhard Bassarak, ed., *Oekumenische Diakonie* (1975). *NZ*, 21 April, 2 November, and 10 December 1972; *NZ*, 8 April and 7 June 1973. An integral goal of the new journal *Standpunkt* was to win the clergy for friendship with the Soviet Union. See CDU archives, 29 January 1973; CDU archives, 2 August 1974; CDU archives, 14 May 1973; CDU archives, 28 March 1973.

[31]"Bericht der KKL . . . ," *epd Dokumentation*, no. 25 (12 June 1973): pp. 15–16; "Ansprache von Landesbischof D. Ingo Braecklein . . . ," *epd Dokumentation*, no. 30 (23 July 1973): p. 10; "Bericht der KKL . . . ," *epd Dokumentation*, no. 52 (11 November 1974): p. 16.

[32]"Bericht der KKL . . . ," *epd Dokumentation*, no. 52 (11 November 1974): pp. 13, 16–17, 21; CDU archives, 15 May 1974; CDU archives, 20 September 1973. For Pabst's request for standing representation in Geneva, see CDU archives, 20 September 1973.

such ties, it continued to place its priority on multilateral ties with world organizations and bilateral ties with the Western churches. It sought permanent representation in Geneva, for example, a request that the GDR rejected, arguing that the Kirchenbund lagged behind other bloc churches in "consciousness."

Despite this skepticism of socialist integration, the Kirchenbund did begin to join in new Soviet-sponsored initiatives addressing peace, namely ad hoc multilateral forums of religious groups. The Soviets realized that the Christian Peace Conference (CPC) had become discredited as a vehicle for mobilizing support among the world's churches since the invasion of Czechoslovakia and the Soviet-manipulated purge of its defiant leadership.[33] Beginning with the Congress of Peace Forces in September 1973 in Moscow, the Soviets demonstrated a preference for an ad hoc forum for the purpose of mobilizing a broader base of European public opinion and providing more flexibility and control than the CPC. At its precedent-setting consultation with the Kirchenbund regarding the CSCE in March 1972, the GDR floated a trial balloon regarding Kirchenbund participation in the 1973 congress. In the person of Christa Lewek, specialist on questions of church and society in the Kirchenbund Secretariat, the Kirchenbund engaged in the planning for the Moscow congress and voted in September 1973 to send a delegation of Lewek, Bishop Gienke, and Bishop Natho.[34]

The churches knew the drawbacks of participating, and opposition was considerable, particularly from Dresden, Magdeburg, and Goerlitz. The visibility and propaganda value to the state from the Moscow congress was considerable and the vast size of the congress would preclude meaningful debate and democratic procedure. Credibility problems for the Kirchenbund would ensue at the grass roots and with the EKD. However, the churches wished to develop a dialogue with the state on European security issues. Many felt that participation would demonstrate, in a limited fashion, the churches' commitment to peace, without the inherent risks of a more extensive commitment, such as joining the CPC. The independence of the churches' participation and the uncensored publication of its contribution were crucial precondi-

[33]Fletcher, pp. 55–56.

[34]Reinhard Henkys, "Eine neue Qualitaet der Zusammenarbeit?," *KiS* 1 (December 1973): 10–11; "Weltkongress unter Moskaus Obhut," *Der Tagesspiegel*, 1 November 1973, reprinted in full in *epd Dokumentation*, no. 2 (21 January 1974): p. 52; CDU archives, 4 April 1973; "Brief Bischof Schoenherrs . . . ," *epd Dokumentation*, no. 2 (21 January 1974): p. 56.

tions for the churches. Another precondition was the participation of ecumenical organizations (especially the WCC and LWF), which alleviated the credibility problem somewhat.[35] By sending two bishops with relatively "progressive" reputations, rather than Chairman Schoenherr, the Kirchenbund also helped limit the damage to its credibility. Most important, however, was the belief that participation on the GDR delegation brought the chance to meet other members—especially its head, Politburo member Albert Norden—and demonstrate the churches' role in society, thereby overcoming the state's mistrust of the church.

The church demonstrated its independence both in protocol and in the substance of its contributions. Issues such as human rights, friendfoe stereotypes, and training for peace were raised, providing a distinctive accent by the Kirchenbund representatives.[36] The level of the state's interest in the churches' participation was reflected in its tolerance of these critical remarks, as well as Honecker's inclusion of the "church officials" in his mandate to the departing delegation.[37]

The Moscow congress represents a significant development in the church-state relationship. Despite its skepticism of socialist integration, the Kirchenbund demonstrated that on the issue of peace and security it was willing to participate in Soviet-sponsored forums of limited commitment. These questions would increasingly dominate the church's international activities in the late 1970s. This heralded future Kirchenbund participation in ad hoc forums—for example, in the June 1977 Conference of Religious Representatives for Lasting Peace, Disarmament, and Just Relations among Peoples, held again in Moscow. On the other side, the 1973 conference demonstrated that the state was willing

[35]"Pressemitteilung des Bundes . . . ," *epd Dokumentation*, no. 2 (21 January 1974): p. 56.
[36]CDU archives, 12 September 1973, "Ansprache OKR Juergenssohns . . . ," *epd Dokumentation*, no. 45 (19 November 1973): p. 11. "Votum von Frau OKR Lewek in der Kommission 4 'Europaeische Sicherheit und Zusammenarbeit,'" in "Information ueber den Weltkongress der Friedenskraefte in Moskau," mimeographed (Berlin, GDR: Sekretariat des Kirchenbundes, 25 October 1973), pp. 15–16; as indicated on pp. 9–12 of this document, freedom of opinion for conscientious objectors, right of assembly and formation of unions, among others, were only mentioned, without being endorsed by the Congress. The other delegates to the Congress also reported on it, employing less visible forums, however. "Beitrag von Frau OKR Lewek . . . ," *epd Dokumentation*, no. 2 (21 January 1974): pp. 57–59. Bishop D. Horst Gienke, "Der Frieden ist unteilbar," *Mecklenburgische Kirchenzeitung*, 9 December 1973, pp. 1–2; Church President Eberhard Natho, "Frieden-Ziel sinnvoller Politik," *NZ*, 30 November 1973; *NZ*, 6 December 1973; OKR Lewek, "Christen als wirkende Kraft," *ND*, 22 November 1973, p. 6.
[37]Reinhard Henkys, "Eine neue Qualitaet der Zusammenarbeit?" *KiS* 1 (December 1973): 10–11.

to tolerate a relatively independent contribution by the churches in order to gain the legitimacy that their participation conferred on such a conference, and indirectly on the state's foreign policy. Reflecting the Schoenherr line, the church hoped thereby to build trust with the state, claiming quasi-recognition of the church's role as a "social force" in GDR society, independent of the state and the CDU.[38]

Of course, this development reflected a step in a longer-term process, one that both sides viewed cautiously and with some skepticism. Certainly the state did not share the church's claim to be a "social force" and continued unsuccessfully to seek church participation in state-dominated organizations, especially the CPC and the Society for German-Russian Friendship.[39] However, when the church requested a position on the Peace Council of the GDR, it was the state's turn to say *nyet*. Moreover, many in the church remained skeptical of the benefits of participating in such Soviet-dominated forums or of the desirousness of the designation "social force."[40] Thus, the Kirchenbund undertook an informational campaign explaining both its motives for participating and the results of the Congress, all to counter the state's one-sided interpretation of it.[41] In 1977, partly as a result of this internal church criticism of the 1973 conference, the Kirchenbund delegation sought only "observer status" and included some more critical church leaders, such as Falcke and Bishop Heinrich Rathke of Mecklenburg.[42] By ceding the Kirchenbund a certain status as an independent societal organization, the state risked the possibility that the Kirchenbund might use this quasi-recognized independent status to make linkages to the domestic GDR Kirchenpolitik and thereby gain domestic advantages. The risks seemed worth taking for the state in its effort to dampen the churches' criticism of human rights, both domestically and in ecumenical forums.

[38]For example, Gienke: "the possibility of common work with other social forces . . . ," *epd Dokumentation*, no. 2 (21 January 1974): p. 60. See CDU archives, 14 December 1973.

[39]For example, Natho favored participation in the Society for German-Russian Friendship, but the Kirchenbund vetoed such action. See CDU archives, 18 February 1974; CDU archives, 28 January 1974.

[40]Most Landeskirchen synods in 1973–74 greeted the Kirchenbund's participation in the Congress; Gorlitz and Saxony-Dresden left it almost unmentioned, suggesting that they entertained doubts. See Werner Raguse, "Friedenskongresse," *DA* 10 (August 1977): 864; "Konzentration ist noetig," *KiS* 1 (December 1973): 29–33; EPC archives, March 1974.

[41]Olaf Lingner, "Die Evangelische Kirche in der Deutschen Demokratischen Republik," *KJ* 1974, p. 481; CDU archives, 17 January 1974.

[42]Daehn, pp. 142–43.

THE HUMAN RIGHTS ISSUE

The heightened emphasis on human rights in ecumenical organizations and the Helsinki Conference challenged the church to address the issue of human rights and the GDR's record on the issue. The spotlight on the issue was intensified in the wake of Helsinki, as over one hundred thousand East Germans invoked the Helsinki Accord in applying to emigrate. Approaches to the issue varied, particularly between church and state.

In the state's view, human rights are a function of the socioeconomic system.[43] Rebutting Western interpretations of human rights, the GDR maintains, "Rights do not have their origin in unreal, heavenly regions, are not granted by supernatural powers. . . . they are a social, in particular a state institution." Human rights are a peculiarly bourgeois concept in the official view. In socialism, these are replaced by "socialist basic rights," which entail, for example, the right to work and education. These rights, however, are conditioned upon meeting of socialist obligations, not intrinsic to man. In the official view, only in socialism can these rights and the concomitant "all-around development of the personality" be realized.

Many church leaders, such as Bishop Fraenkel, directly rejected this conditional view of human rights held by the state. From 1973 until 1978, for example, Bishop Fraenkel applied his advocacy of the church's "guardian office" to human rights.[44] In major addresses between 1972 and 1975, he rejected the notion that the church should provide only the *motivation* for supporting socialism, abdicating all responsibility for the *content* of these stands. For Fraenkel, human rights were God-given, not contingent upon a social system, as argued by the state. In 1973 he argued:

> The essence of human worth and basic rights is misjudged if they are tied to the measure of performance for socialism and thus granted to citizens

[43]Federal Ministry for Inner-German Affairs, *DDR Handbuch*, pp. 1413–14.
[44]Based on Fraenkel's reports to the Goerlitz synods in 1973–1974, as found in "Ein Wort zur Oeffentlichen Verantwortung der Kirche," *epd Dokumentation*, no. 17 (10 April 1973): pp. 40–52; "Die Freiheit des Christen zum Dienst in der Gesellschaft," *epd Dokumentation*, no. 19a (16 April 1974): pp. 2–14; "Das Zeugnis der Bibel in seiner Bedeutung fuer die Menschenrechte," *KJ* 1974, pp. 496–500; and his Annenkirche address, as found in *KJ* 1973, pp. 161–67.

after the fact on the basis of fulfilled conditions. Human rights only have meaning if they are recognized as natural rights and do not presume a certain conviction. This pre-existent character is grounded in God's creation and salvation. The recognition of this pre-existent character of human rights is an unresolved problem in our society."

Later he maintained that "it is a basic error of every total state that man belongs to it body and soul. Therefore every convention of human rights must be measured on the basis of whether it protects people from this illegitimate claim." In this notion of limiting the authority of the state over citizens, Fraenkel comes close to the traditional Western liberal view of human rights. Offering a different accent was Bishop Krusche. He emphasized the dual dimensions of social and individual rights.[45] The socialist states such as the GDR concentrated on social rights, at the expense of individual rights. Because of this systemic bias, Krusche maintained that the churches' role in the GDR was to underscore the protection of individual rights; in capitalist societies, the churches' role would more properly emphasize social rights.

A more cautious approach was taken by the normally circumspect Lutherans in the GDR, acting pursuant to a mandate from the 1970 General Assembly of the LWF.[46] In contrast to Fraenkel's view, the report issued by the GDR National Committee of the LWF described human rights as historically relative rather than God-given or grounded in natural rights. In contrast to Krusche's emphasis on individual rights, the Lutherans gave equal weight to social rights and individual rights. The report also maintained that the Eastern bloc conception of human rights incorporated individual rights, again a different accent than offered by Krusche.

The Kirchenbund's approach reflected an admixture of the Krusche and Lutheran approaches. Its public declaration prior to the WCC consultation on human rights at St. Poelten, Austria, in 1974 was couched in generalities.[47] It viewed dialectical materialism as part of God's process at work in the world and, as such, not foreign to Christians except in certain historical manifestations. Human rights were

[45]"Die Gemeinde Jesu Christi auf dem Wege in die Diaspora . . . ," *epd Dokumentation,* no. 2 (21 January 1974): pp. 18–19.

[46]"Sorge um eine menschliche Welt (Auszug)," *KJ* 1973, pp. 486–95.

[47]"Zur Theologischen Relevanz der Menschenrechte," *epd Dokumentation,* no. 5 (20 January 1975): pp. 75–76.

seen as a concern for Christians, but remained historically conditioned and relative. The St. Poelten statement viewed socialism's emphasis on social rights as a challenge to Christians who have long overemphasized individual rights.

As the basis for its contribution to the closed-door St. Poelten proceedings, the Kirchenbund also issued a study, "for internal consumption," which critiqued GDR society less from the perspective of individual human rights than from a societal perspective, measuring socialism by its own standards.[48] Reflecting strongly the ideas of Falcke, chair of the "Church and Society Commission" of the Kirchenbund, the paper rejected class struggle and partisanship and opted for reconciliation instead. In the form of theses, the paper represented a strong indictment of the regimentation of GDR society, describing the GDR as:

–an *Einheitsgesellschaft* (monolithic society), under the SED's claim to total power, despite the pluralism inherent in the society.

–a society in which power depended not on the ownership of the means of production, but on the possession of information, the SED's monopoly of which was integral to the "monolithic society."

–a society in which democratic centralism limited the cooperation of citizens.

–a *Leistungsgesellschaft* (achievement-society), in which the weak were disadvantaged.

–a *Konsumgesellschaft* (consumption-society), which Christians rejected since they have other views on the value of life.

–an *Erziehungsgesellschaft* (educatory-society), in which pluralism was not respected since this pluralism in education conflicted with a "monolithic society."

–a society in which scientific-technical progress was subordinated to class struggle.

Differences in the church arose not only in terms of the interpretation of human rights, but also in terms of the appropriate means of communicating the church's critique to the state and the priority on human rights vis-à-vis other international goals. Fraenkel, for example, favored public criticism of the human rights situation.[49] In his synodal reports

[48]"Arbeitsbericht Kirchenbund 1972," *Mitteilungsblatt . . .* , no. 1 (30 March 1973): pp. 3–4; CDU archives, 28 March 1973; CDU archives, 1 February 1974.
[49]"Das Zeugnis der Bibel fuer die Menschenrechte," *KJ* 1974, pp. 496–500.

he argued that the SED's goal of a socialist personality was in tension with freedom of conscience and belief, leading to discrimination against Christians, especially in education. He asked for "peaceful coexistence not only of power blocs and peoples, but also of individuals as expressed in elementary human rights."

Schoenherr and the Kirchenbund leadership, on the other hand, preferred to limit public criticism to issues involving the individual Christian and the institutional church; broader political responsibility for human rights was communicated primarily in private discussions with state authorities. This diplomatic approach was explained in Schoenherr's report to the May 1973 synod of the Kirchenbund:

> Church within socialism would be one which in the same freedom of the faith, is ready to cooperate fully in those areas of society in which human life is maintained and improved, and, where necessary, to help deflect danger to human life. It may turn out, as has been the case, that in the light of the promise of God and under His commandment, we Christians see problems and needs in the world and society differently than others, or hear questions which others hear differently. We have then made our inquiries. Those took place primarily in discussion with the responsible authorities, sometimes publicly. We claimed no special social position for Christians. But whoever takes God's will seriously must be attentive to His command and not conceal that which has become clear to him in reflection before God."[50]

The Lutherans were also very cautious, calling in their report to the LWF for more "humanness" in the educational system and greater information in society, but rejecting the idea that it was the task of the church to demand these changes.

Church leaders also differed in terms of the priority given to human rights in relation to other goals of the CSCE.[51] For example, Krusche greeted the signing of the Helsinki Accord and called for adherence to it "in its entirety." Fraenkel hailed the accord as "articulating for the first time the unity of peace and humanity." Schoenherr, on the other hand, emphasized primarily the progress on security and disarmament deriving from the CSCE.

Despite the differing emphases in the church regarding the approach

---

[50]"Bericht der KKL . . . ," *epd Dokumentation*, no. 25 (12 June 1973): pp. 3–4.
[51]*KiS* 1 (December 1975): 12; *KiS* 2 (September 1976): 7.

to the human rights issue domestically, the churches were quite united in responding to the increasing Western attention and criticism of the Soviet bloc's record on human rights. With its greater credibility in the West, particularly with the EKD, the Kirchenbund sought successfully to dampen such criticism. For example, the Kirchenbund's efforts were instrumental in keeping the WCC's St. Poelten consultation on human rights a closed-door session and in gaining support for socioeconomic and racial rights.[52] At the WCC's 1975 General Assembly in Nairobi, at which the religious situation in the USSR came under attack, the Kirchenbund representatives called for "nuanced discussions," rather than plenary discussions and resolutions.[53] Such a tactful approach was justified to "keep our backs covered for witness at home." Thus the Kirchenbund representatives opposed plenary debate on the issue and supported the controversial election of Metropolitan Nikodim of the Russian Orthodox Church to the WCC leadership. Finally, the Kirchenbund began to participate in the consultations of Soviet bloc member churches prior to these WCC meetings, contributing to the greater coordination of these churches.[54] The state responded favorably to the Kirchenbund's posture in these WCC deliberations.[55]

Although grateful for the Kirchenbund's politic posture in ecumenical bodies, the state was infuriated by the Fraenkel's criticisms, particularly his tacit comparison between Nazi Germany and the GDR in his 1973 address at the Annenkirche in Dresden. Focusing on the lessons to be learned from the Kirchenkampf, Fraenkel asserted that "everything depends on faith that Christ the terror-breaker is with us." Although Fraenkel denied any intended comparison, the state demanded that

---

[52]Guenter Wirth, "Mein Standpunkt," *Standpunkt* 3 (February 1975): 57.

[53]Sources on the controversy at Nairobi include Uwe-Peter Heidungsfeld, "Zwischen christlichen Auftrag und Loyalitaet," *KiS* 2 (September 1976): 17–25; Hudson, pp. 286–87; David M. Paton, ed., *Breaking Barriers: Nairobi 1975* (Grand Rapids, Mich.: Eerdmans, 1976); Peter Beyershaus, "Das prophetische Versagen der Fuenften Vollversammlung," and Helene Posdeeff, "Die Rolle des Moskauer Patriarchats in Nairobi," in *Oekumene im Spiegel von Nairobi '75*, ed. Peter Beyerhaus and Ulrich Betz (Bad Liebenzell: Verlag der Liebenzeller Mission, 1976), pp. 254–57 and 240–48. A polemical attack on Nairobi occurs in Peter Babris, *Silent Churches* (Arlington Heights, Ill.: Research Publishers, 1978), pp. 464–78. The official state response to Nairobi can be read in Eberhard Klages, "Zum Ertrag von Nairobi," *Standpunkt* 4 (February 1976): 29–30, and "Die Oekumene in Nairobi . . . ," *Standpunkt* 4 (March 1976): 60–62. Even Christoph Hinz, critic of the system and protege of Krusche, sought to dampen Western criticism. See his contribution in "Den Ruecken fuer das Zeugnis freihalten," *KiS* 2 (February 1976): 14.

[54]Hebly, p. 163.

[55]CDU archives, 12 July 1974.

church leaders publicly reject Fraenkel's views. Church leaders rejected this demand, although some such as Schoenherr and Gienke, did distance themselves from Fraenkel in private discussions with the state.[56]

THE STATE'S IDEOLOGICAL CAMPAIGN AND INSTITUTIONAL CONCESSIONS

The state responded to the rising debate over the proper role of the church in socialism and the increased criticism of human rights in the GDR by intensifying its ideological efforts toward individual citizens and extending institutional concessions to the church during this period.

The state launched an agitational campaign in 1972, using the CDU and the slogan, "socialist state-citizens of Christian belief." Designed to fill the void left by the demise of the Ulbrichtian formula, "the common humanistic responsibility of Marxists and Christians," this formula was introduced by Politburo member Albert Norden at the Thirteenth CDU Party Congress in October 1972. Norden assured the "socialist state-citizens of Christian belief" that they would have a place in the GDR.[57] According to the CDU's exegesis of the formula, Christian faith provided the motivation for social and political participation; the content of this participation, however, came entirely from the scientific laws of Marxism-Leninism, as explicated by the SED. As employed by the CDU over the next two years, the formula had two goals: to oppose those advocating "critical solidarity" as well as those urging political abstinence in the debate over "church within socialism" and to dampen the grassroots' criticism of the treatment of Christians.

Without attacking Fraenkel and Krusche by name, the most important target of the campaign was that segment of the church advocating greater activism on behalf of a Christian concept of socialism or human rights. By addressing the Christians in GDR society, rather than the churches, the formula discounted the church as an independent, critical

---

[56]CDU archives, 8 May 1973; CDU archives, 4 May 1973; CDU archives, 27 November 1973; CDU archives, 14 December 1973.

[57]NZ, 13 October 1972; BS, 22 October 1972. Koch, *Staat und Kirche*, p. 191; Federal Ministry of Inner-German Affairs, *DDR-Handbuch*, p. 593. NZ, 15 June 1973; FAZ, 27 October 1973, p. 24.

actor in society. This continued the CDU's approach of contrasting the alleged "progressiveness" of individual Christians with the "unprogressive" churches and clergy. Any attempt to posit a "guardian role" for the church, a la Fraenkel, was viewed as an attempt to gain power by the church; any "critical solidarity" with "improved socialism," a la Falcke, was considered revisionist and late bourgeois.[58] In its positions on human rights, the church was urged to place emphasis on social rights, rather than individual rights. The CDU also used the campaign to attack notions of free flow of information and people and any ideas of Christian socialism.[59]

The concept thus signaled a shift in the state's "theology." Previously the state had found the CDU's line emphasizing Christian social responsibility to be relatively useful in countering the traditional political abstinence of Lutherans. However, with the rise of an immanent socialist critique of Falcke and Krusche, it began to realize the danger in this doctrine of social responsibility when applied independently by the churches. Thus it began to see advantage in moving back toward a position rooted in the Two Kingdoms Doctrine of Lutherans. This was manifested most clearly in the debate over salvation and welfare between Krusche and Gerhard Bassarak, professor of ecumenicism at the Humboldt University.[60] In his original article, Krusche argued that one's salvation was linked to actions in the welfare sphere; Bassarak attacked the Krusche position, arguing that the state, reflecting reason, is responsible for welfare, the church only for salvation.[61]

---

[58]Gotz Bickelhaupt, "Wiederkehr der Versuchung," *Standpunkt* 1 (March 1973): 61–62; *NZ*, 10 May 1973; EPC archives, 5 April 1973. *NZ*, 15 June 1973.

[59]Carl Ordnung, ed., *Menschenrechte sind Mitmenschenrechte* (1975). *NZ*, 14 May 1973. Goetting spoke to the CDU's celebration of Otto Nuschke's ninetieth birthday, the scaled-down event that replaced the previous annual meetings celebrating the Fuchs-Ulbricht meeting. Gerhard Jung, "Neue Phase in der DDR Kirchenpolitik," *Deutsches Pfarrerblatt* 73 (September 1973): 669–72; *SDZ*, 27 February 1973, p. 6; *FAZ*, 7 March 1974, p. 8.

[60]Werner Krusche, "Heil Heute," and Gerhard Bassarak, "Zur Frage nach theologischem Inhalt und Interpretation von 'Heil heute' in einer sozialistischen Gesellschaft," *Die Zeichen der Zeit* 27 (May 1973): 161–81. The state's shift is also evident in the positive treatment accorded the VELKDDR synod in 1972 and its emphasis on a specific *Biblical* conception of society. See *NZ*, 8 October 1972.

[61]"'Heil heute und Wohl des Menschen.' Referat von Prof. Dr. Gerhard Bassarak . . . ," *epd Dokumentation*, no. 36 (7 August 1974): pp. 58, 61–62. The emerging trend became evident in numerous articles in the CDU media as well. Professor Hanfried Mueller, advocate of a radical Two Kingdoms Doctrine, authored "Zwei Reiche Lehre und sozialistischen Staatsbuerger christlichen Glaubens," *NZ*, 7 November 1973. Other indications are found in *NZ*, 5 May 1974; Gerhard Bassarak, "Zur Protestantischen Theologie heute," *Die Zeichen der*

Ironically, those generally opposing a Christian conception for society, such as traditional Lutherans and the members of the so-called Jesus movement, also found themselves targets of the campaign. The state used it to rebut Braecklein's formula, "Christian citizen in the socialist state," as a "merely geographic description" and a step backwards from Schoenherr's "church within socialism."[62]

In its second thrust to profile "socialist state-citizens of Christian belief," the state counteracted the rising tide of discontent over the treatment of Christians and exhorted Christians to take a partisan stand in support of socialism. The CDU and the state continued to reject publicly the charge that the increasing emphasis on ideology was producing discrimination against young Christians. Implicitly admitting "difficulties" in the education system, Goetting emphasized that "where Christian parents raise their children in the sense of social responsibility and socialist state consciousness and where they cooperate closely and trustfully with the school, there can be no unresolvable difficulties for children of Christian parents."[63] Despite the churches' evidence to the contrary, the CDU continued to maintain that confirmation was not grounds for discrimination. "Progressive" church participation, such as activity in the antiracism program, was no substitute for activity in state organizations, such as the FDJ.[64] The CDU also sought to publicize the "socialist state-citizens of Christian belief" in various occupations, particularly teaching, to show the access of politically correct Christians to those occupations.

Zeit 27 (June 1973); Gerhard Bassarak, *Theologie des Genitivs? Wider falsche Wege des Dienstes am Wort* (Berlin, GDR: Union Verlag, 1975). One observer argues that the CDU, especially via Bassarak's conservative theology and attacks on modern "theology of the genitive," has won new respect and interest among Lutheran clergy in the GDR. See Gerhard Schmolze, "Das Elend der Ost-CDU," in *Das Elend der Christdemokraten*, ed. Gerd-Klaus Kaltenbrunner (1977), pp. 88–89. While the CDU does seem to have become more sophisticated and less polemical in its "theology" in recent years, most clergy realize that Bassarak's conservative Two Kingdoms Doctrine line aligns all too well with the state's post-Falcke desire to depoliticize the church. See for example, Guenter Jacob, *Weltwirklichkeit und Christusglaube: Wider eine falsche Zweireichelehre* (1977), especially pp. 18–26.

[62]*NZ*, 11 February 1973. CDU archives, 15 August 1973; CDU archives, 16 October 1973; CDU archives, 10 October 1973.

[63]*BS*, 22 October 1972; CDU archives, 27 November 1973; CDU archives, 14 December 1973.

[64]Werner Wuenschmann, "Fuer die sozialistische Bildung und Erziehung der jungen Generation," and "Hoeher Ansprueche an die sozialistische Bildung und Erziehung," in *Politisches Jahrbuch der Christlich-Demokratischen Union Deutschlands*, 3rd ed., Sekretariat des Hauptvorstandes der CDU Deutschlands (1973), pp. 13–16, 17, 20–22, 93–96. For example, writers are the focus of *Schriftsteller christlichen Glaubens im antifaschistischen Widerstand* (Berlin, GDR: Sekretariat des Hauptvorstandes der CDU Deutschlands, 1974).

The concept was also an attempt to engender greater political integration based on loyalty to state and nation. By referring to "state-citizens" rather than simply "citizens," the GDR sought to play on traditional German subservience to the state. Reflecting this strategy, the slogan *Burgerpflicht sind Christenpflicht* (civic duties are Christian duties) also became standard usage. Moreover, it sought to transform this not inconsiderable loyalty to the state into loyalty to the "real existing socialism."[65] Likewise the nation became identified with socialism: the constitutional changes in 1974 proclaimed the GDR as a socialist nation, the FRG was defined as a capitalist nation. All of this was an attempt not only to anchor and make irrevocable the socialist character of the GDR, but also to mobilize popular support based on the alleged identification of state-nation-socialism.[66]

Like the slogan "church within socialism," the state's new slogan, "socialist state-citizens of Christian belief," lent itself to differing interpretations, playing upon and fueling the uncertainties of Christian existence in a centralized state dominated by an atheistic ideology. For the CDU, this special status of Christian citizens was viewed as assurance that the state was not, as part of the transition from socialism to communism, undertaking an ideological campaign against Christians and thus indirectly against the CDU. Likewise, the CDU was relieved to learn that for the Christians, Honecker's new emphasis on "socialist personality" required only "socialist state consciousness," not "socialist consciousness," with its implicit acceptance of all components of Marxist-Leninist ideology including atheism. The church, on the other hand, interpreted the special role of Christians in this concept as an indicator of second-class status, part of an ideological campaign against Christians that, depending on one's political perspective, could be used by Christians to qualify their social-political engagement or by the state to justify discrimination against Christians.[67]

The state's claims for equal treatment for "socialist state-citizens of Christian belief" were undercut by the SED's heightened ideological

---

[65]Slogans such as "our state, our socialism" and "identification with the cause of socialism" proliferated. *NZ*, 4 February 1973 and 29 December 1974.

[66]"Nation und nationale Frage," Federal Ministry of Inner-German Affairs, *DDR-Handbuch*, p. 750; *BS*, 24/31 December 1972, p. 5.

[67]Carl Ordnung, "Sozialistische Ideologie und christliche Glaube—Zur geistigen Profil des Sozialistischen Staatsbuergern christlichen Glaubens," in *Tradition und Verpflichtung*, Sekretariat des Hauptvorstandes der CDU Deutschlands (1974), p. 95; CDU archives, 16 October 1973.

campaign. The new youth law, released in draft form in summer 1973, revealed a heightened emphasis on ideology and participation in the FDJ.[68] The new law eliminated the references in the 1964 version to education of youth "independently of world-view and belief," parental rights in upbringing of children, and the voluntary character of the *Jugendweihe*. The increasing criticism by the Kirchenbund of discrimination in the educational system signaled that its fears of the second-class status of Christians were being borne out.[69]

Likewise, the draft version of the new SED party program caused alarm in the church that heightened emphasis on ideology would come at the expense of Christians.[70] Made public in January 1976 in preparation for the Ninth SED Party Congress, the draft dropped earlier references to atheism, but characterized Marxism-Leninism, "in all its components," as the worldview not merely of the Party and the working class, but of all members of the "developed socialist society." References to the freedom of faith and conscience were dropped from the new draft program and the party proclaimed as its goal the "communist education" of the youth, a higher standard than the earlier goal of "socialist education."

Another indication of intensified ideological efforts was the heightened emphasis on scientific atheism in SED activities.[71] Scientific conferences by Marxist sociologists, survey research regarding religious beliefs of youth, and special attention to atheism in the FDJ training seminars all attest to the SED's attempt to shore up the atheistic component of the ideology.

The politic approach of the Kirchenbund leadership regarding human rights was strained not only by the ideological measures of the state, but also by rising internal church criticism of the Kirchenbund's accommodation to the state. For example, Fraenkel aimed his criticism not only at the state but indirectly at certain positions assumed by the church.[72] His rejection of an apolitical church was directed at least as much at conservative Lutheran advocates of the Two Kingdom Doctrine

---

[68]"Stellungnahme der KKL (9.10.73)," *KiS* 1 (November 1973): 19–20; Klaus Machnow, "Alle erreichen—keine zuruecklassen," *DA* 11 (March 1978): 279f, especially 280–81.

[69]"Bericht der KKL . . . ," *epd Dokumentation*, no. 25 (12 June 1973).

[70]Reinhard Henkys, "Der Atheismus fehlt im SED-Programm," *KiS* 2 (February 1976): 9–13.

[71]Ibid., pp. 11–12.

[72]"Bericht der KKL . . . ," *epd Dokumentation*, no. 30 (17 July 1972): p. 28.

as at the state. Yet he also opposed an overemphasis on the social Gospel, criticizing those who promoted social change at the expense of the redemption of individual sinners. In this he was attacking the social activism of not only the WCC, but also the GDR churches, in particular among "progressive" circles. Finally, he indirectly criticized the leadership of the Kirchenbund, warning against engaging in mea culpa for ignoring the working class in the past and allowing this process to immobilize the churches' present social-critical role. He cautioned against righting wrongs far away without challenging those close to home. Bishop Hempel also exercised indirect criticism of misplaced priorities by the Kirchenbund.[73] He maintained that the credibility of the church, both internally and externally, depended on its concretization of the law of God, an implicit vote for less social activism.

More reflective of the views and problems of the laity, the synods during this period were more critical than church leadership of the state's Kirchenpolitik. Rather than the grand perspectives on human rights and social change offered by some church leaders, the synods focused on the treatment of individual Christians and reinforced the church leadership's measured criticism of the state.[74] The reports of the church leadership tended to treat the problem as a limited one involving only the "atmosphere" and a few hard-line teachers; the synod, on the other hand, cited the gap between the declared goal of a socialist education system and the constitutionally guaranteed freedom of belief and demanded that tolerance be practiced.

Some of the Landeskirche synods were also more critical than the Kirchenbund Church Leadership regarding problems in education. Predictably, Saxony-Dresden, Saxony-Magdeburg, and Gorlitz saw intense criticism of the problem.[75] Less predictably, the Thuringian synod

---

[73] Johannes Hempel, "Das Selbstverstaendnis der VELK in der DDR und ihr Beitrag zur Kirchwerdung des Bundes," *Lutherische Rundschau* 21 (January 1974): 16.

[74] "Bericht der KKL...," "Beschluss der Synode...," and "Stellungnahme der Synode...," *epd Dokumentation*, no. 25 (12 June 1973): pp. 8–10, 27–29; "Bericht der KKL...," and "Beschluss der Synode...," *epd Dokumentation*, no. 45 (19 November 1973): pp. 9–10, 14; "Bericht der KKL...," and "Stellungnahme der Synode...," *epd Dokumentation*, no. 52 (11 November 1974): pp. 25, 122.

[75] CDU archives, 17 January 1974; CDU archives, 27 November 1973. "Ansprache von Landesbischof D. Ingo Braecklein," *epd Dokumentation*, no. 30 (23 July 1973): pp. 6–7. On the other hand, the EKU under Gienke's leadership during 1974–76 was less critical. Bishop Fraenkel, among others, criticized Gienke for this, according to "Gottesdienstformen sollen DDR-Situation angepasst werden," *epd Landesdienst Berlin*, no. 94 (13 May 1974): p. 2. "Taetigkeitsbericht der Kirchenkanzlei der EKU-Bereich DDR...," and "Beschluesse der

proved especially forceful in its complaints of discrimination, demanding a bishop's letter to the parishes. Even the VELKDDR, normally quite unpolitical, saw Braecklein vow that the church leadership would work to solve cases of individual discrimination, as long as such cases occurred. Finally, the Berlin-Brandenburg (East) synod heatedly debated Schoenherr's concept "church within socialism" and almost delivered it a tacit rejection. A strongly worded synod resolution "mandating" the church leadership to request equal status for *Bausoldaten* and regular soldiers was softened only after debate and reformulation in committee.[76]

In an attempt to defuse this growing criticism, the state extended significant institutional concessions to the churches beyond those rather meager elite-oriented moves of 1971. The state's overture began in late 1972 and took several forms. The first signal of new movement in the relationship was agreement on the long-standing issue of church construction. In December 1972 the state approved the so-called "Special Building Program" of the Kirchenbund.[77] Previously, the state had given financial support only for the restoration of certain historically significant churches. The new program permitted work on existing church buildings, including the building of parish houses and reconstruction of large churches to create smaller, more useful all-purpose rooms. Prior to 1971 it had been possible on a limited scale for the churches to engage small, privately owned construction firms for such projects. But with the nationalization of small firms by Honecker in that year, such projects had become practically impossible. Under the new agreement, the state agreed to allot the requisite construction capacity in its state plan, under the condition that the churches provide payment in hard currency, in effect from the EKD. The state certainly benefited from the influx of hard currency, which totaled over 15 million marks from 1973 to 1975.[78] Yet the agreement necessitated foregoing other state construction, and it confirmed the "special relationship" between the GDR churches and the EKD, which the state had earlier rejected.

Synode . . . ," *epd Dokumentation*, no. 29 (18 June 1974): pp. 82, 84–86. The resolutions of the synod regarding the Gienke report limited themselves to nonpolitical issues, thus indicating support for his position. See CDU archives, 17 June 1974.

[76]"Beschluesse der Synode . . . ," *epd Dokumentation*, no. 27 (4 June 1974): pp. 51–52.

[77]*Sonderbauprogramm-Zwischenbericht* (Berlin, GDR: Bund der Evangelischen Kirchen in der DDR, 1976), foreword by Stolpe.

[78]"Kirchenbau in der DDR in staatliche Bauplannung aufgenommen," *epd Landesdienst Berlin*, no. 176 (10 November 1976): p. 1.

Moreover, it was the first of several construction agreements that represented the state's acknowledgement of the church's continued existence in the future GDR. In April 1974 the state solicited a wish list of new church structures that the churches hoped to build.[79] In summer 1974, agreement was reached on restoring the heavily war-damaged Berlin Cathedral, which the state desired for aesthetic, nationalistic, and economic reasons.[80] The Special Building Program and the agreement to restore the Berlin Cathedral were the forerunners of the building program in new urban areas, agreed upon in 1976. This agreement was the most significant concession by the state, since it had long rejected the presence of churches in the new "socialist cities" in the GDR. The churches had encountered great difficulties in meeting the religious needs of Christians in these vast new urban developments.[81] In this situation, semispontaneous house churches had often sprung up, a development that the state, fearful of spontaneity and underground religious activity, viewed with concern.[82] Thus, by summer 1976 the state abandoned its opposition and agreed to the program, again based on EKD funding.[83]

Second, the state officially recognized the activities of the churches' social service agencies and struck agreements that gave them greater institutional stability. In March 1973 the minister for health, Dr. Ludwig Mecklinger, met with representatives of the churches' diaconical agency and, in effect, granted it quasi-official acceptance.[84] He designated church hospitals as "components of the socialist health care system" and called for greater coordination between church and state facilities. He assured the church that the state had no intention of eliminating church hospitals or infringing upon doctors' independence of decision in performing abortions. He also guaranteed the training of

[79]"Bericht der KKL . . . ," *epd Dokumentation*, no. 52 (11 November 1974): pp. 25–26; "Bericht der Kirchenleitung der Evangelischen Kirche in Berlin-Brandenburg (Ost) . . . ," *epd Dokumentation*, no. 27 (4 June 1974): p. 30.

[80]"Zahlreiche Kirchen in der DDR werden jetzt wieder hergestellt," *epd Landesdienst Berlin*, no. 197 (1 November 1974): pp. 1–1a; CDU archives, 12 July 1974.

[81]See the resolution of the Berlin-Brandenburg (East) synod in *epd Dokumentation*, no. 27 (4 June 1974): p. 30, for a discussion of problems involved in *Neubau* parish work.

[82]Quoting *Standpunkt, KiS* 2 (November 1976): 29.

[83]Discussion with former Bishop Scharf; Fischer, p. 106; Martin Hoellen, "Kirchen kuenftig auch in Neubaugebieten der DDR," *DA* 10 (May 1977): 466–69. The churches thus translated their dependence on the EKD into clout with the state. The state also agreed to purchase certain unused church buildings for use as concert halls.

[84]*NZ*, 6 May 1973; Gerhard Bosinski, ed., *Zur Antwort Bereit* (1978), p. 46; CDU archives, 26 March 1973.

specialists at church hospitals. Although the state opposed any expansion of the churches into new medical areas, it signaled with this meeting its acceptance of the churches' current role in health care delivery.[85]

The March 1973 meeting presaged further, more concrete agreements with the churches, such as the nurses training agreement in June 1975. The sizable nurses training programs in church hospitals had been endangered by changes in the state curriculum for nursing education in 1973. After long negotiations, the diaconical agency, Kirchenbund, and the state signed an agreement providing joint programs between the church hospitals and the state education system.[86] This agreement, which integrated and stabilized the status of church-trained nurses, was the first one that specifically cited the provision (Article 39.2) in the 1968 constitution for such agreements.

Third, the state reached a compromise with the church over the much-disputed Events Ordinance, perhaps the most important breakthrough in the relationship. Despite the internal differences over the church's proper response and the heavy fines paid particularly by Thuringia and Saxony-Dresden, the unified stance of the Kirchenbund eventually paid off as the state moved in early 1973 to defuse the situation.[87] The state announced an "arrangement," whereby retreats for youth and confirmands would henceforth be considered "religious activities" and thus exempt from the required announcement to the police.[88] As before, they would still be announced to the local civil authorities.

The church leadership also compromised, rescinding its critical resolution of July 1971 and agreeing that for ambiguous events, the content and goal of an event would determine whether it required notification of the police.[89] This concession by the church reflected the greater readi-

---

[85]CDU archives, 10 July 1973; CDU archives, 27 August 1973; CDU archives, 28 September 1973. All indicate the state's reservations regarding a broadening of diaconical work. "Diakonie heute—Stand und Aufgaben," *Evangelischer Nachrichtendienst* 27 (20 March 1974): 2.

[86]Werner Braune, "Diakonische Arbeit in der DDR," *KiS* 2 (November 1976): 12; Bosinski, *Zur Antwort Bereit*, pp. 44–45, 435–42.

[87]Gerhard Jung, "Neue Phase in der DDR Kirchenpolitik," *Deutsches Pfarrerblatt* 73 (September 1973): 669–72; CDU archives, 8 January 1973; CDU archives, 30 January 1973; CDU archives, 28 March 1973; CDU archives, 2 April 1973. Signs of impending movement surfaced in March 1973. Although Fraenkel attacked the ordinance again in March 1973, Schoenherr made no mention of it at the February 1973 Berlin-Brandenburg (East) synod and a frank meeting between Seigewasser and the Mecklenburg leadership in late March revealed some common ground on the issue. See *ND*, 28 March 1973; *BS*, 8 April 1973, p. 5.

[88]"Bericht der KKL . . . ," *epd Dokumentation*, no. 25 (12 June 1973): pp. 10–11.

[89]Based on discussion with Reinhard Henkys, Schoenherr, Krusche, and Braecklein.

ness of church musicians to notify the police in order to avoid jeopardizing church concerts, a not unimportant source of financial support. In effect the church leadership altered its earlier exclusive claim to determine whether an activity was religious or not. In practice, the churches thereafter announced cultural events, such as concerts and plays, to the police.

The informal compromise ended the major source of church-state conflict from 1971 to 1973, although it by no means represented a formal end to disagreement regarding the issue of the churches' right to free assembly. For the most part, the church retreats thereafter encountered no difficulties with the state.[90] Regional church congresses resumed without complication in 1974, following a four-year hiatus due to the political uncertainty surrounding the Events Ordinance and the Abgrenzung efforts of the GDR. The state became much more forthcoming regarding logistical support for church congresses, leading to dramatic increases in attendance figures at congresses in 1976. But the question of the churches' proper role in leisure and cultural activities was by no means solved, as indicated when the state protested church activities at the World Youth Festival in summer 1973. Moreover, despite the informal compromise, the Events Ordinance remained on the books. Should the state wish to tighten control over church activities again, it retained the legal tool to do so.

Finally, in atmospheric terms the state sought to improve the relationship with the church. This was most noticeable in the treatment of the church by the official media. For example, *Neue Zeit* ceased its presynod agitational articles after 1972. Critical leaders, such as Krusche, were able to publish their views on theological matters, such as "salvation versus welfare."[91] The churches' activities were accorded higher status, especially in publications directed for Western consumption.[92] The official media began occasionally to publish articles that were more realistic and balanced. The CDU media even obliquely admitted con-

---

[90]Problems continued in Saxony-Dresden due to its broader interpretation of the agreement. "Bericht der Kirchenleitung der Evangelische Kirche in Berlin-Brandenburg (Ost) . . . , 1974," *epd Dokumentation*, no. 27 (4 June 1974): p. 28; "Konzentration ist noetig," *KiS* 1 (December 1973): 30–31; discussion with Bishop Schoenherr and OKR Stolpe; CDU archives, 23 July 1973; Sibylle Heltau, "Kirchentagsarbeit in der DDR," *KiS* 1 (December 1975): 26–27; *KiS* 2 (September 1976): 6–7.

[91]Guenter Wirth, "Um den Gesellschaftsbezug theologischer Reflektionen," *Standpunkt* 1 (September 1973): 225–26.

[92]For example, *100 Fragen—100 Antworten* (Berlin, GDR: Panorama, 1974).

flicts between Christians and the state, indicating that "Luther's teaching certainly does not guarantee a conflict-free functioning of such an
experiment" (Christians in socialism).[93] Although there was no fundamental shift toward greater objectivity of reporting and analysis in the
state media, the media treatment did represent an overall improvement
in atmosphere.

The state sent a signal of goodwill by disbanding the Pfarrerbund
in November 1974.[94] Though never very large—approximately 125
members, of whom perhaps 35 were active—it had been useful to the
state in agitating for change in the church. However, the few active
members of the Pfarrerbund became overextended and the organization
suffered from leadership problems. Realizing the ineffectiveness of the
Pfarrerbund and indeed its deleterious effect on the state's policy of
direct rapprochement with the churches, the state quietly disbanded it.

Another atmospheric signal was the new emphasis placed on Christians' role in the antifascist resistance. The Committee of Fighters in the
Anti-Fascist Opposition, which was planning the celebration of the
thirtieth anniversary of the end of World War II, increasingly sought out
those persecuted for religious reasons during the Third Reich.[95] This
new emphasis on the historical roots of Marxist-Christian cooperation
also manifested itself in the "new" historiography stressing the historical roots of Marxist-Christian cooperation.

The SED also responded to the criticisms of the Kirchenbund leadership regarding the new SED Program. The clause guaranteeing the right
to free exercise of faith and conscience was restored in the final draft of
the Program.[96]

Finally, in mid-1974 the state dropped the slogan "socialist state-
citizens of Christian belief," replacing it with the less divisive "political-

---

[93]*BS*, 9 December 1973, p. 2; *NZ*, 17 November 1973. CDU archives, 17 November 1973.

[94]A rump group continued to carry on ad hoc conferences, subject to state control. See
"Pfarrerbund aufgeloest," *DA* 8 (February 1975): 117–19. CDU archives, 10 January 1973;
CDU archives, 23 January 1973.

[95]This effort occurred in the context of the upcoming thirtieth anniversary of the end of
World War II and the state's unsuccessful attempts to win high-level church participation.
Bishop Schoenherr, "Errinerung und Vermaechtnis: Gedanken eines Christen zum 8. Mai . . .
1975," *epd Dokumentation*, no. 20 (5 May 1975): pp. 9–11; "Der 30. Jahrestag des 8. Mai in
der DDR und die Stimmen der Kirche," *KiS* 1 (June 1975): 14. See also CDU archives, 5 April
1974.

[96]Hans-Juergen Roeder, "Zwischen Anpassung und Opposition," *KiS* 2 (December 1976):
33; Reinhard Henkys, "Parteiprogramm und Wirklichkeit," *KiS* 2 (June 1976): 15–16.

moral unity" of the people.[97] As discussed earlier, the former slogan had been a vehicle for the CDU to criticize certain church leaders' views and to dismiss allegations of discrimination against Christians. The churches increasingly pointed out that the slogan was inconsistent with the discrimination of Christians in the education system. In addition, Schoenherr interpreted the "Christian belief" aspect to suggest independent political positions by the churches. Whether due to the threat of pluralism allegedly embedded in Schoenherr's interpretation, or to the churches' objection to the CDU's agitational use of the term, the state dropped it from the official rhetoric. The state rationalized that the great majority of Christians already saw themselves as "socialist state-citizens" and that continued use of the term could endanger the "political-moral unity" of the population.[98]

The state hoped to consolidate the gains from this renewed overture by planning a ground-breaking summit meeting between chairman of the State Council, Willi Stoph, and the Kirchenbund leadership on the occasion of the twenty-fifth anniversary of the GDR in 1974. Though Schoenherr was receptive to this breakthrough in protocol, the church's proposed statement emphasized its independent role and the state canceled the plans for the summit.[99] It was to be delayed until 1978 and then acquire even greater significance in terms of protocol.

These agreements and changes in atmospherics reflected a continuation of the state's shift toward a Kirchenbund strategy begun with its recognition of the Kirchenbund in 1971. The state moderated its earlier policy of differential treatment of "progressive" and "reactionary" Landeskirchen: the agreements with the church were Kirchenbund-wide ones; the areas of conflict likewise affected most Landeskirchen equally.

[97]CDU archives, 14 December 1973; CDU archives, 28 January 1974; "Bericht der Kirchenleitung der Evangelischen Kirche in Berlin-Brandenburg (Ost) . . . 1974," *epd Dokumentation*, no. 27 (4 June 1974): p. 39; "Synod Berlin-Brandenburg diskutiert ueber 'Kirche im Sozialismus,'" *Evangelische Nachrichtendienst* 27 (8 May 1974): 11–12; CDU archives, 30 April 1974.

[98]By August 1974 the phrase had disappeared from the CDU media; the September meeting of the National Front's Working Group on Church Questions was canceled to avoid awkward references to it; by the October meeting of this group, Vice President Guenter Grewe referred profusely to its replacement, "political-moral unity." See Reinhard Henkys, "Behutsamere SED Kirchenpolitik?," *Information des Arbeitskreises fuer zeitgeschichtliche Fragen* (November 1974): pp. 1–4; CDU archives, 2 August 1974; CDU archives, 30 August 1974; CDU archives, 30 October 1974.

[99]CDU archives, 21 June 1974; CDU archives, 12 July 1974; CDU archives, 21 October 1974.

The state hoped thereby to strengthen the position of Schoenherr and Stolpe within the Kirchenbund. Especially with the election of a new Kirchenbund leadership in fall 1973, the state sought continuity and stability. Given the variety of viewpoints on the church's role in society, the state feared that a successor to Schoenherr could easily be more, rather than less, critical of the state. For example, the state viewed Fraenkel as trying to form an internal anti-Communist opposition, based on his outspoken advocacy of human rights and his implicit analogies between the GDR and the Kirchenkampf. Though less vocal than Fraenkel, Krusche and Hempel also continued to receive largely negative marks from the state, especially for their refusal to vote in elections.[100]

On the other hand, the relatively "progressive" bishops did not offer the state a strong enough base upon which to build its strategy. Horst Gienke, the successor to Krummacher as bishop of Greifswald, joined Natho as "progressive" in terms of positions on foreign policy issues, domestic political participation by Christians and clergy, and rejection of Falcke and Fraenkel.[101] As the new chairman of the EKU Council (East), Gienke articulated a Lutheran position of a narrowly defined role for the church and dampened the usually critical expressions of the EKU. He lauded the accomplishments of the GDR on the occasion of its twenty-fifth anniversary, barely mentioning the problems in education. Pleased though it was by the actions of these two bishops, the state was careful not to accord them too much profile, fearing a loss of their credibility and a counterreaction in the other much-larger Landeskirchen.

The state's Kirchenbund strategy presumed Thuringia's realignment under Braecklein and Schoenherr's pragmatic leadership of his Landeskirche and the Kirchenbund. Under Braecklein, Thuringia continued a critical, Kirchenbund orientation.[102] Though not pleased with Schoenherr's refusal to rebuke Fraenkel publicly and with his outspokenness regarding "socialist state citizens of Christian belief," the state appreciated his tenuous position in his Berlin-Brandenburg Landeskirche and

[100]"Kritische Debatte in der Synode des DDR-Kirchenbundes," *epd Landesdienst Berlin*, no. 174 (30 September 1974): p. 2; Hempel refused to distance himself from Fraenkel. CDU archives, 15 February 1974; CDU archives, 14 December 1973; CDU archives, 15 May 1974; CDU archives, 28 January 1974.

[101]CDU archives, 22 May 1973; CDU archives, 15 February 1974; CDU archives, 14 December 1973; CDU archives, 27 November 1973.

[102]The acrimonious synod of fall 1973 requested Braecklein to address the discrimination problems in a letter to the parishes. CDU archives, 27 November 1973; CDU archives, 10 October 1973.

his pragmatic cooperation with the state.[103] Moreover, Schoenherr's increasing focus on the need to modernize the "national church" (*Volkskirche*) served to deflect criticism of the state's policy vis-à-vis the church.[104] For example, at the 1975 synod of the Kirchenbund, he greeted the demise of the *Volkskirche* and called for internal changes in the church to cope with the widespread secularization. He argued that "in the secularized world, the atheist who takes God seriously is closer to Him than the self-satisfied church member." Finally, in a precedent-setting speech at the National Front celebration of the thirtieth anniversary of the end of World War II, he hailed the liberation by foreigners in 1945 and cautioned against forgetting the past. The Kirchenbund study on the anniversary picked up the controversial theme of liberation, arguing that May 8, 1945, represented not just a liberation by the Soviet Union but also the beginning of a learning process of inner liberation by the church.

Thus, the state continued to focus on the Kirchenbund and Schoenherr in its strategy. The Kirchenbund had proved itself useful in ecumenical relations and, to a certain extent, in inter-German relations. It had shown itself amenable to pragmatic compromise with the state, even after seeming intransigence. But in its Kirchenbund strategy, the state was at least as interested in the disciplining effects of this process internally in the Kirchenbund as it was in these other benefits of Kirchenbund activity. Rather than relying solely on direct pressure on the critical churchmen, the state sought to influence them by means of the cooperation-oriented leaders in the Kirchenbund. With Fraenkel this approach worked only partially: though criticized in private, he was neither isolated publicly nor silenced. In the cases of Krusche and Hempel, the new rapprochement did promote greater agreement with the Kirchenbund's positions.[105]

---

[103]For example, Schoenherr criticized ideological intolerance during his inaugural sermon as bishop and rejected the formula "socialist state-citizens of Christian belief." "Bericht der Kirchenleitung der Evangelischen Kirche in Berlin-Brandenburg (Ost) . . . 1974," *epd Dokumentation*, no. 27 (4 June 1974): p. 51. CDU archives, 28 March 1973; CDU archives, 14 December 1973.

[104]Schoenherr is quoted in "Religionslose Interpretation als Auftrag," *KiS* 2 (September 1976): 27. Regarding the learning process in the church, see Schoenherr's comments in *KiS* 1 (September 1975): 14. Regarding liberation in the church, see his comments in *KiS* 1 (June 1975): 20, 23.

[105]Krusche turned his attention more toward internal changes in the church facing "ideological diaspora," according to discussion with Bishop Krusche. Hempel tended to go along with the majority in the Kirchenbund leadership.

Although the state still pursued this Kirchenbund-based strategy, it knew the limits of this strategy: the limited effectiveness of the Kirchenbund leadership in disciplining its organization, given its decentralized and relatively democratic character; and the potential volatility of the Kirchenbund should majority relations and/or leadership change. As a result, the state was not displeased by the slowing of church unification during this period. Despite its new cooperation with the Kirchenbund, the state continued to oppose a strong, unified Evangelical Church in the GDR.[106] In discussions with church leaders, it encouraged the independence of the Landeskirchen, directing its efforts particularly at the Lutherans and the small EKU Landeskirchen. By easing the churches' financial and personnel problems, the beginning of pragmatic agreements also had the effect of removing some of the pressure for church unification.

GRASSROOTS DISCONTENT IN THE CHURCH AND THE BRUESEWITZ AFFAIR

There remained areas, however, that did not benefit from the state's extension of rapprochement. Predictably they involved the treatment of the individual Christians in areas of education and the military, the two sacred cows of the ideologists in the SED. The continuing problems revealed the two-tracked strategy of the state: while seeking via compromise on some institutional issues to temper criticism by the church elite, the state sought to foster further erosion in church adherence on the grassroots level, especially among the youth.

The heightened ideological campaign translated into continued discrimination against Christians in the education system, albeit in more

[106]On the problems of church unification, see "Bericht der KKL . . . ," *epd Dokumentation*, no. 52 (11 November 1974): pp. 4–5; "Taetigkeitsbericht der Kirchenkanzlei der EKU-Bereich DDR . . . ," *epd Dokumentation*, no. 29 (18 June 1974): pp. 9–12; "Bericht der KKL . . . ," *epd Dokumentation*, no. 52 (11 November 1974): p. 6; Bishop Albrecht Schoenherr, "Die Kirche als Lerngemeinschaft," *epd Dokumentation*, no. 52 (11 November 1974): pp. 96–97; OKR Fritz Heidler, "Der Beitrag der Lutherischen Kirche zur Gemeinschaft der evangelischen Kirche in der DDR," *epd Dokumentation*, no. 36 (7 August 1974): pp. 37–39. On the state's opposition to greater centralization in the church, see *NZ*, 22 March 1973, 8 October 1972, and 6 July 1974. For example, the state opposed the Leuenberg Concordat and was alarmed at the formation of the Studies Department in the Kirchenbund. See CDU archives, 17 January 1974; CDU archives, 28 March 1973; CDU archives, 10 September 1974; CDU archives, 26 April 1974; CDU archives, 10 October 1973.

subtle fashion. An atmosphere of anxiety was created by teachers, making it extremely difficult for churches to prove discrimination and risky for the individuals involved to seek redress. Christians, even CDU members, were seldom hired as new teachers. Parents continued to be kept out of parents' organizations because they were considered unreliable in supporting the *Jugendweihe*.[107] The state continued to claim that such treatment merely reflected isolated, sectarian tendencies, citing the high percentage of clergy children in the college-track high schools.[108] It continued to maintain that *Jugendweihe* and confirmation were not irreconcilable. The state rectified individual cases in which the churches could document discrimination, but the increasing subtleness of the discrimination made it difficult for the churches to produce such evidence. The state rejected any direct discussion or negotiations with the Ministry of Education. Education was seen as a responsibility of the state and any criticism by the churches was viewed as an "attack on the state and its class-based goals."[109]

On numerous occasions the churches criticized this discrimination; however, the emphasis in their protests shifted from discussing concrete cases of discrimination to addressing the general climate.[110] The state interpreted this shift from specifics to generalities as a sign of greater "realism" by the churches. In fact it reflected not only the increasing subtleness of discrimination, but also conscious moves by the Kirchenbund leadership to downplay the issue following the beginning of the new initiatives by the state. In particular, the agreement on the Events Ordinance and the participation in the Moscow congress encouraged many in the Kirchenbund leadership that a corner had been turned in the churches' relations with the state and that mutual trust could be furthered by showing restraint on the issue of education discrimination. In its official pronouncements, the church leaders showed relative restraint from 1973 to 1976. Indeed the 1974 church leadership report

[107]*FAZ*, 27 October 1973; "Bericht der Kirchenleitung der Evangelische Kirche in Berlin-Brandenburg (Ost) . . . 1974," *epd Dokumentation*, no. 27 (4 June 1974): p. 38; "Bericht der KKL . . . ," *epd Dokumentation*, no. 45 (19 November 1973): pp. 8–10.
[108]*NZ*, 2 March 1974; CDU archives, 14 June 1973. Continued education problems are the subject of "Wort der Information und Seelsorge," Saxony-Magdeburg and Berlin-Brandenburg (East) synod in 1975, both found in *epd Dokumentation*, no. 22 (15 May 1975): pp. 27–28, 45–57.
[109]CDU archives, 29 June 1973; CDU archives, 5 October 1973; CDU archives, 28 January 1974; CDU archives, 23 July 1973.
[110]"Bericht der KKL . . . ," *epd Dokumentation*, no. 25 (12 June 1973): p. 9.

spoke not of atmosphere of anxiety, but of the need "to create an atmosphere of trusting cooperation in the area of education."[111]

The continued discrimination and subtle pressure took a staggering toll on church adherence. Between 1965 and 1973, it was estimated that GDR-wide baptisms dropped 46 percent, participation in Christian religious instruction 34 percent, and confirmations 35 percent. In one relatively representative Landeskirche (Mecklenburg), in a two year period from 1972 to 1974 alone, baptisms dropped 30 percent, confirmations 15 percent. From 1971 to 1973, the number of children participating in Christian religious instruction in Saxony-Magdeburg fell by 26 percent. This erosion of formal adherence among the youth reached even into the religious strongholds in Saxony.[112]

In its youth policy, the ideologically oriented state seemed intent on limiting the free time of youth and the role of alternative socialization agents. In its promulgation of the new youth law, for example, the state's goals of social engineering reigned supreme, with only minor modifications reflecting the concerns of the church and the CDU.[113] The churches' request for recognition of conscientious objection to premilitary training was only indirectly accommodated by including the Red Cross as an option. Their request for inclusion of freedom of belief and conscience in the new law was rejected by the state. At the same time, a certain relaxation of tension over the *Jugendweihe* was seen. To gain greater participation, the state reduced the emphasis on the atheistic component of the *Jugendweihe*.[114] Despite consistently emphasizing the differences in worldview, the state seemed less intent on the ideological content of its *own* socialization agents than on limiting formally the role of *alternative* agents, such as the church. For their part, the churches, realizing the battle was lost, began to soften their opposition

[111]"Bericht der KKL . . . ," *epd Dokumentation*, no. 45 (19 November 1973): pp. 8–10; "Bericht der KKL . . . ," *epd Dokumentation*, no. 52 (11 November 1974): p. 25; "Bericht des Vorsitzenden . . . Bischof D. Horst Gienke," *epd Dokumentation*, no. 29 (18 June 1974): p. 82.

[112]*KJ* 1974, pp. 521–23; Peter Fischer, *Kirche und Christen in der DDR* (1978), p. 102; "Eine Lutherische Unionskirche," *KiS* 4 (February 1978): 24.

[113]*ND*, 29 January 1974. Regarding the CDU's role in the changes, see CDU archives, 15 February 1974. Regarding the requests of the church, see "Vom Entwurf zum Gesetz," *KiS* 1 (1974): 7. See also Klaus Machnow, "Alle Erreichen—keine zuruecklassen," *DA* 11 (March 1978): 279f; Steven R. Bowers, "Youth Policies in the GDR," *Problems of Communism* 27 (March 1978): 78–82.

[114]See the analysis of the new *Handbuch zur Jugendweihe* (1974), in Gerhard Schmolze, "Nach 20 Jahre: Jugendweihe in der DDR," *KiS* 1 (July 1975): 19, and Werner Schnatterbeck, *Aspekte kirchlicher Jugendarbeit in der Deutschen Demokratischen Republik* (1977).

to the *Jugendweihe* and acknowledge that it was not simply an atheistic pledge.[115]

The training of church workers also continued to be a source of conflict with the state. The churches expressed continued concern over the effect of educational discrimination on the numbers of theologians being trained in the state universities.[116] The state denied the existence of a problem, claiming that ample numbers of pastors' children were being admitted to these high schools.[117] The state apparently began an affirmative action program for children of pastors, because they were indeed overrepresented in the college-track high schools.[118] The churches sought to increase the role of the laity through new training programs, including correspondence courses in Saxony-Dresden and Gorlitz, modeled after those in Saxony-Magdeburg. Although designed for non-clergy positions, the possibility of honorary lay ministers was considered. This trend worried the state, which found these courses difficult to oversee compared with formal, full-time programs of study. Although they did not question the correspondence courses per se, local state officials were known to challenge the activity of some individual graduates.[119]

Finally, the question of unarmed military service for Christians also remained a point of contention. More than the Kirchenbund, the Berlin-Brandenburg (East) synod addressed the issue directly. In a harbinger of the petitions of the church in the 1980s, the synod initially called for equal treatment of those choosing "peace service" and those choosing armed service in the NVA. The more moderate forces in the synod managed to soften this to a call for the church leadership to discuss the "problems of peace service of young Christians" with the state.[120]

---

[115]"Konfirmierende Handeln der christliche Gemeinde angesichts der Jugendweihe," *KiS* 1 (December 1973), Document supplement, especially section 2.4; Heinrich Frickel, "Stationen einer 20-jaehrigen Entwicklung," *KiS* 1 (July 1975): 12, 15, 18. On this issue, however, Saxony-Dresden continued to hold a firm line concerning the irreconcilability of the *Jugendweihe* and confirmation.

[116]"Bericht der KKL . . . ," *epd Dokumentation*, no. 25 (12 June 1973): p. 8.

[117]CDU archives, 22 March 1973.

[118]On the positive side, the elimination of residence permits for Berlin following the Four Power Agreement on Berlin in 1971 increased the viability of the church's seminary in East Berlin. See "Bericht der Kirchenleitung der Evangelischen Kirche in Berlin-Brandenburg (Ost) . . . 1974," *epd Dokumentation*, no. 27 (4 June 1974): p. 35.

[119]"Taetigkeitsbericht der Kirchenkanzlei der EKU—Bereich DDR . . . ," *epd Dokumentation*, no. 29 (18 June 1974): pp. 31–32; "Laienarbeit auf neuen Wegen," *KiS* 2 (November 1976): 21–26; "Der 'Idealtheologe'," *KiS* 2 (June 1976): 29; discussion with Bishop Krusche.

[120]"Beschlussvorlag" and "Beschluss," *epd Dokumentation*, no. 27 (4 June 1974): p. 52.

In 1975 the state moved to defuse the protests over the military nature of *Bausoldat* projects by breaking down the units into groups of ten to fifteen men and employing them as replacement service personnel at army bases. This also served to contain the infectious potential of the *Bausoldaten,* who had often organized Bible studies and agitated against militarism among the normal draftees.[121] This shift seemed to ameliorate the church protests over the character of the service, even though discrimination against *Bausoldaten* in education and career continued to pose problems for the relationship with the state. As earlier, the church leadership feared that greater public protest might endanger the *Bausoldat* option entirely.

The continued problems facing ordinary Christians led many in the church grass roots to become increasingly critical of the "Schoenherr course" of accommodation with the regime. The local parishioner, for the most part, felt distant from the Berlin church headquarters. Not able to read the narrowly circulating church press, he or she was forced to rely on the one-sided coverage of church positions by the official media or the often critical coverage of the West German electronic media. Thus church positions that appeared to align with those of the state, such as the antiracism program and Kirchenbund study materials on Vietnam, met with resistance and skepticism in the church grass roots.[122]

Despite the various protests against discrimination against Christians, particularly by the leadership in Saxony-Magdeburg, Berlin-Brandenburg, and Gorlitz, the restraint shown by the Kirchenbund leadership from 1973 to 1976 was not shared by the laity, as demonstrated by the generally more critical debate and resolutions manifested in synods. The 1974 Kirchenbund synod, for example, criticized the thesis of "absence of social antagonism between Christians and Marxists" and beefed up the leadership's mild criticism of discrimination.[123]

[121]Bernd Eisenfeld, "Spaten-Soldaten," *KiS* 10 (September 1984): 24.

[122]"Bericht der Kirchenleitung der Evangelischen Kirche in Berlin-Brandenburg (Ost) am 27.4.74," *epd Dokumentation,* no. 27 (4 June 1974): p. 47. Stolpe hinted at problems on the grass roots with respect to the PCR and social responsibility in his address to the VELKDDR, as indicated in "5 Jahre Kirchenbund—500 Jahre Landeskirchen. Interview . . . mit OKR Stolpe," *epd Dokumentation,* no. 36 (7 August 1974): p. 48. "Vietnam und wir," mimeograph of Facharbeitskreis III—Oekumenische Diakonie, Kirchenbund, 1973. Fraenkel criticized this study as one-sidedly focused on the effects of U.S. war activities in Vietnam. See CDU archives, 17 January 1974.

[123]"Beschluesse der Synode . . . ," *epd Dokumentation,* no. 52 (11 November 1974): pp. 120, 122; "Kritische Debate in der Synode des DDR-Kirchenbundes," *epd Landesdienst Berlin,* no. 174 (30 September 1974): p. 2; Reinhard Henkys, "Achtung und Respektierung des christlichen Glaubens erforderlich," *Berliner Kirchenreport,* October 1974, p. 1.

The clergy, who felt particularly acutely the collapse of the *Volkskirche,* also began to show less restraint. Some of the more dispirited opted to apply to emigrate to West Germany, and the state cooperated by granting permission in most cases. This development caused alarm and admonishment on the part of the church leadership.[124]

This rising sense of frustration with the two-tracked state policy and the church's apparent acceptance of it culminated in a symbolic action that challenged both the church leadership and the state: the suicide by Pastor Oskar Bruesewitz in the town square of Zeitz on August 18, 1976.[125] After unrolling a banner that decried the ruination of the youth and proclaimed a battle between darkness and light, Bruesewitz doused himself with gasoline and set himself afire. He died four days later. The East German news agency labeled Bruesewitz as abnormal and sick, alleging that he used "unorthodox means" in this ministry. "Progressives" close to the CDU trivialized Bruesewitz's action as the "personal failure of a pastor." The Saxony-Magdeburg leadership issued a Word to the Parishes denouncing the state's interpretation and, while not endorsing Bruesewitz's action, refusing to distance itself from it either. The Landeskirche rejected the state's description of Bruesewitz's activities as "fiction" and "shameful denigration of the worth of a human being." In September the Kirchenbund leadership responded with a Letter to the Parishes, indicating that Bruesewitz's action "shows the tensions which run through society and the tests which many face." It urged direct work on these problems not repression of them. The Western media devoted considerable attention to the suicide and the reactions of church and state, largely set in the context of the human rights record of the GDR.

Bruesewitz's message was directed as much at the church leadership as at the state, and his action dramatically crystallized the grass roots' discontent with continued discrimination and institutional-level accommodation. Large numbers of Christians wrote to Magdeburg protesting the Landeskirche's rejection of suicide as a failure to support Bruesewitz. The debate at both the Magdeburg and Kirchenbund synods in fall 1976 was especially heated. The church leadership sought to limit the

---

124*KiS* 2 (February 1976): p. 5; *KiS* 2 (November 1976): pp. 8, 11.
125For a detailed review of the sequence of events surrounding Bruesewitz's suicide, see *KiS* 2 (November 1976): 4–8, and *KiS* 2 (December 1976): 5–42. *Neues Deutschland,* 31 August 1976; Gisela Helwig, "Christ sein in der DDR," *DA* 9 (October 1976): 1020–22; Gisela Helwig, "Kirche im Sozialismus," *DA* 10 (May 1977): 450.

damage from the affair by indicating that the Kirchenbund did not wish a Kirchenkampf with the state. It criticized the sensationalized, propagandistic coverage of the affair by the Western media in the context of the West German elections. As Stolpe put it at the church congress in Halle in September 1976, "We will not allow others to make out of us either a transmission belt of the Party or a Trojan horse of the counter-revolution." The church leadership criticized the state's censorship of its statement in the church newspapers. In the debates during closed sessions of the synod and the resolutions of the synod the more critical views of the clergy and laity became evident. The synod called for "clarification of the tension between the freedom of faith and conscience and the education goal of Communist personality." The Magdeburg synod criticized the one-sided reporting of the state and the absence of real opportunities for substantial, independent participation in society. The synod also called into question the Schoenherr formula of "church within socialism," seeing it as becoming "a mere formula which might produce divisive misunderstandings." The synod distanced itself from the formula, substituting for it the much more neutral term, "church in the *current society*" (emphasis added).

The church leadership realized that, given the democratic organization of the church, rapprochement with the state required greater attention to the impact on the grass roots of high visibility, social-political participation by church leaders. More intensive efforts at communication between church leaders and the grass roots would be required to prevent misperception of the church's actions. As one clergyman put it, "precondition for exercise of critical solidarity in society is the guaranteeing of critical solidarity of the Christian brotherhood within the church." The church leadership also realized that the new relationship with the state required greater efforts to improve the lot of ordinary Christians and clergy.

This internal church criticism in the context of the Bruesewitz affair thus also increased the pressure on the state to seek better relations with the church, strengthening the hand of the church leadership in dealing with the state. The state faced a dilemma. The heightened emphasis on ideology—engendered by Honecker's need to distinguish himself from Ulbricht and the perceived need for Abgrenzung in the face of potentially destabilizing compromises with the FRG—was meeting with resistance from an institution that had begun to prove useful to the GDR and Soviet Union in ecumenical and foreign affairs. This usefulness was, to a great extent, predicated upon its close ties with the West German churches and its relatively unquestioned credibility, both enjoyed at the expense of the GDR's political goals of control and Abgrenzung. But this resistance was occurring in an institution that was sufficiently democratic to transmit the discontent upwards and threaten the church leadership's diplomatic policy of avoiding confrontation with the state, thus forcing the leadership to hew a more critical line vis-à-vis the state.

THE MARCH 1978 SUMMIT BETWEEN CHURCH AND STATE

The Bruesewitz affair, in particular the fallout internationally and within the church, served as an impetus for a new stage in the church-state relationship, symbolized by the unprecedented summit meeting on March 6, 1978, between Honecker and the Executive Board of the Kirchenbund. In addition to the increasing dissent in the church, nonchurch dissent was also rising in the wake of detente, thus providing the context for the state's interest in further consolidating relations with the church.[126] Artistic dissent increased as a result of a more restrictive cultural policy. Wolf Biermann, a leading dissident songwriter and musician, was involuntarily exiled in 1977, shortly after performing in a church in Prenzlau. This produced a wave of protests from other cultural figures, resulting in a crackdown by the state authorities and the emigration of several prominent cultural figures. Marxist dissent also rose, stimulated in 1977 by the critical treatise of SED economist Rudolf Bahro. Bahro's widely read critique of "real existing socialism" stressed the overbureaucratized and alienating structures and called for a democratic "League of Communists" and major cultural change. This rise in dissent extended to the general population, as one hundred thousand applied to emigrate under the new Helsinki guidelines. This dissent, perhaps better described as disaffection, extended to the youth as well. Youth disaffection manifested itself dramatically in October 1977 when youth rioted during a rock concert in East Berlin.[127] Such secular dissent

[126]Rudolf Bahro, *Die Alternative* (Cologne: Europaeischer Verlagsanstalt, 1977). On this Marxist and cultural dissent, see Krisch, *German Democratic Republic*, pp. 129–33, and Roger Woods, *Opposition in the GDR under Honecker, 1971–1985* (1986), pp. 32–36.

[127]Pedro Ramet, "Disaffection and Dissent in East Germany," *World Politics* 37 (October 1984): 90.

doubtless worried the state, particularly given the potential for linkages between secular and religious dissent. This fear, combined with the continued moderate course of the Kirchenbund under Schoenherr, led the state to make the March 1978 overture.

The summit represented a significant breakthrough for the church in terms of protocol. By meeting with the Kirchenbund's executive body, the SED was confirming its Kirchenbund strategy and the authority of the Kirchenbund's leadership to speak for the church, a contrast with earlier attempts to differentiate among the Landeskirchen. The summit was long in planning and the agreements were prepared for ratification well in advance. The reading of prepared statements by both sides was followed by a wide-ranging, three-hour discussion, dominated by negotiating of the final communiqué.[128]

At the heart of the summit were several concrete agreements involving largely institutional perquisites, albeit ones of considerable political and social significance. One of the most significant was television access for the church four times per year for informational programs of a general nature. To be sure, the format precluded actual worship services; for this purpose the church continued to broadcast a weekly service on radio, a privilege it had enjoyed since 1945. The programs have not usually been broadcast in prime time and, even if they were, the fact that most East Germans watch Western television limits the practical impact of this measure. However, the agreement had great symbolic importance: a Communist state that jealously guarded control over the mass media had granted media access, hence social recognition, to an allegedly anachronistic, ideologically taboo institution. In the context of heightened exposure to the West, the state was receptive to the church's argument that it needed a vehicle to credibly combat Western "distortions" of the church's views.

---

[128]Gisela Helwig, "Zeichen der Hoffnung" and Hans-Juergen Roeder, "Absprache zwischen Staat und Kirche," *DA* 11 (April 1978): 351–55; Gisela Helwig, "Neue Chancen fuer Christen?" *DA* 12 (November 1979): 1130–31. For other interpretations of the recent Honecker policy in the context of the 6 March 1978 summit, see George A. Glass, "Church-State Relations in East Germany," *East Central Europe* 6 (1979): 232–49; Stephen R. Bowers, "Private Institutions in Service to the State," *East European Quarterly* 26 (Spring 1982): 73–86; Roger Williamson, "East Germany: The Federation of Protestant Churches," *Religion in Communist Lands* 9 (January 1981); Robert F. Goeckel, "Zehn Jahre Kirchenpolitik under Honecker," *DA* 14 (September 1981): 940–47; and "Church and Society in the GDR: Historical Legacies and 'Mature Socialism,'" in *The Quality of Life in the GDR*, eds. Marilyn Rueschemeyer et al. (Armonk, N.Y.: M. E. Sharpe, 1989).

Another concession offered by Honecker was access by the churches to ministers in certain prisons. Although long a wish of the church, this access in an area of great sensitivity for Communist regimes was dismissed by the state until 1978. Most indications point to only partial fulfillment of its commitment by the state. Honecker also agreed to continue the program of building new churches begun in 1976. Although this represented an acceptance of the churches' role in the future, the fact that all construction was reimbursed in West German marks indicated the state's economic motive in its policy toward the churches. The March 6, 1978, agreement also entailed a state commitment to compensate the church for land tilled by the agricultural cooperatives. Finally, the church and state agreed to integrate clergy and other lifetime workers of the church into the state's pension system. The church was interested in this to guarantee church employees a fixed, stable pension. Although it did give the state a certain amount of control over the church, the arrangements precluded the state's withholding pensions from selected, more critical clergy. Moreover, like the media access, it did represent social recognition of the church by the state.

In addition to these concrete agreements, the atmosphere of the summit spilled over into other areas of interest to the church. For example, the state, which had always viewed church congresses with suspicion since they reflected interchurch cooperation and publicity, now facilitated these congresses.[129] The state cooperated fully with their logistical needs in summer 1978—for example, printing posters, granting space in halls, and allocating special trains. The fifty thousand attending the Leipzig congress represented the largest gathering since the 1961 congress, the last before the Berlin Wall was built. Similarly, international ecumenical travel and cooperation was promoted after the 1978 agreement. This allowed the Kirchenbund to host the precedent-setting WCC Central Committee meeting in August 1981 in Dresden.

However, the primary import of the summit lay not in these concrete agreements and expanding international opportunities but rather in ratifying the basis of the new relationship between church and state that had developed since 1971. This was reflected in the wording of the joint press release of the summit: "Both sides ascertain with satisfaction that

---

[129]*KiS* 4 (October 1978): 7; see *ND*, 27/28 May 1978 for an example of the extensive official coverage of the church congresses in 1978.

the relations of the church to the state have been increasingly marked by objectivity, trust, and forthrightness." It is important to underscore that the March 6 summit did not represent a concordat between church and state, nor did it produce a communiqué with binding character on the participants. The church had long before learned that the 1949 constitutional guarantees or the commitments in communiqués in the 1950s were meaningless unless backed by the political interest of the state. The sole manifestation was a press release in the official media, agreed upon by both sides. Thus March 6 underscored the ad hoc nature of the relationship, a relationship based on the "trusting discrete discussion" of issues so characteristic of the Schoenherr approach. Both sides agreed to cooperate when in agreement, but agreed to disagree when in disagreement. Seigewasser's successor as state secretary, Klaus Gysi, articulated this consensus on process, indicating in 1981 that "we wish a relationship that is constructively cooperative where we agree and that where we do not agree, there is tolerance of the state decisions, a relationship in which each respects the identity and the independence of the other."[130]

The March 6 summit also reflected the shift in the state's strategy toward the church. It had attempted prior to 1973 to limit the church's role in society by such means as the restrictions on the churches' freedom of assembly. Since 1973 the state had come increasingly to accept the church's social presence and indeed to use the church to meet certain goals of the state. Gysi again revealed this in disarmingly honest fashion, proclaiming "the intention to truly root the church in our Republic and gradually to gain its potential both for the stable development domestically in our Republic as well as for our peace policy."[131] Some church leaders maintained that the church had been granted "societal significance" and had been recognized as an "independent societal force." Gysi rejected this, maintaining that the church "will never be completely integrated into our society as a social force, but nonetheless we stand before the task of finding a modus vivendi." Despite the dispute over whether the church had been formally labeled a "social force," with its ideological-political ramifications, the March 6 summit reflected tacit acceptance by the state of the church's social presence.

---

[130]Quoted in Henkys, *Evangelischen Kirchen*, p. 25.
[131]Ibid., pp. 18, 21.

March 6 also represented a further diminishment of the CDU's role in the state's church policy, a process already detectable in 1971. Unlike the meeting between Verner and the Kirchenbund in 1971, CDU Chairman Goetting was not present at the summit, reflecting the general trend toward direct relations between church and state.

Given the Bruesewitz affair and the grassroots discontent in the church, the area in which the March 1978 summit was most crucial—and most controversial—was that of the treatment of individual Christians. In the March 6 communique, Honecker promised that "the socialist society offers security, protection and a clear perspective to cooperate in building the future to every citizen, regardless of worldview and religious confession." Schoenherr sought to press the state by maintaining in the press release that "the relationship of church and state is as good as the individual Christian citizen experiences it in his local social situation." This sent a new impulse for equal treatment to lower-level state authorities, but as Honecker later confided to Schoenherr, translating it into results on the local level was far from simple. The signal may have been clear, but the ideological and bureaucratic blocks to equal treatment for Christians in education and career remained substantial.

The response in the church to the summit was supportive, for the most part. Several clergy disassociated themselves from the new rapprochement. The Catholic church criticized the initiative, charging that the Protestants had been slow to inform them.[132] However, the Catholic church accepted the benefits that were extended to it as well as the Lutheran church. However, most importantly, leading churchmen long known to be more skeptical of the Schoenherr course weighed in on the side of the arrangement. In particular, Bishops Fraenkel, Hempel, and Krusche all supported the March 1978 initiative.

Nineteen seventy-three to 1978 saw an extension of the rapprochement that had begun in 1971. As the inter-German political relationship relaxed, the state's constraints on inter-German church ties also loosened. Indeed, given the increasing attention paid to human rights by the FRG, ecumenical organizations, and the international community, the Kirchenbund's ties to and credibility with the ecumenical community,

---

[132]For views of a confidante of Cardinal Alfred Bengsch, primate of East Germany, see Michael Albus, "Ein konstruktives Gespraech—fuer wen?" *Informationsdienst des katholischen Arbeitskreises fuer zeitgeschichtliche Fragen*, no. 90/1978.

and the West German churches in particular, began to look more attractive to the state. As the international attention turned to the GDR churches, however, the linkages between the Kirchenbund's restraint in international forums and the conflictual domestic Kirchenpolitik became clearer for the state. This linkage was reinforced by the rising tide of criticism—from church elites as well as the grass roots—of the limited rapprochement with the state. Responding to these international and domestic factors, the state extended the rapprochement, making concessions to a variety of church institutional interests.

This modus vivendi between church and state would soon be severely tested by changes in the international environment and rising dissent in the GDR. The next chapter explores the strength of the new-found accommodation in the context of political change.

8 Testing the New Relationship, 1978–1989

The new rapprochement, manifested in the summit of March 6, 1978, and related agreements, was tested quite severely in the coming years. This was to be expected. The March 1978 accord represented not an endpoint in the church-state relationship but one stage in a long-term process. In the years since, the relationship has been buffeted by domestic and international changes. As the embodiment of an alternative value system and as the only institution independent of democratic centralism in the GDR, the church might have developed into a fount of political opposition—as it did in Poland, for example. But in practice the experience of the years 1978–1989 calls for a more nuanced view of the church's role. This chapter argues that, given increasing political dissent and disaffection, the church served as both an umbrella for the expression of oppositional views and a channel for and domesticator of such views. The regime increasingly realized that the church's credibility was useful not only in foreign policy but also in dampening the local effects of domestic dissent. Moreover, the regime sought to incorporate religious-historical figures into the socialist heritage. With this admission the state came to concede the importance of the autonomy and independence of the church as a social force. That this process was not smooth was demonstrated by periodic tensions.

THE LUTHER ANNIVERSARY AND
REHISTORICIZATION

One indication of the extent of change under Honecker was the inclusion of and greater profile granted to the church in the GDR's treatment of history and culture. The most significant example was the five hundredth anniversary of the birth of Martin Luther in 1983.[1] The regime not only revised its negative interpretation of Luther's role but also extended unprecedented assistance to the church in its celebration. The state's handling of the event, particularly when compared to its role in the 450th anniversary of the Reformation in 1967, indicated the regime's adaptation to its inherited political culture, as well as the rapprochement with an inherited institution, the church.

The new official view of Luther upgraded his role and admitted the legitimacy of his subjective religious motivation. This shift in official historiography developed over a period of time and was part of a larger rehistoricization process occurring in the GDR.[2] Such figures as Frederick the Great and Bismarck, long considered reactionary and politically taboo, have been rehabilitated in recent years.[3] In 1949 Alexander Abusch, GDR minister of culture, labeled Luther "the gravedigger of German freedom," a reactionary for his opposition to the peasants and Thomas Muentzer and a contributor to the failures of German development that led to Nazism. By the 1960s, however, Luther's positive contributions to the development of the German nation were conceded, and he was granted an unconsciously progressive role in the "early bourgeois revolution." By 1980 Luther was incorporated into the "socialist heritage of the GDR." Honecker proclaimed him "one of the greatest sons of the German people," a representative of "the progressive traditions which we protect and carry on."[4] Whereas earlier historiography viewed Luther's motivations solely in terms of his class posi-

---

[1] Robert F. Goeckel, "The Luther Anniversary in East Germany," *World Politics* 37 (October 1984): 112–33.

[2] Ronald D. Asmus, "The GDR and Martin Luther," manuscript, 1983; Eleutherius [pseud.], "Luther Rebaptized in Marxist Ideology?" *Occasional Papers on Religion in Eastern Europe*, no. 3 (July 1983): pp. 21–43.

[3] For example, see the new official biography of Bismarck by Ernst Engelberg, *Bismarck, Urpreusse und Reichsgruender* (Berlin, GDR: Siedler, 1985).

[4] *ND*, 14–15 June 1980, p. 3.

tion, the official biography for the 1983 celebration admits a role for his insecurity before God and his theology.

Unprecedented official celebration in 1983 accompanied this shift in the official historiography of Luther.[5] In 1980 the official Martin Luther Committee of the GDR had been constituted with Honecker himself as chairman. The state media showered Luther and the anniversary with attention, including additional television and radio access for the churches and almost daily coverage of the plans in *Neues Deutschland*. Tours, "in the steps of Luther," were promoted heavily by the state, resulting in an estimated 250,000 Western visitors, among them 12,500 Americans. The administrative treatment of the celebration contrasted markedly with 1967, when the state denied most visas for Westerners and forced the cancellation of many church events; in 1983 the state could hardly have been more accommodating to the church.

The church responded with considerable ambivalence to the state's new enthusiasm for Luther and its grandiose jubilee plans. It knew of Luther's negative side and the cloud over pre-1945 Luther anniversaries, which had been demonstrations of anti-Catholicism, German nationalism, and fascism. Many felt that the true needs of the church would be overlooked in this euphoria and that the issues of contention with the state, such as discrimination and militarization of society, should be addressed. Yet the church could hardly ignore the international attention of world Lutheranism, and the increased contact between Marxist and church historians argued for cooperation with the state.

Thus the church sought to coordinate plans with the state while retaining its organizational independence. It maintained a separate Luther committee and held celebrations separate from the state's. The church also sought to balance the new official view of Luther by pointing out his negative dimensions and limiting any damage to ecumenical relations with Catholics by distancing itself from Luther's harsh attacks on the Catholic church. Rebuking the state, the church declared that "Luther does not belong to the GDR, but rather he really belongs . . . to the worldwide community of churches."[6]

The state, in turn, sought to distance itself from church celebrations,

---

[5]Goeckel, "Luther Anniversary," pp. 116–18.
[6]See *Evangelische Nachrichtenagentur* (GDR), 21 January 1982, p. 2.

particularly as the anniversary year approached. Thus, in a belated move in November 1982, the GDR proclaimed 1983 Karl Marx Year, even while it sought to persuade UNESCO to declare 1983 Luther Year. Honecker described Marx as "*the* greatest son of the German people," leaving Luther as only one of many lesser sons. The state delayed meetings of the official Luther committee and downgraded state representation at the church events in 1983, clearly seeking to lower its visibility.[7]

The regime also sought to reemploy the Thuringian strategy during the Luther year. The fact that Braecklein's successor as bishop, Werner Leich, was chairman of the church's committee facilitated this development. At the reopening of Wartburg Castle, which officially kicked off the Luther year, Honecker met with Bishop Leich, praising him for "decisively and successfully continuing the good tradition of Thuringia of bringing constructive elements into the development of church-state relations."[8] The state violated the confidentiality of this meeting by printing some of Leich's words of praise for the GDR's peace policy.

The state also sought to reinforce some traditional Lutheran values in the political culture. For example, it sought to use Luther's deference to the state to build support for the regime among the populace. It also stressed the Lutheran emphasis on the work ethic in an attempt to stimulate work productivity, generally on the decline in the GDR.

The 750th anniversary of Berlin in 1987 provided another case of increased incorporation of the church into historical and cultural inheritance.[9] The state mounted a massive restoration campaign, which included historically significant churches such as the oldest church in Berlin and the Wilhelmine cathedral. As in 1983, separate yet coordinated committees were formed and the church contributed to the anniversary with numerous activities under the rubric of "750 Years of the Church in Berlin." The high point of the church's activities was a church convention in June 1987, the first since the construction of the Berlin Wall. The state's fears of political dissent and unrest had long made such a large church gathering in Berlin unthinkable. Even with the rapprochement and positive experience of the Luther celebrations, the state

[7]Goeckel, "Luther Anniversary," pp. 121–23.
[8]*ND*, 22 April 1983.
[9]Reinhard Henkys, "Einen Schritt vorwaerts," *KiS* 13 (August 1987): 131–32; Matthias Hartmann, "Signale vom evangelischen Kirchentag," *DA* 20 (August 1987): 838–43.

was hesitant to approve the church convention. However, Honecker overrode the concerns of SED security officials and approved the convention. Despite the unrest in the church grass roots (discussed below), the state accorded considerable media coverage to the convention. Thus, in its search to build greater legitimacy based on a more inclusionary historical and cultural heritage, the state accorded the church and its figures increased attention after 1978.

THE CHURCH AND ENVIRONMENTAL ACTIVISM

One issue that provided a test of the new relationship was the environment. Like the peace movement, discussed below, the issue of ecological protection became prominent in the 1980s in the GDR. Likewise, it demonstrated the ambiguity of the church's role under Honecker—as facilitator and articulator, as well as channeler of dissent.

Several factors were involved in the church's increasing activism. Certainly the increasing international attention to environmental deterioration in the 1970s provided the general context.[10] The "limits to growth" argument of the Club of Rome report in 1972 generated a debate in the GDR that included SED dissenters such as Wolfgang Harich. As with the peace movement in the GDR, heightened environmentalism in West Germany and youth disaffection in the GDR also provided a stimulus. In the church itself, early interest in the issue derived from the elite debate about the substance of "church within socialism." The leading figure in the church's activity on ecology has been Falcke, who articulated a position of "critical solidarity" for the church (see chapter 6) and who was instrumental in the Kirchenbund's theses regarding GDR society (see chapter 7). Ecumenical organizations also paid increasing attention to the environment. The Kirchenbund's

---

[10]Wolfgang Harich, *Kommunismus ohne Wachstum? Babeuf und der "Club of Rome"* (Reinbek bei Hamburg: Rowohlt, 1975); Gerhard Timm, "Die offizielle Oekologiedebatte in der DDR," in *Umweltprobleme und Umweltbewusstsein in der DDR*, ed. Deutschland Archiv (Cologne: Verlag Wissenschaft und Politik, 1985), pp. 117–50; Anita Mallinckrodt, *The Environmental Dialogue in the GDR* (1987), pp. 30–39. For general sources on the environmental question, see Joan DeBardeleben, *The Environment and Marxism-Leninism* (1985) and Peter Wensierski and Wolfgang Buescher, eds., *Beton ist Beton: Zivilisationskritik aus der DDR* (1981).

high visibility participation in the WCC Conference on Faith, Science and the Future in Boston in 1979 was a signal event for the GDR church. As in the case of peace, the church's agenda on the environment came to be increasingly affected by external forces.

The church's social criticism on this issue entailed several dimensions, all of which called into question fundamental assumptions of the official political culture of the GDR. First, the church argued that the individual's relationship to nature must be altered. Admitting that the Biblical version of creation has contributed to a culture of exploitation of nature, the church urged cooperation with nature.[11]

Second, the church articulated a position critical of scientific-technical progress. Technological improvements, implemented under the pressure of economic progress, carry negative side-effects. According to Falcke, the "objectification of nature is the origin of the destruction of the living."[12] A "technological convergence" is occurring between capitalism and socialism as a result. Falcke has criticized a "society guided by specialists," endorsing instead "justice, ecological survival, and participation" as the standards for determining permissible technology.

Third, the "pressure to perform," highlighted by the Kirchenbund study in 1974, was seen to be part of the environmental problem. Such pressure came at the expense of all-around personality development and self-sufficiency. As the Kirchenbund Studies Department put it, "if remuneration based on individual performance is the true social principle of distribution and socialist working reality, then ideological propagation of solidarity and general social responsibility can accomplish little."[13] Increasingly, the church, especially the youth, rejected the work ethic so prominent in Protestantism and socialism.

Finally, the church became more critical of the consumer orientation in the GDR. The Kirchenbund Studies Department claimed, "A mere quantitative increase in consumption does not compensate for the loss of quality of life, which the worker loses from modern production methods; rather it has the effect of an additional loss of individuality."[14] The church called for a "conscious reduction of material demands."

[11]Hubertus Knabe, "Gesellschaftlicher Dissens im Wandel oekologische Diskussion und Umweltengagement in der DDR," in *Umweltprobleme*, pp. 172–74.
[12]Ibid., pp. 175–77.
[13]Ibid., pp. 177–80.
[14]Ibid., pp. 180–82.

The church's increasing activism on environmental matters took a variety of forms. The church functioned as an umbrella for grassroots activism.[15] At least forty grassroots groups formed in recent years. In conjunction with individual parishes they began a variety of concrete projects, such as planting trees and cleaning up debris in forests. On an ad hoc basis varying by jurisdiction, the local officials of the state's environmental organization, the Society for Nature and Environment, cooperated with the church-based groups. Sometimes these groups mounted protests against particular state projects, such as a new autobahn in Rostock in 1983. These protests took the form of petition drives or bicycle cavalcades to mobilize public opinion. The church also sponsored a GDR-wide campaign every June, Mobile without Autos, which called upon Christians to forego the use of the automobile for one weekend.

The church also acted to build networks and disseminate information among these groups. Because of the state's near-monopoly on information, the church filled the need for alternative sources of information and organization. The church created a small Environmental Research Center in Wittenberg, which circulated a newsletter and organized conferences. Along with various Evangelical academies, it served to bring together natural scientists and interested church members, thus providing an alternative base of expertise. The church congresses and the annual Peace Workshop in Berlin also provided forums for discussion of the issue and dissemination of information. These institutional bases also criticized society and public policy in the GDR.

At the leadership level, the church also exercised criticism of state policy on the environment. This became more direct in recent years, stimulated by the grassroots movement and the growing fear of environmental disasters. The Kirchenbund had long called for more openness and information regarding the issue.[16] The church increasingly linked the environmental problems to issues such as nuclear arms and poverty in the Third World, as part of a general cultural criticism. The church leadership encouraged the social engagement of Christians in official environmental activities, although this engagement was not always welcomed by the state.

[15]Ibid., pp. 189–95; Mallinckrodt, pp. 34, 53, 92, 105.
[16]Knabe, in *Umweltprobleme*, p. 185, citing the 1980 Kirchenbund synod resolution.

The nuclear disaster at Chernobyl in 1986 challenged the church as never before and precipitated the most direct criticism of state policy.[17] The EKU synod meeting in May 1986 criticized the delay in providing information about the accident and failure to make public the measurements of radioactivity in the GDR. The Kirchenbund leadership proclaimed that "there is no reason for an optimistic assessment of nuclear power" following Chernobyl. Although the Kirchenbund did not call for the abandonment of the GDR's nuclear program, various grassroots groups did so. A petition submitted to Honecker called for a nationwide referendum on the program. Within a year the Kirchenbund followed suit, calling for a "worldwide moratorium on nuclear energy." The Peace Workshop in Berlin in 1986 adopted the theme "Chernobyl Is Everywhere."

The influence of the church on environmental issues was difficult to determine. In terms of the policy process, the state showed a willingness to engage in dialogue with the church. Several of the "informational discussions" that the state granted in the Honecker era dealt with environmental issues (e.g., March 6, 1980, and again following Chernobyl). These permitted the church to present its concerns on this issue. The state permitted considerable cooperation by experts with the church environmental institutions, such as the Wittenberg center. The formation of the official Society for Nature and the Environment in 1980 was an indicator of not only the increasing attention paid by the state to the issue but also its fear that church-based grassroots groups would enjoy a monopoly of environmental activism. Like the FDJ and church youth work, the Society had a competitive relationship with church environmental groups, although on occasion they did cooperate on projects.[18] In some cases the church groups' protests resulted in the halting or altering of state construction projects. However, the continued priority on economic growth by the state limited this impact to marginal matters. Certainly the GDR's nuclear program remained intact despite Chernobyl. The church's greatest impact has lain in changing the political culture of the GDR by providing an alternative value structure to the consumerism pervasive in the "goulash communism" of the "niche-society." Of course, this impact is difficult to measure.

[17]Mallinckrodt, pp. 136–39; *epd Dokumentation*, no. 33 (28 July 1986): pp. 42–48.
[18]Peter Wensierski, "Die Gesellschaft fuer Natur und Umwelt," in *Umweltprobleme*, pp. 151–68.

The issue of environmentalism in the GDR tested the new rapprochement of church and state under Honecker. The church articulated a view diverging from the official political culture and the policy of the state and served as an umbrella for grassroots activism on ecological concerns. Yet the church acted to channel this dissent, in some cases disciplining it. For example, the church terminated the employment of Jochen Rochau—who protested heavy chemical pollution in the Halle area by leading a bicycle procession with gas masks and protest signs in 1983—thus disassociating itself from such demonstrative tactics. Moreover, the church's appeal for reduced consumption and greater civic mindedness converged with the state's interest in dampening expectations of the GDR's economic performance in the 1980s. Thus, the church's role was ambiguous: the state tolerated increased church visibility outside the narrow cultic sphere, but such activity also served as a stabilizing force in GDR society.

THE CHURCH AND THE PEACE MOVEMENT

The most significant challenge to the new modus vivendi arose from the deterioration of East-West relations in the late 1970s and the development of an independent peace movement in the GDR in the 1980s. The issue of peace, including domestic and international dimensions, came to overshadow the conflict over discrimination against Christians as a source of tension in the church-state relationship. However, the new rapprochement not only survived this conflict, but the church functioned to channel rising grassroots dissent on this issue, thereby proving useful to a conservative regime interested in political stability without sacrificing ideological purity or loyalty to the USSR.

The issues of peace and foreign policy had been a chronic source of conflict between church and state. However, the detente process in the 1970s and the churches' refocusing on their role in socialism had reduced this considerably. The emphasis in the church's international agenda shifted from that of improving relations between the two Germanies to improving the quality of life within the GDR. As noted in chapter 7, after Helsinki deliberations on the issue of human rights preoccupied church and state.

However, in this period the institutional framework for a greater profile on peace issues was begun. Already in 1970 the Kirchenbund had created a full-time post responsible for peace issues in the Secretariat. Associated with this position is a Working Group on Peace Questions, a representative subcommittee of the Kirchenbund's Committee on Church and Society. The Kirchenbund also engaged in considerable ecumenical and bilateral diplomacy on peace, as indicated in chapter 7. One must conclude that the church's concern and activity on behalf of peace long antedated the rise of the peace movement in the 1980s. Moreover, in this activity the church had articulated a position linking the issues of peace and human rights, proclaiming its dissatisfaction with a "cold peace" and arguing that violations of human rights endangered peace.

Despite this broader view of peace held by the church, the narrow definition returned to center stage in the late 1970s for several reasons. First, the increasing militarization of GDR society by the regime led the church to speak out. In particular the introduction in fall 1978 of military instruction as a required subject in the ninth and tenth grades prompted an energetic response by the Kirchenbund.[19] Although military preparedness had long been emphasized in the educational system, this represented a significant intensification on a formal basis and included summer camp training for both boys and girls. After rumors of its introduction circulated, the Executive Committee asked for clarification from State Secretary Seigewasser. Seigewasser met with representatives of the Executive Committee in June 1978 and confirmed the plans to introduce such instruction. In a letter to the government, the church leadership protested this policy, arguing that it would fixate the youth's consciousness on categories of friend and foe and encourage force as the means of conflict resolution. Moreover, the leadership argued that it would erode the credibility of the GDR's peace policy internationally. It asked that the decision be rescinded and, if not, that the state respect the decisions of those who refuse to participate on grounds of conscience.

As a test of the church's clout following the March 1978 summit, the church's criticism of the state action failed. The regime refused to

---

[19]Theo Mechtenberg, "Die Friedensverantwortung der Evangelischen Kirchen in der DDR," in Henkys, *Evangelischen Kirchen,* pp. 365–68; Wolfgang Buescher, Peter Wensierski, and Klaus Wolschner, eds., *Friedensbewegung in der DDR* (1982), pp. 69–77. Joachim Garstecki and Hans-Juergen Roeder, "Aus unterschiedlicher Sicht: Die katholischen und evangelischen Bedenken gegen die Wehrerziehung in den Schulen in der DDR," *KiS* 4 (December 1978).

reconsider, not surprising given the bureaucratic interests at stake in the Ministries of Defense and Education. Privately, the state agreed to exempt those with ethical qualms and the church sought to publicize this agreement among parishioners. However, here also the church's efforts failed. Few parents asked to exempt their children from the training, reflecting widespread resignation in the face of the state's measure. In a failure reminiscent of that surrounding the church's efforts to combat the *Jugendweihe* in the 1950s, the church leadership realized that parishioners did not possess the "civil courage" to oppose the measure.

In a more indirect manner, however, the churches' response to the military training did have a significant impact. Realizing its lack of efficacy and the need for greater consciousness among the parishioners, the Kirchenbund introduced an educational program, Educating for Peace, in the parishes.[20] This multifaceted program entailed a justification of the church's concern for peace as well as suggested formats for seminars and programs at the parish level. Designed for all age levels, these programs entailed role-playing exercises, exercises in peaceful conflict resolution, critical discussion of school books, and discussion of peace and security issues at the international level. It is difficult to measure the impact of such efforts, but they did represent the church's first systematic attempt to counter militarization, and they likely helped to create a more receptive context for the peace movement that soon arose.

The focus of the peace issue was soon to shift from the increased militarization to international developments that raised East-West tensions. In December 1979 two events in particular precipitated this heightened tension: the escalation of the arms race, particularly through the NATO decision to deploy intermediate-range nuclear missiles, and the Soviet invasion of Afghanistan. Both signaled the beginning of what is often termed the "new Cold War," a development producing particular anxiety in Europe, with its greater interest and investment in detente. Given the clear connection, particularly after 1971, between East-West detente and the improvement in the church's relationship with the state,

[20]Mechtenberg in Henkys, *Evangelischen Kirchen*, p. 368; Reinhard Henkys, "Verantwortung fuer den Frieden," *KiS* 5 (October 1979): 21–28; "Erziehung zum Frieden—Anregung und Vorschlaege fuer die Durchfuehrung von Gemeindeveranstaltungen," *epd Dokumentation*, no. 41 (1979): pp. 1–76.

it is not surprising that the Kirchenbund should have registered its alarm at the developments. In a "Declaration on the World Political Situation" in January 1980, the Kirchenbund called for "the restoration of a climate of trust and cooperation, which is indispensable for a policy of detente."[21] It attempted to avoid direct political attacks by not referring specifically to the Soviet intervention and only generally to "the stationing of atomic intermediate-range missiles in Europe." Following a pattern since its founding, the Kirchenbund also sought to express its voice in an ecumenical context, in this case with an expression of concern regarding "the conflicts associated with the events in Afghanistan and Iran" by all Soviet-bloc member churches in the WCC. Although the statement garnered support from the Russian Orthodox Church, certainly a novel development, it was considerably weaker than the Kirchenbund's own position and it paved the way for a watered-down statement by the WCC Central Committee later in 1980.

The state's own interest in limiting the damage in East-West relations led it initially to greet the church's peace efforts. In an August 1980 letter to Bishop Schoenherr, Prime Minister Willi Stoph praised the church's responsibility in dealing with "questions of securing peace, detente, and effective military disarmament," claiming that all previous activities of the Kirchenbund were "an expression of the fact that the consistent and constructive peace policy of the GDR is borne by both Christians and churches in our land."[22] Given the Kirchenbund's particularly strong contacts with leaders of the governing SPD in the FRG, such as Herbert Wehner and Helmut Schmidt, the state hoped to use the Kirchenbund to persuade the FRG to rescind its support for the NATO deployment decision. Indeed, considerable Kirchenbund diplomacy pursued this goal, entailing meetings between Schoenherr and Schmidt and SPD participation at conferences at Evangelical academies in West Germany. The "special relations" between the East and West German churches, a target of intense state attacks in the early 1970s and gradually accepted by the state, now came to be seen as useful by the state in its efforts to influence public opinion in the FRG. The Kirchenbund itself became bolder in this context, as evidenced by the first joint statement issued with the EKD in 1979, on the occasion of the fortieth anniversary of the

[21]Mechtenberg in Henkys, *Evangelischen Kirchen*, pp. 372–73, 378.
[22]Ibid., pp. 371–72.

beginning of World War II. In this statement both churches "acknowledged their common responsibility for peace, a responsibility conditioned particularly by their location at the interface of two world systems." There followed a March 1980 agreement to consult regularly on
questions of peace and a common worship service for peace on November 9, 1980.[23] The Luther anniversary also entailed considerable exchange between EKD and Kirchenbund, facilitating the state's lobbying
efforts regarding the INF deployment.

Political instability in neighboring Poland during 1980 and 1981 led
to a partial crackdown on the church's peace efforts.[24] The strikes in
August 1980 and the formation of the independent trade union Solidarity worried the GDR leadership, which feared ideological infection
and spillover effects. The state quickly attenuated contacts with Poland
and raised the minimum exchange requirements for Western visitors to
the GDR. It criticized the Polish developments, even to the point of
resurrecting long-standing prejudices against Poles. In its report to the
Kirchenbund synod in September 1980, the church leadership cited not
only the NATO decision but also "the military intervention of the Soviet
Union in Afghanistan" as contributing to the worsening world situation. It also criticized the effect of higher minimum exchange requirements on inter-German contacts and the official media treatment of the
Polish events. In the state's effort to limit the impact of this criticism,
Western reporters were denied access to the synod, and publication of
the leadership's report was forbidden in church newspapers. Later, in
November 1980, the state demanded that the church cancel plans to
ring church bells as part of the Peace Week agreed upon with the EKD.
The church acquiesced, acknowledging the state's fears of the development of a Polish-like opposition. This crackdown did not end the new
rapprochement, but did reveal that the relationship was affected by
international currents and changes and that the state was still willing to
circumscribe the church's independence.

By 1981 a new challenge to the March 1978 modus vivendi arose, the
independent grassroots peace movement in the GDR.[25] Earlier, as the

[23]Ibid., pp. 379–80; "Wort zum Frieden," *epd Dokumentation*, no. 37a (1979): pp. 1–3.
[24]Mechtenberg in Henkys, *Evangelischen Kirchen*, p. 373.
[25]For treatments of the role of the church in the independent peace movement, see
Ronald D. Asmus, "Is There a Peace Movement in the GDR?" *Orbis* 27 (Summer 1983): 301–
41; Joyce Marie Mushaben, "Swords into Ploughshares," *Studies in Comparative Commu-*

dispute over the introduction of military instruction indicated, the church had taken the lead on the issues of peace and militarization, albeit not always with success. From 1981 to 1984, however, grassroots groups of peace activists, often only loosely associated with the church, assumed the role of impetus and catalyst on these issues. The church hierarchy reacted more than it acted during this period.

Several factors explain this phenomenon. One permissive factor was certainly the development of widespread youth disaffection in the GDR in the 1970s.[26] Partly a function of generational conflict, partly of political rebellion against the rigid organization of society, this latent youth disaffection became manifest in the context of the modest liberalization associated with detente. Although it had been channeled primarily into cultural expressions, such as rock music and alternative styles of dress, the October 1977 riots during a rock concert had indicated its explosive potential. The youth disaffection became politicized in the early 1980s as a result of both the rising East-West tension and the example of the West German peace movement. Although the East German peace movement certainly had its roots in the GDR situation, there is little doubt that it drew inspiration and sustenance from the massive peace protests and political success of the Greens in West Germany. A heightened sense of efficacy on the part of the East German youth and lower perceived costs of political dissent combined to produce a peace movement, another expression of an alternative political culture.

Although remaining outside the traditional culture of church and state, this movement tended to use the church as a forum in which to articulate and express its views, since the democratic nature of the church structure and its "church-for-others" orientation led it to be receptive to such social outsiders. As a result the church leaders found themselves continually confronted by initiatives and pressure from below. Although these grassroots pressures threatened to disturb the working relationship with the state, the spirit of March 1978 survived. Indeed, they demonstrated the church's usefulness to the state as a

---

nism 17 (Summer 1984): 123–35; Pedro Ramet, "Church and Peace in the GDR," *Problems of Communism* 33 (July–August 1984): 44–57; Woods, pp. 36–41.

[26]On the rise of dissent, see Ramet, "Dissent and Dissaffection," pp. 85–111; Michael Sodaro, "Limits to Dissent in the GDR: Cooptation, Fragmentation, and Repression," in *Dissent in Eastern Europe*, ed. Jane Leftwich Curry (New York: Praeger, 1983), pp. 82–116; Goeckel, "Church and Society in the GDR."

means of channeling and managing societal dissent. In some instances the church responded to these initiatives by embracing them and transmitting such criticism of the state; in other instances it acted to domesticate or discipline dissent.

An early example of grassroots initiative developed in May 1981, the proposal for a "social peace service."[27] The issue of military service without weapons had been relatively dormant since the mid-1970s. Few had opted to join the *Bausoldaten* units and, since the unofficial arrangements of 1975, criticism of the military nature of the projects on which the *Bausoldaten* were employed had declined. In the new atmosphere of the 1980s, however, the issue of alternative service was raised anew. Church-affiliated peace activists in Dresden called for the church leadership to request an alternative "social peace service" analogous to that available to conscientious objectors in West Germany. The proposal, supported by five thousand petitioners, called for this service to be performed in social service and health care and, to guarantee the sincerity of the participants, would entail a twenty-four-month commitment, as opposed to the eighteen-month obligation in the East German army. Both the Saxony-Dresden Landeskirche and the Kirchenbund raised the issue with the state while realizing that the state was unalterably opposed to compromise. Seigewasser's successor as state secretary for church questions, Klaus Gysi, rejected the proposal, arguing that military commitments to the WTO precluded alternative service. Gysi claimed that the proposal defamed Christians opting for armed service, since it implied that such service is "antisocial war service." Werner Walde, Politburo member, was more blunt, arguing propagandistically in a speech in Cottbus that "our whole Republic is peace service," hence alternatives to armed service were unnecessary and indeed endangered peace. The CDU and other adjuncts of the SED chimed in the chorus opposing pacifism.

In the church, however, the state's rejection of the "social peace service" did not resolve the issue but rather stimulated a renewed debate regarding the Christian response to military service.[28] The 1958 Hei-

---

[27]"Appeal from the Initiative Group 'Social Service for Peace'" (9 May 1981), in Woods, pp. 193–94; Buescher, Wensierski, and Wolschner, pp. 169–75, 209–11, 230, 238–41.

[28]Eberhard Kuhrt, *Wider die Militarisierung der Gesellschaft: Friedensbewegung und Kirche in der DDR* (1984), p. 68; *KiS* 7 (September 1981): 4; *KiS* 6 (December 1980): 60; Mechtenberg in Henkys, *Evangelischen Kirchen*, pp. 385–86. For recent affirmations of this

delberg Theses, which had endorsed both armed and unarmed service as ethically responsible, were challenged anew. Strong segments of opinion in the church, particularly in the Saxony-Magdeburg and Berlin-Brandenburg Landeskirchen, advocated pacifism and unarmed service as the "clearer signal of peace" by Christians. Bishop Rathke of Mecklenburg issued a statement strongly supportive of pacifists in the church. Although the church did not expressly reject the Heidelberg Theses and its either/or approach to military service, the center of gravity in the church shifted in the direction of the unarmed option, a view reflected in the Kirchenbund's discussions with the EKD.

The dispute over the "social peace service" foreshadowed even greater conflict in early 1982. The church became embroiled in a conflict with the state over the use of the motif "Swords into Ploughshares."[29] Though Biblical in origin, the motif had been the subject of a Soviet sculpture presented to the United Nations and had long been officially accepted in the GDR. The churches employed it in the materials for their second peace week in November 1981. However, as a sign of protest, youths began to wear badges based on this motif and the state cracked down. With no clear legal basis, the police in many cases forcibly removed the badges and arrested some for "anti-state activity." The FDJ initiated a counteroffensive under the rubric "The peace must be armed." The church leadership and synods defended the use of the symbol but indicated that they were no longer in a position to protect those wearing it. Seeking to avoid conflict with the state and Western publicity, the church agreed to remove the symbol from public use. The state indicated that its actions were directed not at the motif per se but at the "weakening of defense readiness" that the badges represented. The state eventually permitted the church to use the motif again in its printed materials. Caught between the state and grassroots activists, the church backed off from the politically charged symbol.

Simultaneously the church acted to domesticate dissent even while providing a forum for its expression.[30] On the occasion of the anniversary of the bombing of Dresden (February 15), peace activists planned a

---

position in Saxony-Magdeburg and Saxony-Dresden, see *KiS* 11 (April 1985): 41, and *KiS* 11 (December 1985): 273.

[29]Mechtenberg in Henkys, *Evangelischen Kirchen*, pp. 389–91; Buescher, Wensierski, and Wolschner, pp. 290–97.

[30]Buescher, Wensierski, and Wolschner, pp. 265–81; Mechtenberg in Henkys, *Evangelischen Kirchen*, pp. 392–93.

silent march in Dresden. To avoid a confrontation between marchers and the security forces, the Saxony church leadership offered to sponsor an open forum on peace at the Church of the Cross. Five thousand youth jammed the forum, and church representatives freely discussed issues and responded to questions. A confrontation between the state and peace activists was avoided. Thus the church provided an umbrella for the alternative political culture but, on the other hand, prevented a show of political opposition that might have polarized the situation even more.

Another example of this dual role of the church regarding the peace movement was the so-called Berlin Appeal.[31] This petition—circulated by Berlin pastor Rainer Eppelman and supported by the late, prominent dissident Robert Haveman, among others—called for the withdrawal of "occupation troops" from and neutralization of both Germanies as a means of guaranteeing peace and self-determination. More than two thousand signed the petition; certainly many more sympathized with its position. The Berlin-Brandenburg Landeskirche distanced itself from both the form and substance of the petition, labeling it a "distorted view" and "positions unsupportable in the discipleship of Christ." Yet it recognized that the petition reflected an "expression of unrest and concern for peace," and it succeeded in obtaining Eppelman's release from detention and in preventing further litigation against him. In this case the church distanced itself from grassroots peace initiatives that, in its view, went too far.

The church also demonstrated the limits of its role in cases of unorthodox protest.[32] For example, in Jena a group of activists, organized around Roland Jahn, engaged in several unorthodox peace activities, including bicycle parades featuring peace symbols. The state security forces reacted to this "spontaneous demonstration" with arrests. Although Jahn was only remotely involved in the church, church peace activists in Thuringia appealed to Bishop Leich to help in obtaining Jahn's release from custody. Leich claimed that no appeal ever reached him and that the activists turned to the Western media without engaging

[31]For the text of the Berlin Appeal, see Woods, pp. 195–97; also Buescher, Wensierski, and Wolschner, pp. 242–44, 283, 290; Mechtenberg in Henkys, *Evangelischen Kirchen*, pp. 393–94.

[32]*KiS* 9 (1983): 71; *FAZ*, 9 November 1982, 17 and 21 February 1983, and 9 August 1983; Krisch, *German Democratic Republic*, p. 129.

the church first. The details of the case remain unclear even today, but Leich's handling of the case established distance from peace activists who did not operate within the framework of the church. The Rochau case discussed earlier indicates that sometimes the church may discipline even its own employees in such cases.

It would be a mistake to view the church's role solely as reactive to actions taken by activists, either within the church or outside it. The church evolved a substantive position on issues of peace that reflected its Christian beliefs and the independence of the institution, as well as the international environment and changes in popular attitudes in both Germanies.[33] The church consistently supported the rights of conscientious objectors, including those who, having served earlier in the military, later rejected reserve service and those whom the state rejected for *Bausoldat* status on the basis of a narrow religious test of conscience, such as church baptism. The church grappled with the ethical question of nuclear deterrence. At its 1982 synod in Halle, the Kirchenbund condemned "the logic, spirit, and practice of nuclear deterrence," a position that it repeatedly reaffirmed and that the Kirchenbund delegation successfully lobbied the WCC to assume at its 1983 General Assembly in Vancouver. Strong forces in the church pressed the Kirchenbund to declare opposition to nuclear weapons a "question of doctrine and confession." The Kirchenbund synod in 1981 debated this question, but conservative Lutherans, from Saxony and Thuringia in particular, prevailed, fearing that those opting for military service would then be guilty of a violation of doctrine. However, the Kirchenbund did come to specifically condemn the INF deployment in 1983. The Kirchenbund supported proposals for a nuclear-free zone in Central Europe, such as that offered by the Palme Commission, and a ban on chemical weapons. It opposed new weapons systems, such as the neutron bomb and strategic nuclear defense. Thus the church, while not making nuclear weapons an issue of doctrine, became more radical in its rejection of them and more supportive of a "security partnership" between East and West

[33]Opposition to deterrence is expressed in "Beschluss der Synode . . . ," *epd Dokumentation,* no. 47 (11 October 1982): pp. 30–33; opposition to the NATO missiles in "Erklaerung zur Stationierung von atomaren Mittelstreckenwaffen in Europa," *epd Dokumentation,* no. 43 (10 October 1983); denunciation of the "logic, spirit, and practice of deterrence," rejection of strategic defense, and calls for a nuclear-weapon-free zone in central Europe can be found in "Bericht der KKL" and "Beschluesse der Synode," *epd Dokumentation,* no. 43 (7 October 1985): pp. 1–19, 43–44.

Germany. In this it closely paralleled the thought of the West German Greens and the left wing of the SPD. It is not surprising that contacts with both West German parties have been relatively close, leading even to cooperation by Gottfried Forck, Schoenherr's successor as Bishop of Berlin-Brandenburg (East), in the Greens-sponsored plan to present a petition protesting the INF arms buildup to both U.S. and Soviet embassies in November 1983. The state ambivalence regarding this link was reflected in its coercion against the planned demonstration and periodic harassment of Greens' ties to the peace movement in the GDR.[34]

The domestic stabilizing role of the church was demonstrated most clearly in the aftermath of the INF deployment in 1983. In early 1984 the state began to permit large numbers of East Germans to emigrate.[35] Most emigres did not represent humanitarian cases of family reunification. Rather, they were young dissenters, particularly those active in the independent peace movement. In many cases the state arrested activists and left them little choice but to leave; in other cases, activists, demoralized by the apparent failure of the peace movement and their own bleak economic prospects, became frustrated and applied to leave voluntarily. For the state this unprecedented forthcomingness provided a relatively easy means of cleaning house. In total, 41,000 were allowed to emigrate legally in 1984 and another 30,000 in 1985. But the state feared that this massive wave of emigration might stimulate others to apply to leave.

The church faced ethical and practical implications since a significant portion of emigres (52 percent according to a West German study) cited Lutheran church membership.[36] Practically, the emigration cost the church some of its most active members, even some clergy. Ethically, the church had long maintained that its members' obligations to family and community argued for remaining in the GDR, except in extreme cases. In this case the voices from the church were divergent. Some acknowledged the disillusionment of peace activists due to the failure to make an impact on state policy, domestic or international, and called on the state

---

[34]*FAZ*, 11 November 1983.

[35]Woods, pp. 32–36.

[36]Wolfgang Buescher, "Warum bleibe ich eigentlich?" *DA* 17 (July 1984): 683–88; *KiS* 10 (June 1984): 48; Gerhard Rein, "Zum Bleiben ermuntert," *KiS* 10 (September 1984): 9–14; Theological Study Department, "Leben und Bleiben in der DDR," Information und Texte No. 14 (July 1985), in *epd Dokumentation*, no. 41a (23 September 1985): pp. 9–14. Leich is quoted in *KiS* 11 (December 1985): 274.

to create the conditions under which citizens would opt to remain in the GDR. However, others, such as the Thuringian church newspaper, criticized those leaving, arguing that they should give up "dreams of self-realization in the West" and that "Christians have good prospects in the GDR and are not forced to leave the country."[37] The Kirchenbund repeated its call for citizens to consider the ethical advisability of leaving. Bishop Leich of Thuringia went so far as to argue that emigration was no escape for Christians; freedom was not greater in the FRG, only curtailed differently than in the GDR. In its entreaty to remain and work for change in the GDR, the church functioned to stabilize the political system.

This supportiveness was manifest in the church's response to Honecker's dramatic assertion of GDR interests in 1984.[38] At several points Honecker signaled the GDR's reluctance to be swept into the new Cold War between Moscow and Washington. He spoke of "limiting the damage" to detente from the NATO deployment, arguing that "security is not guaranteed by weapons alone." Later Honecker indicated that the GDR was less than enthusiastic in its support for the deployment of new short-range missiles in the GDR. This subtle position might have been calculated to influence the debate in the FRG. In 1984, however, it became clear that a divergence of view had developed in the wake of deployment: the Soviets attempted to punish the West, while the GDR continued its beneficial economic ties with West Germany. The showdown in this intrabloc dispute occurred over the planned visit of Honecker to the FRG in September 1984. The Soviets forced the cancellation of the visit at the eleventh hour, but the public assertion of GDR independence by Honecker, although unsuccessful, engendered considerable credibility with the population and the church. The Kirchenbund proclaimed that a "fundamental consensus" existed between church and state on the issue of peace. This supportiveness of the state reached its zenith at the February 1985 summit between Honecker and Bishop Hempel, chairman of the church leadership. In the name of the Kirchenbund, Hempel

---

[37]*Glaube und Heimat* (Thuringia), 15 April 1984; Radio Free Europe RAD, Background Report no. 64 (21 April 1984).

[38]Hempel is quoted in *ND*, 12 February 1985. For a treatment emphasizing Honecker's new self-confidence and advantageous position in inter-German relations, see McAdams, pp. 161–92. See also Krisch, *German Democratic Republic*, pp. 60–61; Ronald Asmus, "East Berlin and Moscow: The Documentation of a Dispute," *RFE Background Reports*, no. 158 (31 August 1984).

maintained that "all other issues in dispute between church and state must be subordinated to the shared interest in peace."[39]

In the late 1980s the church set a new accent on international justice in its stance on peace issues. The underlying context was provided by the international "conciliar process," designed to lead to a 1990 world conference for justice, peace, and the preservation of creation sponsored by the WCC.[40] Increasingly the church linked the arms race to poverty in the Third World and called for greater aid to the Third World. Falcke called for "ploughshares for the Third World."[41] Church aid, via Bread for the World collections, increased, entailing state approval for the assignment of church personnel for specific development projects in the Third World, a novel development.

Differences with the EKD also sharpened.[42] The consultations with the EKD since 1980 did not always lead to common positions, often resulting in an agreement to disagree. For example, the EKD did not share the Kirchenbund trend toward viewing unarmed service as the "clearer signal of peace," holding to its position of supporting "peace service, with or without weapons." Although both reached a consensus opposing strategic missile defense and supporting bans on atomic testing and chemical weapons, the EKD has been more reluctant to reject nuclear weapons in any form.[43] The Kirchenbund's outsider role in GDR society enabled it to take bolder positions on the peace issue than the EKD's, with its inclusionary claim and ties to West German political elites in various parties.

The issue of peace and the rise of an independent peace movement tested the church-state rapprochement in the period 1978 to 1989 and revealed the ambiguity of the relationship. On the one hand, the church disagreed with the state on matters of substance, especially regarding domestic militarization, and guarded its independence on matters of process. However, the church also functioned as a stabilizing force by channeling dissent and by expressing support for the state's policies.

[39]Detlef Urban, "Spitzengespraech Staat-Kirche," *DA* 18 (March 1985): 231–32.
[40]*KiS* 11 (December 1985): 245.
[41]Quoted in Mathias Hartmann, "Untypische Schlagzeilen," *KiS* 11 (December 1985): 237.
[42]Reinhard Henkys, "Dialog-Gemeinschaft," *KiS* 10 (November 1984): 11–20; Henkys, "Wirksamer Dialog," *KiS* 10 (July 1984): 7–8; see Forck and Demke, quoted in *KiS* 10 (July 1984): 60. See Werner Krusche's critical comments in *epd Dokumentation*, no. 30a (4 July 1984): pp. 1–32.
[43]*KiS* 12 (April 1986): 91.

THE CHALLENGE OF THE
"CHURCH FROM BELOW"

Despite resignation in the peace movement following the INF deployment and emigration to the West in 1984 and 1985, the grassroots dissent in the church continued to pose a dilemma for the church leadership. Indeed, given the church's vote of confidence in Honecker from 1984 to 1986, the gap between the leadership and the various grassroots groups tended to widen. The most pressing question for the church became that of defining and maintaining a viable relationship with these groups, loosely labeled the "church from below."

Under the umbrella of the church, scores of these grassroots groups developed in the early 1980s, focusing on human rights, homosexuality, and women's issues, as well as peace and the environment.[44] They achieved a high degree of organization, holding regional and GDR-wide meetings and circulating *samizdat* newsletters among members. For some they reflected the sociological phenomenon of the "reproduction of religion" in socialism, marking the end of the secularization process.[45] For others, they represented an opportunity for the church, a means of concretizing the general social and political positions of the church.[46] Bishop Leich, chairman of the Kirchenbund since 1986, reflected a more widespread view that the "church should be open to all, but not endorse all views." For many traditional parishioners in the shrinking "national church," the unorthodox groups represented a disturbance of church norms by individuals with little commitment to Christianity.

As noted earlier, the state was interested in the church's channeling of these groups, domesticating them and disciplining them, if necessary. The church began to admit this function more openly.[47] Falcke, a

---

[44]Ruediger Rosenthal, "Groessere Freiraeume fuer Basisgruppen," *KiS* 13 (October 1987): 189–91.

[45]Ehrhart Neubart, "Sozialisierende Gruppen im konziliaren Prozess," *KiS* 11 (December 1985): 241–45.

[46]Heino Flacke, "Unsere Kirche und ihre Gruppen," *KiS* 11 (August 1985): 145–52. Falcke's support for a role for peripheral groups in the church is captured in his pronouncement: "our institutional church with its pluralistic inclusiveness must grasp that it can represent the bond of peace of God only together with these groups and can live its openness as a national church if and because in it there are groups which live according to the dictates of a voluntary church." Quoted in Neubart, p. 242.

[47]Falcke, quoted in *KiS* 12 (June 1986): 137; Manfred Stolpe, "Modell fuer deutsch-deutschen Dialog," *KiS* 10 (June 1984): 20.

leading supporter of such group activity, argued that the state sees the church as a "conservative force," which it expects to "influence young people in the peace scene." Stolpe, architect of the rapprochement and leading church negotiator with the state, endorsed a "critical-stabilizing role" for the Kirchenbund; the "church within socialism contributes to making the socialist society more stable, more just and better."

The church, as part of its stabilizing function, curtailed the activity of such groups after 1986, shied away from bold initiatives regarding peace, and addressed more clearly the concerns of mainstream parishioners. The curtailment of grassroots groups was demonstrated in the planning for the 1987 church convention in Berlin.[48] Seeking to assuage the fears of the security forces and without consulting grassroots groups, the Berlin-Brandenburg church canceled the 1987 Peace Workshop, an annual potpourri of activities and exhibits by grassroots groups held every summer in a Berlin parish. A bitter exchange ensued, with one church official labeling the groups as irresponsible and the groups charging the leadership with sacrificing the workshop to obtain state approval for the church convention. Threatening to occupy a church to mount their own "Church Convention from Below," the groups pressured the church into allowing them a forum during the convention and rescheduling the workshop for November. Other planned meetings in churches by grassroots groups, such as human rights groups and dissident singers, were canceled by the church under state pressure.

The church also modified course to reflect the concerns of mainstream parishioners. For example, it halted the trend toward pacifism.[49] Although reaffirming its support for *Bausoldaten* and the "social peace service" option, the Kirchenbund synod in 1986 paid new attention to those opting for armed service, petitioning the regime for "regular worship services, religious literature, and pastoral access" for those in the military. Although this position aligned more closely with the vast majority of Christians who continued to serve in the East German army, it relativized the church's earlier support for unarmed service as the "clearer signal" of peace and contradicted its earlier doctrinal position rejecting nuclear deterrence. The Kirchenbund also moderated its rejec-

---

[48]Hans-Juergen Roeder, "Rebellische Kirchenbasis," *KiS* 13 (June 1987): 87–88; Reinhard Henkys, "Einen Schritt vorwaerts," *KiS* 13 (August 1987): 131–32.

[49]Reinhard Henkys, "Phase der Selbstbesinnung," *KiS* 12 (October 1986): 193–94; Henkys, "Grundvertrauen," *KiS* 10 (November 1984): 8.

tion of nuclear weapons: the 1984 synod admitted that "despite our 'no' to military force as a means of solving conflicts and our 'no' to the spirit, logic and practice of deterrence, we cannot abandon the strategy of deterrence immediately."

The church also began to focus anew its attention on the continued discrimination against Christians in education and career. Although not always supportive of the "church from below" groups, the synod took to task the increasing participation of the church leadership in the official peace movement in the GDR (for example, 1986 criticism of the Kirchenbund delegates to the annual meeting of the Peace Council of the GDR and the manipulation of the church's contribution by the state media).[50]

The church's stabilizing role was overtaken by the reform process in the USSR under Gorbachev, which provoked a counterreaction of intransigence on the part of the Honecker regime. In some areas Honecker made perfunctory bows to *glasnost*. For example, relations with the world Jewish community were improved, as in the Soviet case.[51] In February 1986 the GDR also eased travel regulations for millions of East Germans with relatives in the FRG. The church hailed this liberalization but asked for greater clarity and accountability in the visa process.[52]

The general direction of GDR policy, however, was a rejection of the need for reform in the GDR. Kurt Hager, responsible for ideology on the Politburo, encapsuled this rejection obliquely yet unmistakably: "Just because your neighbor redecorates his apartment does not mean that you must renovate yours."[53] Particularly during the late Honecker period (1987 to 1989), the GDR rejected reform at home, a stance that could hardly leave the church unaffected.

The state's crackdown on the church manifested itself in various forms. One form was the increased interference with and censorship of

[50]Hans-Juergen Roeder, "Sorge vor Vereinnahmung," *KiS* 12 (October 1986): 195–96.
[51]Barbara Donovan, "GDR Offers 'Symbolic' Compensation to Jewish Victims," *RFE Background Reports*, no. 211 (20 October 1988): 1–2; Gerhard Rein, "Annaeherung," *KiS* 14 (June 1988): 83–84; *New York Times*, 5 May and 19 October 1988.
[52]*KiS* 12 (April 1986): 91–92.
[53]Barbara Donovan, "Gorbachev's Reforms and the GDR," *RFE Background Reports*, no. 32 (6 March 1987): 1–5; Hager quoted in "Jedes Land Waehlt seine Loesung," *Stern*, no. 16 (9 April 1987): 142. Hager later explicitly rejected Soviet reforms as "not transferable" to the GDR. See *ND*, 29 October 1988. The GDR began to ban certain Soviet publications and undertook diplomatic overtures with such hard-line states as Romania, Czechoslovakia, and even China. See Barbara Donovan, "The SED Becoming More Outspoken," *RFE Background Reports*, no. 6 (12 January 1989): 1–5.

church publications.[54] Critical topics became taboo; reports of church synods were forbidden on a routine basis. Renewed prospects for a meeting with educational officials and an authoritative pronouncement on discrimination were dashed again in November 1987.

The chill in relations also affected the churches' social presence. For example, church congresses, earlier facilitated by the state, now met with official impediments.[55] The state made it difficult to obtain public meeting places and curtailed publicity for the congresses; the state also objected to the content of some events. At the 1988 congress in Erfurt, the SED packed the forum featuring Erhard Eppler and Egon Bahr, prominent West German politicians, in order to forestall a demonstration of support for freedom of travel to the West. Also the state halted new church construction, invoking various pretexts such as economic shortages.

Security forces also began to interfere with church activities.[56] In late November 1987 security police stormed a Berlin church in the early morning hours, arresting several individuals involved in grassroots groups and confiscating duplicating equipment allegedly used in publishing an underground newspaper. Grassroots activists mobilized protest vigils involving hundreds. The Berlin-Brandenburg church leadership managed to gain the release of some; the others were charged with "organizing anti-state activity." This was followed by numerous arrests of those attempting to march with critical slogans in an official parade honoring Rosa Luxemburg and Karl Liebknecht. Finally, security forces interfered with parishioners' attendance at worship services in March 1988. Such a draconian measure had not been seen since the conflicts in 1953. Honecker sought to reassure the Kirchenbund leadership that the arrangement of March 1978 was still valid, but such developments seemed to violate its spirit. State Secretary Klaus Gysi, identified with the rapprochement with the church, was replaced by ideologue Kurt Loeffler in July 1988.[57]

For its part the church became increasingly critical of the regime,

[54]*KiS* 14 (June 1988): 124. For example, an issue of *Der Sonntag* of the Saxony-Dresden church was confiscated because it mentioned the existence of consumer queues in the GDR. See Matthias Hartmann, "Hier aendert sich nichts," *DA* 21 (October 1988): 1026. Reinhard Henkys, "Deutliche Signale," *KiS* 13 (December 1987): 221–22.

[55]*KiS* 14 (August 1988): 129.

[56]*KiS* 12 (February 1986): 46; "Zwischen ADN und Eigenstaendigkeit," *KiS* 14 (February 1988): 2–4; Reinhard Henkys, "Wenig Zukunftweisendes," *KiS* 14 (April 1988): 41–43; Reinhard Henkys, "Deutliche Signale," *KiS* 13 (December 1987): 221–22.

[57]*FAZ*, 18 July 1988.

initially focusing on the right to travel. Some church leaders, led by Falcke, became more critical than the Kirchenbund leadership, submitting to the 1987 synod a petition rejecting the policy of Abgrenzung.[58] The petition called for reopened borders with Poland, increased opportunities to travel generally, and recognition of the right to travel to the West regardless of age, job, or family status. Bishop Leich, chairman of the Kirchenbund since 1985, opposed this as overburdening the improving relationship with the state and the synod rejected the petition. By 1988, however, the Kirchenbund became bolder, advocating the right to travel independent of age and familial relationships.

After 1987 the church became increasingly critical of the GDR's failure to introduce Gorbachev-style reforms at home.[59] At the Halle church congress in summer 1988, Stolpe maintained that "it will not work without *perestroika,* even in the GDR." Even conservative Bishop Leich, at the September 1988 Kirchenbund synods, pleaded for "a society which has a human face in its daily experience." An internal group in the church, the Church in Solidarity, propounded theses on reform, including calls for democratic elections, state authority based on law and an independent judiciary, freedom of information, and economic reforms.[60] Although the church leadership did not officially endorse these recommendations, they reflected widespread thinking in the church, a debate that was moving increasingly in the direction of Falcke's "critical solidarity" position articulated in 1972.

The state reacted harshly. Incensed at Leich's Prague Spring–like formulation, Honecker retorted that "the countenance of socialism on German soil has never been as human as today."[61] In February 1988 Politburo member in charge of relations with the church, Werner Jarowinsky, charged the church with violation of the principle of separation of church and state. By November of the same year he alleged that counterrevolutionary forces were afoot in the church. The degree of polarization was best demonstrated by the state's attack on Stolpe, the architect of the improved relationship with the state. *Neues Deutsch-*

[58]Barbara Donovan, "East German Church Synod Debates Approach to the State," *RFE Background Reports,* no. 173 (28 September 1987): 1–4. *KiS* 14 (October 1988): 171.

[59]*KiS* 14 (October 1988): 130; Matthias Hartmann, "Hier aendert sich nichts," *DA* 21 (October 1988): 1025.

[60]Susan Sanders, "The Independent Reform Debate in the GDR," *RFE Background Reports,* no. 137 (3 August 1989): 1–5.

[61]*KiS* 14 (June 1988): 124; *FAZ,* 14 November 1988.

land urged him to undergo a "learning process in the free exercise of religion," rather than engaging in political affairs.[62] By May 1989 the church's critique of election fraud in the local elections seemed a logical extension of church activism. The stage was set for the wave of protests, again not surprisingly originating among grassroots church groups, particularly in Leipzig, and the dramatic collapse of SED authority in the fall of 1989 that was to bring an end to the Honecker era. The stabilizing role of the church proved inadequate to staunch the hemorrhage in authority suffered by the SED in the context of bloc-wide political liberalization.

The years 1978 to 1989 demonstrated the extent as well as the limits of change in the church-state relationship. This period saw considerable societal unrest and the rise of popular dissent. The state granted the church new visibility in historical and cultural terms and freedom of articulation on social-political issues such as peace and the environment. For its part, the church showed increasing willingness to cooperate with the state, even to the point of assuming a stabilizing role with respect to dissent. However, the state also demonstrated that the rapprochement was an institutional one; it would not tolerate the church acting as a vehicle for *glasnost*-like initiatives in the GDR. The Honecker regime, reluctant to follow Gorbachev's lead on internal political change, clearly continued to share the Leninist preference for control, in this case, controlled institutional change with a conservative purpose.

[62]*ND*, 11 January 1989.

9 The Character and Limitations of Change

This book has described the relationship between the Evangelical Lutheran church and the postwar regime in East Germany. Significant change occurred in this relationship in the period under study. Before the 1970s the relationship was characterized largely by confrontation and conflict, deriving primarily from the state's domestic goals of socialist transformation in the 1950s, increasingly a function of the state's foreign policy of Abgrenzung from West Germany in the 1960s. After 1969 a process of pragmatic cooperation led to the evolution of a symbiotic relationship. Expressions of political dissent tested this relationship in the 1980s but also demonstrated its resilience. Bloc-wide liberalization in 1989 undermined the SED regime's legitimacy and demonstrated the limitations and conservative nature of this change under Honecker.

THE PROCESS OF CHANGE IN THE CHURCH-STATE RELATIONSHIP

The early postwar years saw the Communist regime pursue a relatively mild policy toward the churches. Many traditional privileges were restored, and the all-German character of the church's organization coincided with the regime's avowal of German reunification. After the founding of the GDR in 1949, however, the regime began to pursue the goal of Stalinist transformation of society and the economy, which in turn led to increased ideological and political conflict with the churches. Nonetheless, the churches' all-German ties remained unchallenged by the regime. After 1958, however, the source of conflict shifted. The state's attempt to build greater legitimacy via Abgrenzung led to increased pressure on the churches' ties to the allegedly "NATO–tied EKD," even as the domestic issues receded somewhat with the state's appeal to the "common humanistic responsibility of Marxists and Christians."

In 1969 the churches yielded to state pressure by formally separating from the all-German umbrella organization, the Evangelical Church in Germany. They formed the Federation of Evangelical Churches in the GDR, or Kirchenbund. However, the separation was not complete: the churches retained strong informal ties, and the Evangelical Church of the Union, a confessional organization, and the Berlin-Brandenburg provincial church remained formally all-German. As a result of these continuing ties and the regime's ambivalence regarding the political orientation of the new Kirchenbund, the state refused to recognize it.

By 1971 the state began to shift toward a Kirchenbund-based policy. It officially recognized the Kirchenbund and began to deal with it, at the expense of previously intense relations with the provincial churches as well as the regime's own mass organizations. The state began to promote international activity by the churches and promised pragmatic agreements on various issues. For its part, the church continued moving toward formal separation from the West German churches and turned increasingly to defining its new-found role as a "church within socialism."

But the state's initiative stalled with the Honecker succession. The promises of pragmatic agreements went unfulfilled, and the few state concessions were elite-oriented. In many areas the heightened emphasis on ideological and military vigilance led to increased conflict with the churches. For example, the state imposed new restrictions on freedom of assembly, discrimination against Christians in education increased, and conscientious objectors faced new barriers.

Within the church, criticism of the state's policy—as well as of the church leadership's accommodation to the regime—increased. This development, combined with heightened attention in the FRG and worldwide to the issue of human rights, led the regime to deepen the rapprochement from 1973 to 1978. Yet this deepening brought primarily

institutional benefits to the churches: inter-German ties were accepted
and ecumenical relations allowed to flourish; strictures on the churches'
right of assembly were eased; church construction projects were approved, even in new urban areas designed to be free of religion; and the
churches' diaconical agencies received official sanction. In terms of the
treatment of individual Christians, however, little relaxation occurred.
The state agreed to resolve individual cases but refused to alter its
general policy of ideologically based discrimination. Not until the suicide burning of Pastor Oskar Bruesewitz in August 1976 highlighted the
credibility gap between the church hierarchy and the grass roots did the
churches' demands cause the state to extend the rapprochement to the
grassroots level. This took the form of the unprecedented summit between Honecker and the Kirchenbund leadership.

The March 6, 1978 summit ushered in a new era of cooperation
between church and state. It brought some improvement in the treatment of individual Christians, although the major elements were again
institutional (for example, television access, state pension assistance,
reimbursement for church land used by the state, access to prisons, and
facilitation of church conventions). Discrimination against Christians
moderated, but the state continued to refuse an authoritative meeting
between the church and the Education Ministry.

The new relationship was both challenged and confirmed by the rise
of nonreligious dissent and disaffection in the 1980s. Due to both
domestic and international factors, dissent from the official policies of
the GDR and generalized disaffection threatened the regime. Independent social movements formed to address the issues of peace and militarization, as well as the environment. The church provided an umbrella
for the expression of these alternative views; but it also served to
domesticate and channel such dissent. Thus the church played a crucial
role in facilitating political dissent but also served to partially limit the
expression of such dissent to politically acceptable dimensions. The
state also increasingly incorporated the church and religious and cultural figures from history, such as Luther, as part of a general rehistoricization designed to develop greater legitimacy for the GDR among the
population. The regime did not curtail the churches' ties with the West
German churches and indeed continued to allow them to flourish.
However, even when these attempts failed to influence West German
policy, as in the case of the INF deployment decision, the regime for the

most part left the inter-German church ties intact. The church remained implicitly a defender of the German historical and cultural nation, as the Luther year celebration in 1983 demonstrated.

Thus, rather than erode the cooperative relationship that developed between church and state in the early 1970s, the increased dissent in the early 1980s and the churches' role in it reinforced the relationship and strengthened the argument that significant, sustained political change had occurred in the GDR. This change occurred on two dimensions, international and domestic. On the international level, the regime, which had castigated and curtailed the East German churches' ties with the West German churches in the late 1950s and 1960s, came not only to permit them but even to foster them. On the domestic dimension, the regime, which earlier had planned on the elimination of the churches' presence in social and political life, found itself sanctioning an active role for this institution.

THE NATURE OF THE RELATIONSHIP

The process and dynamics of this change in the church-state relationship yield insight into the character of the relationship that had developed prior to the momentous political changes in the fall of 1989. It was best described as a symbiotic institutional relationship, based on informal arrangements rather than legal or ideological commitments. It did not result from major dramatic shifts by either state or church. Indeed the state's declaratory overtures to the church were often not matched by equivalent actions on its part. Similarly informal negotiations often led to considerable amelioration of conflict. The pragmatic arrangement developed over time, and this long-term process was a precondition for the role of the church in the recent rise of nonreligious dissent. Several conclusions can be drawn regarding the nature of the relationship that developed.

First, the state tacitly treated the Kirchenbund as an interest group. The Kirchenbund has aggregated and articulated demands upon the political system and is relatively representative of the evangelical population. However, the state was not willing to grant this status *officially*, since this would have undermined the leading role of the party. For their part, the churches usually refrained from articulating their demands publicly, choosing often to represent their institutional interests and the interests of their members, as well as broader normative positions on societal issues, in private meetings with the state. The state rejected any claim by the church to represent the interests of nonreligious dissenters but tolerated the church's role as a forum for such dissent in hopes of channeling it.

Second, the rapprochement did not result from, or reflect, a change in the regime's ideological position regarding religion, but rather it represented an accommodation with the church *as an institution*. The Marxist-Leninist ideology gives vague and contradictory signals on the Kirchenpolitik. Marx, Engels, and Lenin all advocated at some points the pragmatic cooperation with "progressive" Christian elements. Marx was vague on policy toward the churches and religion after the revolution, since he felt the conditions of socialism would resolve the issue by eliminating the need for religion. Lenin, however, was less willing to leave religion to a voluntary death and tended to view the struggle against religion as an integral part of the total class struggle. Regarding religion and the churches, the ideology could as easily explain the Kirchenkampf in the early 1950s as the rapprochement of the 1970s.

Nor does it seem very applicable to the situation in the GDR. Marx assumed that the decoupling of the church from politics and the decline of religion would be quite advanced in the bourgeois capitalist stage. Lenin's point of reference was the powerful Russian Orthodox Church in a backward society. Neither seems very applicable to a socially oriented Lutheran church in a developed socialist society.

The contemporary ideologists of scientific atheism have seemed no less ambiguous than the classics. An example is Olof Klohr. On the one hand, he says, "religion and the church do not die totally until the transition to communism. Thus this is a slow process, the time frame of which depends upon this or that historical precondition in the individual socialist lands." On the other hand, "this dying away does not proceed spontaneously."[1]

Some observers have emphasized apparent shifts in Marxist approaches to the nature and attraction of religion.[2] While one cannot

[1]Quoted in Fischer, pp. 22–24.
[2]Ruth Zander, "Abkehr vom dogmatischen Atheismus," *KiS* 4 (June 1978): 15–28; Almut Engelien, "Keine einheitliche Linie," *KiS* 6 (September 1980): 29–38.

deny that official scholars have taken a more realistic and differentiated view of the roots of religion, this did not alter the component of materialistic atheism in the official ideology. Indeed the growth of a relationship based on pragmatic arrangements was predicated upon the mutual affirmation of continuing differences in basic philosophy. The party feared the effect of any ideological erosion of party discipline; the churches wished to demonstrate their autonomy from the state. Thus it was not surprising that the state's concessions in this process largely involved the institutional interests of the churches (media, ecumenical ties, exemption from police notification for certain church events); the church found it considerably more difficult to defend the interest of individual believers. Nor is it surprising that the party intensified the study of atheism within its ranks or that the Christian-Marxist dialogue found elsewhere in Eastern Europe was limited in the GDR.[3]

Thus, the state's moves toward rapprochement were directed toward the church as an institution and did not reflect a change in the Marxist-Leninist view of religion. Despite its weakened position in terms of church adherence, the institutional church showed remarkable resilience, and the state came to respect this. It grudgingly conceded the church a role in society beyond that of mere ritual. The institutional church had certain chips that the state was interested in: ties with the West German churches and international organizations in Geneva; access to information and media, both East and West; potential to express organized political criticism, thus affecting the broader population.

Third, another ramification of the informal basis of the rapprochement was that it was not anchored in constitutional-legal guarantees, nor did it reflect changes in the legal status of the churches and Christians.

Legal provisions in the GDR, as in most traditional Communist systems, have been vague and conditional.[4] They have been usually worded in general terms, thus lending themselves to arbitrary interpretation and application. For example, the Events Ordinance of 1971 allowed both harsh application from 1971 to 1973 and more lenient application thereafter. Moreover, legal rights have been conditioned by obligations in the socialist understanding of law. For example, the *right*

[3]Friedrich Ebert Stiftung, *Kirche und Staat in der DDR und in der Bundesrepublik* (Bonn: Verlag Neue Gesellschaft, 1977), p. 37.
[4]Federal Ministry of Inner-German Affairs, *DDR-Handbuch*, pp. 488–99, 893, 1119.

to political participation depends on the *duty* to participate in socialist democracy.

This vagueness and conditional character yield a second problem: constitutions in Communist systems have been designed to codify the stage of development toward communism not to protect rights. Thus they have been violated in practice, since there has been no effective appeal. The use of administrative measures to undermine the constitutionally guaranteed rights of the churches in the 1950s was a case in point; the discrimination against Christians in education and career has been another.

Moreover, the church-state relationship may often have transcended the legal reality and improved without legal changes. The growth of pragmatic cooperation in the Honecker era was in large part based on private, ad hoc agreements: both sides, especially the state, benefited without risking the embarrassment of future shifts as occurred in 1988, requiring major ideological gymnastics to justify the reversal.

The constitutional and legal status of the churches has usually been a function of some other factor. For example, party ideology has explained many of the constitutional provisions. The changes in the 1968 constitution that pointed toward a break with all-German church organizations reflected another factor, the GDR's Deutschlandpolitik.

Rather than constitutional-legal provisions, the rapprochement was based on the informal exchange of legitimacy of church and state elites. Although philosophical/ideological differences prevented each side from conceding the other's claims in their entirety, they did not prevent the elites from exchanging at least partial legitimacy. Despite the continuation of the state's ideological polemic and "expectations" of the churches and the churches' criticism of certain aspects of GDR socialism, the elites often found pragmatic solutions and valence issues (e.g., antifascism, peace, Third World issues) on which they at least partially agreed publicly. Yet at the same time, they were aware of the limits to the relationship and of the implicit rules of the game. The relationship was not characterized by overt bargaining but rather by "focal point solutions" in which the expectations of the other side played a large role. The state elite expected the church to dampen public criticism, in part to limit the potential for a counterreaction by other elements in the wider state elite against the pragmatic arrangement with the churches; the church elite expected the state to avoid actions that might have caused an increase in lower-level church criticism of the relationship with the state.

Fourth, this elite-level rapprochement was predicated upon the credibility of the respective elites with their mass base. The state elite sought to retain credibility with the party masses by emphasizing the ideological basis for pragmatic cooperation with the churches, even while continuing to propagate the SED's atheistic materialism. Given their democratic character internally, it was even more crucial for the churches to retain credibility with the grass roots. The churches sought to maintain this credibility by several means, including emphasizing differences in basic philosophy, couching decisions in terms of ecumenical resolutions, justifying actions nonideologically, and occasionally criticizing state policies. The church was forced to continually renew its distance from the state. In this question of credibility, the role of the Western electronic media in publicizing the churches' positions in the GDR cannot be underestimated.

Fifth, the relationship has not been immune to external disturbances, although the source of such disturbances has increasingly been within the Soviet bloc rather than West Germany. A general decline in sensitivity of the relationship to the changing Deutschlandpolitik has been evident since the 1950s and 1960s. After 1971 the normalization of East-West German relations was accompanied by greater stability in the church-state relationship. However, the political instability in Poland in 1980 and 1981 and, more recently, the political liberalization in the USSR occasioned cooling in the relationship. The regime sought thereby—unsuccessfully as it turned out—to dampen expectations of change that might overreach the bounds of the institutional change in the church-state relationship.

THE STATE'S MOTIVATION

Several factors explain Honecker's motivation for rapprochement with the church, especially the Deutschlandpolitik of the GDR and the shifts in this policy in response to changes in the Deutschlandpolitik of the FRG and the Soviet Union.[5] The basic dilemma confronting GDR

---

[5]This discussion of the Deutschlandpolitik is based on numerous sources found in the bibliography, including Griffith and McAdams.

foreign policy has derived from its ambivalence toward the FRG. On the one hand, for both international and domestic reasons, the GDR has sought international legitimacy, which the FRG's commitment to a unified Germany impedes. On the other hand, the GDR has often found the commitment to German unity, or at least a special relationship with the FRG, politically expedient.

From its inception in 1949, the GDR suffered a "legitimacy deficit," both in international and in domestic terms. Not only the Western powers but to a certain extent the Soviet Union itself considered the FRG and the GDR provisional entities, to be replaced by a reunified Germany as a result of a formal peace treaty. Unlike the FRG, which through the EEC, NATO, and its increasing international economic presence was able to overcome this provisional status, the GDR continued into the 1960s to suffer from this legitimacy deficit. Political contacts with the Arab states multiplied, as did economic and cultural representation; yet formal diplomatic recognition did not extend beyond the other socialist bloc states. The FRG's Hallstein Doctrine, which mandated a break in relations with any state recognizing the GDR, hindered broader-based recognition.

Concurrent with its goal of international recognition, however, the GDR formally proclaimed the goal of German reunification.[6] Yet, except in several instances in which the GDR made certain tentative proposals, such as Ulbricht's confederation proposal of 1957, no practical initiatives to realize this general goal were undertaken. Indeed, from time to time some who favored more forthcomingness on the German question were purged. In the case of the tentative initiatives, there was little chance of a positive result, given the intransigent position of the FRG government until 1966.

The GDR operated within the limitations set by Soviet foreign policy. The Soviets too pursued an ambivalent policy toward Germany. On the one hand they showed considerable interest in hindering the rearmament and integration of the FRG into NATO. Yet with the ambiguous exception of the note of 1952, they did not seem ready to take any concrete steps that might lead to a reunified Germany, a development that they understandably feared.[7]

---

[6]This goal was anchored in the 1949 constitution. See Mampel.

[7]Johannes Kuppe, "Phasen," in *Drei Jahrzehnte Aussenpolitik der DDR*, ed. Hans-Adolf Jacobsen et al. (Munich: R. Oldenbourg Verlag, 1979), p. 179.

Until 1958 at least, this formal commitment to German unity and the desire to hinder FRG integration into NATO led the state to tolerate the all-German EKD. Considerable criticism of rearmament and NATO originated in EKD circles in these years. After 1958 these issues receded somewhat in public attention, especially in the SPD. This tendency, as well as the EKD's Military Chaplaincy Agreement with the FRG, decreased the attractiveness of the GDR churches' inter-German ties. The state made these ties more difficult in practical terms but did not directly challenge the churches' all-German organizational character.

However, after 1966, the new Grand Coalition government in Bonn began to pursue a more forthcoming approach toward Eastern Europe. This aroused fears of isolation in the GDR foreign policy apparatus. Ulbricht responded by attacking West German revanchism and proclaiming his own "Ulbricht Doctrine," whereby socialist state relations with the FRG were to be established only after the FRG had abandoned its claims on the GDR and revanchism with respect to the territories occupied by Poland and the USSR. Ulbricht sought increased delimitation (Abgrenzung) from the FRG, as reflected in the constitution of 1968.

The Abgrenzung campaign intensified even more in reaction to the Ostpolitik of the Brandt government from 1969 to 1971. The GDR hewed a hard line in initial talks, demanding nothing less than full diplomatic recognition at the meeting between Prime Minister Stoph and Chancellor Brandt in Kassel in May 1970. Organizations with an all-German basis were disbanded accordingly. Naturally this harsh Abgrenzung campaign led to increased pressure on the all-German ties of the GDR churches, leading to the division of the EKD and the formation of the Kirchenbund (1969), as well as moves toward greater separation and independence by the GDR regions of the VELKD (1968), the EKU (1972), and the Landeskirche Berlin-Brandenburg (1970–72).

However, increasingly this Abgrenzung policy ran counter to Soviet policy. In the late 1960s, the Soviets showed an increased interest in ratifying the postwar European status quo, in particular their sphere of influence in Eastern Europe. They also sought greater economic ties with the FRG.[8] Thus the Soviets were more receptive to the initiatives of

---

[8]Adam B. Ulam, *Expansion and Coexistence: Soviet Foreign Policy, 1917–73* (New York: Holt, Rinehart and Winston, 1974); Joseph Nogee and Robert H. Donaldson, *Soviet Foreign Policy since World War II* (New York: Pergamon Press, 1984), pp. 248–300.

the SPD-led FRG in 1969. Although in the wake of the intervention in Czechoslovakia, Ulbricht was successful in braking this process, the conflicts with the Soviets led eventually to his removal under Soviet pressure in 1971.

With the assumption of the SED leadership by Honecker, the two policy goals of recognition and special inter-German relations were brought into a new semblance of balance. Although internally the GDR propagated even more intensively the ideological Abgrenzung with respect to the FRG, externally it became more forthcoming in inter-German negotiations, leading to the Transit Agreement and Basic Treaty in 1971 and 1972, respectively. In this process the GDR fell short of attaining the desired international legal recognition by the FRG, yet it was thereby able to make rapid advances in realizing this international recognition from other states and international organizations. While claiming to have achieved normal international relations with the FRG, in practical terms the GDR has acknowledged the continued special inter-German relationship.

This greater forthcomingness toward the FRG had a marked impact on the state's Kirchenpolitik. It explains why the state dramatically reduced pressure for Abgrenzung from the West German churches and accepted the incomplete solutions of the EKU and Berlin-Brandenburg. In order not to disturb the FRG's ratification of the Eastern treaties and the Basic Treaty, the state sought rapprochement with the churches to keep peace on the church front. Over time, the regime even moved to facilitate such all-German contacts.

Honecker sought in two ways to compensate for these concessions to the FRG. First, he initially attempted increased ideological Abgrenzung, countering the Brandt conception of "two states, one nation" with his own formulation of two nations, the "socialist nation" and the "capitalist nation." This class-defined nature of the nation closed out any "drawing-together or commonalities with the socially conflicting capitalist nation in the FRG."[9] Thus the GDR appeared to have abandoned the goal of German unity. This policy of ideological Abgrenzung likewise affected the Kirchenpolitik. While showing increasing tolerance of the practical ties with the West German churches, the state media

[9]Federal Ministry of Inner-German Affairs, *DDR-Handbuch*, pp. 748–50; Hermann Axen, *Zur Entwicklung der Sozialistischen Nation in der DDR* (Berlin, GDR: Dietz Verlag, 1973), pp. 18–23.

continued to underscore the GDR churches' "new orientation," a form of implicit Abgrenzung. Second, Honecker placed increased emphasis on friendship with the USSR and socialist integration, which led the state to promote church ties with churches in other socialist states, particularly with the Russian Orthodox Church.[10]

A second permissive factor explaining the state's motivation for the rapprochement was the impact of international nongovernmental organizations (INGOs). The GDR churches are members of various INGOs, such as the World Council of Churches and Lutheran World Federation. Although not as autonomous as other INGOs, such as multinational corporations or the Catholic church, these largely Protestant bodies may nonetheless affect the tradeoffs facing the regime in its domestic church policy.[11]

Compared with other churches in the Soviet bloc, the East German Lutheran church has had relatively intense and long-term ties to these various INGOs. As part of the EKD it had enjoyed representation and active participation since 1948—contrasting, for example, with the Russian and other Orthodox churches in the bloc, which did not join the WCC until 1957. This exposure left the state more vulnerable to international church criticism than most others in the bloc.

Yet these INGOs also offered the state certain benefits as instruments of state policy.[12] For example, in the context of the state's goal of increased international legitimacy, GDR church participation in these functional INGOs, particularly those in Geneva, offered the state an *ersatz* for full membership in international governmental organizations, such as the United Nations. Bilateral ties of the churches also promoted the international profile and recognition of the GDR. This explains my finding that the state made early concessions to the Kirchenbund in the area of INGO activity.

Church participation in INGOs also offered the state the opportunity

---

[10]Harald Neubert, "Die Dialektik von nationalen und internationalen in der Politik der sozialistischen Staatengemeinschaft," excerpted in Hermann Weber, *Die SED nach Ulbricht* (Hannover: Fackeltraeger Verlag, 1974), pp. 100–101.

[11]Ivan Vallier, "The Roman Catholic Church: A Transnational Actor," and Kjell Skjelsbaek, "The Growth of International Non-Governmental Organization in the Twentieth Century," *International Organization* 25 (Summer 1971): 479–502, 420–42; Joseph S. Nye, Jr., "Multinational Corporations in World Politics," *Foreign Affairs* 3 (October 1974): 153–75.

[12]Samuel P. Huntington supports this view that INGOs are useful to states and that by controlling access, states can limit the loss of sovereignty to INGOs. See his "Transnational Organizations in World Politics," *World Politics* 25 (April 1973): 355–65.

to pursue certain specific foreign policy goals. For example, the INGOs provided hospitable forums for the regime on issues such as support for African liberation movements, European security, and more recently nuclear disarmament.[13]

Participation in INGOs may also lead indirectly to increased legitimacy of the GDR as a political community. Especially among the church leadership, the contact with Western church leaders cued the GDR participants to their distinctive identity and likely served to strengthen identification with the GDR as a political community. It is likely that such international contact would cue the grassroots members as well.

Despite these advantages, GDR participation in these INGOs also brought distinct disadvantages from the state's perspective. They pursued a private foreign policy by lobbying the GDR government; they also helped set the agenda in the Kirchenpolitik by their access to the GDR, as the human rights debate in the mid-1970s demonstrated.

As Ramet concludes, this participation has provided external resources that strengthen the organizational independence of the church in question.[14] For example, Western materials and personal contacts advanced the theological independence of the Kirchenbund. INGOs provided the churches with independent justifications for politically sensitive positions on political and social issues. By defending the social concerns of the church, such international church organizations helped protect the social presence of the churches. Finally, allowing such contact represented an acknowledgment of a transnational belief system other than Marxism-Leninism.

The churches' participation in INGOs also strengthened the churches' representations to the state regarding the treatment of individual Christians and the institutional interests of the churches.[15] Ecumenical organizations established contacts with individual Christians in the GDR,

[13]The GDR's "anti-imperialist" policy in the Third World is treated in Michael Olszewski, "The Framework of Foreign Policy," in Lyman Legters, ed., *The German Democratic Republic: A Developed Socialist Society* (1978), pp. 188–94. This is, of course, derivative of heightened Soviet interest in Southern Africa. See William Griffith, "Soviet Policy in Africa and Latin America," in his *The Soviet Empire: Expansion and Detente* (Lexington, Mass.: Lexington Books, 1976), pp. 337–39. The SED increasingly praised the progressive role of believers in revolutionary struggle and the importance of demonstrating cooperation between Christians and atheists in socialism. See Reinhard Henkys, "Parteiprogramm und Wirklichkeit," *KiS* 2 (June 1976): 18.

[14]Pedro Ramet, *Cross and Commissar* (1987), p. 193. See also Hebly, p. 8; Fletcher, pp. 150–53.

[15]The Russian case is rather different. See Hudson, pp. 265–70, 279.

thereby helping the Kirchenbund make the linkage between its credibility in these organizations and the domestic Kirchenpolitik. Desiring to retain this international credibility as a means of shoring up its human rights record (and thereby defending the process of detente), the state moderated its Kirchenpolitik.

This was most visible not in terms of increased interactions outside the regime's control but rather in the way such ties altered the tradeoffs facing the state.[16] The churches' ties to INGOs did alter these tradeoffs: they offered the state opportunities to pursue certain international and domestic goals, but they also challenged the sovereignty of the state and raised the cost of doing business with the GDR churches. The state was willing to accept the price to obtain the benefits. To be sure, the GDR's foreign policy needs and the nature of Protestantism affect the tradeoffs in this issue of INGOs and state sovereignty. But without these ties, the state would have been less likely to seek rapprochement with the church, as revealed by other Soviet bloc states with limited international contact, for example the USSR and Romania. Thus sovereignty was eroded, but it was sacrificed by the state to achieve other goals.

The changes in the Deutschlandpolitik of the GDR and the impact of INGOs provide only a partial explanation for the state's policy shift. They are permissive causes of the political change. For a fuller explanation of the state's motivation one must look to domestic factors that constrained the state to seek rapprochement, particularly with the Evangelical-Lutheran church.

First, the confessional homogeneity of the GDR, and the concomitant absence of reinforcing social cleavages, increased the state's incentive for an arrangement with the church. The predominant confession in the GDR is Evangelical-Lutheranism; the Catholic church and other Protestant churches are quite weak. When religion does not disappear, as predicted by the ideology, and the costs of a Kirchenkampf become too high, states confronting a confessionally homogeneous society—such as Poland, Romania, Bulgaria, and the GDR—are pressed to seek an arrangement with the predominant church. States facing confessionally heterogeneous societies, such as Czechoslovakia and Hungary, can more easily play off the churches one against the other, especially the smaller Protestant churches against the large Catholic churches. The

[16]In the author's view, Ramet overemphasizes the erosion of sovereignty by concentrating on interactions outside regime control. Ramet (1987), p. 193.

Lutheran predominance in the GDR raised the cost of a Kirchenkampf and reduced the potential for a divide-and-conquer strategy. The state was constrained to coopt the church or seek rapprochement with it.

The homogeneous religious situation in the GDR also precludes confessional differences reinforcing national differences, as in Czechoslovakia, Yugoslavia, and the USSR. These reinforcing cleavages may make it risky for a regime to seek rapprochement with the church, since this may stimulate national unrest and expectations.[17] Thus this absence of reinforcing cleavages made church-state rapprochement more likely. Of course, the Lutheran fortress in the GDR may raise another problem, namely German unity as a cultural nation. Like many Germans, the church has rejected the glorification of the nation and has counseled against demands for reunification and return of lost territories. Yet the church is certainly perceived by the broader population as an important element in a German cultural nation and has manifested this role, for example, during the Luther celebration, and supported GDR assertion of national interests in the 1984 dispute with the USSR. The regime fought this identification, although at times it paradoxically attempted to use such identification to promote its foreign policy goals.

A second factor, however, made difficult the cooptation of the church that has occurred in some confessionally homogeneous states such as Romania, Bulgaria, and the USSR; namely, the internal organization of the church. The Lutheran church is hierarchical yet still democratically organized and decentralized. Bishops and church leaderships, the executive bodies, are elected by synods composed of officials, who are in turn elected by church parishes. The Kirchenbund is a confederation of provincial churches. On both levels the church leaders enjoy a certain flexibility but are accountable to the provincial church establishment and the activist grass roots in the church. Thus there exists a process of internal democracy within the church that permits feedback and criticism from the grass roots. Criticism of church elite accommodation to the regime in the early years after the formation of the Kirchenbund strengthened the hand of the church leadership in dealing with the state, which explains the state's eventual deepening of rapprochement with the church. The rise of societal dissent regarding issues of peace and the environment also increased the church's clout with the regime. This

[17]Ramet, *Cross and Commissar*, pp. 40, 187–88.

democratic element sets the churches in the GDR apart from others in Eastern Europe. The Catholic and Orthodox churches have relatively authoritarian structures. In the case of the Catholic church this hierarchical structure has seemed to strengthen its position; in the Orthodox case the opposite seems to have occurred. The GDR Lutheran churches, as Ramet notes, are more "modern" institutions, adaptable to social and cultural change.[18]

Moreover the creation and development of the Kirchenbund increasingly constrained the state to seek an arrangement with it. Although Lutheranism was the predominant confession, this had not translated into a monolithic position vis-à-vis the state. After the state withdrew recognition of the EKD as the GDR churches' spokesman in 1958, the eight territorially based Landeskirchen were left with no official joint representation. This allowed the state to pursue a strategy of differentiation among the Landeskirchen, using in particular the "progressive" Thuringian Landeskirche. As Ramet and chapter 4 find, this factionalization resulted in "fragmented and disjointed church policy." The formation and consolidation of the Kirchenbund and the end of the "Thuringian Way" represented a centralization of interchurch structure. This centralization clearly increased the unity and leverage of the churches vis-à-vis their environment, the state.[19] The state was forced to largely abandon its Landeskirche-based strategy and develop a cooperative relationship with the Kirchenbund.

Finally, the failure of the state's mobilization organizations led it to seek an arrangement with the churches. The CDU and Pfarrerbund had served a useful purpose in pressuring the church for separation from the EKD. But these organizations failed to gain any considerable credibility with the vast majority of Christians and clergy. As a result, their influence in this key segment of society remained minimal: CDU membership among the clergy hovered around 4 percent; Pfarrerbund membership never exceeded one hundred and the active core was considerably smaller. This situation contrasts with the success that other states in

---

[18]Ibid., p. 186. Interestingly, in the case of the Russian Orthodox Church, dissent outside the church establishment has strengthened the hand of the church vis-à-vis the state. See Bohdan Bociurkiw, "Religious Dissent and the Soviet State," in Bociurkiw and Strong, p. 85.

[19]Ramet, *Cross and Commissar,* p. 190. James Q. Wilson makes the point that voluntary organizations facing a centralized political structure are likely to become centralized themselves. See his *Political Organizations* (New York: Basic Books, 1973), p. 249.

Eastern Europe have enjoyed in integrating the churches and clergy in such mobilization organizations. Thus these organizations were limited in their effectiveness, making a direct overture to the churches by the state advisable.

The Church's Motivation

All of these factors—the shift in Deutschlandpolitik, impact of international nongovernmental organizations, confessional homogeneity and internal organization of the churches, and failure of the state's mobilization organizations—suggest a state in a weakened position vis-à-vis the church, one constrained to seek rapprochement with it. However, unlike in Poland, church-state accommodation in the GDR was conditioned by certain factors that made the church seek a modus vivendi.

The most significant was the decline in church adherence after the 1950s. As a result of state discrimination against Christians and processes of secularization common to modern societies, many left the church or, among the youth, failed to become members.[20] As a result the church has encountered problems of organizational maintenance, such as declining financial support and clergy replacement. This led the church to seek greater state support, which explains why many of the agreements with the state dealt with institutional needs of the church, such as support for church publications and social service agencies.

Another factor motivating the church has been the theological currents in the churches, or religious culture. The GDR churches are characterized by divergent theological currents. By tradition they have been strongly influenced by Lutheran passivity grounded in Luther's separation of the spiritual and secular kingdoms, the so-called Two Kingdoms Doctrine. However, since the 1920s, and particularly since the Third

[20]Donald Smith offers a standard developmental approach to the relationship between political modernization and religion. According to this view, secularization is part of the social differentiation that accompanies the modernization process. However, Smith uses the term "secularization" primarily to describe the increasing independence and dominance of the state and nation over religion and the church. See his "Religion and Political Modernization: Comparative Perspectives," in *Religion and Political Modernization*, ed. Donald E. Smith (New Haven: Yale University Press, 1974), pp. 1–28. More appropriate for the meaning of the term here, namely a decline in subjective religious adherence, is Peter L. Berger, *The Social Reality of Religion* (London: Faber and Faber, 1967), pp. 105–25.

Reich, Barthian social activism has become a strong influence in the church. Paradoxically, both currents have lent legitimacy to the rapprochement with the state. The Lutheran passivity helped facilitate the separation from the EKD, justifying it as deference to the secular kingdom rather than as an issue of creed, as many Barthians in the church viewed it. After the separation, however, the Barthian influence in leaders, such as Schoenherr, justified rapprochement with the state on the basis of the church's witness to society. Although the Barthian position has also justified criticism of the state on various issues such as peace and the environment, it has been more important than traditional Lutheran views in motivating church cooperation with the state. Thus the Lutheran churches had certain theological bridges for accommodating to socialism, unlike the spiritualized Orthodox churches and the totalistic Catholic church.[21]

A third factor leading the church to seek an improved relationship with the state was the generational change in the church leadership. Many of the older church leaders—such as Fraenkel, Noth, and Dibelius—saw the GDR in terms of the Nazi regime, a totalitarian, atheistic regime to be opposed on the basis of creed. In the period of the foundation of the Kirchenbund, however, a new generation assumed power in many of the provincial churches, including Schoenherr, Krusche, Hempel, and Braecklein. They too had experienced the Third Reich, but they attained prominence and political maturity primarily in the postwar period. As a result they have tended to no longer view the GDR as provisional, and in seeking the proper role of the "church in socialism," they have tended toward pragmatic cooperation with the state.

Despite the regime's materialist ideology and its Leninist principles of organization, both the East German state and church sought rapprochement. This finding, in turn, raises the question to what extent this reflected the Soviet Kirchenpolitik or a church-state model in Eastern Europe. A brief review of the church-state relationship bloc-wide indicates that the political change in the GDR did not reflect a replication of Soviet policy either at home or in the bloc.

---

[21]Ramet, *Cross and Commissar*, pp. 186, 188–89, emphasizes Protestantism's proclivity toward dissent and modernization, in contrast to the Catholic and Orthodox churches. See also William C. Fletcher, "Backwards from Reactionism . . . ," in *Religion and Modernization in the Soviet Union*, ed. Dennis J. Dunn (1977), pp. 205–38; Bohdan Bociurkiw, "Religious Dissent and the Soviet State," in Bociurkiw and Strong, pp. 58–90; Hans-Jakob Stehle, *Eastern Politics of the Vatican* (Athens: Ohio University Press, 1979).

The GDR policy was clearly not a replication of the Soviet Kirchen-politik at the time.[22] The Russian Orthodox Church has until recently been coopted by the regime. The church remains quite weak as an institution, dependent on state subsidy and extremely limited in its opportunities to train clergy. With a ritual-oriented theology, the church has claimed little social presence. Despite relaxation during World War II, the regime's policy remained repressive until the millennial celebration under Gorbachev in 1988. The churches' political strength cannot be compared to that of the GDR Lutheran church.

Nor did the East German case seem to reflect a uniform bloc-wide policy. The church-state relationships in the bloc reflected considerable diversity.[23] Large Orthodox churches—in the USSR, Romania, and Bulgaria, for example—have been largely coopted by their respective regimes. Their emphasis on ritual and limited ties to the West have weakened them in their dealings with the regime.

Until recently Czechoslovakia too contrasted with the GDR.[24] Divided confessionally and weak institutionally, the Catholic and Reformed churches were the target of a continuous Kirchenkampf after 1948, relieved only briefly during the liberalization of the Prague Spring.

In Poland one finds the opposite situation.[25] The Catholic church has long enjoyed great institutional strength, favorable treatment of religious adherents, and considerable political clout. When it has struck a modus vivendi with the regime, it has been on the basis of the strength of the church vis-à-vis the regime, unlike the mutual weakness in the GDR case.

[22]Albert Boiter, *Religion in the Soviet Union*, Washington Papers 8, no. 78 (1977); Jane Ellis, *The Russian Orthodox Church* (1986), especially pp. 251–84.

[23]Marin Pundeff, "Church-State Relations in Bulgaria under Communism," and Keith Hitchens, "The Romanian Orthodox Church and the State," in Bociurkiw and Strong, pp. 328–50, 314–27; Irwin T. Sanders, "Church-State Relations in Southeastern Europe," *Eastern European Quarterly* 16 (March 1982): 63–69; Beeson, pp. 23–88, 329–79; Trond Gilberg, "Religion and Nationalism in Romania," and Spas T. Raikin, "Nationalism and the Bulgarian Orthodox Church," in *Religion and Nationalism in Soviet and East European Politics*, ed. Pedro Ramet (1984), pp. 170–206.

[24]Beeson, pp. 219–55; Peter A. Toma and Milan J. Reban, "Church-State Schism in Czechoslovakia," in Bociurkiw and Strong, pp. 273–91.

[25]Suzanne Hruby, "The Church in Poland and Its Political Influence," *Journal of International Affairs* 36 (Fall/Winter 1982–83): 317–28; Giovanni Barberini, "Relationship between the Socialist State and the Roman Catholic Church," in *Poland: Church Facing Socialism* (Rome: IDOC International, 1979), pp. 13–20; Vincent Chrypinski, "Church and Nationality in Postwar Poland," in Ramet (1984), pp. 123–39.

Hungary presents perhaps the closest parallel to the GDR case.[26] Predominantly Catholic, Hungary pursued a relatively moderate policy toward the church after the Vatican's removal of Cardinal Mindszenty in 1974. Because of the high level of secularization and a strong economy, the church was not in a position to challenge the regime. However, the regime, as in the GDR, was solicitous of the Vatican, and pragmatic cooperation developed. Among Lutherans the proclivity for dissent in the Protestant religious culture was overshadowed by Lutheran deference to the regime: a small Lutheran church found itself weak and supportive of the regime, in contrast to the GDR Lutherans.

Thus with the possible exception of Hungary, the political change in the church-state relationship in the GDR found no parallel in the bloc and did not reflect either a uniform policy in the bloc or a direct application of the Soviet policy. To be sure, Soviet policy toward the bloc is likely a permissive factor in the change. The Soviets' desire for viable regimes, particularly since Stalin, has led them to accept greater national variation in the bloc.[27] Moreover, their interest in detente and the dampening of the human rights issue certainly had consequences for the GDR regime's policy toward the church. Certainly the renewed chill in church-state relations in 1988 and 1989 reflected rejection of a uniform bloc-wide policy, in this case a liberal policy in Moscow. Nonetheless, the change in the GDR case reflected the particular factors operating in the GDR context.

SIGNIFICANCE AND CONCLUSIONS

The Evangelical-Lutheran church in the GDR, a relatively autonomous actor outside the official system and ideology, has served as a source of significant political change. In the 1970s the regime came to grant the church tacit recognition as an institutional force in society, despite continuing ideological conflict. This represented a significant change in a Leninist system in which the Communist party arrogates for

[26]Beeson, pp. 256–87; Leslie Laszlo, "Towards Normalization of Church-State Relations in Hungary," in Bociurkiw and Strong, pp. 292–313; Leslie Lazlo, "Religion and Nationality in Hungary," in Ramet, *Religion and Nationalism* (1984), pp. 140–48.

[27]James F. Brown, "Detente and Soviet Foreign Policy in Europe," *Survey* 20, nos. 2–3 (1974): 46.

itself the role as the sole institution legitimately organizing atomized individuals. Analysis of the process of this change yields several general conclusions.

First, change in the international system can effect change in the domestic systems of Communist states. During the 1960s the loosening of bipolarity in the transition from Cold War to detente affected Germany in particular. The GDR was reluctant to accommodate this shift by the USSR and continued a policy of Abgrenzung from 1969 to 1971, resulting in the formal separation of East German and West German churches. However, with the East German accommodation to the Soviet position favoring Ostpolitik and detente, the GDR increasingly accepted the inter-German church ties and even promoted them. These ties, particularly given the escalating human rights debate in the 1970s, pressed the GDR to reach an accommodation with the church in order to limit international criticism.

The GDR was not alone in this respect; other states in the Soviet bloc also felt domestic effects from the detente process. The economic effects of this international change were great in Poland and Hungary, leading eventually to political instability in Poland. Increased political dissent affected many regimes as the Helsinki movement manifested itself. However, in the GDR the Helsinki process benefited an institution, the church, rather than simply ad hoc human rights groups. Thus it carried greater potential for long-term political change in the system.

Second, study of the church-state relationship gives considerable support to the assumption of the West German Ostpolitik, particularly the Brandtian version: that domestic liberalization would follow international rapprochement with the GDR. The churches and Christians certainly constitute a significant dimension of East German society. Improvement in their situation in the late 1970s signaled liberalization, however limited. The GDR denied any connection between the treatment of the churches and foreign policy toward the FRG, but the linkage and erosion of GDR sovereignty are clear. The GDR under Honecker accepted the linkage and even tried to exploit it for economic and international advantage. But the rapprochement with the church was clearly an effort to limit the damage from detente.

This liberalization in the case of the church appears to have promoted the West Germans' longer-term goal of reunification as well. To be sure, the separation from the EKD and the Kirchenbund's international activity worked to build greater legitimacy for the GDR internationally.

The regime maintained that the GDR constitutes a separate "socialist German nation." However, the GDR's policy betrayed this at times, attempting to use the special all-German ties to influence debate in the FRG. This was obvious during the debate over the Eastern treaties and more recently in Honecker's appeals regarding the NATO Euromissile debate and the chill in East-West relations in the early 1980s. The churches' ties to West German churches, while not free from controversy, were facilitated after the early 1970s, a trend that belied the state's official policy on the national question. Thus the church has continued to form part of a German *Kulturnation*. Although the state under Honecker accepted this ambiguity, large-scale emigration and demands for freedom of travel and even reunification in 1989 suggest that a large portion of the GDR population has not accepted this ambiguity.

Third, the churches' participation in international nongovernmental organizations (INGOs), such as the World Council of Churches, has affected the tradeoffs facing the state in its policy toward the church. On the one hand, like the churches' special ties to West German churches, the INGOs have raised the costs of a harsh Kirchenpolitik. Even though only loosely organized above the state level, the Evangelical-Lutheran churches have been strengthened by this international attention, particularly in the context of the human rights debate. However, sovereignty was hardly at bay for the GDR as a result. The GDR limited formal international contacts at times, when such contacts conflicted with other state dictates. Moreover, this international contact contributed to the achievement of the state's goal of international recognition. Nonetheless, even after achieving this goal, the GDR solicited approval of these INGOs, a policy that narrowed its options regarding the domestic church policy. Rapprochement with the church again proved a prudent way of limiting any criticism from the INGOs.

Finally, the church-state relationship provides insight into the sources and nature of political change in Communist systems. This case of political change seems to conform to the development approach,[28] which describes the evolution of revolutionary one-party systems into

[28]Samuel P. Huntington, "Social and Institutional Dynamics of One-Party Systems," in *Authoritarian Politics in Modern Society*, ed. Samuel P. Huntington and Clement H. Moore (1970), pp. 24–40; Kenneth Jowitt, "Inclusion and Mobilization in European Communist Regimes," in *Political Development in Eastern Europe*, ed. Jan Triska and Paul M. Cocks (1977), pp. 93–118.

established one-party systems through the stages of transformation, consolidation, and finally inclusion. In the transformation stage, the old order is destroyed and the bases of an ideological, homogeneous society are laid. In the consolidation stage, ideology declines in importance and state and party institutions grow in significance. The inclusion stage sees the party deal with social complexity by either incorporating such groups into the party or "devolving its functional overload upon a variety of governmental and autonomous or quasi-autonomous groups."[29]

The East German case seems to support the argument that, during the period under study, the regime was moving through an inclusion stage, devolving areas to social groups such as the church. Yet there are major flaws in this application. First, the developmental approach emphasizes modern functional groups, not premodern attachments such as religion and the church. In fact, however, the present case suggests that the regime was more likely to include a premodern nonfunctional group, such as the church, than some functional groups such as workers. By maintaining the irreconcilability of their respective belief systems, church and state were more successful at striking a modus vivendi than in the case of a social group that claims to share the regime's "modern" belief system. Second, such a modus vivendi between church and state may actually *inhibit* the inclusion of other groups or devolution of politics in functional areas. Indeed the GDR case offers support for this argument. During the period under study, the GDR economic model was characterized not by devolution but by centralized control and steering mechanisms.[30] Cultural life likewise was characterized by tight central control by party organs. In fact, despite Brandt's hope, the liberalization that occurred in the area of church-state relations was a profoundly conservative one, foreclosing as many possibilities of further change as it opened.

In order better to explain this conservative political change one must adduce Hirschman's analysis of market dynamics in a near-monopoly situation.[31] Communist states, like the corporations Hirschman analyzes, fear too much exit, which may cause collapse. Yet if exit is foreclosed, as in the GDR after 1961 and in the case of monopolies,

[29]Samuel P. Huntington and Clement H. Moore, "Conclusion: Authoritarianism, Democracy, and One-Party Politics," in Huntington and Moore, p. 515; see also p. 41.

[30]Thomas A. Baylis, "Explaining the GDR's Economic Strategy," *International Organization* 40 (Spring 1986): 381–420.

[31]Albert O. Hirschman, *Exit, Voice, and Loyalty* (1970).

voice becomes heightened as a response of those dissatisfied. This voice may be uncomfortable to the entity. It may no longer want to maintain a total monopoly—in the case of a Communist regime, state control over an atomized society. Rather it may become a "lazy monopolist" seeking to deteriorate the product—in the case of a Communist system, diminish revolutionary fervor and goals. Such a lazy monopolist thus may paradoxically find it in its interest to tolerate a limited amount of competition to foster the exit from the system of those whose voice is discomforting. The GDR churches represent a limited amount of competition. Thus the state's acceptance of the churches in the period under study may be explained by its realization not only that the church was likely to exist for some time, but also that this limited competition served to channel and contain political discontent.

The state was hardly pleased by criticism, even when it came from the churches. Yet criticism from the churches was less radical and more limited to the interests of Christians and the churches. When it was wider in focus—as on abortion, peace and militarization issues, the environment, even human rights—it became increasingly tempered by a long-term-oriented, positive attitude toward socialism. As Falcke has argued, "because Christians did not expect socialism to lead directly to a reign of freedom, disappointment in its performance would not lead them to reject it totally or to lapse into cynical disapproval."[32] Although it is not clear whether the state perceived this statement as a blessing or a curse, it reflected the fact that the church was more tolerant of socialism's failures and took a longer-term view than Marxists themselves.

Moreover, the state's ties with the church gave the state a certain oversight over such criticism. The state hoped to dampen dissent among elements of the church leadership as well as the grass roots. By making the linkage, whether explicit or implicit, between the interests of the individual Christians and the churches with the issue of political criticism, the state sought to exert pressure on the churches to discipline the political dissenters within the churches. Although the church leadership has limited power to stop such criticism, this discipline function has also operated through internalized self-disciplining within the churches.

Not only did the state view the churches (along with expulsion to

[32]Heino Falcke, "Christus befreit—Darum Kirche fuer andere," *epd Dokumentation*, no. 30 (17 July 1972): p. 11.

West Germany) as a means of dealing with uncomfortable voices, it saw exit to the church as a way to discredit the arguments of such dissenters. System-immanent criticism was delegitimized by identifying it with the still extrasystemic church. Thus the state was interested in maintaining the churches' status outside the system; the state's rejection of a "socialist church" was understandable since this designation might have given greater credibility to those espousing system-immanent criticism who exited to the churches. But while stopping short of a "socialist church," the state found it expedient to cease fighting the church and even to stabilize the church. This normalization of the status of the Evangelical churches brought them great advantages: not only institutional benefits and some benefits for individual Christians, but also a relatively autonomous position and considerable room to take official positions critical of state policy.

Under certain circumstances the institutional church, ordinarily a source of ideological and political challenge to a Leninist regime, can be tacitly accepted by such a regime and effect significant political change. The GDR case suggests that increases in Western attention and activity by international church organizations, internal democracy in churches, and noncultic theological thought, among other factors, can increase the likelihood of such political change.

In the final analysis, the stabilizing effect of the limited exit that the church represented was overwhelmed by the demonstration effect of reform in the Soviet bloc, particularly in Moscow, Warsaw, and Budapest. Given the option of exit to the West, a massive hemorrhage of emigration occurred in the fall of 1989. In this context the church assumed a far larger role than one of limited exit; it began to serve as the vehicle for the articulation of voice for change in the political system, manifested in massive street protests. The resulting combination of exit and voice toppled the SED regime and threatened the viability of the GDR itself as a sovereign state. The developments revealed that the basis for the essentially conservative nature of the regime's change in its relationship to the Lutheran church in the 1970s had been undermined by new Soviet pressure for liberalization and rising popular expectations of democratization. In the liberalizing context, the autonomous institution of the church played a key role in challenging SED authority. It may continue to play a key role as a relatively stable institution in a period of considerable political instability and uncertainty.

Bibliography

PERSONAL INTERVIEWS, FEBRUARY–NOVEMBER 1979

Elisabeth Adler, Evangelical Academy, Berlin, GDR.
Dr. Johannes Althausen, member of Berlin-Brandenburg (East) Consistory.
Christfried Berger, director of Ecumenical-Missionary Center, Berlin, GDR, former member of Saxony-Magdeburg Consistory.
Prof. Dr. Karl-Heinz Bernhardt, Humboldt University, Berlin, GDR.
Bishop Niklot Beste, former bishop of Mecklenburg.
Bishop Ingo Braecklein, former bishop of Thuringia.
Dr. Siegfried Braeuer, Evangelical Publishing Company, Berlin, GDR.
Bishop Christoph Demke, Saxony-Magdeburg, former president of Kirchenbund Secretariat.
Prof. Dr. Helmut Dressler, Humboldt University.
Provost Heino Falcke, Erfurt.
Bishop Gottfried Forck, Berlin-Brandenburg (East).
Bishop Hans-Joachim Fraenkel, former bishop of Goerlitz.
Superintendent Hans-Otto Furian, provost in Berlin, GDR, former superintendent of Zossen.
Bishop Horst Gienke, Greifswald.
Pastor Gustav-Adolf Gloeckner, Greifswald.
OKR Christa Grengel, member of EKU Consistory, Berlin, GDR.
OKR Reinhard Groscurth, former president of EKU (West) Chancellory, Berlin.
OKR Hans-Martin Harder, member of Greifswald Consistory.
OKR Uwe-Peter Heidungsfeld, president of EKD Church Chancellory, West Berlin branch, formerly member of EKU (West) Consistory.
Bishop Johannes Hempel, Saxony-Dresden.
Reinhard Henkys, Evangelical Press Service, Berlin.
Karl Hennig, National Front of Democratic Germany, Berlin, GDR.
Prof. Dr. Erich Hertzsch, former professor of theology, Jena.

Dr. Erwin Hinz, Magdeburg.
Pastor Martin Hohman, Magdeburg.
Dr. Kurt Johannes, former president of Provincial Church Office, Saxony-Dresden.
Eberhard Klages, *Neue Zeit,* Berlin, GDR.
Dr. Olof Klohr, Rostock/Warnemuende.
Pastor Wilhelm Knecht, Berlin, GDR.
Pastor Martin Kramer, president of Saxony-Magdeburg Consistory.
Dr. Gerhard Krause, former president of Saxony-Magdeburg Consistory.
Bishop Werner Krusche, former bishop of Saxony-Magdeburg.
Pastor Heinz Langhoff, Brandenburg.
Bishop Werner Leich, Thuringia.
OKR Christa Lewek, member of Kirchenbund Secretariat.
OKR Hartmut Mitzenheim, President of Provincial Church Office, Thuringia.
Church President Eberhard Natho, Anhalt.
OKR Walter Pabst, former member of Kirchenbund Secretariat.
OKR Ernst Petzold, former director of Domestic Mission and Aid Society.
OKR Siegfried Plath, member of Greifswald Consistory.
Manfred Punge, member Kirchenbund Studies Department.
Bishop Heinrich Rathke, former bishop of Mecklenburg.
Provost Siegfried Ringhandt, former provost of Berlin, GDR.
Hans-Juergen Roeder, correspondent of Evangelical Press Service (West) in Berlin, GDR.
Dr. Joachim Rogge, bishop of Goerlitz, former president of EKU (East) Chancellory.
Pastor Georg Schaefer, Weimar.
Bishop Kurt Scharf, former bishop of Berlin-Brandenburg and chairman of EKD.
Bishop Albrecht Schoenherr, former bishop of Berlin-Brandenburg (East).
Provincial Superintendent Otto Schroeder, Parchim/Mecklenburg, former head of GDR Church Congress.
OKR Harald Schultze, member of Saxony-Magdeburg Consistory.
OKR Walter Schulz, former member of Mecklenburg Provincial Church Office.
Pastor Reinhard Steinlein, Nauen, former member of Berlin-Brandenburg (East) Church Leadership.
OKR Manfred Stolpe, president of Berlin-Brandenburg Consistory, former president of Kirchenbund Secretariat.
Lothar Teichman, Karl-Marx-Stadt, former member of Conference of Church Leaderships, Kirchenbund.
Prof. Dr. Herbert Trebs, Humboldt University, Berlin, GDR.
Dr. Wulf Trende, Department of Church Affairs, Secretariat of the Executive Committee of the CDU.
Dr. Wolfgang Ullman, professor at Sprachenkonvikt, Berlin, GDR.
Prof. Dr. Guenter Voegler, Humboldt University, Berlin, GDR.
OKR Ulrich von Brueck, member of Provincial Church Office, Saxony-Dresden.
Pastor Axel Walter, Rostock.
Dr. Wolfgang Weichelt, Director, Institute for Theory of State and Law.
Hans Wilke, Office of the State Secretary for Church Affairs.
Dr. Friedrich Winter, president of EKU (East) Chancellory, former provost of Berlin-Brandenburg (East).
Ruth Zander, former member of Kirchenbund Studies Department.

OKR Helmut Zeddies, president of Lutheran Church Office and GDR National Committee of the Lutheran World Federation.
OKR Friedrich Zilz, member of Provincial Church Office, Thuringia.
Pastor Ralph Zorn, former LWF representative in West Berlin.

UNPUBLISHED SOURCES

*Documents from the Archive of the Executive Committee
(Hauptvorstand) of the Christian Democratic Union of
Germany (East) (CDU archives)*

3 August 1966. Zur Taetigkeit der Arbeitsgruppe 'Christliche Kreise,' no author.
8 September 1966. Wie hat der Druck der westdeutscher Militaerkirche leitende kirchliche Persoenlichkeiten an ihrer eigenen Entwicklung gehindert? no author.
1966. Die politische-ideologische Arbeit der CDU auf kirchenpolitischen Gebiet im Jahre, no author.
1967. Fuerstenwalde file, no author.
17 March 1968. Information bez. Verfassungsfragen von der Synode Kirchenprovinz Sachsen, signed Reinelt.
20 March 1968. Wie ist der Einfluss der CDU in kirchenleitenden Kreisen gewachsen? no author.
22 March 1968. Informationsbericht, CDU Presse-Berliner Redaktion, 1. Tagung der 6. Synode der Evangelische Kirchenprovinz Sachsen.
16 April 1968. Aktenvermerk betr. Beteiligung von kirchlichen Amtstraeger am Volksentschied, no author.
16 August 1968. Memorandum, Heikisch—Unionsfreund Wiedeman.
1 November 1968. Aktenvermerk, Gespraech mit OKR Stolpe betr. Synode Berlin-Brandenburg und Strukturkommission, signed Quast.
13 November 1968. Argumentationsthesen fuer die Arbeit mit kirchlichen Amtstraegern und Theologen in Vorbereitung des 20. Jahrestages der DDR, signed Heikisch.
1968. Aktenvermerk, "Evangelische Fruehjahrssynoden," signed Quast.
6 January 1969. Aktennotiz, betr. Gespraech Schoenherr mit Prof. D. Gehlen und Pfarrer Bruehe, signed Quast.
24 January 1969. Aktenvermerk, betr. Ruecksprache mit Flint (24 January 1969), betr. Aussprache mit Schoenherr vom 21 January 1969, signed Quast.
5 February 1969. Aktenvermerk, betr. Aussprache beim Vize-Praesident des Nationaler Rates Werner Kirchhoff (4 February 1969), signed Quast.
15–19 March 1969. Bericht ueber Synode der Evangelische-Lutherische Kirche Sachsen, signed Deputy Regional Chairman, CDU.

*Key figures in the Kirchenpolitik files of the CDU archives: Willi Barth, head, Working Group on Church Questions, Secretariat, SED; Rudi Bellman, deputy, Working Group on Church Questions, Secretariat, SED; Fritz Flint, CDU representative in State Secretariat for Church Questions; Kurt Huettner, deputy, Working Group on Church Questions, Secretariat, SED; Eberhard Klages, *Neue Zeit*; Gerhard Quast, head, Department of Church Questions, CDU Executive Committee; Wolf Trende, Deputy, Department of Church Questions, CDU Executive Committee

31 March 1969. Bericht ueber die Synode der Goerlitzer Kirche vom 21. 3. bis 24. 3. 1969, signed Dressler.

11 April 1969. Aktenvermerk, betr. Gespraech Seigewasser mit der Kirchenleitung Sachsens (27 March 1969).

18 April 1969. Aktenvermerk, betr. Aussprache Barth, Bellmann, Huettner (17 April 1969), signed Quast.

21 April 1969. Aktenvermerk, betr. Aussprache mit Flint (17 April 1969, betr. Gespraech Seigewasser-Krummacher vom 1 April 1969), signed Quast.

21–23 April 1969. Entwuerfe, Diskussionsbeitraege zum Kongress der Nationalen Front des demokratischen Deutschland.

24 April 1969. Aktenvermerk, betr. Seigewasser Gespraech mit Reformierten Vertretern, signed Hoffman.

3 June 1969. Aktennotiz, betr. Aussprache Goetting, Seigewasser, Bellman, Weise, und Quast (no date given), signed Quast.

5 June 1969. Aktenvermerk, betr. Aussprache mit Stolpe (3 June 1969), signed Quast.

17 June 1969. Aktenvermerk, betr. Zentralrat der FDJ, signed Viererbe.

26 June 1969. Aktenvermerk, betr. Aussprache mit Stolpe (26 June 1969), signed Quast.

30 June 1969. Aktenvermerk, betr. Aussprache Flint (27 June 1969), betr. Gespraech Bischof Beste-Seigewasser vom 17 June 1969), signed Quast.

24 July 1969. Aktennotiz, betr. Gespraech mit Stolpe (23 July 1969), signed Hoffman.

26 July 1969. Aktenvermerk, betr. Gespraech mit Flint (21 Juli 1969, betr. Aussprache Stolpe-Seigewasser vom 17. Juli 1969), signed Heikisch.

6 August 1969. Einschaetzung der Weiterentwicklung des sozialistischen Staatsbewusstseins in den Kerngemeinden, no author.

11 August 1969. Der Beitrag der CDU in Vorbereitung des 20 Jahrestages der DDR, no author.

19 August 1969. Entwurf, Rede Seigewassers, no author.

24 September 1969. Aktenvermerk, betr. Aussprache mit Huettner betr. Bund der Evangelischen Kirchen in der DDR, signed Quast.

5 December 1969. Aktenvermerk, betr. Aussprache mit Flint (4 December 1969), signed Quast.

23 December 1969. Aktenvermerk, betr. Aussprache Bellman, Huettner,Heyl, Quast (19 December 1969), signed Quast.

23 January 1970. Aktenvermerk, betr. Evangelische Lutherische Kirche in Thueringen, Gespraeche mit Flint (22 January 1970) und Lotz (23 January 1970), signed Quast.

26 January 1970. Aktenvermerk, betr. Aussprache mit Stolpe (23 January 1970), signed Quast.

23 February 1970. Aktenvermerk, betr. Aussprache mit Stolpe (18 February 1970), und De Maiziere (23 February 1970), signed Quast.

3 April 1970. Einschaetzung der Berlin-Brandenburg Synode, no author.

28 June 1970. Informationsbericht der Bezirkssekretariat Magdeburg, signed Fahl.

30 June 1970. Aktenvermerk, betr. Aussprache Goetting, Seigewasser, Huettner, and Bell (22 June 1970), signed Quast.

13 July 1970. Aktenvermerk, betr. Aussprache mit Flint (6 Juli 1970), signed Quast.

1 August 1970. Berichterstattung, signed Quast.

20 August 1970. Aktenvermerk, betr. Gespraech mit Flint (no date given), signed Heikisch.

7 September 1970. Aktenvermerk, betr. Aussprache mit Flint und Weise (3 September 1970), signed Quast.

17 September 1970. Aktenvermerk, betr. Aussprache Barth, Bellman, und Huettner (10 September 1970), signed Quast.

1 October 1970. Gedaechtnisprotokoll, bez. Tagung der Arbeitsgruppe Kirchenfragen beim Hauptvorstand der CDU (30 September 1970), signed Trende.

8 October 1970. Erste Konzeption und Ziele. Erste Gedanken zu einer Konzeption betr. 9.2.71, signed Quast.

16 October 1970. Aktenvermerk, betr. Gespraech mit Praeses Haase (Anhalt) (15 October 1970), signed Fahl, CDU District Chairman, Magdeburg.

28 October 1970. Aktenvermerk, betr. Information von Dr. Schneider und Unionsfreund Berthold (Halle), signed Quast.

5 November 1970. Aktenvermerk, betr. Aussprache Bellman, Barth (4 November 1970), signed Quast.

10 November 1970. Zweite Konzeption und Ziele betr. 9.2.71, signed Quast.

13 November 1970. "Kirchenpolitische Probleme," Abteilung Kirchenfragen, Sekretariat des Hauptvorstandes der CDU, no author.

26 November 1970. Aktenvermerk, betr. Aussprache Natho-Fahl-Quast (25 November 1970), signed Quast.

15 December 1970. Aktenvermerk, betr. Aussprache mit Wilke (14 December 1970), betr. Aussprache Bischof Krusche, Schoenherr, Ammer, Krause, Vorsitzender der Rat des Bezirks Erfurt Gote, Seigewasser, Wilke, u.a. vom 9. 12. (1970), signed Quast.

16 December 1970. Aktenvermerk, betr. Aussprache mit Dr. Schneider, Ministerium fuer Fach- und Hochschulwesen, (11 December 1970), signed Quast.

17 December 1970. Aktenvermerk, betr. Aussprache mit Huettner, Barth, and Bellman betr. 9.2.71 (16 December 1970), signed Quast.

1970. Einschaetzung der evangelischen Fruehjahrssynoden, no date given, no author.

1970. "Einschaetzung der evangelischen Herbstsynoden 1969," Anlage zur Information der Sekretariat des Hauptvorstandes der CDU, no. 5, no date given, no author.

11 January 1971. Aktenvermerk, betr. Aussprache mit Barth, Huettner, Bellman, and Weise (8 January 1971), signed Quast.

12 January 1971. Einladungsliste 9.2.71, Abteilung Kirchenfragen der Sekretariat des Hauptvorstandes der CDU.

13 January 1971. "Bewusste Neuorientierung erfordert entschiedene Auseinandersetzung mit Sozialdemokratismus und Konvergenztheorie," address by Carl Ordnung to Arbeitsgruppe Kirchenfragen beim Hauptvorstand der CDU, Protokoll der Sitzung der Arbeitsgruppe Kirchenfragen, 21 January 1971, no author.

14 January 1971. Aufzeichnungen von dem Gespraech am 14.1.71 zwischen Seigewasser, Wenzel (SED), Klein (SED), Kind (CDU), and Generalsuperintendent Lahr (Potsdam) und Superintendent Stubbe, betr. Referat am 15.3.71 von Lahr, no date, no author.

9 February 1971. Brief, OKR Stolpe an die CDU, betr. Ablehnung der Einladung zu Veranstaltung am 9.2.71, no date.

29 March 1971. "Bericht ueber ein Gespraech der Bezirksvorstaende der CDU

Magdeburg and Halle mit der Kirchenleitung der Evangelische Kirche der Provinz Sachsen am 10.3.71 in Magdeburg," Informationsbericht des Bezirksvorsitzenden an den Vorsitzender der CDU zum 1. April 1971.

3 April 1971. Aktenvermerk, betr. Theologische Literatur, signed Quast.

14 April 1971. Brief, Bishop Rathke to parish church councils.

25 May 1971. Aktenvermerk, betr. Aussprache mit Barth, Huettner, und Bellman im Zentralkommittee (21 May 1971), signed Quast.

14 June 1971. Aktenvermerk, betr. Aussprache mit Flint (no date, betr. Aussprache Seigewasser mit Schoenherr, Braecklein, Rathke vom 17 June 1971), signed Quast.

30 June 1971. Aktenvermerk, betr. Aussprache mit Flint, signed Quast.

1 July 1971. "Bericht ueber den Mecklenburgische Kirchentag," Informationsbericht des Bezirksvorsitzenden Schwerin an den Vorsitzender der CDU zum 1 Juli 1971, signed Friedrich.

23 July 1971. Aktenvermerk, betr. Ruecksprache mit Bellman (22 July 1971, betr. Fusion von *Pfarrerblatt* und *Glaube und Gewissen*), signed Quast.

23 July 1971. Aktenvermerk, betr. Auswertung des VIII. Parteitages der SED und Aussprache mit Bellmann vom 22. Juli 1971, signed Quast.

28 July 1971. Bericht ueber ein Gespraech zwischen der Kirchenleitung Mecklenburgs und Seigewasser, Stellvertretender Vorsitzender der Rat des Bezirkes, und Referent Kirchenfragen bei der Rat des Bezirks am 27 Juli 1971, signed Hans Koch, Vorsitzender des BV der CDU, Schwerin.

3 August 1971. Bericht ueber ein Gespraech der Stellvertreter des Vorsitzenden des Rates der Bezirk Magdeburg, Kollege Steinbach, mit Bischof Krusche, Informationsbericht des Vorsitzenden des BV Magdeburg an den Parteivorsitzender zum 1. Juli 1971.

20 October 1971. Aktenvermerk betr. Ergaenzung zur Frage der Haltung kirchlichen Amtstraeger und Theologen zur Zivilverteidigung, signed Heikisch.

22 October 1971. Sinnprotokoll der Sitzung der Arbeitsgruppe Kirchenfragen beim Hauptvorstand der CDU am 13 Oktober 1971, no author.

26 October 1971. Aktenvermerk, betr. Aussprache mit Flint (15 October 1971), signed Quast.

1 November 1971. Aktenvermerk betr. Meinungsbildung, Abteilung Kirchenfragen der Sekretariat des Hauptvorstandes der CDU.

2 November 1971. Bericht betr. die Herbstsynode der saechsische Landeskirche, signed Quast.

3 November 1971. Aktenvermerk, betr. Gespraech zwischen Goetting und Schoenherr, Pabst, und Stolpe (2 November 1971), signed Quast.

5 November 1971. Erste Information des Bezirksverband Magdeburg an den Hauptvorstand der CDU Berlin.

8 November 1971. Memorandum an die Abteilung Kirchenfragen, signed Straubing (CDU Berliner Redakteur).

15 November 1971. Bericht von der 6. Tagung der VII Synode der Evangelischen Kirche der Kirchenprovinz Sachsen, signed Lenz.

16 November 1971. Bericht ueber die Greifswalder Synod. Aeusserungen zu Fragen Volksbildung, signed Klages.

1 December 1971. Aktenvermerk, betr. Gespraech mit Dr. Sjollema (WCC) (30 November 1971), signed Dr. Zachmann, DDR-representative in Geneva.

13 December 1971. Aktenvermerk, betr. Aussprache mit Flint, signed Quast.

28 December 1971. Aktenvermerk. betr. Aussprache mit Dr. Huettner am 23.12 und Rudi Bellmann am 20.12., signed Quast.

29 December 1971. Aktenvermerk, betr. Erste Meinungsbildung zum Beschluss des Politburo des ZK der SED und Ministerrats ueber die Ausarbeitung neuer gesetzlicher Bestimmungen zur Schwangerschaftsunterbrechung, Abteilung Parteiorgane CDU.

1971. Einschaetzung der Berlin-Brandenburg (West) Synode, no date given, signed Klages.

1971. Information ueber die Herbstsynoden, no date given, no author.

10 January 1972. Aktenvermerk, betr. Meinungsbildung zum Beschluss . . . , Abteilung Parteiorgane CDU.

21 January 1972. Aktenvermerk, betr. Information von Flint (13 January 1972, betr. Informierung der leitender Amtstraeger der evangelischen Landeskirchen ueber die VVO und Schwangerschaftsunterbrechung am 5.1.72), signed Quast.

11 February 1972. An die Teilnehmer der Tagung des Praesidiums des Hauptvorstandes der CDU Deutschlands mit der Arbeitsgemeinschaft Kirchenfragen, signed Prof. Dr. Stefan Doernberg, Generalsekretaer des DDR Kommittees fuer Europaeische Sicherheit.

24 February 1972. Brief Goettings an Rolf Damman, head of East German Baptists.

29 February 1972. Brief Goettings an Albrecht Schoenherr.

29 February 1972. Brief Goettings an Alfred Kardinal Bengsch, head of the Berlin Conference of Catholic Bishops.

13 April 1972. Sinnprotokoll der Sitzung der Arbeitsgruppe Kirchenfragen beim Hauptvorstand der CDU am 12 April 1972, no author.

9 May 1972. Aktenvermerk, betr. Gespraech mit Huettner (4 May 1972), signed Quast and Trende.

11 May 1972. Aktenvermerk, betr. Beratung mit dem Vorstand des Bundes und Vertretern der KKL am 10.5 von 10:00 Uhr bis 13:30 Uhr (11 May 1972), Abteilung Kirchenfragen der Sekretariat des Hauptvorstandes der CDU.

26 May 1972. Aktenvermerk, betr. 4. Kirchenbund Synod, Aussprache mit Stolpe, signed Quast.

13 July 1972. Aktenvermerk, betr. Aussprache mit Flint (13 July 1972 betr. Gespraech zwischen Vorstand des Bundes und Seigewasser vom 26.6.72), signed Quast.

25 July 1972. Aktenvermerk, betr. Gespraech zwischen Goetting, Heyl, and Quast und Krummacher und Gienke (18 July 1972), signed Quast.

28 July 1972. Aktenvermerk, betr. Aussprache mit Flint (27 July 1972, betr. Gespraech Seigewasser-Natho am 26 July 1972), signed Quast.

18 October 1972. Notiz an Quast betr. Artikel vom 18. 10. 1972, signed Klages.

20 October 1972. Aktenvermerk, betr. Aussprache mit Bellman, Barth, Huettner, und Fritz Naumann (19 October 1972), signed Quast.

3 November 1972. Aktenvermerk, betr. Gespraech mit Kollegen Janott (23 October 1972), signed Quast.

9 November 1972. Aktenvermerk, betr. Gespraech mit OKR Stolpe und Lewek, signed Quast.

1972. Bericht ueber ein Gespraech zwischen Werner Wuenschmann an der Zentralausschuss fuer die Jugendweihe, no date given but likely early 1972, no author.

8 January 1973. Aktenvermerk, betr. Gespraech mit Diakon Kerst (8 January 1973), signed Carl Ordnung.

10 January 1973. Aktenvermerk, betr. Vorbereitung fuer das Gespraech mit dem Bund der Evangelischen Pfarrer in der DDR am 12. January 1973, signed Quast.

23 January 1973. Aktenvermerk, betr. Aussprache mit dem geschaeftsfuehrenden Ausschuss betr. Bund der Evangelischen Pfarrer in der DDR (12 January 1973), signed Quast.

29 January 1973. Aktenvermerk, betr. Aussprache mit Bellman (26 January 1973, betr. Berlin-Brandenburg Synod), signed Quast.

29 January 1973. "Zum Erscheinen der Evangelischen Monatsschrift 'Standpunkt,' " Information des Sekretariats des Hauptvorstand der CDU no. 2/73.

30 January 1973. Aktenvermerk, betr. Aussprache mit Stolpe (29 January 1973), signed Quast.

22 March 1973. Aktenvermerk, betr. Aussprache mit Barth, Huettner, and Bellman (21 March 1973), signed Quast.

26 March 1973. Aktenvermerk, betr. Aussprache des Ministers fuer Gesundheitswesen Prof. Dr. Mecklinger mit Vertreter der Inneren Mission am 22.3.73, Burgscheidung, no author.

28 March 1973. Aktenvermerk, betr. Aussprache zwischen Heyl (CDU), Quast, and Huettner (27 March 1973), signed Quast.

2 April 1973. Aktenvermerk, betr. Aussprache mit Flint (30 March 1973), signed Quast.

4 April 1973. "Zum Weltkongress der Friedenskraefte in Moskau," Information des Sekretariats des Hauptvorstandes der CDU no. 6/73.

4 May 1973. Aktenvermerk, betr. Aussprache mit Flint (3 May 1973), signed Quast.

8 May 1973. Aktenvermerk, betr. Aussprache mit Stolpe (7 May 1973, betr. Kirchenbund), signed Quast.

14 May 1973. Memorandum, an die Abteilung Kirchenfragen betr. Analyse der Zentralorgan, Abteilung Agitation CDU.

15 May 1973. Aktenvermerk, betr. Aussprache Bellman, Huettner, Barth, und Naumann (9 May 1973), signed Quast.

22 May 1973. Aktenvermerk, betr. Vorschlag fuer eine Konzeption fuer das Gespraech mit Kirchenpraesident Natho am 24 May 1973, signed Quast.

14 June 1973. Sinnprotokoll der Sitzung der Arbeitsgruppe Kirchenfragen beim Hauptvorstand der CDU am 13 Juni 1973, no author.

29 June 1973. Aktenvermerk, betr. Aussprache mit Huettner, Janott, und Bellman (29 June 1973), signed Quast.

10 July 1973. Aktenvermerk, betr. Aussprache mit Flint (9 July 1973), signed Quast.

23 July 1973. Aktenvermerk, betr. Aussprache mit Flint (20 July 1973), signed Quast.

3 August 1973. Aktenvermerk, betr. Oekumenische Gottesdienst anlaesslich des X. Weltfestspiele, signed Trende.

9 August 1973. Aktenvermerk, betr. Zusammenfassende Einschaetzung der X. Weltfestspiele im Blick auf die glaeubige Jugend, signed Trende.

15 August 1973. Aktenvermerk, betr. Zur Meinungsbildung unter kirchlichen Amtstraeger und Theologen zu den Aussagen des 9. ZK Plenum in unserer Partei, signed Abteilung Kirchenfragen.

20 August 1973. "Zu den Ergebnissen der X. Weltfestspiele der Jugend und Studenten," Information des Sekretariat des Hauptvorstandes no. 14/73.

27 August 1973. Aktenvermerk, betr. Aussprache mit Flint (24 August 1973), signed Heikisch.

12 September 1973. Stenograph der Veranstaltung am 12 September 1973 aus Anlass der Abreise der Delegation nach Moskau, no date given, no author.

13 September 1973. Aktenvermerk, betr. Aussprache mit Flint (7 September 1973), signed Quast.

20 September 1973. Aktenvermerk, betr. Aussprache mit Pabst (18 September 1973), signed Quast.

28 September 1973. Aktenvermerk, betr. Aussprache mit Flint (27 September 1973), signed Quast.

5 October 1973. Aktenvermerk, betr. Aussprache mit Huettner (5 October 1973), signed Quast.

10 October 1973. Bericht der Tagung des Aktivs "Kirchenfragen" des BV Schwerin am 10.10. 1973, no author.

10 October 1973. Beschlussvorlage des Sekretariat des Hauptvorstand der CDU: Bericht ueber die Tagung vom 10 October 1973 der Arbeitsgruppe Kirchenfragen.

16 October 1973. Sinnprotokoll der Sitzung der Arbeitsgruppe Kirchenfragen beim Hauptvorstand der CDU am 10. October 1973.

25 October 1973. "Information ueber den Weltkongress der Friedenskraefte in Moskau," Sekretariat des Hauptvorstandes der CDU.

17 November 1973. Entwurf einer Artikel fuer die *Neue Zeit*, am 17.11.73 erschienen, Prof. Norbert Mueller.

27 November 1973. Aktenvermerk, betr. Aussprache mit Flint (27 November 1973), signed Quast.

14 December 1973. Aktenvermerk, betr. Aussprache mit Flint (no date given), signed Heikisch.

14 December 1973. Aktenvermerk, betr. Aussprache mit Huettner (13 December 1973), signed Quast.

17 January 1974. "Information ueber die evangelischen Herbstsynoden, 1973," Information des Sekretariats des Hauptvorstandes der CDU no. 1/74.

28 January 1974. Aktenvermerk, betr. Aussprache mit Flint (25 January 1974, betr. Gespraech Seigewasser-Vorstand des Kirchenbundes), signed Quast.

1 February 1974. Aktenvermerk, betr. Aussprache mit Pabst (31 January 1974), signed Quast.

15 February 1974. "Aenderung im Jugendgesetzentwurf," Information des Sekretariat des Hauptvorstandes der CDU no. 3/74.

15 February 1974. Aktenvermerk, betr. Aussprache mit Flint (15 February 1974), mit Anlage, "Referat Seigewassers vom 7.2.74 mit Beratung der Stellvertretern fuer Innere Angelegenheiten und Mitarbeiter der Bezirksleitungen," signed Quast.

18 February 1974. Aktenvermerk, betr. Gespraech mit Stolpe (no date given), signed Quast.

5 April 1974. "Erweiterung des Taetigkeitsbereiches und Veraenderung der Struktur des Kommittees Antifaschistischen Widerstandeskaempfer der DDR," Information des Sekretariat des Hauptvorstandes der CDU no. 6/74.

26 April 1974. Aktenvermerk, betr. Aussprache mit Huettner (24 April 1974), signed Quast.

30 April 1974. Aktenvermerk, betr. Synod Berlin-Brandenburg—2. Zwischeninformation, signed Quast.

15 May 1974. Aktenvermerk, betr. Aussprache mit Flint (15 May 1974), signed Quast.

28 May 1974. "Zur wahlbeteiligung kirchlichen Amtstraeger und Theologen," no author.

17 June 1974. "Information ueber die evangelischen Fruehjahrssynoden, 1974," Information des Sekretariat des Hauptvorstandes der CDU no. 11/74.

21 June 1974. Aktenvermerk, betr. Aussprache mit Flint (21 June 1974), signed Quast.

10 September 1974. Beschlussvorlage des Sekretariat des Hauptvorstand der CDU: Bericht ueber die Tagung der Arbeitsgruppe Kirchenfragen beim Hauptvorstand der CDU vom 3. July 1974.

12 July 1974. Aktenvermerk, betr. Aussprache mit OKR Stolpe (11 July 1974), signed Quast.

2 August 1974. Aktenvermerk, betr. Aussprache zwischen Bellman, Huettner, Heyl und Quast (no date given), signed Quast.

16 August 1974. Aktenvermerk, betr. Aussprache mit Flint (15 August 1974), signed Quast.

26 August 1974. Aktenvermerk, betr. OeRK-Zentralausschuss Tagung in Westberlin, 11.–18.8.74, signed Abteilung Kirchenfragen CDU.

30 August 1974. Aktenvermerk, betr. Aussprache mit Grewe (29 August 1974), signed Quast.

10 September 1974. Aktenvermerk, betr. Aussprache mit Flint (9 September 1974), signed Quast.

21 October 1974. Protokoll der Dienstbesprechung des Sekretariats des Hauptvorstandes der CDU mit den Bezirksvorsitzenden vom 21 Oktober 1974, no date given, no author.

30 October 1974. Zuarbeit, Grewe Referat an die Arbeitsgruppe Kirchenfragen beim Hauptvorstand der CDU am 30.10.74, no date given, no author.

1974. Kommunalwahlergebnisse.

No date. CDU Argumentationsthesen bez. theologische Argumente gegen Abtreibung, no author.

No date. Hinweise und Anregungen zum Entwurf des Gesetzes ueber die Unterbrechung der Schwangerschaft und zu seiner Durchfuehrung, no date given, no author.

No date. Zum Beitrag der CDU zur Neuorientierung der Kirchen, no author.

Documents of the Evangelical Press Service, West Germany
(EPS documents)

15 January 1968. "Die kirchenpolitische Situation in der DDR an der Jahreswende 67/68," *epd Gelber Brief,* no. 2/68.

20 January 1968. "Undurchsichtige Verordnung," *epd Gelber Brief,* no. 5/68.

16 March 1968. "Verfassungsgespraeche abgesagt," *epd Gelber Brief,* no. 23/68.

17 October 1968. "Regionalsynoden und Ratssektionen der EKU," *epd-Vertraulich,* no. 28.

18 December 1968. "Die Haltung der Lutherischen Kirchen," *epd-Vertraulich,* no. 37.

31 March 1969. "Die Kirchenbundverhandlung der Synoden in Dresden, Schwerin, und Goerlitz," *epd-Vertraulich,* no. 11.

21 April 1969. "Undurchsichtige Kirchenpolitik Seigewassers," *epd-Vertraulich,* no. 14.

8 May 1969. "DDR Kirchenbund und kirchliche Ost-West Gemeinschaft," *epd-Vertraulich* no. 16.

14 May 1969. "Synodale Opposition in Thueringen," *epd Vertraulich,* no. 17.

4 June 1969. "Konferenz der Kirchenleitung in der DDR berat am 10. Juni," *epd-Vertraulich,* no. 20.

26 September 1969. "Verlauf der Synode des DDR-Kirchenbundes," *epd-Vertraulich,* no. 26.

3 October 1969. "EKU will fest bleiben," *epd-Vertraulich,* no. 27.

28 November 1969. "DDR-Bischoefe duerfen nicht nach Kopenhagen," "Vor Maerz kein Termin," and "Synode ausgepunktet," *epd-Vertraulich,* no. 31.

21 January 1970. "EKD orientiert sich auf den Westen," *epd-Vertraulich,* no. 2.

10 February 1970. "EKU soll nicht getrennt werden," *epd-Vertraulich,* no. 3.

18 March 1970. "Teile eines Ganzen," *epd-Vertraulich,* no. 6.

5 May 1970. "Verstaerkte Trennungstendenzen in der EKU-Ost," *epd-Vertraulich,* no. 7.

25 June 1970. "Massnahmen gegen Goerlitzer Kirche," "DDR fordert Sozialismus-Praeambel fuer die Verfassung des Kirchenbundes," and "DDR Pfarrerblatt mit neuer Leitung," *epd-Vertraulich,* no. 10.

21 September 1970. "Erleichterung nicht zu erwarten," *epd-Vertraulich,* no. 14.

5 November 1970. "Zunaechst weiterhin 5 Jahre Theologiestudium in der DDR," and "Kirchentagserfahrungen 1970 in der DDR," *epd-Vertraulich,* no. 19.

24 November 1970. "Akzentverschiebungen in der DDR," *epd-Vertraulich,* no. 20.

29 January 1971. "Das DDR-Idealbild vom systemgerechten Pfarrer," *epd-Vertraulich,* no. 2.

19 February 1971. "DDR-Veranstaltungsverordnung nicht nur gegen Kirchen," and "DDR erkennt demnaechst Kirchenbund formell an," *epd-Vertraulich,* no. 6.

16 July 1971. "Zur kirchlichen Situation in der DDR," *epd-Vertraulich,* no. 8.

September 1971. "Erleicherung nicht zu erwarten," *epd-Vertraulich,* no. 14.

*Documents in the Press Archive of the Evangelical Press
Center, West Berlin (EPC archives)*

5 January 1967. Rede D. Schoenherrs beim Empfang durch den Bezirk Frankfurt/Oder.

22 April 1968. Aktennotiz der EKU (Ost-Mitglieder) Kirchenkanzlei.

3 September 1968. Entwurf einer Ordnung des 'Bundes der Evangelischen Kirchen in der DDR,' Anlage 1 zu G10-1820/68 II.

9 November 1968. Taetigkeitsbericht der Ev.-Luth Landeskirchenamtes Sachsen . . . , Teil II; Beschluesse der Synode der Landeskirche Sachsens (1968).

1968. Rechenschaftsbericht der Evangelischen Kirchenleitung Berlin-Brandenburg.

15 November 1968. Bericht, Bischof Krummacher an die Greifswalder Synode.

26 September 1969. Notizen, signed Reinhard Henkys.

22 November 1969. Geheimgehaltener Beschluss der Konferenz der evangelischen Kirchenleitungen in der DDR vom 22.11.69.

22 November 1969. Protokollauszug aus der Sitzung der Konferenz der Kirchenleitung von 22. November 1969, signed Lingner.

15 December 1969. Protokoll ueber die Sitzung des Vorstandes der Konferenz der Kirchenleitung der evangelischen Kirchen in der DDR mit der Beratergruppe des Rates der EKD-West am 15 Dezember 1969, signed Lingner.

1969. Bericht Bischof Noths vor der saechsischen Landessynode; Beschluesse der Synode.

5 January 1970. Skizze fuer einen Gespraechsgang in der Januar 5 Ratssitzung, signed Walter Hammer, President of the EKD Chancellory.

1 February 1970. Anmerkung zum Kirchenbund Besuch in Genf.

December 1970. Weihnachtsbotschaft—Auftrag zur Bewaehrung, Sekretariat des Hauptvorstandes der CDU, signed Carl Ordnung.

1970. Beschluesse der Landessynode Sachsens.

1970. Der kuenftige Weg der EKU. Entwurf zu einem Beitrag, signed Synod President Lothar Kreyssig.

28 October 1971. Taetigkeitsbericht des Ev.-Lutherischen Landeskirchenamtes Sachsens der Ev.-Lutherischen Landessynode auf ihrer Herbsttagung vom 22. bis 28. Oktober 1971, section 2.

4–7 November 1971. Bericht der Kirchenleitung fuer die 5. Tagung der 5. Landessynode Greifswald vom 4.–7. November 1971, Section 2; Beschluss der Synode, 4 November 1971.

1971. Bishop Heinrich Rathke, "Kirche fuer Andere -Zeugnis und Dienst der Gemeinde," address delivered at 1971 synod of the Kirchenbund.

31 December 1972. Interview des Westdeutschen Rundfunks mit Bischof Scharf am 31.12.72.

5 April 1973. Reinhard Henkys' Broadcast over Deutschlandfunk.

1973. Information aus der Arbeit des Kirchenbundes, Sekretariat des Kirchenbundes 2501–1139.

March 1974. Taetigkeitsbericht der Kirchenleitung fuer die Synode der Evangelischen Kirche des Goerlitzer Kirchengebietes.

No date. Bedarf die Zustimmung der Bundes der Evangelischen Kirchen in der DDR einer 2/3 Mehrheit der Synode der Evangelische Kirche in Berlin-Brandenburg?, signed President Ranke, Consistory of Berlin-Brandenburg (West). No date. Kein Termin vor Maerz, signed Reinhard Henkys.

PUBLISHED SOURCES

Adler, Elisabeth. *A Small Beginning: An Assessment of the First Five Years of the Program to Combat Racism.* Geneva: World Council of Churches, 1974.
Asmus, Ronald D. "The GDR and Martin Luther." *Survey* 28 (Autumn 1984): 124–56.
——. "Is There a Peace Movement in the GDR?" *Orbis* 27 (Summer 1983): 301–41.
Barth, Karl, and Johannes Hamel. *How to Serve God in a Marxist Land.* New York: Association Press, 1959.
Bassarak, Gerhard, ed. *Oekumenische Diakonie.* Berlin, GDR: Evangelische Verlagsanstalt, 1975.
——. "Zur Frage nach theologischem Inhalt und Interpretation von 'Heil heute' in einer sozialistischen Gesellschaft." *Die Zeichen der Zeit* 27 (1973): 161–81.
Beeson, Trevor. *Discretion and Valour: Religious Conditions in Russia and Eastern Europe.* 2d ed. Philadelphia: Fortress Press, 1982.
Bertinetti, Ilse. "Mein Standpunkt." *Standpunkt* 1 (1973): 225.
Black, Hilary. "The Church in East Germany." *Religion in Communist Lands* 1, nos. 4–5 (1973): 4–7.
Bociurkiw, Bohdan R., and John W. Strong, eds. *Religion and Atheism in the USSR and Eastern Europe.* London: Macmillan, 1975.
Bosinski, Gerhard, ed. "*. . . und tue desgleichen.*" Berlin, GDR: Evangelische Verlagsanstalt, 1975.
——. *Zur Antwort Bereit.* Berlin, GDR: Evangelische Verlagsanstalt, 1978.
Bowers, Stephen. "Private Institutions in Service to the State." *East European Quarterly* 26 (1982): 73–86.
——. "Youth Policies in the GDR." *Problems of Communism* 27 (1978): 78–82.
Braeuer, Siegfried. *Martin Luther in marxistischer Sicht von 1945 bis zum Beginn der achtziger Jahre.* Berlin, GDR: Evangelische Verlagsanstalt, 1983.
Brand, George. "Accommodation and Resistance: A Study of Church-State Relations in the German Democratic Republic." Ph.D. diss., Colgate University, 1974.
Braune, Werner. "Diakonische Arbeit in der DDR." *Kirche im Sozialismus* 2, no. 5 (1976): 9–14.
Brendler, Gerhard. *Martin Luther: Theologie und Revolution.* Berlin, GDR: VEB Deutscher Verlag der Wissenschaft, 1983.
Buescher, Wolfgang. "Warum bleibe ich eigentlich?" *Deutschland Archiv* 17 (July 1984): 683–88.
Buescher, Wolfgang, Peter Wensierski, and Klaus Wolschner, eds. *Friedensbewegung in der DDR: Texte, 1978–1982.* Hattingen: Scandica Verlag, 1982.
Bussiek, Hendrik. *Notizen aus der DDR.* Frankfurt/Main: Fischer Taschenbuchverlag, 1979.

Childs, David. *The German Democratic Republic: Moscow's German Ally.* Boston: Allen & Unwin, 1983.

Christians and Churches in the GDR. Berlin, GDR: Panorama DDR, 1983.

Christlich-Demokratische Union Deutschlands. *Zu den Beziehungen zwischen Kirche und Staat in der DDR.* Berlin, GDR: Union Verlag, 1956.

Croan, Melvin. "After Ulbricht: The End of an Era?" *Survey* 17 (1971): 74–92.

———. *East Germany: The Soviet Connection.* Washington Papers 4, no. 36. Beverly Hills, Calif.: Sage, 1976.

———. "Kirchenkampf in East Germany." *Soviet Survey,* no. 31 (1960): 81–87.

———. "A Quarter Century of the Two Germanies." *Survey* 21 (1975): 79–84.

Daehn, Horst. *Konfrontation oder Kooperation? Das Verhaeltnis von Staat und Kirche in der SBZ/DDR, 1945–1980.* Opladen, FRG: Westdeutscher Verlag, 1982.

Dahlgren, Sam. *Das Verhaeltnis von Staat und Kirche in der DDR waehrend der Jahre 1949–1958.* Uppsala: CWK Gleerups Forlag, 1972.

DeBardeleben, Joan. *The Environment and Marxism-Leninism.* Boulder, Colo.: Westview, 1985.

Dibelius, Otto. *Obrigkeit.* Stuttgart: Kreuz Verlag, 1963.

Dillenberger, John, ed. *Martin Luther: Selections from His Writings.* Garden City, N.Y.: Doubleday, 1961.

Drummond, Andrew L. *German Protestantism since Luther.* London: Epworth, 1951.

Dunn, Dennis, ed. *Religion and Modernization in the Soviet Union.* Boulder, Colo.: Westview, 1977.

Eisenfeld, Bernd. "Spaten-Soldaten." *Kirche im Sozialismus* 10 (September 1984): 20–29.

Eleutherius [pseud]. "Luther Rebaptized in Marxist Ideology?" *Occasional Papers on Religion in Eastern Europe,* no. 3 (July 1983): 21–43.

Evangelisches Staatslexikon. Stuttgart: Kreuz Verlag, 1975.

Evian 1970: Offizieller Bericht der fuenften Vollversammlung des Lutherischen Weltbundes. Witten/FRG: Eckart Verlag, 1970.

Falcke, Heino. "Place of the Two Kingdoms Doctrine in the Life of the Evangelical Churches in the GDR." *Lutheran World* 24 (1977): 23–31.

———. "Unsere Kirche und ihre Gruppen." *Kirche im Sozialismus* 11 (August 1985): 145–52.

Federal Ministry of Inner-German Affairs. *DDR-Handbuch.* Cologne: Verlag Wissenschaft und Politik, 1985.

Fischer, Peter. *Kirche und Christen in der DDR.* Berlin: Verlag Gebr. Holzapfel, 1978.

Fletcher, William. *Religion and Soviet Foreign Policy, 1945–1970.* London: Oxford University Press, 1970.

Frickel, Heinrich. "Stationen einer 20-Jaehrigen Entwicklung: Konfirmandenunterricht und Konfirmation in der DDR." *Kirche im Sozialismus* 1, no. 3 (1975): 9–17.

Friedrich-Ebert Stiftung. *Kirche und Staat in der DDR und in der Bundesrepublik.* Bonn: Verlag Neue Gesellschaft, 1977.

Frielinghaus, Dieter. "Menschenrechte und Menschenpflichte." *Standpunkt* 2 (1974): 30–31.

Geiger, Max. *Christsein in der DDR.* Theologische Existenz heute, no. 185, ed. Trutz Rendtorff and Karl Gerhard Steck. Munich: Chr. Kaiser Verlag, 1975.

Glass, George A. "Church-State Relations in East Germany: Expanding Dimensions of an Unresolved Problem." *East Central Europe* 6 (1979): 232–49.

Goeckel, Robert F. "Church and Society in the GDR: Historical Legacies and 'Mature Socialism.'" In *The Quality of Life in the German Democratic Republic,* ed. Marilyn Rueschemeyer. Armonk, N.Y.: M. E. Sharpe, 1988.

——. "Detente and Conservatizing Liberalization: The State and the Evangelical Churches in the German Democratic Republic, 1968–1974." Ph.D. diss., Harvard University, 1982.

——. "Domestic Dissent in the GDR: The Role of the Evangelical Church." In *East Germany, West Germany, and the Soviet Union: The Changing Relationship,* ed. Thomas A. Baylis. Western Societies Program Occasional Paper no. 18, Cornell University, 1986.

——. "Is the GDR the Future of Hungary and the Baltics? Dissent and the Lutheran Church in Eastern Europe." In *East Germany in Comparative Perspective,* ed. Thomas Baylis, David Childs, and Marilyn Rueschemeyer. London: Routledge, 1989.

——. "The Kirchenpolitik of the GDR and the Evangelical Churches, 1968–1978." In *Studies in GDR Culture and Society,* vol. 1, ed. Margy Gerber. Washington, D.C.: University Press of America, 1981.

——. "The Luther Anniversary in East Germany." *World Politics* 37 (October 1984): 112–33.

——. "Zehn Jahre Kirchenpolitik unter Honecker." *Deutschland Archiv* 14 (1981): 940–47.

Goetting, Gerald. *Christians and Politics in the German Democratic Republic.* Berlin, GDR: Union Verlag, 1966.

Griffith, William. *The Ostpolitik of the Federal Republic of Germany.* Cambridge: MIT Press, 1978.

Gust, Kurt. "East German Protestantism under Communist Rule, 1945–1961." Ph.D. diss., University of Kansas, 1966.

Hanhardt, Arthur. *The German Democratic Republic.* Baltimore: Johns Hopkins Press, 1968.

Hartmann, Matthias. "Signale vom evangelischen Kirchentag." *Deutschland Archiv* 20 (August 1987): 838–43.

Hebly, J. A. *The Russians in the World Council of Churches.* Belfast: Christian Journals, 1978.

Heltau, Sibylle. "Kirchentagsarbeit in der DDR." *Kirche im Sozialismus* 1, no. 5 (1975): 24–30.

Helwig, Gisela. "Christ sein in der DDR." *Deutschland Archiv* 9 (1976): 1020–22.

——. "Kirche im Sozialismus." *Deutschland Archiv* 10 (1977): 449–51.

——. "Neue Chancen fuer Christen?" *Deutschland Archiv* 12 (1979): 1128–32.

——. "Zeichen der Hoffnung." *Deutschland Archiv* 11 (1978): 351–53.

Helwig, Gisela, and Detlef Urban, eds. *Kirchen und Gesellschaft in beiden deutschen Staaten.* Cologne: Verlag Wissenschaft und Politik, 1987.

Hempel, Johannes. "Christen im Sozialismus." *Deutschland Archiv* 10 (1977): 1336–40.

———. "Das Selbstverstaendnis der VELK in der DDR und ihr Beitrag zur Kirchwerdung des Bundes." *Lutherische Rundschau* 21 (1974): 10–17.

Henkys, Reinhard. "Der Atheismus fehlt im SED-Programm." *Kirche im Sozialismus* 2, no. 1 (1976): 9–13.

———. "Dialog-Gemeinschaft." *Kirche im Sozialismus* 10 (November 1984): 11–20.

———. "Eine neue Qualitaet der Zusammenarbeit?" *Kirche im Sozialismus* 1, no. 2 (1973): 5–15.

———. "Einen Schritt vorwaerts." *Kirche im Sozialismus* 13 (August 1987): 131–32.

———. *Gottes Volk im Sozialismus*. Berlin: Wichern Verlag, 1983.

———. "Irritationen im Herbst." *Kirche im Sozialismus* 6 no. 5–6 (1980): 53–62.

———. "Kapitalistisches Ueberbleibsel: Kirchenpolitik nach dem letzten SED-Parteitag." *Evangelische Kommentar* 5 (1971): 215–18.

———. "Parteiprogram und Wirklichkeit." *Kirche im Sozialismus* 2 (June 1976): 13–18.

———. "Verantwortung fuer den Frieden." *Kirche im Sozialismus* 5 (October 1979): 21–28.

Henkys, Reinhard, ed. *Bund der Evangelischen Kirchen in der DDR: Dokumente zu seiner Entstehung*. Witten and Berlin: Eckart Verlag, 1970.

———, ed. *Die Evangelischen Kirchen in der DDR*. Munich: Chr. Kaiser Verlag, 1982.

Hermann, Friedrich-Georg. *Der Kampf gegen Religion und Kirche in der Sowjetischen Besatzungszone Deutschlands*. Stuttgart: Quell Verlag, 1967.

Hertz, Karl H., ed. *Two Kingdoms and One World: A Sourcebook in Christian Social Ethics*. Minneapolis: Augsburg, 1976.

Heyl, Wolfgang. *Christen im Engagement—heute und morgen*. Berlin, GDR: Sekretariat des Hauptvorstandes der CDU, 1976.

———. *Christen und Kirchen in der DDR*. Berlin, GDR: Panorama, 1975.

Hinz, Christoph. "Den Ruecken fuer das Zeugnis freihalten." *Kirchen im Sozialismus* 2, no. 1 (1976): 14.

Hirschman, Albert. *Exit, Voice and Loyalty*. Cambridge: Harvard University Press, 1970.

Hoellen, Martin. "Kirchen Kuenftig auch in Neubaugebieten der DDR." *Deutschland Archiv* 10 (1977): 466–470.

Hoffman, Stephen. "East Germany." In *Three Worlds of Christian-Marxist Encounters*, ed. Nicholas Piediscalzi and Robert G. Thobaben. Philadelphia: Fortress Press, 1985.

Hudson, Darrel. *The World Council of Churches in International Affairs*. Leighton Buzzard, England: Faith Press, 1977.

Huettich, H. G. "Dissent and Systemic Stability in East Germany." *Studies in Comparative Communism* 12 (1979): 254–62.

Huntington, Samuel P., and Clement H. Moore, eds. *Authoritarian Politics in Modern Society*. New York: Basic Books, 1970.

Hutten, Kurt. *Iron Curtain Christians: The Church in Communist Countries Today*. Minneapolis: Augsburg, 1967.

"Der 'Idealtheologe,'" *Kirche im Sozialismus* 2 no. 3 (1976): 25–32.

Immer, Karl, ed. *Kirche in diesen Jahren: Ein Bericht*. Neukirchen-Vluyn, FRG: Neukirchener Verlag, 1971.

Innere Mission und Hilfswerk der Evangelischen Kirchen in der DDR. *Froehlich helfen: Handreichung der Innere Mission.* Berlin, GDR: Evangelische Verlagsanstalt, 1975.

Jacob, Guenter. *Der Christ in der sozialistischen Gesellschaft: Theologische Probleme und Folgerungen.* Stuttgart: Evangelisches Verlagswerk, 1975.

——. *Weltwirklichkeit und Christusglaube: Wider eine falsche Zweireichelehre.* Stuttgart: Evangelisches Verlagswerk, 1977.

Jacobsen, Hans-Adolf, et al., eds. *Drei Jahrzehnte Aussenpolitik der DDR.* Munich: R. Oldenbourg Verlag, 1979.

Jaenicke, Johannes. *Ich konnte dabeisein.* Berlin: Wichern Verlag, 1984.

Jenssen, Hans-Hinrich. "Nach zehn Jahren: DDR-Spezifik in der Theologie." *Evangelisches Pfarrerblatt,* no. 2 (February 1971): 33–34.

Jenssen, Hans-Hinrich, and Herbert Trebs, eds. *Theologisches Lexikon.* Berlin, GDR: Union Verlag, 1978.

Jung, Gerhard. "Neue Phase in der DDR Kirchenpolitik." *Deutsches Pfarrerblatt* 73 (September 1973): 669–72.

Kaltenbrunner, Gerd-Klaus, ed. *Das Elend der Christdemokraten.* Munich: Herder, 1977.

Kirchliches Jahrbuch fuer die Evangelische Kirche in Deutschland. Gutersloh, FRG: Gerd Mohn, various years.

Klages, Eberhard. "Organtrennung und Divergenz." *Evangelisches Pfarrerblatt,* no. 6 (June 1972): 165.

——. "Wie der 'stille Amerikaner'." *Standpunkt* 1 (1973): 117.

——. "Zum Ertrag von Nairobi." *Standpunkt* 4 (1976): 29–30.

Klausener, Erich. *Sie hassen Gott nach Plan.* Berlin: Morus Verlag, 1962.

Klohr, Olof. *Marxismus-Leninismus, Atheismus, Religion.* Rostock-Warnemuende: Ingenierhochschule fuer Seefahrt, 1978.

——. "Religion und Marxismus unvereinbar!" *Kirche im Sozialismus* 2, no. 2 (1976): 23–25.

——. "Ursachen und Tendenzen des Absterbens von Religion und Kirche im Sozialismus." *Voprosy Filosofi* (1974): 147–54.

Klohr, Olof, ed. *Religion und Atheismus Heute.* Berlin, GDR: Verlag der Wissenschaften, 1966.

Knauft, Wolfgang. *Katholische Kirche in der DDR: Gemeinden in der Bewaehrung, 1945–1980.* Mainz: Matthias-Gruenwald Verlag, 1980.

Koch, Hans-Gerhard. *Luthers Reformation in Kommunistischer Sicht.* Stuttgart: Kreuz Verlag, 1967.

——. *Neue Erde ohne Himmel.* Stuttgart: Quell Verlag, 1963.

——. *Staat und Kirche in der DDR.* Stuttgart: Quell Verlag, 1975.

Koehler, Guenter, ed. *Pontifex nicht Partisan: Kirche und Staat in der DDR von 1949 bis 1958: Dokumente aus der Arbeit des Bevollmaechtigten des Rates der EKD bei der Regierung der DDR Propst D. Heinrich Grueber.* Stuttgart: Evangelisches Verlagswerk, 1974.

Koehler, Hans. *Pseudo-Sakrale Staatsakte in Mitteldeutschland.* Witten: Luther Verlag, 1962.

Kosok, Paul. *Modern Germany.* Chicago: University of Chicago Press, 1933.

Krisch, Henry. *The German Democratic Republic: The Search for Identity*. Boulder, Colo.: Westview, 1985.

——. *German Politics under Soviet Occupation*. New York: Columbia University Press, 1974.

Krummacher, Friedrich-Wilhelm. *Ruf zur Entscheidung: Predigten, Ausprachen, Aufsaetze, 1944–1945*. Berlin, GDR: Union Verlag, 1965.

Krusche, Werner. "Heil heute." *Die Zeichen der Zeit* 27 (1973): 161–81.

Kuhrt, Eberhard. *Wider die Militarisierung der Gesellschaft: Friedensbewegung und Kirche in der DDR*. Melle, FRG: Verlag Ernst Knoth and Konrad-Adenauer Stiftung, 1984.

Kulbach, Roderich, and Helmut Weber. *Parteien im Blocksystem der DDR*. Cologne: Verlag Wissenschaft und Politik, 1969.

Lamberz, Werner. *Ueber ideologische Arbeit heute*. Berlin, GDR: Sekretariat des Hauptvorstand der CDU, 1975.

Larrabee, F. Stephen. "The Politics of Reconciliation: Moscow and the West German Ostpolitik, 1966–1972." Ph.D. diss., Columbia University, 1975.

Legters, H. Lyman, ed. *The German Democratic Republic: A Developed Socialist Society*. Boulder, Colo.: Westview, 1978.

Lenin, V. I. *Religion*. New York: International Publishers, 1933.

Lewek, Christa, Manfred Stolpe, and Joachim Garstecki, eds. *Menschenrechte in christlicher Verantwortung*. Berlin, GDR: Evangelische Verlagsanstalt, 1980.

Lidtke, Vernon L. "August Bebel and German Social Democracy's Relationship to the Christian Churches." *Journal of the History of Ideas* 27 (April–June 1966): 245–61.

Lobkowicz, Nicholas, ed. *Marx and the Western World*. Notre Dame: University of Notre Dame Press, 1967.

Ludz, Peter Christian. *Die DDR zwischen Ost und West: Politische Analysen, 1961–1976*. Munich: C. H. Beck, 1977.

——. *The German Democratic Republic from the Sixties to the 1970s: A Socio-Political Analysis*. Cambridge: Center for International Affairs, Harvard University, 1970.

McAdams, A. James. *East Germany and Detente*. Cambridge: Cambridge University Press, 1985.

McCauley, Martin. *The German Democratic Republic since 1945*. New York: St. Martin's Press, 1983.

Machnow, Klaus. "Alle Erreichen, keine zuruecklassen." *Deutschland Archiv* 11 (1978): 279–85.

Mallinckrodt, Anita. *The Environmental Dialogue in the GDR*. Lanham, Md.: University Press of America, 1987.

Mampel, Siegfried. *Die Verfassung der sowjetischen Besatzungszone Deutschlands: Text und Kommentare*. Frankfurt/Main: Metner Verlag, 1966.

Marx, Karl, and Friedrich Engels. *On Religion*. Introduction by Reinhold Niebuhr. New York: Schocken, 1964.

——. *Werke*. Vol. 2. Berlin, GDR: Dietz Verlag, 1958.

Maser, Werner. *Genossen Beten Nicht: Kirchenkampf des Kommunismus*. Cologne: Verlag Wissenschaft und Politik, 1963.

Matern, Hermann. *Unser gemeinsamer Weg zur sozialistischen Menschengemeinschaft*. Berlin, GDR: Union Verlag, 1969.

Meinecke, Werner. *Die Kirche in der volksdemokratischen Ordnung der Deutschen Demokratischen Republik*. Berlin, GDR: Union Verlag, 1962.

Meyer, Christian. "Das Verhaeltnis zwischen Staatsgewalt und Kirche im Lichte der Glaubens und Gewissensfreiheit in der Sowjetischen Besatzungszone Deutschlands." Diss., University of Mainz, 1964.

Mueller, Hanfried. *Der Christ in Kirche und Staat*. Hefte aus Burgscheidung no. 4. Berlin, GDR: Christlich-Demokratische Union Deutschlands, 1958.

Mueller-Roemer, Dietrich. *Die neue Verfassung der DDR*. Cologne: Verlag Wissenschaft und Politik, 1974.

Mushaben, Joyce Marie. "Swords into Ploughshares." *Studies in Comparative Communism* 17 (Summer 1984): 123–35.

Naimark, Norman. "Militarism, Pacifism, and the GDR's Peace Policy." Paper presented at Hamilton College conference "A New Germany?" April 1985.

Nationale Front des Demokratischen Deutschland. *Kongress der Nationalen Front des Demokratischen Deutschland*. 21–22 March 1969, Protokoll. Vol. 1. Berlin, GDR: Nationalrat der Nationalen Front des Demokratischen Deutschland, 1969.

Neubart, Ehrhart, "Sozialisierende Gruppen im konziliaren Prozess," *Kirche im Sozialismus* 11 (December 1985): 241–45.

"Die Oekumene in Nairobi Gespraech mit OKR Ulrich von Brueck." *Standpunkt* 4 (1976): 60–62.

Oekumenisches Institut Berlin. *Die Kirche im Gespraech der Kirchen*. Berlin, GDR: Evangelische Verlagsanstalt, 1975.

Ordnung, Carl. *Christen in der Friedensbewegung* Hefte aus Burgscheidungen no. 215. Berlin, GDR: Hauptvorstand der CDU, 1983.

——. "Genf 1973." *Standpunkt* 1 (1973): 282–84.

——. "Oekumene in Westberlin." *Standpunkt* 2 (1974).

——. "Ueber das spezifische 'Christliche.'" *Standpunkt* 1 (1973): 5–6.

Ordnung, Carl, ed. *Menschenrechte sind Mitmenschenrechte*. Berlin, GDR: Union Verlag, 1975.

Piechowski, Paul. *Proletarische Glaube*. Berlin: Furche Verlag, 1927.

Raguse, Werner. "Friedenskongresse." *Deutschland Archiv* 10 (1977): 861–65.

——. "Pfarrerbund aufgeloest." *Deutschland Archiv* 8 (1975): 117–19.

Ramet, Pedro. "Church and Peace in the GDR." *Problems of Communism* 33 (July–August 1984): 44–57.

——. *Cross and Commissar*. Bloomington: Indiana University Press, 1987.

——. "Disaffection and Dissent in East Germany." *World Politics* 37 (October 1984): 85–111.

Ramet, Pedro, ed. *Religion and Nationalism in Soviet and East European Politics*. Durham: Duke University Press, 1984.

Rein, Gerhard. "Zum Bleiben ermuntert." *Kirche im Sozialismus* 10 (September 1984): 9–14.

Richter, Klemens. "Erziehung zum Frieden? Die DDR-CDU und die sozialistische Wehrerziehung." *Deutschland Archiv* 14 (1981): 899–903.

——. "Kirchen und Wehrdienstverweigerung und in der DDR." *Deutschland Archiv* 12 (1979): 39–46.

——. "Die vatikanische Ostpolitik und die DDR." *Deutschland Archiv* 12 (1979): 742–47.

Roeder, Hans-Juergen. "Absprache zwischen Staat und Kirche." *Deutschland Archiv* 11 (1978): 353–55.
——. "Churches and Religious Groups in the GDR: An Overview in Figures." *Kirche im Sozialismus* 5 (June 1979): 32–38.
——. "Rebellische Kirchenbasis." *Kirche im Sozialismus* 13 (June 1987): 87–88.
——. "Signale der Basis." *Kirche im Sozialismus* 8 (February 1982): 31–38.
——. "Sorge vor Vereinnahmung." *Kirche im Sozialismus* 12 (October 1986): 195–96.
——. "Zwischen Anpassung und Opposition." *Kirche im Sozialismus* 2 (December 1976): 27–38.
Rommel, Kurt. *Religion und Kirche in sozialistischen Staat der DDR.* Institut für Recht, Politik und Gesellschaft der sozialistischen Staaten, University of Kiel, 1975.
Rosenthal, Rudiger, "Grossere Freiraeume fuer Basisgruppen." *Kirche im Sozialismus* 13 (October 1987): 189–91.
Sandford, Gregory. *From Hitler to Ulbricht: The Communist Reconstruction of East Germany, 1945–46.* Princeton: Princeton University Press, 1983.
Schaefer, Georg. "Standort und Engagement." *Standpunkt* 1 (1973): 7–10.
Schaefer, Hans-Peter. "Chancengleichheit und Begabtenforderung in der DDR." *Deutschland Archiv* 10 (1977): 818–28.
Schapiro, Leonard, and Peter Reddaway, eds. *Lenin—the Man, the Theorist, the Leader, a Reappraisal.* London: Pall Mall Press, 1967.
Scharf, C. Bradley. *Politics and Change in East Germany.* Boulder, Colo.: Westview, 1984.
Schelz, Sepp. "Loyal, aber doch kritisch: Der Ertrag von Eisenach." *Lutherisches Monatsheft* 10 (1971): 377–78.
Schmolze, Gerhard. "Nach 20 Jahren: Jugendweihe in der DDR." *Kirche im Sozialismus* 1, no. 3 (1975): 18–22.
Schnatterbeck, Werner. *Aspekte kirchlicher Jugendarbeit in der Deutschen Demokratischen Republik.* Munich: Verlag Ernst Vogel, 1977.
Schoenherr, Albrecht. *Horizont und Mitte: Aufsaetze, Vortraege, Reden, 1953–1977* Berlin, GDR: Evangelische Verlagsanstalt, 1979.
Schulz, Eberhard, et al., eds. *GDR Foreign Policy.* Armonk, N.Y.: M. E. Sharpe, 1982.
Schwarz, Hans-Peter. *Handbuch der deutschen Aussenpolitik.* Munich: R. Piper Verlag, 1975.
Schweigler, Gebhard. *National Consciousness in a Divided Germany.* Beverly Hills, Calif.: Sage, 1975.
Sekretariat des Bundes der Evangelischen Kirchen in der DDR. *Kirche als Lerngemeinschaft: Dokumente aus der Arbeit des Bundes der Evangelischen Kirchen in der DDR.* Berlin, GDR: Evangelische Verlagsanstalt, 1981.
Sekretariat des Hauptvorstand der CDU Deutschlands. *Antirassismus–Antiimperialismus.* Berlin, GDR: Union Verlag, 1971.
——. *Buergerpflicht und Christenpflicht.* Berlin, GDR: Union Verlag, 1974.
——. *Dokumente der CDU.* Berlin, GDR: Union Verlag, various editions.
——. *Martin Luther—Beitrag der CDU zum 500: Geburtstag des Reformators.* Berlin, GDR: CDU, 1982.

——. *Politisches Jahrbuch der Christlich-Demokratische Union Deutschlands.* 3d. ed. Berlin, GDR: Hauptvorstand der CDU Deutschlands, various editions.

——. *Tradition und Verpflichtung.* Berlin, GDR: Union Verlag, 1974.

Smith, Jean Edward. *Germany beyond the Wall: People, Politics and Prosperity.* Boston: Little, Brown, 1969.

Sodaro, Michael. "Limits to Dissent in the GDR: Cooptation, Fragmentation, and Repression." In *Dissent in Eastern Europe,* ed. Jane Leftwich Curry. New York: Praeger, 1983.

——. "Ulbricht's Grand Design: Economics, Ideology, and the GDR's Response to Detente, 1967–1971." *World Affairs* 142 (1980): 147–68.

Solberg, Richard. *God and Caesar in East Germany.* New York: Macmillan, 1961.

Sonderbauprogramm–Zwischenbericht. Berlin, GDR: Federation of Evangelical Churches in the GDR, 1976.

Sorgenicht, Klaus, et al., eds. *Verfassung der Deutschen Demokratischen Republik: Dokumente, Kommentar.* Vols. 1 and 2. Berlin, GDR: Staatsverlag der DDR, 1969.

Spotts, Frederick. *The Churches and Politics in Germany.* Middletown, Conn.: Wesleyan University Press, 1974.

Stackhouse, Max. "The Religious Situation in the German Democratic Republic." *Occasional Papers on Religion in Eastern Europe* 1 (February 1981): 1–8.

Starrels, John M., and Anita M. Mallinckrodt. *Politics in the German Democratic Republic.* New York: Praeger, 1975.

Stolpe, Manfred. "Modell der deutsch-deutschen Dialog." *Kirche im Sozialismus* 10 (June 1984): 15–24.

Suckut, Siegfried. "From Oppression to Alliance." *Occasional Papers on Religion in Eastern Europe* 3 (December 1983): 1–9.

"Synodaltagung des DDR-Kirchenbundes." *Deutschland Archiv* 11 (1978): 1225–29.

Tilford, Roger, ed. *The Ostpolitik and Political Change in Germany.* Lexington, Mass.: Lexington Books, 1975.

Triska, Jan, and Paul M. Cocks, eds. *Political Development in Eastern Europe.* New York: Praeger, 1977.

Troeltsch, Ernst. *The Social Teaching of the Christian Churches.* New York: Macmillan, 1931.

Umschau '74: Evangelische Christen in der DDR—Zwischenbilanz in 40 Streiflichtern. Berlin, GDR: Evangelische Verlagsanstalt, 1974.

Umweltprobleme und Umweltbewusstsein in der DDR. Cologne: Verlag Wissenschaft und Politik, 1985.

Urban, Detlef. "Spitzengespraech Staat-Kirche." *Deutschland Archiv* 18 (March 1985): 231–32.

Urban, Detlef, and Hans-Willi Weinzen. *Jugend ohne Bekenntnis: 30 Jahre Konfirmation und Jugendweihe in anderen Deutschland, 1954–1984.* Berlin: Wichern Verlag, 1984.

Vajta, Vilmos, ed. *The Lutheran Church: Past and Present.* Minneapolis: Augsburg, 1977.

Verner, Paul, and Gerald Goetting, eds. *Christen und Marxisten in gemeinsamer Verantwortung.* Berlin, GDR: Union Verlag, 1971.

Ward, Carolyn. "Church and State in East Germany." *Religion in Communist Lands* 6 (Summer 1978): 89–95.

Weber, Hermann. *Kleine Geschichte der DDR.* Cologne: Verlag Wissenschaft und Politik, 1980.

"Wehrunterricht in der Schulen in der DDR." *Deutschland Archiv* 11 (1978): 890–94.

Wendelborn, Gerd. *Versoehnung und Parteilichkeit: Alternative oder Einheit?* Berlin, GDR: Union Verlag, 1974.

Wensierski, Peter. "Nach Alternativen wird gefragt." *Kirche im Sozialismus* 6, nos. 5–6 (1980): 29–43.

——. "Theses on the Role of the Church in the GDR." *Occasional Papers on Religion in Eastern Europe* 3 (May 1983): 1–19.

Wensierski, Peter, and Wolfgang Buescher, eds. *Beton ist Beton: Zivilisationskritik aus der DDR.* Hattingen: Scandica Verlag, 1981.

Werner, Fred. "Wehrdienstverweigerung in der DDR." *Die Nationale Volksarmee,* ed. Studiengruppe Militaerpolitik. Reinbek bei Hamburg: Rowohlt, 1976.

Williamson, Roger. "East Germany: The Federation of Protestant Churches." *Religion in Communist Lands* 9 (1981): 6–17.

Winter, Beatrice. "Zur Problematik der Mitarbeit der Evangelischen Kirche im Rundfunk der DDR in den Jahren 1946–1958." Diss., Fachbereich Philosophie und Sozialwissenschaften, Free University of Berlin, 1979.

Wirth, Guenther. *Auf dem Weg zur gemeinsam humanistischen Verantwortung: Eine Sammlung kirchenpolitischer Dokumente, 1945–1966.* Berlin, GDR: Union Verlag, 1967.

——. "Bemerkungen zur Bilanz." *Standpunkt* 1 (1973): 86–88.

——. "Ein Seminar ueber Engagement? Ein Seminar des Engagements!" *Standpunkt* 1 (1973): 234–35.

——. "Mein Standpunkt." *Standpunkt* 3 (1975): 57.

——. "Ueber einen Erkundungsausflug." *Standpunkt* 1 (1973): 143.

——. "Um den Gesellschaftsbezug theologischer Reflektionen." *Standpunkt* 1 (1973): 225–26.

——. "Die Versuchung des Nationalismus." *Standpunkt* 1 (1973): 115–17.

——. "Zu Kernfragen des ideologischen Kampfes." *Standpunkt* 1 (1973): 131–32.

—— et al., eds. *Auf dem Wege der sozialistischen Menschengemeinschaft: Eine Sammlung von Dokumenten zur Buendnispolitik und Kirchenpolitik 1967–1970.* Berlin, GDR: Union Verlag, 1971.

Woods, Roger. *Opposition in the GDR under Honecker, 1971–1985.* New York: St. Martin's Press, 1986.

"Wort zum Frieden: Gemeinsame Erklaerung der evangelischen Kirchen in beiden deutschen Staaten." *Deutschland Archiv* 12 (1979): 1115–16.

Zander, Ruth. "Abkehr vom dogmatischen Atheismus." *Kirche im Sozialismus* 4, no. 3 (1978): 15–28.

Zimmerman, Hartmut. "Kirche im Sozialismus—Zur Situation der evangelischen Kirche in der DDR." *DDR Report,* no. 12 (January 1979).

Zimmermann, Wolf-Dieter. "Nicht ohne kritische Distanz." *Lutherisches Monatsheft* 11 (1972): 399.

Index

Library of Congress Cataloging-in-Publication Data

Goeckel, Robert F., 1951–
    The Lutheran Church and the East German state : political conflict
and change under Ulbricht and Honecker / Robert F. Goeckel.
        p.   cm.
    Includes bibliographical references.
    ISBN 0-8014-2259-0 (alk. paper)
    1. Bund der Evangelischen Kirchen in der DDR—History.   2. Church
and state—Germany (East)—History.   3. Germany (East)—Church
history.   I. Title.
BX4844.82.A4G64   1990
284.1'431—dc20
                                                              90-31313

DATE DUE		
DEC 3 '80		
APR 3 0		